MINISTRIES EXAMINED

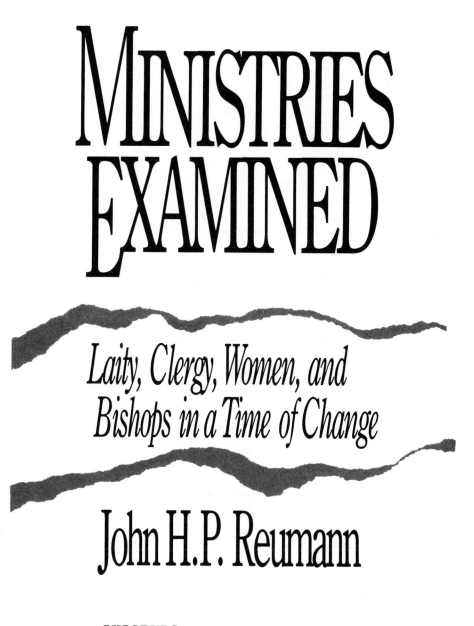

MINISTRIES EXAMINED

Laity, Clergy, Women, and Bishops in a Time of Change

John H.P. Reumann

AUGSBURG Publishing House • Minneapolis

MINISTRIES EXAMINED
Laity, Clergy, Women, and Bishops in a Time of Change

Copyright © 1987 Augsburg Publishing House

Scripture quotations, unless otherwise noted, are from the Revised Standard Version of the Bible, copyright 1946, 1952, and 1971 by the Division of Christian Education of the National Council of Churches.

Chapter 2 includes materials originally published in an article by John Reumann, "Ecclesial Recognition of the Ministry of Women: New Testament Perspectives and Contemporary Application," in *Ministering in a Servant Church,* Proceedings of the Theology Institute of Villanova University (Villanova University Press, 1978), pp. 99-150, used by permission of The Rev. Francis A. Eigo, O.S.A.

Chapter 2 also includes materials originally published in an article by John Reumann, "What in Scripture Speaks to the Ordination of Women?" in *Concordia Theological Monthly* 44/1 (January 1973), pp. 5-30, used by permission of the Editorial Committee of *Concordia Journal.*

Chapter 3 includes materials from an article by John Reumann, "A Further Report on the Title and Office of Bishop in the Lutheran Church in America, 1970–1980," reprinted by permission from the Minutes, Tenth Biennial Convention of the Lutheran Church in America, June 25–July 2, 1980, Seattle Center, Seattle, Washington.

Library of Congress Cataloging-in-Publication Data

Reumann, John Henry Paul.
    MINISTRIES EXAMINED.

    Bibliography: p.
    Includes index.
    1. Pastoral theology—Lutheran Church. 2. Lutheran
Church—Clergy. 3. Ordination of women.   I. Title.
BX8071.R45   1987   262'.1441   87-19537
ISBN 0-8066-2296-2

Manufactured in the U.S.A.   APH 10-4433

1   2   3   4   5   6   7   8   9   0   1   2   3   4   5   6   7   8   9

To the many in God's people who have ministered to me
and for those whom I have served as minister,
and to colleagues on the Commission for a New Lutheran Church
and its Coordinator, Arnold R. Mickelson,
where the ministry was discussed without end
but with some new beginnings

Contents

Abbreviations

AELC	The Association of Evangelical Lutheran Churches (1977–1987)
ALC	The American Lutheran Church (occasionally "TALC" in its documents) (1960–1987)
BEM	*Baptism, Eucharist and Ministry*
CA	*Confessio Augustana,* the Augsburg Confession
CBQ	*Catholic Biblical Quarterly*
CLU	The Committee on Lutheran Unity
CNLC	Commission for a New Lutheran Church
CTM	*Concordia Theological Monthly,* later shortened to *CTM*
DPL	Division for Professional Leadership, Lutheran Church in America
DTS	Division of Theological Studies, Lutheran Council in the USA
ELCA	Evangelical Lutheran Church in America (1988–)
ELCC	Evangelical Lutheran Church of Canada
Enc. Luth. Ch.	*The Encyclopedia of the Lutheran Church*
HNT	Handbuch zum Neuen Testament
HNTC	Harper New Testament Commentaries
IDB	*The Interpreter's Dictionary of the Bible*
IDBS	*The Interpreter's Dictionary of the Bible, Supplementary Volume*
JAAR	*Journal of the American Academy of Religion*
JES	*Journal of Ecumenical Studies*
JBL	*Journal of Biblical Literature*
KEK	Meyer, Kritisch-Exegetischer Kommentar
LCA	Lutheran Church in America (1962–1987)
LCAM	*Lutheran Church in America Minutes*
LCMS	Lutheran Church–Missouri Synod (1847–)
LCUSA	Lutheran Council in the USA (1966–1987)
LED I, II	Lutheran–Episcopal Dialogue in the United States, Round 1, Round 2
LQ	*Lutheran Quarterly*
LSTC	Lutheran School of Theology at Chicago
LW	*Lutheran World*
LW-AE	Luther's Works, American Edition
LWF	Lutheran World Federation

LWM	Lutheran World Ministries (USA National Committee of the Lutheran World Federation)
NTS	*New Testament Studies*
PE	Philadelphia edition, Works of Martin Luther
RGG	*Die Religion in Geschichte und Gegenwart,* 3rd ed.
SBT	Studies in Biblical Theology
TDNT	*Theological Dictionary of the New Testament*
TFT	Task Force on Theology, CNLC
TLZ	*Theologische Literaturzeitung*
TWNT	*Theologisches Wörterbuch zum Neuen Testament*
ULCA	United Lutheran Church in America
WA	Weimarer Ausgabe of Luther's works
WCC	World Council of Churches
ZNW	*Zeitschrift für die neutestamentliche Wissenschaft*

Spellings and punctuation follow the document being cited, in most cases. Thus, while *episkopē* may be preferred as a transliteration of the Greek word for "oversight," *episcopē*, episcopé, and episcope all appear.

Introduction

Ministering is something the church cannot get along without, for it is of the essence of Christianity. Yet it is also something Christians have had great trouble getting along with. This is so not merely because doing is always harder than willing or thinking a thing. Rather, the fact is that the ministry has often been a source of strife within denominations, and it certainly is a divisive element—perhaps the greatest point of difference among the various churches—to be resolved in any ecumenical reunion.

The root terms for "minister" in both Hebrew and Greek (*shārath* or *ʿābed*, and *diakonein*, respectively) mean "to serve." Ministry is service. Ministers are vehicles for God's serving us and for our serving God and the neighbor in response. This basic nature of ministry—for God's speaking to and enlivening us and for our response of service—makes it indispensable for Christendom.

Yet ministry cannot be simply spontaneous (though it is sometimes). It must somehow be structured and organized; it needs to be carried through "decently and in some sort of order" (cf. 1 Cor. 14:40). Who shall speak for God? Where does authority lie? How is the believing community to save, support, admonish, and, where necessary, discipline its members and through them address the world? Here lies the rub. The ways in which the church's ministering function has been conceived and carried through in practice often divide Christian groups, especially with regard to the role and nature of ordained ministers and the acceptability (or unacceptability) of one church's clergy by another church. To an irritating degree, those who wear their collars backwards, put on vestments, lead worship, preach, and administer the sacraments are therefore the unresolved barrier to fuller Christian fellowship.

All this is no new problem. For already in the New Testament period we hear "the elder" (traditionally, John) protesting that another church leader, "Diotrephes, who likes to put himself first, does not acknowledge my authority" (3 John 9). Another letter laments those who "went out from us, but . . . were not of us" (1 John 2:19); our fellowship is with one another (1:7), not with such "antichrists" (2:19); since there are false prophets claiming to be of God and for Christ, such leaders ("spirits") must be tested (4:1). The New Testament abounds with warnings against false teachers and prophets (Matt. 7:15; 24:11,24; 2 Peter 2:1). Paul urges utmost opposition to those presenting another gospel (Gal. 1:6-9; Phil. 3:2,18-19).

In our own day, it has been common to hold in recent decades that "ministry is in crisis." The ordained clergy have lost a sense of identity, it has been said as long as I can recall. Or, it is maintained, we are on the edge of a great breakthrough in lay leadership; an exciting "era of the laity" is at hand. But that judgment has never quite materialized. As for bishops, take your choice: "This hierarchical office is an anachronism, on the way out, like monarchy," or, "Episcopacy is the only way to go in church governance." The growth in the number of denominations ordaining women and of the number of women clergy in these churches has been hailed as the wave of the future—or by others as a sign of temporary secularization of the true tradition of priesthood, the greatest barrier to ecclesial reunion. Or again, how often is it said that we are facing a crisis of authority in the ministry?

While it is always rash to see one's own day as unusual, let alone unique, it is probably true that there has been more change in the doctrine of the ministry in the past five decades or so—in my lifetime—than for many centuries, perhaps more change than since the turbulent days of the 16th-century Protestant Reformation in Europe. Yet, the modern currents are too diverse simply to call the many changes taking place a "new reformation" or by any other single term.

The six studies that follow all examine the ministry of the church in one form or another. They were written about various aspects of this topic in crisis times over the last 20 years, between 1969 and 1987. All were written "on assignment," as it were, for ecclesiastical or academic occasions, except the final one, which has been prepared specifically for this collection of essays. Two of the five reprinted here were composed for the national Lutheran–Roman Catholic dialogue in the United States. Two were written at the request of Lutheran groups or officials, one for a study by the Lutheran Council in the USA (a cooperative agency involving the major bodies of that denomination) on the ordination of women, the other for discussion within the decision-making process of my own church, the Lutheran Church in America, concerning the title "bishop." The fifth was originally assigned for a symposium on the issue of "church recognition for women's ordination" at the Theology Institute of a Catholic university.

In varying degrees, all these writings are thus rooted in the specific situation of American Lutheranism (though not unaware of the larger world-Lutheran scene), and in one way or another all of them are stamped by an ecumenical concern for all of Christianity. Even what seems the most parochial of the topics, "Shall the LCA employ the title Bishop?" (Chap. 3), could not be discussed without knowledge of the range of positions in the *oikoumēnē* on that usage. Those essays that were originally addressed to an audience that was especially composed of Roman Catholics were not framed, I add, without some awareness of non-Roman Christianity of the Eastern Orthodox type, as well as that of the Evangelical variety.

To a considerable extent the first five studies can also claim to have been written "in the eye of the storm." They were part of public debates, usually within a corporate process of seeking conclusions, among Lutherans or with others, especially Roman Catholics in dialogue. To at least some degree, several of these essays can claim to have been part of a process in the course of which a momentous decision was made, at least for Lutherans: to ordain women; to use the title *bishop* officially; to distinguish clergy and laity so as to lay claim to an ordained ministry in the "catholic" sense but also to view the clergy within the total ministry of all God's people in the church.

Perhaps in each instance age-old positions were simply being reiterated, but there was also something decisive as well as divisive in the positions taken by a dialogue, a convention, or a Lutheran Council statement, of which these essays were a part. Dividing lines must sometimes be drawn, yes or no. Time must judge how significant a part these words played and how momentous in the long run the direction taken proved to be. It is clear, however, that Lutherans in the United States, since 1969, have divided over the issue of ordination of women, have drawn closer in some ways in convergence with Anglicans, Roman Catholics, and others on mutual recognition of ministries, and face new discussions about the ministry in the years ahead.

Details concerning the original publication of these essays are given at the beginning of each. Except for minor corrections, the essays have been reprinted as each originally appeared (so that they are in some sense historical documents) but with the appending of "Supplementary Comments" to each. This approach removes the temptation of rewriting in retrospect and allows the reader to trace both consistency and development in thought. For the record, let it be said that there is little I wish to repudiate. Where "updating" is necessary, opportunity is provided in the new comments and the fresh essay in Chapter 5 about current "crisis questions," especially in light of the 1982 Faith and Order statement on Ministry and experiences on the commission that worked in the years 1982–1986 to plan a new Lutheran Church in the United States.

In editing each essay I have allowed myself occasional improvements in the direction of more inclusive language (a concern scarcely on our consciences in the 1960s or early 70s). In the "Supplementary Comments" to each of the first five chapters there is noted first of all what the result of the piece was in the study or process of which it was a part. Second, some bibliographical additions are usually provided, but only of the most crucial sort. It would be pedantic here to update each footnote with subsequent titles. Third, there is usually some indication of how the essay points toward further issues or discussion. The new concluding chapter has provided the occasion to bring up to date a few issues which were broached with a certain tentativeness a decade or two before or which seemed settled then but have since proven lively.

Before it is asked, one other question needs comment. Though I am, by training and career, a student of the Bible, teaching New Testament in a seminary, there is no essay on "Ministry in Holy Scripture." Why not? The simplest reply is that such an assignment was never called for in the dialogues, studies, and academic settings in which I have been involved. The fuller answer is that to undertake such a study would result in a volume far bigger than this one, if exegesis were thorough and attention given to later developments and the kinds of questions that are of interest to modern church people and ecumenists. Perhaps some day. . . . Meanwhile, I have availed myself of references to a few of the existing treatments, often excellent, on ministry as seen biblically by writers of various church backgrounds and outlooks. Finally, I would like to think that, in addressing the topics assigned, I have kept in mind a biblical perspective and at times have dealt with pertinent scriptural material.

As part of this Introduction, it is in order here to comment on the sequence of the essays and how they fit together. Generally they are arranged chronologically, but there is a further logic that moves from a basic, historic overview to specific issues that reflect some of the current crises about ministry. In the following paragraphs the endeavor is to suggest what I see the collection of essays to be addressing and what not.

In what is now Chapter 1 an effort is made to set forth *a Lutheran view of ministry,* ministry both by lay people and by clergy, that is foundational for the other essays to follow. The origin of this essay lies within the fourth round of the Lutheran–Roman Catholic dialogue in the United States, which took place between 1968 and 1970. That context and the assignment there account for my starting point at the Reformation and the emphasis on "the ordained" or, as the dialogue was later to distinguish, "the Ministry" (capital "M"), in contradistinction to "ministry" (lower case "m"; Greek, *diakonia*) that belongs to the "task or service of the whole church" (see §9 in the Common Statement of the dialogue volume, cited in the introduction to Chap. 1 below).

As to the exact role of this essay in the dialogue as a whole, we are fortunate in having for this round an account of developments written by a participant at the conclusion of the process: "Stages in Questions and Development" by Maurice C. Duchaine, in *Eucharist and Ministry,* Lutherans and Catholics in

Dialogue (1970, repr. Minneapolis: Augsburg, 1979), pp. 34-68. Rarely has a dialogue been so reported for its inner workings.

After treating, in a pioneering way, the Nicene Creed (1965) and baptism (1966), the U.S. dialogue turned to what had been more divisive between Catholics and Lutherans, the Lord's Supper or eucharist. In what was hailed widely as a breakthrough, the dialoguers treated the issues of "(real) presence" (something which Catholics had long doubted that Lutherans really believed) and "sacrifice" (where Protestants traditionally saw unevangelical sentiments in Catholic belief and practice). The volume from round three was published in 1967 under the title *The Eucharist as Sacrifice* (reprinted by Augsburg Publishing House as Part III of *Lutherans and Catholics in Dialogue I–III*). After an unsuccessful session on "intercommunion" (where the importance, indeed the necessity, for Roman Catholics of having as celebrant a priest ordained by bishops under the see of Rome became apparent), we turned to ministry. The focus was on the "Special [or ordained] Ministry," specifically with regard to the eucharist.

As background for discussion of the theme, I had provided (as we often do in the dialogue, to share existing material that might be helpful) a paper entitled "*Diakonia*: Scriptural Foundation." It had been prepared originally for an anniversary of the deaconess movement in the Lutheran Church–Missouri Synod and was made available in mimeographed form in the proceedings of a celebratory symposium at Valparaiso University in 1964.[1] Those observations helped lead to a presentation for the dialogue in February 1969, by Father Raymond E. Brown, s.s., on the possibility of "a variety of patterns of church structure in the first and early second centuries." Crucial issues for the dialogue, however, were to be found more in the developments during the patristic centuries and the Reformation (Duchaine, pp. 35, 36, 38-39).

In the dialogue we sometimes employ the device of asking each other questions in order to attain clarity. Thus, in this round, it was my task to answer a Catholic inquiry as to how important it is in a Lutheran view of the church that there be "presbyterial succession," i.e., that pastors are always ordained by other pastors. (If not episcopal succession or ordination by bishops, Lutherans have prized this sort of sequence from pastors to pastors.) The answer asserted that "for Lutherans 'succession' is first of all succession in the gospel" but that "there is also regularly a succession of ministers to ministers. . . . Clergy are regularly ordained by clergy" (Duchaine, pp. 44-45). Very well, then, Catholics asked, their interest peaked, "What difference does Lutheranism see between the ordained Lutheran minister and the Lutheran layperson?" That was the assignment for the paper to be read at the Baltimore meeting in September 1969, my first major paper for the dialogue, ironically covering almost everything but New Testament data! (See Duchaine, p. 60.) The paper was part of a process that led to a statement on "areas of agreement and disagreement between Lutherans and Roman Catholics in the question of eucharist and ministry, without attempting to cover all the bases on the subject of ministry" (ibid., p. 67).

This attempt to sketch a basic Lutheran position on ministry, ordained and lay, while admitting to the tremendous variety that had obtained historically and even varied strands of emphasis that go back to Luther himself—e.g., on the "universal priesthood of all the baptized" and the "public office of minister"—was discussed within the dialogue and deemed important enough to include in the dialogue report. It has also enjoyed a useful subsequent history. The paper has sometimes been shared with participants from other churches in dialogue with Lutherans in order to provide them with a basic orientation on this involved topic. The essay has also been separately reprinted as a resource for the continuing education lectures given by Dr. Joseph A. Burgess in the audiocassette "Select" series from Trinity Seminary, Columbus, Ohio, in 1984. I regard this 1969 paper as both introductory and foundational to grasping the Lutheran view (or views) on ministry of all sorts.

Does such a historical and descriptive paper have anything to do with a "crisis" in ministry? Yes, in the sense that for some Lutherans (and other churches) it was news to discover that Lutherans had regularly insisted on their ministers being ordained by other ministers in a presbyterial succession, and that the office of public ministry is thus not a haphazard creation at the whim of each local congregation. Conversely, others have had to give heed to the fact that recovery of the role of the laity in ministry has a pedigree that goes back to Luther.

Chapter 2 below combines two essays on *the crisis issue of ordaining women*. The first, Part A, written in 1968 for an inter-Lutheran study, concentrates on the biblical evidence, pro and con, for such a step. Part B presents part of a paper read nine years later at Villanova University in a summer Theology Institute on *Ministering in a Servant Church*. While the biblical data are reexamined there from a different angle, certain portions have been omitted to avoid repetitions with the 1968 paper. The 1977 essay was able to reflect on the positive Lutheran experience in ordaining women as well as men since 1970 and broaches an argument that may have appeal to Orthodox as well as Roman Catholic theology, that women might be ordained, even though ecclesial custom has been against it, on the grounds of the principle of "economy." This device permits, out of merciful condescension, what canonically is not allowed. It could be a way to validate ministries of other churches in a divided Christendom and to deal with an otherwise unprecedented step (in these traditions) of allowing women into the priesthood.

I regard the two parts of this chapter as an exegetical and hermeneutical discussion that sets forth why women can, in spite of centuries of contrary practice, be a part of the church's Ministry at all levels. The case is presented both for the Lutherans and all others who have a penchant for the supreme importance of what the Bible says (Part A) and for other Christians ecumenically whose ecclesial tradition seems to demand opposing such a step (Part B). The arguments presented should not be regarded as past history, even for churches that have already begun to ordain persons without respect to gender, for the ecumenical movement raises afresh the question whether these churches should continue to insist on women's ordination if it blocks progress with those in the Catholic and Orthodox traditions. The 1982 Faith and Order statement raises that very issue, as we shall see in Chapter 5. The temptation may be for some ecumenists to scrap further ordinations of women in order to secure consensus with a long tradition of solely male priesthood. Put bluntly, those favoring women in ministry had better continue to know the reasons for so doing, particularly the exegetical and theological arguments.

The two essays combined in Chapter 2 came about in different ways. While Free Church groups had for some decades been permitting women into their clergy ranks, Lutherans and Anglicans, like the Roman Catholics and Orthodox, for two-thirds of this century continued to follow the practice of the past: men only. By 1960, however, a number of Lutheran churches in Europe authorized the ordination of women, and during the sixties voices were increasingly heard within Lutheran circles in the United States urging such a step (see section B, Part III, below, for details and documentation). The American Lutheran Church asked the then newly formed Lutheran Council in the U.S.A. to study the question in 1967. This was done through a subcommittee of the Council's Division of Theological Studies.

The ecclesiastical situation in the Lutheran churches that were involved differed considerably at the time. The LCA, which seemed ready to take the step without any LCUSA study, actually delayed consideration of women's ordination in 1968 in hopes of broader Lutheran agreement. The ALC was regarded as less persuaded, but likely also to vote such a step. The Lutheran Church–Missouri Synod had a policy of opposing women in the church's public ministry on scriptural grounds. There was, however, within the LCMS, discussion of whether women could vote in congregational elections, as men did. (One needs to recall that even in the United States women had not had political suffrage for most of the history of the Republic, and in democratic Switzerland women had no vote until 1971.) Moreover, the Missouri Synod's history included longtime controversy over the numerous parochial school teachers who were deemed not lay people but not clergy either (see below, Chap. 1, §§66, 75). Many of these Christian day-school teachers were women. To have decided for the ordination of women and the inclusion of such teachers as ministers would have automatically given Missouri the largest number of women on the clergy roll of any church in North America!

The Lutheran Council study went thoroughly into sociological and psychological factors and ecumenical praxis as well as theological arguments, especially in the Lutheran tradition (for a list of papers, see Chap. 2, B, note 118, below). My own assignment was to write on "What in Scripture Speaks to the Ordination of Women?" As a result of discussion in the Division of Theological Studies a statement emerged that, by agreement, was middle-of-the-road and, one hoped, could be acceptable to all involved: it held that scripturally and theologically "there are no conclusive grounds for forbidding the ordination of women and no definitive ones for demanding it"; social and other factors could allow churches to have differing practices but still remain in fellowship.

When these findings were examined at a further LCUSA consultation in 1969, the chief Missouri Synod opposition to the paper on the scriptural data came on the grounds of the "orders of creation" and passages about the "headship" of men over women. It was argued that, by the very way God has structured creation, women are unable to engage in rule and leadership over men. To satisfy a request that passages said to take this line ought to be more fully treated in my paper, a new section was added (below, Part A, IV. B. 6-8) before the papers from the study process went to the member churches.

At the annual meeting of the Lutheran Council in February 1970, it was likely that the representatives of ALC, LCA, and the LCMS would have voted for the ordination of women as a recommendation to all three churches. But the motion was left merely at the level of transmission of the findings and a call for study by each church. A further resolution mandated, however, a popularized summary of our work for wider distribution. Unfortunately, this summary,[2] in its effort to be popular, struck too glib a note, and President J. A. O. Preus of the Lutheran Church–Missouri Synod used what he termed its "flippant" style to raise questions about the whole report.

Subsequently, the ALC and LCA voted to ordain women (in 1970). The LCMS, in 1969, while allowing women to vote and sit on boards where "the order of creation" is not violated, continued to reject women in the pastoral office. It is scarcely a secret that the ALC's action was especially responsible for the Missouri Synod's withdrawing from formal ties of fellowship that had begun with ALC. The use of Scripture in the decision to ordain women has often been cited as a dividing line between Missouri and the other Lutheran churches.[3] It is not too much to say that the work on ordaining women in 1968–1970 contributed to the present configuration of Lutherans in the United States—a uniting new Lutheran church made up of ALC, LCA, and some congregations that left Missouri (the Association of Evangelical Lutheran Churches) in contrast to the LCMS with its scriptural opposition to women in ordained ministry.

In Part B of Chapter 2 some of this fuller story is recounted, but with a vastly more ecumenical audience in mind. The conference theme at Villanova of a "servant church" immediately put one back into a positive New Testament perspective, as did a presentation earlier in the week by Prof. Reginald H. Fuller on "The Son of Man Came to Serve, Not to Be Served." But my assignment, to deal with "ecclesial recognition" of the ministry of women, confronted one with the stubborn fact of Christian differences about recognizing each other's ministries as valid and with the long tradition against women in ministry.

Ecclesiology and ministry intertwine. And ecclesiology includes the structure and governance of the church. There must be leadership for units larger than the local parish. Historically, this role has usually fallen to a clergyman (almost never women, over 2000 years). This ordained minister presided over congregations and church institutions of a region, often in concert with fellow leaders of like units and usually was assisted (or perhaps checked) by a collegium, a church council, synod, or other group. Traditionally, this regional leader was called a bishop. The Greek term, *episkopos,* which may—but need not—be so translated, appears already in the New Testament (e.g., Phil. 1:1; 1 Tim. 3:2), basically for one who "oversees" the church's work. It later took on further connotations. Eventually there appeared a threefold pattern of "bishop," presbyter or priest, and deacon.

While the medieval pattern of episcopal government and much that such a structure had come to mean continued after the Reformation in parts of Protestant Europe like Sweden and England, most Lutheran settlers in America brought with them other customary titles, like "superintendent," or adopted the more democratic terminology of America, "president." Lutherans in the United States, therefore, with few (and usually unhappy) exceptions, like "Bishop" Martin Stephan (see Chap. 1, §59), did not employ the term *bishop.*

But occasionally voices began to be heard for change here too. I recall that my father, a parish pastor in the ULCA, had spoken for it in the 1930s. By 1970 the ALC began using it informally. The LCA, as usual, opted for the route of constitutional change, but rejected the title at conventions in 1972 and 1974 (it required a two-thirds vote and got only a majority). But for consideration at the 1980 convention I was asked by the Division for Professional Leadership to prepare a paper on this issue.

Chapter 3, therefore, takes up *the title "bishop"* within an ongoing LCA and broader Lutheran debate. The paper itself details the history involved. On the one hand, the decision cannot be regarded as a "crisis"; on the other hand, emotions did run high, as they had for some years. Shall it be democracy or ecclesiastical tyranny? Is it a distinctive churchly title or another catholicizing trend? Even though no change in power of the leaders involved was at issue, a number of subtle psychological and social factors was at stake.

Moreover, issues were raised that are still before Lutherans and other churches concerning the office of more-than-local-congregational leadership.

That the 1980 discussion had an affirmative outcome, adopting the title, was probably due to a variety of factors, including the 450th anniversary of the Augsburg Confession celebrated that year (which challenged Lutherans to be both evangelical and catholic) and the use of the term elsewhere in Lutheranism, including (informally) the ALC and the AELC, and the impact of the Catholic dialogue. I regard the decision in 1980, to use the title in the LCA, as one small step in putting the Lutheran house in better order—though without all the connotations or the same accouterments that adhere to episcopal order for Anglicans, Roman Catholics, Methodists, or others. *Bishop* has had many institutional meanings in the long history of the churches. Lutherans ought to be free to define a specific sense of the term for themselves, within their general view of ministry.

The adoption of the title *bishop* by the LCA constitutionally and the ensuing years of experience with it no doubt eased the way for use of the term in the new Lutheran church that took shape in the 1980s. But it also provoked comments about the need for "real bishops" (a phrase seldom defined) and debate over their power and authority and hence the authority of the Ministry as a whole within the church. The final essay that is reprinted in this volume as Chapter 4, while dealing with a rather specific area within "authority," that of the grounds for the church's teaching ministry, raises what is a perennial concern: by what right (or rite, some would say) do ministers speak and act?

The U.S. Lutheran–Roman Catholic dialogue has become more intentional and precise in its use of Scripture over its 20 years of existence. Although, from the first, attention was given to biblical aspects of a topic and at times a Catholic and a Lutheran exegete were each asked to write on the same subject, it was increasingly discovered that in the Bible a great meeting ground was shared and that our use of modern methods of historical criticism had much in common. Accordingly, it was possible, in connection with the treatment of papal ministry, to employ an approach where a group of biblical scholars outside the dialogue looked in depth at "Peter in the New Testament." Their study,[4] published in 1973, was used by the dialogue as a whole, and since the task force included others than Lutherans and Catholics, the report on Peter became a resource for other dialogues. This method proved so successful that a second task force produced a collaborative assessment on Mary[5] in 1978 that was of value to the U.S. dialogue in its work on infallibility (since it is in Marian dogma that papal infallibility is chiefly to be seen) and in the eighth round of discussion, on "Mary and the Saints" (1984–   ).

In discussing infallibility the dialogue early determined that some scriptural work would be needed but, since "infallibility" as a concept involves all sorts of post–New Testament developments, one can scarcely do a paper on such a theme in the Bible. But the linkage with the previous round on the papacy readily suggested that treatment was needed on teaching authority in the New Testament. What is the basis for the authority to teach definitively? Is there a specific "office" or locus whence teaching for the whole community emanates? The matter was regarded as especially a "Catholic problem," and it was clear that a Catholic should write on it (just as, in the next round, "justification" was deemed a Lutheran theme and so a Lutheran should write on it). It was also established that this work did not call for a task force to investigate the matter; rather, it should be done within the dialogue itself. The Rev. Joseph A. Fitzmyer, s.j., was designated to present the Catholic paper on "The Office of Teaching in the Christian Church according to the New Testament."

Chapter 4 below consists of the response I was assigned to make to Professor Fitzmyer's paper at the September 1974 meeting of the dialogue in Princeton, N.J., on *authority in the teaching office*. It is the shortest of the essays reprinted here, except for that on the title *bishop*. It may seem the least able of the collection to stand on its own feet, since it is a response to someone else's work (though enough of a summary of Father Fitzmyer's findings is given that the response is, I believe, comprehensible). It may seem the least relevant of the essays, because of the connection with "infallibility" (a term applied to pope or Bible but which tends to rub off as a concept onto the ministry).

Yet the discussion raises some issues that might be said to constitute a somewhat hidden crisis for the ministry. Though we may not use the word *infallible* or even think much of "teaching office" in an age not prone to church doctrine, the fact is that ordained Ministry frequently faces questions about its authority. We question the credentials of the leaders in sect groups— and then discover, no matter what our denomination, that other churches question the credentials of our clergy. We live in a time when it has become common for people to question their own authority. Clergy doubt their own office! Even tight-knit hierarchical structures have somewhat broken down under the acids of modernity. And even if we are clear on our identity, the world certainly questions it. Not just clergy, however. Laypersons too must face uncertainties and insecurities about their right to do this or that in ministry in Jesus' name.

The focus in this chapter on authority in the teaching office turns out to be no superfluity either. What Jesus taught was at the center of his identity; it prompted responses of yes or no to him, and led to his death. What churches teach is a matter of identity too, a vital one—what to teach authoritatively, how to arrive at this, how much variety to tolerate in teaching. In much recent discussion teaching authority has been related especially to the role of the bishop, but there has also been increasing attention to the role of the laity here. And the teaching ministry of the clergy can be said to have come to the fore in the last decade too. Hence teaching authority is a matter in which all Christians have a stake.

Chapter 5 has been written specifically for this book. It seeks to introduce the *issues posed on ministry in the late 1980s* by the major ecumenical statement on the subject in this century, that on *Baptism, Eucharist and Ministry* from the Faith and Order Commission of the World Council of Churches in 1982. The chapter presents also some *reflections of* the experiences I and some 70 other U.S. Lutherans had from 1982 till 1986 working on *the Commission for a New Lutheran Church*, from whose proposals came the Evangelical Lutheran Church in America (which begins operations on January 1, 1988).

Neither topic can be treated definitively here. The *BEM* statement is worthy of—and has received—treatment in numerous articles and books. Having dealt with its eucharist section elsewhere,[6] I am keenly aware of the need for much fuller discussion on the ministry and of the problems surrounding it—far more complicated than for baptism or the Lord's Supper, in my opinion. But what *BEM* proposes is on the agenda—or ought to be—of all churches and of all Christians. Nor do I wish the few pages on the intra-Lutheran discussions of the CNLC to be regarded as a full chronicle or insider's interpretation of those four years of work by what was one of the largest and most egalitarian committees ever to plan a church. To take up "ministry," however, in a group that was predominantly lay, balanced between women and men, and inclusive of minorities was already to provide a nontraditional setting for discussion.

Yet the two events—*BEM* and CNLC—go together in several ways. The commissioners for the new Lutheran church were often aware of what had been said ecumenically. Indeed, the Director of the Secretariat on Faith and Order when the report on *Baptism, Eucharist and Ministry* was completed, Dr. William Lazareth, was one of the 70 on the CNLC. The commission, unable to settle all disputes about the ministry, built in a required study by the ELCA in its first six years on the ministry, including attention to precisely what *BEM* suggests: "the possibility of articulating a Lutheran understanding and adaptation of the threefold ministerial office of bishop, pastor, and deacon and its ecumenical implications."[7]

For that task of study, practice, and lived ministry that lies ahead for the ELCA—not just by a commission but by all segments of its membership—perhaps these pages will be of some help. Perhaps too that study will show, as these chapters often suggest, a symbiosis as well as a tension, in the ellipse between a specific tradition (like the Lutheran) and the ecumenical whole, between a specific church and the churches together. For one suspects that we shall not get our Lutheran view of ministry clear without attention to the ecumenical aspects—or get the ecumenical household in order without involvement in ministry of Lutherans as well as Anglicans, Reformed, Roman Catholics, Methodists, Orthodox, and all others who name the name of Christ.

For Christians in other churches who likewise face the ongoing task of relating established patterns of ministry to a changing world, perhaps these pages will be of some help by documenting the Lutheran struggles of recent decades, which often parallel what other churches have gone through or may experience. The "ecumenical implications" of "a Lutheran understanding," called for in the ELCA study, may be a gift to others of how to relate tradition and freedom. But there is obviously a flip side of how ecumenical understandings have implications for Lutherans. And so with other traditions.

In concluding, two notes in the personal realm. First, my thanks to the staff of Augsburg Publishing House, without whose vision and suggestions these essays would not have come together in this book. Likewise to Dr. Joseph A. Burgess, who encouraged the project, and the Rev. Constance F. Parvey, from whom I learn much about women in the churches. To Ms. Laurie Pellman, faculty secretary at the Philadelphia Seminary, I am grateful for deciphering my manuscript of new materials for this book and amending my own input on the word processor.

Second, a personal confession. I have probably been known over the years in many circles as an advocate of a positive view of the office of the Ministry, of the ordained, the *ministerium verbi divini*, for I have often said in addresses, sermons, and forums that every formal statement on the ministry of my church—the LCA or its predecessor body, the United Lutheran Church in America—has seemed to knock down or throw into confusion the self-understanding of the pastor, so that there have been needless identity crises. I have long been convinced that the Ministry of the Word, in preaching, sacraments, and pastoral care, could and should be lifted high, so that it can proclaim the gospel for which it is called. But I have never thought that this needs to be done by denigrating the ministering of all the baptized, the work of the whole people of God in the world.

In thinking through positions over the past 20 years or so I have come to see, I must confess, laity in ministry as the cutting edge, the new discovery that we have not adequately conceptualized in theology or done justice to in reality. My period of service on the CNLC has strengthened that conviction while not diminishing my understanding of the necessity of those who are ordained in their crucial task of "ministering to the ministers." These pages will not work out a theology and praxis for unleashing laypersons to serve God in their callings—as ministers—but perhaps they can lay some groundwork for what Luther and most recent ecumenical statements advocate or at least give lip service to, the ministry of the whole people of God, within which that of the clergy is a necessary part—but only a portion of the whole—under God, "whose service is perfect freedom" (*cui servare regnare est,* literally, "whom to serve is to reign"). May ministry be service in the reign of God.

1

The Ministries of the Ordained and of the Laity in Lutheranism

This essay, which seeks to give an overall Lutheran view on the topic of "ministry," was originally published as "Ordained Minister and Layman in Lutheranism," in *Eucharist and Ministry*, Lutherans and Catholics in Dialogue IV, published jointly by Representatives of the U.S.A. National Committee of the Lutheran World Federation and the Bishops' Committee for Ecumenical and Interreligious Affairs (Washington, D.C.: United States Catholic Conference, and New York: U.S.A. National Committee of the Lutheran World Federation, 1970): 227-82; Augsburg Publishing House edition, 1979.

An answer to the question posed by the Catholics, "What differences does Lutheranism see between the ordained Lutheran minister and the Lutheran layman?" could be ventured simply by jotting down impressions one has. But such an answer might vary with the Lutheran making it.

Accordingly, in order to do justice to the complex evidence, noting the tendencies and tensions which have appeared in the Lutheran understanding of "ministry," it is necessary (1) to examine the topic in the Reformation, especially in the confessions; (2) to see something of the historical development since the 16th century, in Europe and more particularly in America, especially the discussion in the 19th century; (3) to summarize what constitutions, commission reports, and other documents of Lutheran bodies in America say on ordained ministry and laity, and then to draw on what further evidence is available from sociological surveys, current periodical literature, and other sources on how Lutherans are thinking about what is a question in all Christendom, the relation of the ordained and the unordained in ministry.

This survey of theological, historical, constitutional, sociological, and other material will be presented generally along chronological lines, from past to present, and in a way which concentrates geographically more and more on the United States. No attempt is made to encompass many developments in other parts of the world, and backgrounds prior to the Reformation period, especially in discussion of the biblical sources, are only alluded to, not evaluated.

I. "Ministry" in the Reformation Era

1. What the Reformers have to say about "ministry" must be seen in light of the theology and practices of the church of the Middle Ages. This means both that they were influenced by earlier and current views of the ministry— in the case of conservative reformers like Luther the tendency was to hold on to many existing structures—and were in reaction against certain existing understandings. (Then, and to this day, Lutheran views on ministry are often stated against the foil of medieval, or later, Catholic positions.) In particular, Reformation statements about the ministry are reacting to a clear and rigid distinction between laity and clergy, the latter structured in a graded hierarchy.[1]

2. Nonetheless, it is to be noted, the doctrine of the ministry cannot be called a major item in Reformation controversy with Rome. There is in the Lutheran confessions, for example, "surprisingly little about the office of the ministry," it is "incidental and secondary to the real controversy."[2] Accordingly, the Lutheran Reformation did not devote major attention to the topic, and there is a tendency today to regard what was done as "makeshift" or "temporary," or to claim that what Luther envisioned was never carried through.[3]

3. Coupled with this is the fact that for Lutherans matters of church structure and ministerial organization were and are adiaphoral. No one theory of church organization was espoused by the Lutheran Reformers as essential to the nature of the church or as *the* "biblical" one. What mattered instead was the word or gospel. This freedom about ministerial structure led inevitably, in different situations, to a variety of practices regarding the ordained ministry.

4. In particular, as a general impression, it has been claimed that two strands of thinking appear in Luther and the Lutheran confessions about the ministry, and that these two factors are repeatedly affirmed in succeeding centuries by Lutherans: (1) the universal priesthood of all the baptized, on the basis of which Lutheranism rejected as unbiblical any "qualitative distinction of clergy and laity grounded *de jure divino* in a special power of ordination" and any "clerical rank set over the laity . . . in hierarchic steps";[4] (2) the necessity of the public office of the ministry of the word, instituted by God, through the church.

Sometimes one pole in this tension is emphasized more than the other, but extremes whereby only one strand is present have regularly been repudiated within Lutheranism. To the extent that both elements were present in the 16th century, some of the uncertainty in present-day discussion over the doctrine of the ministry among Lutherans can in part be traced.

5. Finally, by way of general comment, it needs to be added that the emphatic point in the Reformation view of the ministry is an understanding of it as ministry of the word of God, i.e., the gospel, or, to put it in terms of the confessions, justification and the forgiveness of sins (shorthand expressions of what the gospel means). What is said about ministry in the "structure of Lutheranism" is bound firmly to "the impact of the gospel" *(evangelischer Ansatz),* to use Werner Elert's characteristic phrase.[5] A key to the thinking of the confessions is the realization that the controversy is not "ministry versus ministry" but "the word versus the ministry"—i.e., ministry, in the sense of the hierarchy, had come to occupy, in the medieval church's life, the central place which belonged to the word of God. Edgar M. Carlson puts it thus:

> . . . in Rome the ministry (i.e., the hierarchy) presided over the Word; in the Reformation view the Word presided over the ministry. In Rome the Word was an instrument through which the ministry functioned; in Luther the ministry was instrumental to the Word. . . . Therefore, the counterpart in Reformation theology to the hierarchy in Roman theology is not the ministry but the Word.[6]

This formulation is admittedly oversimplified, but it makes the necessary point that Lutheranism is accustomed to discuss the ministry in light of the word, not to defend a divine order of ministers, as central.

A. Luther on "Ministry"

6. In summarizing Luther's views it makes a considerable difference for the outcome whether one begins with and emphasizes statements from his voluminous writings about the universal priesthood of all the baptized, e.g.,

> We are all priests, as many of us as are Christians. But the priests, as we call them, are ministers chosen from among us, who do all that they do in our name,[7]

or statements about the public office of minister or preacher, e.g.,

> It is true that all Christians are priests, but they are not all pastors. Over and above that he is a Christian and priest, he must also have an office and a field of work *(Kirchspiel)* that has been committed to his charge.[8]

> . . . A distinction is given between preacher and laymen.[9]

7. One recent study concludes that these two lines of thought coexist in Luther in an irreducible tension, but that the "more prominent notion" is of ministry as a divine institution, while the idea of it as "derived from the common priesthood" is a "subordinate line in Luther's thinking."[10]

8. Another study which appeared about the same time attempts to show development in Luther's thought on the ministry in three stages: (1) up through 1519 there is little evidence that his view differed from that of the medieval

church; (2) a great change took place in 1520–1525, so that Luther, in protest against the "clerical priesthood of the papal system," vigorously championed the universal priesthood and local congregation, arguing that it transfers from itself whatever functional authority the ordained ministry possesses; then (3) Luther, because the notion that the ministry derives from the universal priesthood "did not wear well" and the universal priesthood "failed in maintaining the preachers," began again to give greater authority to the ministry as an office, different from the spiritual priesthood of all believers. [11]

9. Real question can be raised, however, as to whether the pictures of stages (2) and (3) are accurate. Attractive as it may be to assume that outbursts in Wittenberg (1521–1522), the Peasants' Revolt (1524–1526), and the Saxon Visitation (1527–1528) convinced the "older Luther" of the need for an order of ministry, the fact is that the Luther of 1520–1525 seems to have had no intention of doing away with an ordained ministry or of putting clergy under laity or of allowing the local congregation to eclipse the larger fellowship of the church. What is more, what is called "new" after 1526 in this picture of development can be well established in Luther in the earlier period. [12]

10. If such a "development" in Luther is thus unlikely, so also is the notion of an irreducible tension between two theories, for the theories as foisted on Luther prove "spurious." While later Lutherans were to debate a "theory of transfer" *(Übertragungslehre)* of authority from the universal priesthood to its ordained ministers, there is considerable agreement that for Luther the "universal priesthood" [13] did not imply transfer of priestly rights from laity to the clergy or even a "delegation theory." [14] As for the greater prominence assumed in Luther for the "divine institution" idea, the few texts offered as proof seem not to "prove anything of the kind." [15]

11. Thus we are left in Luther not with a wavering course of development back and forth or a tension for interpreters to resolve in one way or another, but a commitment to the fact that God instituted both the church (a universal priesthood) and its public ministerial office, [16] but not an office independent of the church, and not a priesthood merely of the laity but of the church as a whole. Thus, *"the church is a priesthood; it has an ordained ministry."* To ask whether the special ministry rests on the common priesthood of believers or on a direct divine institution, whether its authority comes "from below" or "from above," is to ask the wrong question of Luther. The real tension is the "wonder of God's working in and through men." The ambiguity often stems from two uses of the expression "ministry of the word," as (1) "the church's (the priesthood's) task of proclaiming the gospel," (2) "the public office in the church; the clergy are the special ministers of the church, around whom the church's order is built." [17]

Historians will probably continue to debate precisely where Luther stood, when, on the ministry and priesthood, seizing on phrases here and there, even those in a summary such as that just noted by Robert H. Fischer. It is significant that Fischer himself concludes by referring to a summary on the Lutheran confessions.

12. A note on Melanchthon: though (because?) he was a layman, Melanchthon seems to have stressed the dignity of the ministerial office more than Luther did and was more emphatic about its divine institution, omitting connections with the universal priesthood. The point is worth noting in that Melanchthon was author of some of the confessional writings and because his formulations were often stressed in Lutheran Orthodoxy.[18]

B. In the Lutheran Confessions

13. The pertinent sections in the confessional writings (where the structure of the church and the relation of clergy to laity were generally not primary issues) include Augsburg Confession (1530), Articles 5, 14, and 28; Apology of the Augsburg Confession (1531), Articles 13, 14, and 28; Smalcald Articles (1536–1538), Part III, Articles 9 and 10; and the "Treatise on the Power and Primacy of the Pope" (1537).[19]

14. (1) The starting point in the Augsburg Confession for such references as do occur is striking: Article 5, "The Office of the Ministry" (Latin, "The Ministry of the Church"; it really concerns the means of grace), comes immediately after the central article on justification:

> To obtain such faith God instituted the office of the ministry, that is, provided the Gospel and the sacraments. . . (Latin, "In order that we may obtain this faith, the ministry of teaching the Gospel and administering the sacraments was instituted. . ."),

and just before Article 6 on "The New Obedience" ("It is also taught among us that such faith should produce good fruits and good works. . ."). The ministry is thus thought of in light of the gospel ("justification") and of bringing people to faith which produces fruits; it is seen in relation to salvation and the means of grace.[20]

15. Coupled with this starting point is the fact that when the church is discussed in Article 7 (". . .the assembly of all believers among whom the Gospel is preached in its purity and the holy sacraments are administered according to the Gospel") "no mention is made of the office of the ministry"[21] as constitutive for the church. Ministry is spoken of only in light of the gospel (Article 5) and in connection with good order (Article 14, "nobody should publicly teach or preach or administer the sacraments in the church without a regular call") and the power of bishops, which turns out to be the power of the gospel (Article 28, the power of bishops or of the keys is to preach the gospel, forgive sins, administer the sacraments, by divine right, and is

not to be confused with jurisdiction granted by virtue of human right; the functions of spiritual and of temporal power are not to be mingled or confused). This means that, while a ministry is implied in the church, it is "not an independently existing institution but only a service to the Gospel."[22]

16. (2) The royal priesthood of all the baptized—the emphasis on which in Reformation writings is "due in some measure to the claims made for the Roman priesthood"[23]—is presupposed, even in Article 14. The gospel and its functions are given to the church as a whole.

17. But while all justified Christians have a right and duty to proclaim the word, a special office of preaching is also assumed. "Because the spiritual office has been entrusted to all believers, its administration is not left to the whim of every individual believer. The public administration depends, rather, on the authorization of the assembly of believers. Because the ministry is entrusted to the church, the church calls the particular believer into the office of public preaching and administration of the sacraments" ("Treatise on the Power and Primacy of the Pope" 60-72).

18. Involved here is a distinction between "private" and "public" functioning and also a distinction between "priestly" and "ministerial." As Edmund Schlink puts it, " 'Ministerial' . . . means that in the congregation the preacher of the Gospel serves the priestly commission which God has given the whole congregation."[24] The fact that there is a public ministry does not, however, abolish the right of all believers to, or excuse them from, their priestly functioning.

19. (3) Within the total priesthood of the church there is thus, under the word of God, a functional office of the ministry which is completely necessary in the life of the church for proclaiming God's word in its various forms. This "office of preaching the Gospel and administering the sacraments" in the church is viewed as "spiritual government" in parallel with "civil government," in terms of the "two realms," both of which derive their dignity from the word of God. However, the *ordo* in the spiritual office is not that of the civil government (cf. Augsburg Confession 16); it is not merely "created and instituted" (*geschaffen und eingesetzt,* as 16, 1, says of civil government) for good order, but is instituted by God's command and promise, originally in the calling of the apostles and thereafter through God's call in the church— "wherever God gives his gifts, apostles, prophets, pastors, teachers" (Treatise 26)—to set forth the gospel.[25] "Wherever the church exists, the right to administer the Gospel also exists. Wherefore it is necessary for the church to retain the right of calling, electing, and ordaining ministers" (ibid. 67).

20. The functions especially noted for this ministry within the priesthood of the church include preaching, teaching, administration of the sacraments, prayer with parishioners, etc.[26] One recent examination of "ministry" in the confessions led to the answer, "unexpected" and perhaps different from "the

way in which we who are ministers have conceived of our office," that the "official and essential function" of the office of minister is "to absolve from sin" (Augsburg Confession 25, 28; Apology 11, 12). Absolution would thus be "the central core of the conception of ministry," and the minister is a "forgiveness-man." This understanding of the ministry is then related to the universal priesthood by seeing the "mutual conversation and consolation of brethren" (Smalcald Articles, Part Three, 4) as "a sort of lay equivalent of the office of the keys for the clergy."[27]

21. As one 19th-century theologian, Charles Porterfield Krauth,[28] summed up the import of Article 5 in the Augsburg Confession: "there is such a thing as the ministry," it is "an institution" which did not "expire with the apostleship," but is "founded by authority," "exists by necessity," and "is intended to be permanent"; this ministry is "instituted by God" with its functions "to teach the Gospel" and "impart the Sacraments"; this ministry, which no one enters without a call of God mediated through the church, is "the ordinary medium by which men, led by the Word and Sacraments to a living faith, obtain salvation."

22. (4) This special office of ministry, instituted by God, called through the church, is regularly regarded as one office, where all are equal, without ranks and grades (which arise only by human authority). Though this ministry represents Christ—not itself (Apology 7 and 8, 28 and 47)—it is not above the church ("the church is above the ministers," Treatise 4). It is, further, a ministry where all ministers are on an equality (ibid.; also Treatise 63), whether they are termed "pastors, presbyters, or bishops" (Treatise 61). The "distinction between the grades of bishop and presbyter (or pastor) is by human authority" (Treatise 63, citing Jerome) and "not by divine right." Involved here is a view of New Testament ministry reflecting, for all its variety, one office, the "proclamation of the divine word," and not a fixed hierarchy; cf. Luther's "Prayer of a Pastor," in WA 43, p. 513, "Lord God, Thou hast made me a bishop and pastor in the church. . . ." Just as no distinction between all the universal priests ("laity") and the public ministry ("clergy") is envisioned, except functionally, so also no distinctions within the public office of ministry are assumed, except functionally by human authority.

23. If we ask why the Lutheran Reformation insists on an office of the ministry, even though it has so radically changed the structures of the medieval church by emphasizing universal priesthood and the equality within the one office of proclaimer *(Predigtamt)*, the answer is twofold, not merely on pragmatic grounds but because of a divine institution.[29] (1) There is, admittedly, a purely practical, utilitarian side—aesthetically, for the sake of good order, lest there be "a confused bawling such as. . . among frogs" (WA, 10, I, 2, p. 239, 25), and ethically, for the sake of the brother, so that no one claim what is the right also of every brother, at his expense. (2) The office of

preaching, as already noted, is regularly traced back to divine institution (Augsburg Confession 5).

Schlink sums up, "The church does not transfer its office of preaching the Gospel and administering the sacraments to individuals in its membership, but it fills this office entrusted to it by God, it calls into this office instituted by God."[30]

24. This office, it should be noted, is not only conceived of in light of the gospel, but also in terms of service. No attempt is made to establish the ministry as a priesthood, differentiated from the laity, on the basis of the words of institution for holy communion; this Luther repudiates as destroying the *fraternitas Christiana* which is an essential feature at the Lord's Supper.[31] Thus, even though there is a special ministry which exists on more than pragmatic grounds and "proclaims the Lord's death" sacramentally as well as in other forms of the word, this office of the ministry is not differentiated even here from the laity in the priestly church, except functionally. "Priests are not called to make sacrifices that merit forgiveness of sins for the people, as in the Old Testament, but they are called to preach the Gospel and administer the sacraments to the people" (Apology 13, 9).

25. (5) Of ordination, the Apology goes so far as to say on one occasion, "we have no objection to calling [it] a sacrament" (Apology 13, 10, cf. 12), if it is "interpreted in relation to the ministry of the Word."

Luther himself, however, while taking over the term from the medieval church, denied the rite has sacramental character. All Christians are "ordained" through baptism. In any further sense, "to ordain means to select an individual for the sake of order and to confer on him the right to preach and to administer the sacraments" publicly.[32]

The confessions elsewhere stress that ordination belongs to the whole church (Treatise 24; 66-69), and, while Jerome is quoted to the effect that "apart from ordination, what does a bishop do that a presbyter does not do?" (Treatise 62), the position of the Treatise is that pastors (= presbyter-bishops, in the argument there) administer ordination validly "by divine right" (Treatise 65).

26. Nowhere else in the confessions, however, in listing the sacraments, is ordination considered for inclusion, and the context in Apology 13 is contrasting an ordination to the ministry of the word with the positions of (1) "our opponents," who interpret the priesthood "in reference to sacrifice," and (2) the "fanatics," who do not favor such an office as ministry of the word (Apology 13, 7-13). Schlink calls the term "sacrament" as a designation for ordination "questionable inasmuch as the *mandatum* [command] by which God instituted the ministry does not comprise an external sign; the laying on of hands at ordination, for example, was not commanded by Christ like water, bread, and wine."[33] The thrust of the entire section in the Apology (13, 7-

13) is to underscore the fact that "the church has the command to appoint ministers . . ., God approves this ministry and is present in it" (Apology 13, 12), but the sacramental type of ordination in the medieval church, which made "priests" in contradistinction to "lay people," is rejected, as is the rejection of a ministerial office by the *Schwärmer*.

27. (6) What do the confessions say about the laity? Very little, even in comparison with the little said about the ministry. The cup should not be withheld from them at celebration of the Lord's Supper (Augsburg Confession 22)—this is one of the few places where an issue specifically mentioning lay-people comes to the fore, and the Reformation position is not merely that "among us both kinds are given to laymen in the sacrament" but also that the words of institution ("drink of it") do not "apply only to priests," as if there were thereby a distinction between clergy and laity (cf. also Formula of Concord, Epitome 7, 24).

Further, "in an emergency" a layperson can absolve and become "the minister and pastor of another" (Treatise 67).[34] The whole church, the royal priesthood, has the power of the keys, and even though it elects and ordains ministers, there may be occasions when the priest-layperson must function as minister in that office for the brother's sake.

28. (7) While there is thus comparatively little on the ministry in the confessions, less on the laity, and very little directly on the relationship of the two, a few references do point up differences between ministers and laypersons assumed in these documents. For one thing, the layperson is not expected to be so well trained theologically as the minister; he or she would not be expected to know the confessions themselves, for example, in detail, but only their more popularized forms, the Small (and Large) Catechism(s)—these are termed "the layman's Bible" and "contain everything which Holy Scripture discusses at greater length and which a Christian must know for his salvation" (Formula of Concord, Epitome, Rule and Norm 5); the Catechisms serve "ordinary people and laymen," pastors and theologians have the other confessional writings (Solid Declaration, Rule and Norm 8).[35]

29. Also to be noted is the expectation that laypeople will honor and be obedient to the ministry (Augsburg Confession 28, 55). Even though "some louts and skinflints" may "declare that we can do without pastors and preachers"—"what one can expect of crazy Germans" (Large Catechism, Preface, 6)—the obligations to give "double honor" to ministers, care for them, pray for them, and have patience with them are repeatedly emphasized (Large Catechism, 10 Commandments, 161; Lord's Prayer, 28; Apology 4, 234).

30. Particularly suggestive is the order of the Table of Duties in the Small Catechism. Sections are paired in terms of subordination and reciprocal relation, as in the New Testament *Haustafeln* [tables of household duties];

Bishops, Pastors, and Preachers	Duties Christians Owe Their Teachers and Pastors
Governing Authorities	Duties Subjects Owe to Governing Authorities
Husbands	Wives
Parents	Children
(Masters and Mistresses)	(Laborers and Servants, Male and Female)[36]

The table was probably suggested to Luther by John Gerson, and not all of the material was prepared by Luther himself (Tappert, p. 354, notes 8 and 9); the material consists simply of a catena of New Testament verses ("those who proclaim the gospel should get their living by the gospel," 1 Cor. 9:14; "respect those who . . . are over you in the Lord," 1 Thess. 5:12; "obey your leaders and submit to them," Heb. 13:17). The net effect, however, from this "Bible of the Lutheran layman," on which generations of catechumens were trained, was to inculcate in laypersons a high regard for the office of the ministry.

31. (8) This picture of ministry and laity which emerges in the confessions has by no means been exempt from criticism, even on the part of those most loyal to the confessional writings. We have already noted the obvious fact that the positions hammered out were wrought often in the heat of conflict, in opposition to positions of the medieval church, sometimes with awareness that it was an "emergency situation." Some have felt that Luther's daring reemphasis on the universal priesthood and the positions in writings of 1520–1525 were stultified by later events, and the "real Reformation position" was never carried through with regard to ministry. Others have felt that the "true Lutheran emphasis" was on the divinely instituted office of ministry and that this aspect needed further development. For such reasons, the ministry in the Lutheran church—precisely because it never was an article on which the church stands or falls but is in so many aspects a matter of human ordinance—could be subject to trends and change in ensuing centuries, with a variety of forms which in the eyes of some were almost an embarrassment—the embarrassment of freedom.

32. In our own day, questions have been raised on New Testament grounds, e.g., by Schlink and Goppelt, whether the confessions "have a biblical basis for teaching only one ecclesiastical office and concentrating in it the multiplicity of New Testament offices" (cf. 1 Cor. 12:28, Eph. 4:11), or "take too little account of the factors which make necessary the special ministry of the apostles alongside the ministry of all."[37] Goppelt would lay more emphasis than the confessions have occasion to, on the church "as a complete organism," where every member participates in serving, and "a special ministry

. . . is responsible for the church as a whole"; "only this definition of the special ministry," he goes on, "can clarify something which is basically given no motivation in the confessions—the restricting of the administration of the sacraments to the ministry."[38]

33. Finally, a word about the "chicken-and-egg" question which, in one form or another, was to plague much future discussion among Lutherans: which came first, the ministry or the church (*Gemeinde*, priesthood of all believers)? An either/or is out of order. The position presumed above is that the word or gospel precedes and creates both. Schlink sees a reciprocal relation, like that of the church and preaching, in Augsburg Confession 7.[39] Luther, in speaking positively of the institution of the office of ministry by Christ, just as he does with regard to the universal priesthood, ties it together with the gospel and the sacraments, all bound to the "impact of the Gospel."[40] Both congregation and pastor are governed by the Lord in royal sovereignty. Ordained ministry and general priesthood of the baptized are properly not contrasts but function together. The church must have a ministry, but the forms are open, except for the requirement that it be a serving ministry of the word.

34. Summary: In the context of the priesthood of all believers and in order to proclaim the gospel, the Lutheran Reformation regards a functional ministry, instituted by God, as necessary in the church, a ministry of the office of the word, ordained normally by pastor-presbyter-bishops. Like the laity, this special ministry serves the gospel. Ministry and laity work reciprocally, but the ministry has functions which differentiate it from the general priesthood of the baptized.

II. Historical Development in Lutheranism

35. For reasons noted above, the concept of ministry among Lutherans has been subject to change, and that in several possible directions, as time passed after the Reformation and conditions changed. This development is noticeable in the European countries where the Reformation took hold—each land disparate, with its own history and development—and even more so in the new world of America. Factors other than theological were often at work, and there is truth in Elert's statement that in the intervening years "Luther's theological doctrine of the spiritual office flows unnoticed into the domain of sociology."[41]

36. If many changes from the medieval church's positions ensued in Reformation lands through the Evangelical understanding of universal priesthood and ministry, nonetheless some of the most radical proposals by Luther, e.g., in the Preface to his *Deutsche Messe* (1526), for voluntary *ecclesiolae in ecclesia* [little church assemblies within the church], a "truly Evangelical

church order"—that "those who mean to be real Christians and profess the Gospel with hand and mouth, should record their names on a list and gather in a house by themselves in order to pray, read, baptize, receive the sacrament, and to practice other Christian work" (a kind of gathering which Luther himself realized "I cannot and do not yet dare organize")[42]—failed to materialize:

37. Instead, there arose a variety of patterns for church structure and ministry, including the consistory in German territories, the involvement of bishops and king in Sweden, the "free church" developed in Amsterdam, etc. There arose also, in fidelity to the Reformation's emphasis on ministry as a serving proclaimer of the word, a new concept of "clergyman," the *minister verbi divini* [minister of the divine word], the *Prediger, Praedikant,* or *Pfarrer* (older terms like "priest" lingered, but that usage for Evangelical clergy was "reintroduced or at least aimed at" only really "at the time of Rationalism";[43] "pastor" became popular in the 18th century under the influence of Pietism;[44] "clergy" itself as a term can be said to reflect Anglican preference, "minister," the Free Churches).[45] In the Lutheran minister a "new social and vocational class" arose, drawn neither from the nobility nor generally from the peasantry. In particular, this special ministry in Lutheran lands was characterized by a high educational training. The Reformation's emphasis on allowing the clergy to marry led to the creative development of the Lutheran parsonage. In these ways a distinct concept of ministry developed, akin to all other lay priests in the church, but set off by calling, function, and such factors as theological education, public position, etc.

We note for our purposes the trends which set in under Lutheran Orthodoxy, Pietism, and then during the 19th-century Confessional Revival in Europe before turning to see how American Lutheranism is heir of all these developments.

A. European Lutheranism Generally

38. (1) Lutheran Orthodoxy endeavored to follow the Reformation heritage in *(a)* viewing the office of ministry, instituted by God, as the property of the church as a whole, and in *(b)* seeing that "the call to the office carries with it no class distinction before God and affords no . . . *character indelebilis* [possession that cannot be lost]"[46]—i.e., is not a special order apart from the universal priesthood (though Lutheran Orthodoxy, while preserving Luther's concept of a priesthood of all the baptized, "never helped it make a breakthrough" in church life).[47] The basic relationship of office to gospel was preserved, and Luther's successors were aware of the flexibility required in transitional times, but there was often unclarity over where what is essential for the church ends and where freedom in form begins.

39. The Lutheran fathers, of course, further emphasized scriptural proof to develop their view of ministry.[48] Thus Hollaz availed himself of Matt. 18:16 to distinguish the "representative church" (an "assembly of Christian teachers") from the "collective church" (consisting of "teachers and hearers"). This "representative church" could then be identified with the ministry, in distinction from the whole number of church members. Hutter voiced the view that "the aristocratic form of government" is best in the church—i.e., under Christ, "one equal ministry of teachers or pastors, or bishops of the church," as in apostolic times (but not changed into a monarchy, as the Catholics do). Schmid's summary on these scholastic theologians speaks of "the Ministry" as the "instrumentality" through which the entire number of those in Christ (who "cannot equally participate in all the affairs of the church by giving counsel, direction, or decision") can be represented. On this view, the ministry not only makes public proclamation but also leads the church. However, the texts Schmid cites scarcely require so complete an identification of ministry with leadership, and he himself, quoting Hollaz and Baier, speaks of a governing council which includes laymen, "provided they be experienced and skillful in sacred affairs, godly and peace-loving."

40. These Orthodox theologians refer frequently to the *status ecclesiasticus* as one of the three estates or hierarchies of the church (along with the political or civil authority, and the domestic).[49] They maintain, with fuller precision, Reformation definitions of the ministry of the church, ordination, etc.[50] There is, however, a more definite emphasis on differing ranks and grades assigned to individual ministers, for reasons of outward order. Elert sees departure from Luther "in the fact that later dogmaticians divide spiritual authority into 'power of office' *(potestas ordinis)* and 'power of jurisdiction' *(potestas jurisdictionis),*" and now the power of jurisdiction is seen to add something to the office of the ministry, a power in which "ordination of ministers" and "censorship of morals" appear as accessories in Melanchthon's *Loci* (XIII, 16).[51] In this period the officeholder therefore sometimes becomes also a custodian of morals, and there is a tendency (e.g., in Johann Benedikt Carpzov I) to see the preacher also as judge and one who disciplines.[52] There is also a revival in the 17th century of the medieval concept of *Seelsorge,* the care of souls, and with it a tendency to govern and judge, not just to preach, on the part of those who held the *Predigtamt.*[53]

One has the impression that Lutheran Orthodoxy generally enhanced the status and concept of the ordained ministry and minimized the universal priesthood of the baptized.

41. (2) Pietism redressed this imbalance and stressed, as might be expected, the priesthood of all believers, often at the expense of any special clerical office. Already in 1675 Spener advocated in his *Pia Desideria* the restoration

of universal exercise of the "spiritual priesthood" of all Christians, a Reformation theme which had lain dormant. Laypeople should be built up in the word of God and, further, share in the administration of the church. Under Pietism cell movements, *ecclesiolae, collegia pietatis* [little gatherings of the pious or of true believers], conventicles arose in many places, in many forms, throughout Evangelical territory and beyond, sometimes within the organized (state) church, sometimes apart from it. On the whole, Pietism did not lead, in the Lutheran church, to a full development of "universal priesthood," nor did it result in the loss of the Reformation sense of office of the ministry.[54] But it had the effect, like the Reformation itself, of opening the structures and reemphasizing the laity's role. It was from Pietist circles that many of the early European Lutheran settlers in America were to come, e.g., already in 1683, separatists from Spener's Frankfort group who came to Pennsylvania.

42. While pietistic movements always carried with them the twin dangers of separatistic tendencies and opposition to clergy (because of the predominantly lay participation in conventicles and the emphasis on universal priesthood), it must be remembered that Pietists varied considerably and many stayed within existing church structures, even among the ranks of the ministers. Spener, for example, "broke with the separatists for love of his church and his pastoral office."[55] Often these leaders themselves within the church promoted a new and fuller religious expression of faith among the lay priests. In connection with efforts at securing greater lay participation in church government, the principle of "collegialism" may also be mentioned, a principle which many Pietists endorsed. It argued that neither state nor church are divine institutions but corporate unities founded by means of a social compact of people voluntarily (contrast the medieval idea of a unity of church and state as *unum corpus christianum*). In a society which is often pluralistic religiously, each church group has the right to govern itself. In the church there are two classes of members: teachers and hearers (not three estates: nobility, clergy, and people), "and these two classes stand side by side with equal rights, the teachers having no sovereign authority over the hearers."[56] Such a view encouraged greater importance for the laity than one where the clerical estate was emphasized.

43. The general picture of development traced out above for Germany also applies elsewhere, e.g., in Sweden.[57] Luther's emphasis on "universal priesthood" was taken over in principle, but never effected, for theoretical and practical reasons. Accordingly, Lutheran Orthodoxy came to dominate, with its "orders"—family, government, and clergy (representing the church). The clergy were a separate class in society, the *ecclesia representativa*. They exercised a power of the keys, not only to "loose" (absolve), but also to "bind," in the sense of discipline, even in the general community down to 1686. The clergy were self-perpetuating in the sense that synods were made

up only of clerics, and ordination (at times vested with a sacramental meaning) was at the hands of the bishop and chapter. Pietism challenged this with an emphasis on universal priesthood, new birth (rather than baptism), and sanctification (more than justification); only a regenerate minister could rightly proclaim the gospel, it was understood. Thus the Swedish church reflects two strands of thought: *(a)* the ministry is a divine institution, the officeholders, in direct line, followers of the apostles; *(b)* this ministry, however, does not depend on the *potestas ordinis* of the bishop but the activity of God who calls men, with the universal priesthood (church) a feature of some importance.

44. (3) A final factor in European developments to be noted here is the Confessional Revival in the 19th century and the ensuing debate involving "high church" and "low church" wings on the ministry in Lutheranism.

Justus Henning Boehmer (1674–1749), a jurist who sought to apply older principles of canon law to post-Reformation conditions, initiated, according to Schlink, the "theory of transference," i.e., that the priesthood of believers transfers in the local congregation its authority to one of its members who then serves as its minister.[58] This theory, building on the Reformation theme of universal priesthood, revitalized and actualized in Pietism, was further developed during the next century, e.g., by J. W. F. Hoefling (1802–1853), of Erlangen. Hoefling, though he "regarded the office of the ministry as the sacramental office of dealing with men in the name of God," thought that this ministerial office rests solely on the universal priesthood, "the only office which exists by divine right."[59] Here the public ministry becomes but an "organization" or "concentration" or even "emanation" of the priesthood of all believers, "a 'community office' based on the 'collective right' of the whole congregation"; the pastor functions for and on behalf of the community; as Ritschl put it, he "represents" it in the divine service.[60] Such views were opposed—rightly, Schlink feels,[61] in light of the confessions—by such 19th-century theologians as Loehe, Klieforth, Vilmar, Dieckhof, and Stahl.

45. However, in the face of this "transference theory," in light of the revival of interest in the confessions, and amid the often revolutionary events of the day (1848!), some of these theologians forged a view of the office of the ministry with a "priestly significance almost in the Catholic sense."[62] A. F. C. Vilmar (1800–1860), of Marburg, a champion of confessional orthodoxy and the *"Theologie der Tatsachen"* ("facts"—vs. "rhetoric"), maintained that the statements on congregations ordaining ministers in the "Treatise on the Power and Primacy of the Pope" are merely "superfluous remarks about the emergency rights of the congregation in the practically inconceivable emergency of the absence of all pastors called by pastors."[63] Hence Vilmar held to an "inviolate rule" that only a pastor can decide whether someone is fit to be a pastor and install him in the office. In an age, the post-Napoleonic, when many institutions were crashing to the ground and the Lutheran church

in Germany was menaced by "unionism" (forced mergers with the Reformed), Vilmar clung to a personal certainty about the "presence of Christ in the Church on earth"[64] and the need for a ministry which is not dissolved into a quintessence of congregationalism. F. J. Stahl (1802–1861), the jurist, who criticized the Augsburg Confession for omitting in its definition of the church (Article 7) "the organic side," namely, "office and government," regarded both state (conceived as "Christian") and church as resting on divine ordinance, favored episcopacy because "it alone can guarantee authority of administration and spiritual care" ("no majority but authority"), and deduced from the confessions that there is not merely a functional office of preaching but also a class of preachers, divinely instituted, "in the specific ecclesiastical sense of a special profession which determines also the entire orientation of life."[65] Here we have emphasis on a ministerial office, over against the laity, as constitutive of the church, with the universal priesthood minimized.

46. It may be remarked that this discussion over church office in German Lutheranism of the 19th century has its ramifications in study of the early church. The outcome of the views of men like Boehmer and Hoefling was the position of Rudolf Sohm (who held that the church was originally charismatic, with no "ministry" or *Kirchenrecht* [church law]). The alternative position (excluding the traditional view that later orders, the threefold ministry, etc., were there at the outset) is that expressed by Adolf Harnack, that "ministry and legal ordinances were present from the beginning; they do not contradict the nature of the church." This dispute epitomized by Harnack and Sohm "has governed down to the present time" work on the character of the primitive church.[66]

47. Schlink dismisses both the 19th-century positions sketched above as guilty of exaggeration, compared with the confessional position, and regards Adolph von Harless (1806–1879) of Erlangen (opponent of Loehe on some issues) and Theodosius Harnack (1817–1889, the father of Adolf Harnack) as the figures of the period who "came closest to avoiding the twin dangers of denying either the universal priesthood or the divine institution of the public ministry."[67] Needless to say, both extremes still find expression today, sometimes in the opinions of "high church" versus "kerygmatic" theologians.[68] Moreover both 19th-century views were carried by Lutheran emigrants to the United States.

48. While our arrangement here of material may suggest, by moving at this point to the American scene, that the Loehe-Vilmar "high" view of the ministry would be dominant, it has already been noted that the immigrants prior to the Confessional Revival of 1817 and following years were usually pietistic in outlook. Moreover, other events have served to give impetus in more recent times to the "universal priesthood" side of the coin—e.g., the outburst of lay power (John R. Mott), the Pentecostal movement, the "lay

apostolate" in Roman Catholicism, "theologies of the laity," and all emphases on worldly engagement and secular Christianity[69]—just as some aspects of liturgical revival, the search for meaning for the professional ministry, etc., have given support to the stress on ministerial office.

B. *In American Lutheranism*

49. All of the patterns of ministry and laity in church life and government plus all of the disputes over universal priesthood and public ministry noted above were brought to the New World by Lutheran settlers. In addition, the absence of a state church or *Landeskirche* [territorial churches, as in Hannover or Bavaria], to which many of them had been accustomed, the religious pluralism now encountered, the influence of the American frontier and the spirit of democracy (at time, perhaps, also antiintellectualism and anticlericalism, so that an educated ministry concerned about theological issues of past centuries was scarcely regarded as a necessity), and the frequent paucity of trained, properly called and ordained pastors exacerbated the situation.[70] All these factors help explain Conrad Bergendoff's statements, "In no area of doctrine has the Lutheran church in America had greater difficulty than in the matter of ministry,"[71] and again, ". . . there is no clear doctrine of the laity in the Lutheran Church."[72]

50. Needless to say, the Lutheran pastor in the American scene had certain social and theological dynamics going for him: a particular, committed understanding of the gospel and its centrality; an education often far in advance of most people in the neighborhood; a set role in the liturgy (though this varied with trends in worship) and in the proclamation of the word and administration of the sacraments; an accustomed place in confirmation and instruction leading up to it; and a pastoral relationship with his people. In spite of all this inheritance, however, the minister, transplanted across the sea, having to adapt to new conditions, often had a difficult time sustaining any proper notion of office in a society where many a person conceived "no other idea of a clergyman than that of a hired man."[73] Muhlenberg, who arrived in Pennsylvania in 1742 to gather together the Lutheran settlers and minister to them and who found all sorts of itinerant "ministers" preying upon them and great churchly laxity, wrote, "A preacher must fight his way through . . . if he wants to be a preacher and proclaim the truth [in America]."[74] In spite of widespread depreciation of a "European ministry" and frequent opposition (in the spirit of the free churches and democracy) to office, doctrine, and liturgy, Muhlenberg, it can be said, "held to a high standard of the ministerial office."[75]

51. Typical of the difficulties faced in new, almost emergency situations are the ordination of the first Lutheran clergy and the efforts to provide pastors

under such conditions. Justus Falckner, the first Lutheran to be ordained in America, was ordained in 1703 by the Swedish clergy in Pennsylvania for the Dutch churches in New York—not apparently on commission from the bishops in Sweden but according to the custom of the Amsterdam church. The one acted for the other, according to the customs of the latter church. As for providing pastors, because of the shortage of pastors, candidates who were still studying (usually under some pastor in his home) were sometimes "licensed" to preach, administer sacraments, etc.—although some Lutherans (in North Carolina) questioned the practice, and some later immigrants "looked askance at a type of clergy who could administer sacraments before proper ordination."[76] Such were the irregularities caused by the conditions in America.

52. Almost inevitably, Lutherans in America took on a coloring from their surroundings, even though opposing it at points and seeking to remain true to the Reformation. An interesting case is S. S. Schmucker's "Plan for Catholic Union on Apostolic Principles," issued in 1838 from the then new seminary at Gettysburg, which sought for an "American Lutheranism" in ecumenical context. Schmucker drafted an "Apostolic, Protestant Confession," seeking to update the Augsburg Confession and at times to correct "errors" in it. His "Article on the Church" does refer to the ministry, and the "Fraternal Appeal" from his pen envisions "free sacramental, ecclesiastical, and ministerial communion among the confederated churches."[77] We may note that even in a time when much of Lutheranism in America looked to some observers like a kind of "Methodistic Presbyterianism," Schmucker's projections included an office of the ministry.

53. However, not all Lutherans—and in particular many of the immigrants from Europe during the period of the Confessional Revival—agreed with what Schmucker proposed or with the church life and ministry which had developed among the earlier Lutheran settlers in America. Here we must reckon with the variety of views coming from 19th-century Europe, which blossomed and developed yet further mutations in the freedom of the American scene. At one extreme might be placed the followers from Finland of the theories of Lars Levi Laestadius (1800–1861), who in the 1870s formed the "Apostolic Lutheran Congregation" in Michigan (later, the Finnish Apostolic Lutheran Church of America, numbering in 1965, with related groups, some 20,000 members; in 1985 the Apostolic Lutheran Church of America was listed as having fewer than 5000 members).[78] Here spiritual priesthood of all believers was more important than any special group of pastors. Every Christian is held to have the power of the keys. There is little stress on training for professional ministry, leaders rise directly out of the congregation. The universal priest-

hood, emphasized by the Reformation, reawakened in Pietism, is in this group radically developed along congregational lines.

54. At the opposite extreme, emphasizing the authority of the pastor, might be cited the position of the Buffalo Synod, organized under J. A. A. Grabau (1804–1879), who left Prussia in 1839 with a thousand sympathizers after he was arrested for opposing Friedrich Wilhelm III's attempted union of Lutherans and Reformed. In this group, ministers were looked upon as a rank or class, constituted by the word of God, to rule over the congregation, by divine right. Only pastors can decide doctrine, they alone have the power of the keys. The laity obey. One of the groups later to make up the American Lutheran Church formed in 1930 (subsequently merged into a larger body, The American Lutheran Church, 1960), the Buffalo Synod found its views especially opposed by the Missouri Synod because it thus subordinated congregations (universal priesthood) to the ordained ministry.[79]

55. Within these extremes, many other positions appeared. The bulk of Lutherans probably reflected the twin Reformation emphases of ministerial office and universal priesthood, to one degree or another. Typical might be the Theses on the Ministry by the Joint Synod of Ohio (later, part of the American Lutheran Church), 1868–1870:

1. In the Christian Church there is a universal priesthood. . . .

2. In the Church there is also a public office of the ministry . . . instituted of God. . . .

3. There is a distinction to be made between the evangelical pastoral office and the universal priesthood . . . not . . . that the public office of the ministry possesses a word of God, a Baptism, an Absolution and a Eucharist different from those given to the entire Church, but . . . that it publicly administers this word, baptism, absolution and eucharist. But . . . all Christians have the right and duty to make use of God's Holy Word, and, in cases of necessity, also to baptize and to absolve.

4. The Church, i.e., all Christians, have the keys . . . but it does not follow from this, that every Christian is a pastor.

5. The pastoral office is not a human arrangement, but a divine institution, although the external appointment . . . is a work of the spiritual priesthood.

6. The call to the pastoral office comes from God . . . but mediately, through men, i.e., through the Christian congregation.

7. Ordination . . . is not a divine command . . . there is no absolute necessity for it, and yet it is necessary from a churchly point of view . . . and, in the regularly organized condition of the Church, is only to be administered by those who are already in the ministerial office.[80]

56. Sometimes, where the church being planted was not yet in a "regularly organized condition" but in an emerging, missionary situation, the results, while yielding some irregularities, worked out in unexpected ways. Settlers from Norway, for example, included both those from the state church with its university-trained pastors (who formed the Norwegian Synod in 1853) and

those touched by the lay revivals of Hans N. Hauge (1771–1824); the latter, under the lay preacher Elling Eielsen (1804–1883), formed in 1846 an "Eielsen Synod" (later largely absorbed into Hauge's Norwegian Evangelical Lutheran Synod). (To abbreviate a long story, there also emerged a more middle-of-the-road Norwegian group in the United States, in fact two of them; eventually most of these merged and became part of The American Lutheran Church). The significant thing is, however, that Eielsen, the lay preacher, sought ordination in America and secured it from a neighboring pastor. Bergendoff comments that, even in this group where the "universal priesthood" was strongly emphasized and amid the religious freedom and pluralism of America, "the American Haugeans still preferred an ordained clergy for the administration of sacraments."[81]

57. Another example: Muhlenberg, trained at Halle, and many early settlers in Pennsylvania and New York, reflected a Pietist background, but their development of a ministerium as the pattern of church government on the synodical level has been called an influence from Lutheran Orthodoxy.[82] Thus, the first Lutheran synod formed in North America, under Muhlenberg, at Philadelphia in 1748, involved 6 pastors and 24 laymen representing 10 congregations, but the laymen were simply visitors, with no vote. The organization was first called the "United Pastors," later the Evangelical Lutheran Ministerium of North America (still later, the Ministerium of Pennsylvania, a name which survived until 1962; cf. "New York Ministerium," etc.). Thus, how the ministry was understood, especially in relation to the laity, does not always follow predictable patterns, and takes a profuse variety of forms.

58. Two other understandings of ministry must be mentioned as significant for U.S. Lutheran development. Wilhelm Loehe[83] has already been mentioned as a proponent of a "high" view of the office of ministry in 19th-century discussion in Germany. Loehe had great influence in the American scene through pastors, missionaries, deaconesses, and other leaders trained at the institutions he created at Neuendettelsau, Bavaria, and sent to the United States, where they were instrumental in forming the Iowa Synod (later, part of the American Lutheran Church). Loehe was shocked at the "Americanization" of the ministry, the trend toward "democracy" and "majority votes," etc., eroding away pastoral authority. He was, moreover, favorable to episcopacy (for him, the episcopacy found in Scripture, i.e., an episcopacy "identical with the presbytery"; he wrote, "Nor can we see how a congregation can be rightly cared for where such an episcopate does not enter into its full rights"). "Universal priesthood" meant for Loehe simply the prerogative of direct access to God and the offering of intercession and thanksgiving by every Christian. However, for all these emphases, Loehe did not think that differing opinions on the ministry need disturb confessional unity; to be in doctrinal agreement, Lutherans need not agree on every detail about church

order. Loehe's position on the ministry, nonetheless, helped bring about a break with C. F. W. Walther, and helped prevent agreement of the Iowa Synod with yet another German immigrant group, the Missouri Synod.

59. Under the Dresden pastor, Martin Stephan, some 800 Saxon Lutherans, including 6 pastors, 10 theological candidates, and 4 teachers, had come to St. Louis in 1839, in part because of their opposition to the rationalism then widespread in the German churches. Stephan, however, was soon deposed for hierarchical tendencies and charges of immorality, and C. F. W. Walther (1811–1887) became leader of the group which eventually developed into The Lutheran Church–Missouri Synod.[84] In light of its experiences in the American scene, the Missouri immigrants developed a thoroughgoing congregationalism. Here conditions allowed—at last!—fuller implications to be drawn and practiced from the "universal priesthood" emphasis of the Reformation. The "transfer theory" was widely espoused. The public ministry was retained, termed a divine institution, and congregations were said to consist of pastors and laymen, but the public ordained ministry was not always conceived of as "absolutely necessary." In line with this congregational emphasis, a local congregation was deemed able to call a pastor of its own without the cooperation of some other pastor. Walther and Loehe were unable to agree on the office of the ministry, even after a personal meeting in Germany in 1851, and theologians of the Iowa and Missouri Synods differed, as a series of theses and treatises put forth over the rest of the century shows.

60. Walther's position, which became normative for the Missouri Synod, is well summed up in his Thesis VII in "On the Ministry" (1851–1852): "The holy ministry is the authority conferred by God through the congregation, as holder of the priesthood and of all church power, to administer in public office the common rights of the spiritual priesthood in behalf of all." Walther went on to elaborate this definition: ". . . the spiritual priesthood which all truly believing Christians possess, and the holy ministry [*Predigtamt*] or the pastoral office [*Pfarramt*], are not identical." An "ordinary Christian" is not a pastor just because he is a priest, and a pastor is not a priest because he holds the *Predigtamt*. Spiritual priesthood is not a public office in the church; however, the public ministry is "not an order different from that of Christians, but it is a ministry of service." Ministers differ in that they do publicly, in behalf of all, what every Christian originally possessed.[85]

61. It would require too much retracing of history to outline here debates among Lutherans in America over how the ordained ministry was regarded in the various groups in contradistinction to the unordained church members or spiritual priesthood. Typical of the reaction to Walther's position is that enunciated by the Synod of Iowa in its "Davenport Theses" (1873): ". . . we cannot concede that, according to the confession of our Church, the ministry originates through the transfer of the rights of the spiritual priesthood

possessed by the individual Christian. In opposition to this view, we maintain that the public office of the Ministry is transmitted by God through the congregation of believers in its entirety and essence by means of the regular call, because the 'mandatum de constituendis ministris' [the command to ordain preachers] is not given to the individual members, but to the Church as such." [86]

62. As Lutherans closed ranks in the late 19th and in the present century, statements often had to be worked out which safeguarded both the emphasis on public ministry and that on universal priesthood cherished by one group or another. Thus among Norwegians, the doctrinal agreements written for the United Church included a statement on "Lay Ministries in the Church" (1907):

> 1. God has given the Church, also the individual congregation, the means of grace, the power of the keys, the office of the ministry and the gifts of grace. The congregation and the individual Christian in it therefore possess all things. . . .
>
> 2. For the purpose of administering the means of grace in the congregation God has instituted the public office of the ministry, which the congregation by its call commits to one or more persons, who are qualified for it according to the Word of God. . . .
>
> 3. When the congregation has committed the office of the ministry to one or more persons, no one, except in a case of emergency, should publicly teach, or administer the Sacraments, without the call of the congregation. . . .
>
> 4. This office of the ministry does not, however, do away with the universal priesthood of believers; but it is the right and duty of every Christian as a spiritual priest to work for mutual edification . . . in accordance with the . . . gifts which God has bestowed. . . .
>
> 5. God also wills that the special gifts which He has bestowed upon certain individuals in the congregation . . . shall be employed by the congregation . . . called to this service in the congregation at its request . . . and . . . under the supervision of the congregation. . . . [Such] Christian lay activity . . . shall not be considered unchurchly practice or religious fanaticism. . . . [87]

63. It is impossible to state in detail any single view of the ministry on which all Lutherans in this period would have agreed, between the Scylla of extreme congregationalism and universal priesthood (Laestadius) and the Charybdis of a class or order of minister-priests, minimizing the place of the laity (Grabau). Perhaps much of the position which would have gained general assent from a large number of Lutherans is outlined in C. P. Krauth's "Theses on Ordination," relevant items in which include these:

> 1. No one should preach publicly and ordinarily, and administer the Sacraments, unless he be rightly and legitimately called with the ordinary calling. . . .
>
> 7. The perpetual practice of the Apostolic and Primitive Church was, that the call should be given by the Church through distinctive parts of its organism, by clergy and people, each estate virtually possessing the power of veto, and every act requiring the concurrence of both.

8. They who commit the vocation to ministers alone or to the people alone, give to a part which belongs to a whole. . . .

9. [Ordination, like calling,] belongs to the whole church. In the Lutheran Church ordination ordinarily was performed by the Superintendent with the co-operation of his colleagues in the ministry, and in this country is performed by the officers of the Synod in connection with other presbyters. . . .

16. An orthodox candidate cannot seek ordination from a heterodox minister without scandal and just suspicion of collusion. It is absurd that those whose doctrine is impure should examine and testify to the purity of the doctrine of others. . . .

18. The person ordaining should himself be an ordained minister [10 reasons are given].[88]

64. It is perhaps worth adding that, as usual in churches, finely wrought distinctions and principles did not always work out in practice, and what a group advocated, through theses or statements, did not always fully obtain in actuality. Thus, for example, in spite of Walther's clearcut position, the Missouri Synod, in practice, often had congregations where great deference was given to "Herr Pastor" (just as in other Lutheran bodies). In the period between 1860 and 1900, when waves of immigrants were coming from Germany and there was great growth of membership in Missouri congregations, there frequently just was not time to teach and train the laity adequately and integrate them into the fuller role developed in America. The leadership of the pastor could then reach "exaggerated dimensions," for people were trained by the confessional writings and Orthodox fathers to honor him and respect him. Thus even in a group particularly committed to the primary place of the universal priesthood (congregation over ministry), the public office of the ministry was often of far greater significance than public statements suggest.[89]

65. One other matter within Missouri Synod circles, a further ramification of Walther's views, deserves note: the position of the teacher in the parochial schools of the church.[90] With the confessions, the point was accepted that there is but "one divinely instituted ministry" in the New Testament, that of *minister verbi domini,* though forms of this can vary from time to time and place to place. The term *Predigtamt* had been used in the confessions, but Walther tended to equate *Predigtamt* with *Pfarramt* and to use *Predigtamt* for both the pastoral ministry and for the ministry of teachers. Hence, when he spoke of *das Predigtamt* as the highest office in the church, this was taken by some to mean that the pastorate is the highest office, and that any other functions, such as teaching, must derive from it as auxiliary to it, while others held that the teaching office was just as legitimate an expression of ministry as the pastoral office.

66. The settlers who came with Stephan included teachers of religion. Over the years the system of parochial schools grew in Missouri congregations, with teacher-training institutes created, etc. In Germany, at least in some places

and under Orthodoxy, the teacher had been considered a member of the clergy. Hence two positions emerged in Missouri, voiced in debate during the 19th century and down to the present decade: (1) the pastorate is the one divinely instituted office (even if called through the universal priesthood in the local congregation), and any teaching ministry is subordinate to it; (2) God has instituted the office of the ministry, but not the forms, and if the pastorate is one form descended from the single all-embracing office, teaching is another—teachers are part of the ministry and should be ordained, even if they teach secular subjects, and might even preach or assist at holy communion. While the practice was usually to install the teacher, there has been agitation to ordain him also (though these two terms have been used synonymously by some in this discussion)—and, we must add, these proposals have been made regarding male teachers, women called to teaching would not be ordained "for scriptural reasons." The net result with regard to the position of teacher in Missouri Synod circles has been to create a third category: a ministerial office that is not of the laity and not—at least in the opinion of all, or in certain ways—of the clergy. It constitutes an exception to the usual division into ordained ministry and unordained laity. "Special ministries of the word" is the phrase sometimes used to cover this and other varieties of service.

67. We have therefore reflected in Lutheranism "three rather definite concepts of the ministry": the episcopal (Church of Sweden, the early Swedish colony on the Delaware—otherwise not found in North America); the congregational (pietist groups, Missouri theory); and the presbyterial (most common in U.S. Lutheranism).[91] The source of ministerial power has been seen in three different places: (1) the local congregation (Hoefling, Walther); (2) the ministry as a class separate from the local congregation (Vilmar, Stahl, Loehe, Grabau); (3) the church considered as a whole, in which the congregation and the ministry both take their place ("Lutherans in general").[92] Bergendoff concludes that for Lutheranism in America the presbyterial system prevails, and that while Walther and Missouri "interpreted the presbytery to include lay elders elected by the congregation" with no place for a "ministerium," most Lutherans in the United States developed "a college of ministers which perpetuated itself by providing for the education and ordination of their successors," ordination being by ministers alone.[93] One can thus speak of "two theories of the ministry existing today side by side in the Lutheran church," as Bergendoff does, depending on whether the emphasis is put on universal priesthood or the office of the ministry, but the general practical agreement among Lutheranism is somewhat surprising, given the fact that the Lutheran confessions prescribe no rigid doctrine here.

68. Chapters on "the ministry" in recent symposia by Lutheran professors of theology[94] refer, in one case, to the "remarkable unanimity by the Lutheran churches of the world" at this point, but also admit, in the other essay, that

the Reformation point of view of the ministry, not as "an authority, but a service," is an answer "the Church is still trying to give" but has not yet been fully articulated, especially in a period when "the Church . . . tends to shape and use 'ministries' which forget to be 'ministries of the Word.' "

69. Accordingly, the topic continues to be one of lively debate among American Lutherans—in the Missouri Synod, especially on the status of teachers; in The American Lutheran Church (in the ALC as recently as 1950 it was discussed whether a layman could be president of a church college;[95] the ALC has requested the Lutheran Council in the U.S.A. to undertake a full study of ordination and ministry [see below, n. 97 and in the Supplementary Comments on this essay]); and in the Lutheran Church in America, where there has been a number of commissions studying the ministry (1938, 1952, 1966ff.).[96] We take the LCA as an example here of such official study.

70. Study of the ministry in the Lutheran Church in America and its predecessor bodies seems not to have been oriented to the question of the relation of ordained ministry to laity, though more recent discussion has raised the question repeatedly, What is the ordained ministry within the context of the whole people of God? Rather, these reports usually dealt with practical questions, such as licensure (it should be discontinued, according to the 1938 Report); the proliferation of men in special ministries which were not, however, "valid" by past definitions for retaining ministerial status, and the increasing number of those engaged in entirely secular work and not under church jurisdiction who insisted on being carried on the ministerial roll because their concept of ministry was that of an "order" with "indelible character" (the 1952 Report urged a broader view of ministry but at the same time more precise discipline so as to exclude those not actually functioning in the ministry of the word—"there is no ministry where there is no ministering"); or the place of commissioned, part-time ministries (the 1966 Report distinguished within "the whole set-apart ministry of the church," of which "the ordained clergy are only a part," among [1] the commissioned, limited-time ministry—officers or committee members of the local congregations, representatives on boards; [2] the commissioned, full-time ministry—business managers, parish workers, lay associates in local congregations, synodical staff members, lay missionaries; [3] the ordained ministry—clergy, in ministry of the word, in administration, supervision, etc.). Generally these LCA statements reflect the Lutheran position consistently noted above through the centuries, with repudiation of a strictly congregational view where the office is derived from the universal priesthood ("The whole church is priestly because it is the body of Christ, the true and only priest," but the ordained ministry "cannot be derived from the priesthood of all believers; the individual is not everything

the church is," 1952). Perhaps the clearest reference to ordained minister and layman comes in the 1952 Report:

> The minister is not a priest with an indelible character upon whose ministrations in the sacraments the layman is dependent. Neither is he just another member of the congregation. But he stands before the congregation as the bearer of the office of Word and Sacraments upon which the congregation is dependent. It is, however, the living Word upon which the congregation is dependent, . . . the living Christ who must be brought to men in the "mediated immediacy" of Word and Sacrament.

The 1966 Report, while speaking of ministries (commissioned, of limited term) where laypersons and ministers have equal authority, and proposing expansion of the practice of commissioning for certain tasks, had "no intention to suggest any major changes in the ordained ministry, either in the direction of an elimination of the clergy or a greater separation of the ordained from the laity." Thus it speaks in a manner similar to the 1952 Report: clergy "do not stand over the people as lords, neither do they stand under the people as mere functionaries"; the clergyman receives "no indelible character that distinguishes him from the laity," but "remains, even after ordination, one of the people of God." The 1966 Report and its recommendations, however, were not as a whole adopted by the LCA convention, and the matter has been referred to a new "Commission on the Comprehensive Study of the Doctrine of the Ministry," to report in 1970 [see below, Supplementary Comments].

III. In Contemporary Thinking

71. While the doctrine of the ministry continued to be under study among Lutherans as part of the church's task "to rethink, renew, and reform the ministry entrusted to her,"[97] there is meanwhile further evidence from constitutions and other documents, surveys, books, and periodical literature about how Lutheranism regards the ordained ministry and the laity. It needs to be said that much in this current picture reflects the variety of positions already noted in light of the two prime emphases which we have traced since the Reformation (universal priesthood and public ministry), and that contemporary Lutheran thinking is at many points one with ecumenical wrestlings today, especially Roman Catholic discussion, on ministry. We shall proceed in this survey generally from official documents to private and individual expressions of opinion.

A. Church Constitutions

72. The constitutions and bylaws of the three major Lutheran bodies in the United States did not offer much direct evidence on how the ordained Lutheran

minister differs from the Lutheran layperson. It might be claimed that these documents, like every Lutheran, assumed the minister does differ—just as it was also known that there are other ways in which the minister does not differ from lay believers—but these differentiations were not spelled out. Indeed, no definition of the terms appeared to be offered except in the ALC *Handbook;* here "clergy" denoted "the body of men set apart, by ordination, to the service of God, in the Christian Church, in distinction from the laity" ("pastor" was used for a clergyman "in charge of a congregation . . .," "clergyman" for any ordained man), and "laity" denoted "the people, as distinguished from the clergy" or "members of the church who are not ordained."[98]

73. A few generalizations can be made (see below for details). All three bodies assumed a public office of the ministry, with clergymen ordained by clergymen, regardless of the emphasis on the universal priesthood. All three churches understood the ministry in explicit statements or implicitly from Scripture and the Confessions, which form the basis of the church's witness and life, to be rooted in the gospel, as a functional instrument for its proclamation. In the LCA the pastor might constitutionally enjoy more power in the local congregation. In all three churches, to varying degree, on the synodical level (both nationally and in adjudicatories between the local and national levels) clergy generally could outvote the laity and play a greater role in carrying out the church's work and decisions.

74. More specifically, The Lutheran Church–Missouri Synod reflects not only the 16th-century confessions and the Orthodox fathers, but also more particularly Walther's exposition in his 10 theses on the ministry (and 9 on the church) as a basis for presenting the ministry; cf. the "Brief Statement" of 1932 and the "Common Confession" of 1950, as well as in the 1959 convention's discussion of the ministry, though these recent statements seem to put more emphasis on the office of ministry as a "divine ordinance" than as something merely derived from the general priesthood.[99] In line with Walther's views, the local congregation is emphasized as the group which, through the voters' assembly, calls a pastor. Indeed, there is some uncertainty constitutionally over the precise role of the district president, whether he acts on his own in ordination or is simply an extension of "the Synod itself" (Bylaws 3.07e; the Synod presumably having received the authority transferred from the general priesthood), and his signature is not required on a call (the 1967 convention turned down a request to put more power into the hands of the district president at this point).[100] Important as the congregation is, however, care is taken to carry out Walther's thesis that "the congregation is not permitted, and dare not abrogate to itself the right, arbitrarily, to depose its minister."[101] (In most Lutheran churches, a congregation calls a pastor for life, theoretically, but has a right of recall—almost never exercised.) In the guidelines for congregational constitutions, the parish pastor is not expected

to be president of the congregation and may not even be required to be at the meetings of the voters' assembly. The role of the laity is in this and other ways stressed. A pastor, we may note, is permitted to fill temporarily the pulpit of a non-Lutheran congregation, but "will not publicly celebrate the Lord's Supper in that congregation." [102]

75. At times the phrase "pastors, teachers, and laymen" occurs in Synodical documents, reflecting the particular position of the "God-given ministry and office of the teacher" in the schools of the Missouri Synod, noted above (see §§65-66). Thus, teachers are advisory members of both Synod and district (while laymen are only when elected as delegates) and may not serve as lay delegates. [103] Their present status, similar to that of the pastor—a development which seems a departure from Walther's own ideas—has come in part of necessity in connection with government classifications for the draft and income tax regulations. [104]

76. Other ministries may be seen in such emerging groups as "full-time Church Staff Workers" (trained at the "Lutheran Lay Training Institute" for two years at Concordia College, Milwaukee), "full-time Lutheran Parish Workers" (two years at St. John's College, Winfield, Kansas), deaconesses (Valparaiso University), and the "lay apostolate" (emphasis at Concordia Teachers College, River Forest, Illinois). On policy-making levels, laymen are said to have considerable numerical representation, but are less noticeable in administration. [105] Hence, there are frequent overtures to use the laity more, and some suggestions that a gap exists between proclaimed principles and actual clergy-lay relationships, so that charges of "clericalism" and "laicism" can arise. [106]

77. The American Lutheran Church, as noted above, provided definitions of "clergy" and "laity" in its *Handbook,* and in a 1964 "Statement on Ordination and Clergy Roster" spoke with great clarity on the gospel as the basis for ordination (Augsburg Confession 5, 7, and 14 are cited) and of ordination as consisting of three elements, "calling, sending, and blessing." [107] The constitution stated, "The pastor and laity constitute the membership of the congregation, the pastor's status differing only as to function." [108] The district president had a role not noted in the Missouri Synod: he had to countersign all letters of call. This provision led some congregations of the Lutheran Free Church (a Norwegian group, the result of the spiritual awakening movement, stressing universal priesthood) to split off in 1962 (when the LFC joined The ALC, itself the result of a three-way merger in 1960) and create an "Association of Free Lutheran Congregations"; they regarded involvement of a district president as "a restriction on congregational freedom." [109]

78. The ALC Constitution held that to the clergy "is committed the public administration of the Means of Grace" (Paragraph 701), a point stressed in

fellowship talks between The ALC and the Missouri Synod (1966).[110] The 1964 "Statement on Ordination and Clergy Roster" elaborated this, but also was open to "specialized ministries" of all sorts, "based on the ministry of the divine Word":

> As Luther pointed out to the Bohemian Christians, the office of the ministry is based upon the need of the church as understood under the enlightenment of the Holy Spirit rather than upon the fact that all believers are priests.
> Since the ministerial office is not precisely defined in the New Testament and the duties . . . and needs . . . are subject to variation, we are led to Luther's conclusion: namely, that God has left the details of the ministerial office to the discretion of the church, to be developed according to its needs and according to the leading of the Holy Spirit.[111]

79. In ALC congregations the pastor was an advisory member of boards of trustees and deacons, but without vote. In district conventions, where clergy usually outnumbered lay delegates, it was proposed to restrict the vote to clergy who were parish pastors, thus insuring a lay majority. In The ALC's "United Testimony on Faith and Life," the royal priesthood of all "members of the church" was noted and defined (as "full access to the throne of grace with no mediator save Jesus Christ"), and laypersons were said to "exercise their royal priesthood and in no sense surrender it" when they call a pastor.[112] The list of "lay activities in the church" cited at another point in the same document stated specifically:

> (6) The Means of Grace have been given to the congregation, and, for the purpose of administering Word and Sacraments, God has instituted the public office of the ministry, which, by the official call of the congregation, is committed to one or more qualified persons. . . .
> (7) The doctrine of the priesthood of all believers gives the individual member no right to assume any of the functions which belong to the public ministries of the congregation. . . .[113]

80. References in documents of the Lutheran Church in America set the public ministry in the context of the church's total ministry and the world: the primary objective of the church is "to proclaim the Gospel through Word and Sacraments, to relate that Gospel to man's need in every situation, and to extend the ministry of the Gospel to all the world" (Constitution, Article V, Section 1,a); "there is a sense in which the ministry is one of all believers . . . there is also a special ministry . . . a 'ministry within a ministry,' which through Word and sacraments directs the general ministry of all the laity in all relationships of life" (1964 Report, Board of Theological Education, based on a composite response from seminary faculties).[114] The Commission report in 1966 on the ministry can be said to have stressed a broadening scope of the ministry of all believers, while stressing less the significance of the ordained ministry. If so, then the rejection of that report by the 1966 convention

can be said to reflect the mood of a church "wanting to safeguard and recognize the status of the ordained ministry" and prevent further "loss of identity" on the part of the clergy.[115] Hence Franklin Clark Fry's comment that ". . . with the tide flowing so strongly toward lay vocations and the accent falling so heavily on the universal priesthood," he thought "the next declaration of the church needed to be on the Ministry, with a capital 'M,' to redress the balance."[116] In convention debate, some saw too much emphasis already on universal priesthood, the current trends being "not accurate to the normative Lutheran understanding of the minister, proclaiming the Word of God. You cannot be the laity to the world, unless you have first received the word of absolution. And it is this that constitutes the integrity of the holy office of the ministry" (William Lazareth).[117]

81. A greater emphasis could be seen on the authority of the pastor and of the national church in the LCA documents, compared with those of the other two Lutheran bodies. Dagny Ohlekopf saw the former in the fact that "the LCA documents accorded the pastor a role in the direction and administration of congregational affairs which considerably exceeds that of an ALC or LCMS pastor"—e.g., he was normally president of the church council and had voice and vote on all congregational committees. The latter point she saw exemplified in the fact that the LCA put its ordination requirements not only in its model constitution for congregations (as ALC did) but also in the Bylaws (II, 1) of the Constitution for the national church.[118] As in other Lutheran bodies, it was assumed that only the ordained ministers would administer the Lord's Supper; this is implicit in the careful regulation provided in a 1964 statement on "Communion Practices" (intended to "liberalize" provisions in some areas but also to regulate any existing "abuses"):

> A lay person may assist in the distribution of the elements by administering the cup, but this privilege must be carefully guarded. Whenever a lay person so assists, with the exception of a seminarian when approved by the church council, he must be a communicant member of the parish, be approved by the church council for this purpose, be instructed by the minister, and be commissioned for this ministry only in his own congregation and his appointment must be renewed annually by the church council.[119]

82. One point in the LCA Constitution where a difference between ordained ministers and laymen came to the fore was in the matter of membership in secret societies. Article VII, section 4 provided ". . . no person, who belongs to any organization which claims to possess in its teachings and ceremonies that which the Lord has given solely to His Church, shall be ordained or otherwise received into the ministry of this church. . . ." Clergy were thus forbidden to join such societies, though there was no statement forbidding laypersons to do so. The background was the "lodge issue," especially the

strong feeling against the Masons, found in many 19th-century immigrants during the period of confessional revival and many Lutheran groups thereafter in the United States. The provision was also found in the church's "standards" for the ministry ("no minister . . . shall become a member of a group which because of its oath of secrecy makes it impossible for the church to determine if its 'teachings and ceremonies' are consistent with what 'the Lord has given solely to His Church'").[120]

83. The laity were not frequently referred to in the LCA documents. "Church vocations," a term which, as noted, has received much emphasis in recent times, was understood as a collective term, used to unite "the ordained, the set-apart, the commissioned, the certified, and elected, and so forth, into a multiple yet ordered ministry"; "calling," as a term, was here used of all Christians, "vocation" (in this parlance) of a specific task or occupation.[121] "Lay readers" could be designated in synods. There were proposals to "put into more effective practice the Christian doctrine of the priesthood of all believers," even for a "department of lay ministry," and study of the laity's role in worship. In synods and on boards, while the principle was equal representation, the specific provisions and actual results were usually weighted on the clergy side. Dagny Ohlekopf was led to conclude that by and large "the LCA presently offers the laity a lower standing than do the other two major Lutheran bodies,"[122] though constitutional statements may be misleading compared with actual situations.

84. Related to these constitutional reflections of Lutheran understanding of the ministry was actual liturgical practice at the ordination service. W. A. Ewing, in working out this analysis, found that the "duality" of "divine institution and the human appointment" appears throughout the "Order for Ordination."[123] In particular, in the order provided in the occasional services of the LCA and The ALC (1962), the whole was set in the context of the gospel and of the service, emphasizing worship and devotion (so that there cannot be just an "ordination service"). "Nothing is here directly said, either of a special function or office within the congregation of Christ which separates that office from the prophetic, apostolic, and divine mandate laid upon all persons within range of this Word."[124] Yet, the office is not thereby "derivative from the priesthood of believers," for there are ample references to "this holy office," "the holy ministry of the Word and sacraments," and "the office and work of a minister in the church of God"; rather, the intention was to see this ordained ministry, here given authority to minister publicly, within the context of the church's total ministry. Here "the congregation of Christ takes upon itself the responsibility" to minister, and here gives to the ordinand "the *authority* to minister," which can be withdrawn when not exercised.[125] The rubrics, incidentally, provided that the order for ordination "shall be conducted by the President of the Synod or District, or by a Minister whom he shall

appoint," and that only ministers, one or more, participate in the laying on of hands.

B. Recent Discussions

85. What other ways exist for examining how Lutheranism looks at the ministry? Portraits of the clergy in fiction and short stories might be revealing of attitudes, but I have found little of significance for our purposes.[126] Sociological surveys on how laypeople look upon the ordained ministry would also be helpful, but I do not find any study like that compiled about Methodists in 1947, or even like an analysis in Lund, Sweden, which reported that "lay people showed more esteem for the minister than ministers showed for themselves."[127] One suspects, however, that a similar regard would show up for the clergy in American Lutheranism. Lutheran clergy probably continue to see many of the roles traditionally connected with the ministry, such as preaching and the leading of worship, as basic, but increasing value is no doubt assigned to newer roles such as counseling, administration, and community activity; for many, however, clergy and lay alike, there is probably an identity crisis about what the ministry is today in its ordained form.[128] One relevant study, by Ross P. Scherer, in 1959, of 572 Missouri Synod clergymen, concluded that ministers tended to look on themselves often very much in the way Synodical literature ideally pictured them, e.g. as primarily "mediator of the Word and sacrament," thus disputing the picture of the ministry as disintegrating, then being given in the popular press. The ministers polled thought "laymen would disagree with ministers most in wanting a minister who was primarily a 'generalist' (skilled in many things), had a pleasing personality, and sacrificed his own convenience for his members," and that ministers would clash with laypersons most when the minister wanted to be "an independent-thinking theologian, an expert in only a few pastoral functions, a go-getter for new Synodical programs, or to take additional university work." Sons of clergymen who enter the ministry seem to provide proportionally more occupants of leadership positions than sons of laypersons; "apparently there is a kind of indelibility which is stamped on an individual by the parsonage or teacherage which clings to him throughout his life."[129] There is some evidence to suggest that Protestant and Catholic attitudes about the ministry are often similar in a given locality and can influence each other.[130]

86. It is chiefly to periodical literature and recent books that one must turn to find Lutheran views today. First of all, let it be noted that the characteristic Lutheran views on the ministry which we have noted continue to be expressed. In the United Lutheran Church in America, for example, the first of the "Knubel-Miller Lectures," in 1945, by the then secretary of the ULCA, set forth a popular summary, in succinct terms, on the Lutheran position as commonly understood.[131] The second set of lectures in the same series also dealt

with the ordained ministry and reflected the high opinion of a layman, and of 30 other laymen responding to a survey, about the pastor: the minister is "God's unique representative," he is "as Christ going about and among his flock . . . an ambassador of the Most High God."[132]

87. Let it also be said that some of the tensions we have noted over the centuries continue to be displayed and some of the same characteristic differences of opinion. Thus in the same encyclopedia, one article avers that "the ministry is not derived by transfer of function from a general priesthood of all believers but it is derived from the authority of the keys," while another states, "Believers delegate and transfer the public exercise of this office to called servants of the Word."[133]

88. As a further example, we may note different points of view in two treatments of ministry, each by Swedish churchmen. (Both of them, it may be noted, frame their statements against traditional Roman Catholic understandings.) Ruben Josefson[134] emphasizes that the ministerial office is basically one office, of proclamation of word and sacraments, established by God, in Christ, and sustained by the Spirit. He insists it is never based on "the concept of sacrifice," either in the Roman sense (since "the office of sacrifice is abolished in Christ") or in the pietistic sense (the priest "offers his heart to God"). But he then goes on to add that this office, really a "divine order," "a God-given order," is "antecedent to the faith," "the fulcrum by which [God's redemptive] work exercises its continuing effectiveness," and thus is "one of the church's constitutive factors," and is of its *esse*. Per Erik Persson, on the other hand, poses the issue as whether gospel or ministry is central: "Either salvation is provided through the ministerial office, and therefore word and sacrament are provided, the presence of Christ being dependent on his presence in the bearer of the office, or else salvation comes through the gospel in word and sacrament, and on this account there is a ministry in the church."[135] Thus two views are contrasted by Persson: the Roman, where the ministry represents Christ, there is a differentiation between priests and laity which is constitutive of the church (so that proper consecration and succession are vital), and what is said christologically also applies to the ministry—there is cooperation of the human with the divine; and the Evangelical, where ministry exists so the gospel may function, Christ's presence in the Lord's Supper is not by virtue of the ministerial office but by the word, and there is no redemptive significance to ordination or a valid succession—"cooperation" between human beings and God is here an impossibility in the sense presented in the other view.

89. Secondly, however, we must note that, for all these characteristic assertions and tensions, the present is a time of change, as most writers on ministry are aware. Symptomatic of this change and the questions it raises is

the fact that four Lutheran periodicals have devoted major space or an entire issue to the question of the ministry in the present decade: the *American Lutheran,* in its "Symposium on Authority," in 1963; *Lutheran World,* with an issue on "The Ministry Today" (dealing with the pastor, not the laity) in 1964; *The Lutheran Quarterly* in 1966, "Ministry and Ministries," focusing especially on ordination, LCA discussion, and the place of women in the ministry; and *Dialog,* on "Ministry as Vocation and Profession," 1969 (ordination and women).[136] None of these was oriented to clergy/laity as chief topic, however.

90. Periodicals of The Lutheran Church–Missouri Synod particularly exhibit a growing discussion over ministry. The centennial year of that church (1946) emphasized "royal priesthood." Articles about that time examined the theme of general priesthood and the pastor.[137] A report to the Synodical Conference in 1948 continued to stress the local congregation, but there were differences of opinion on points of application—study on which was encouraged—as to whether the public ministry is divinely instituted "on its own," so to speak, or is to be viewed in light of the *Übertragungstheorie,* and whether Christ instituted simply the *genus* of the ministry, "in the abstract," the *Predigtamt,* or more specifically the *species,* or pastorate in the local congregation, the *Pfarramt.*[138] We have already noted how LCMS church commissions began to take up the questions in the late 1950s. Sometimes individual treatments sought to transcend traditional hang-ups—e.g., by speaking, in biblical terms, of "the ministry of reconciliation" which belongs to all the saints (instead of "universal priesthood"), and, with criticism of the "transfer theory," by stressing a "ministry to the ministers" in the manner of Eph. 4:8-13.[139] This type of language was at times reflected in the American Lutheran symposium, where there also appeared protests against "clerical domination" in The LCMS, reaffirmation of the "ministry of the laity," and assertions that the church of the writer in this case has the answer—but one layman saw this "definite answer" in the universal priesthood; another in obeying the minister, who is God's intended ambassador, with authority "from God down, and from the Royal Priesthood on up."[140]

91. Is there, amid such change and debate, any "image" today of the Lutheran clergyman? Yes, one pastor wrote in 1961, in spite of rapid change, decline in the prestige of the ministry and the church, expanded duties for the clergy, and the often unflattering image in the mass media; there is an "image that seems to go without saying" of the clergy "as men of God, dedicated to their tasks, specialists from personal experience in the things of the spirit . . . the embodiment of compassion." The picture here is of the clergyman as "the keeper of the keys of morality, the comforter of the bereaved, friend of lonely and sick, the ear open to trouble, the pocket open to the wayfarer."[141] Absent here seems any central stress on proclamation. An

article the next year in the same periodical by a layman (!) took the position that "laymanship" is not confined only to laymen and that there is a "lay perversion of the church": the danger that we lose sight of "the primary function of the church: to preach the Word and administer the sacraments through which God speaks, not man." [142]

92. Certainly we live in a time when the role of the laity has been redis-covered. It is commonplace to regard the clergy as "enablers" of the "real ministry," by the laity out in the world. Sometimes the analogy is employed of the clergy as "commissioned officers with special training" in comparison with the rest of the troops; other times it is said, "the distinction between clergymen and laity cannot be sharply drawn." [143] It is perhaps typical that the LCA Manifesto, "God's Call to the Church in Each Place," drafted by the "Commission on the Nature and Mission of the Congregation" and ap-proved at the LCA's 1966 convention, spoke mostly of the laity ("to equip its members . . . to perform their ministries") and little of the clergy, except that, as the Study Guide to the Manifesto said, "the traditional image [whose?] of the role of the clergy" must change. [144]

93. Exegetically, as part of the current changes, there have been reexam-inations of biblical bases traditionally cited in discussions about the ministry. A dissertation by a Lutheran New Testament scholar, for example, challenged the traditional use of 1 Peter 2:5, 9, on the "royal priesthood," to support the idea of a "universal priesthood of believers" (dear to the Reformers but also to recent Catholic theologians), by claiming the verses refer to election and holiness, eschatologically, of the community, and its witness to the world, not to priesthood—Levitical, spiritual, or otherwise—individually. But the author adds that Luther and others may well be correct on universal priesthood, even though not on the basis of this passage. [145] The Old Testament too has been invoked at times to provide perspective on ministry. One article, avowed-ly championing the "special priesthood" or ministry against the erosion of "classical Lutheranism" in America, argued, invoking recent Old Testament insights, that "as a priest, the clergyman alone" has the right to "absolve sins . . . or to excommunicate" and "to celebrate the Eucharist"—all Chris-tians may "forgive one another," but the clergy have the "gift of absolu-tion." [146] In reply, others denied the applicability of this Old Testament priest-hood idea to the New Testament or to present-day ministry. [147] The New Testament evidence, in its variety, charismatic setting, kerygmatic emphasis, and tendency toward order but not orders, undergirds—though here there is enormous difference of opinion—the general picture which has kept recurring in this chapter, of variety, centered in the gospel, with some sort of public office and a general ministry for all believers. [148]

94. The debate goes on. The traditional Lutheran emphasis on the ministry as a functional office continues to be reasserted; ordination is a conferring of

"the authority publicly to proclaim the gospel and administer the sacraments on behalf of those who call a man to do this," not "the most vital of the sacraments," without which "there is no sacrifice of the mass, and . . . the flow of grace . . . is cut off." [149] Others want "other answers." [150] Such answers are proposed. One writer wants a view of ministry not only "in conformity with the Word of God" but also "relevant to the present cultural situation." [151] He seeks it, however, by going back to orders of creation (as understood from "the sphere of Christ")—which turn out to be two divinely established orders in the church, the ministry and the laity, which correspond to the proclamation of, and response to, the word, in the priesthood of all believers. However, it is also asserted that the parish is scarcely the only or the "primary valid formation of Christ's body," "there is no primary valid form of the church"; and laypeople, although placed in a different order from ministers, are nonetheless allowed to be included in "task forces of ministers" and indeed ought to have "consecration" (annually?) as a parallel to ordination for ministers. (It is rather difficult, it appears, to get away from the two points we've seen constantly: universal priesthood and a public office of ministry!)

95. One other article proceeds more radically, however, and takes up the "universal priesthood" side. It is argued that "the ordained ministry" is not essential to the life of the people of God, laypersons can do everything without clergy; hence, baptism really amounts to ordination for every believer; it is a person's initiation and commissioning. "Baptism as ordination" is thus seen as the watchword for A.D. 2000. [152] Meanwhile, news dispatches report other proposals and events: it was proposed that laypersons in Norway be authorized to administer the Lord's Supper, and vicars in Germany have refused to accept ordination until any ceremony in the rite which suggests sacramental misinterpretation is omitted and until overstress on the pastorate in comparison with other ministries is omitted. [153]

96. In this welter of reports and ideas I single out two more. (1) The notion of the Lutheran ministry as a "presbyteral succession" has appeared in several of the historical references above—i.e., that ministers are regularly ordained by other ministers. It reappears in current discussion, based on the confessions. [154] (2) Peter Brunner suggested that the "apostle" in the early church was to the charismatic ministries there as the "ordained ministry" today is to the layperson. [155]

97. According to Brunner, in the early church there was clearly an apostolic ministry, appointed by the Lord, in living confrontation after Easter through his word of command (*jure divino*), to proclaim the gospel. It had priority temporally as well as in its eyewitness character. Proclamation of the gospel goes back to this ministry in a way that it cannot to the charismatic ministries. These apostles served as "missionary messengers" (*apostellō = mitto,* send forth), and it is from their missionary office (Matt. 28:19-20) that the pastoral

office developed. After this apostolic-missionary-pastoral office, charismatic ministries might flourish. But while every Christian has the Spirit and his own charisma and must have a part in the church's ministry and the extension of the apostolic message, preservation of the gospel "dare not be left to the charismatic ministries by themselves," and "to do justice to the Lord's apostolic commission," the church "must select, call, authorize, and send out individuals as bearers of the office of preacher."[156] Thus, *Predigtamt (Pfarramt)* succeeds the apostolic ministry and continues its work of preserving and spreading the gospel; the laity, under the Spirit too, continue to carry out all sorts of ministries for which they are charismatically equipped. In Brunner's presentation, the ministry is free to structure itself with all sorts of "helpers" and offices, *de jure humano*, but celebration of the Lord's Supper is one of the functions of the ministerial-pastoral office. Thus we have the office of public ministry, fitted into the ministry of all Christians, the twin concerns of Lutherans through the centuries. Brunner's is a presentation favorably regarded in several recent articles.[157]

GENERAL LITERATURE CONSULTED

Enc. Luth. Ch. = The Encyclopedia of the Lutheran Church. Edited by Julius Bodensieck for the Lutheran World Federation. 3 volumes. Minneapolis: Augsburg, 1965. "Lay Activity," by Otto W. Heick, pp. 1275-80 (deals only with those Christians "not members of the official ministry of the church"). "Ministry," by Robert Paul Roth, pp. 1574-84 ("the ministry is *not derived by transfer* of function from a general priesthood of all believers but . . . from the authority of the keys given to the church by the Lord Jesus Christ"). "Priest and Priesthood," by William H. Lazareth, pp. 1964–1966 (" 'Through Baptism all of us are consecrated to priesthood . . . and there is no difference at all but that of office' "). "Keys, Office of," pp. 1206-7; is reprinted from the *Lutheran Cyclopedia* (the office is given to the church from Jesus Christ, and "believers . . . delegate and transfer the public exercise of this office to the called servants of the Word").

Lutheran Cyclopedia. Edited by E. R. Lueker. St. Louis: Concordia, 1954. Cf. "Laity," pp. 565-66 (the division into clergy and laity is valid if the words "stand for the distinction of those who have been called by the church into the ministry of the Word from those who have not been so called"); "Laymen's Activity in the Lutheran Church," p. 576; "Ministerial Office," pp. 682-83; "Teachers," pp. 1036-41 (the length of the article reflects discussion in the Lutheran Church–Missouri Synod over the status of teachers in church schools).

RGG = Die Religion in Geschichte und Gegenwart, 3rd ed. Edited by Kurt Galling and others. 7 volumes. Tübingen: J.C.B. Mohr (Paul Siebeck),

1957–1965. "Amt," III, by E. Schott, 1, esp. cols. 339-40. "Gemeinde,"
I. Begrifflich, by G. Gloege, and II. Rechtlich, by Erik Wolf, 2, cols.
1325-38. "Klerus und Laien," 3. In der ev. Kirche, by G. Wendt, 3, cols.
1663-64. "Laienbewegung, christliche," by H. H. Walz, 4, cols. 203-206.
"Priestertum, allgemeines," by R. Prenter, 5, cols. 581-82. "Priestertum,"
III. In der christlichen Kirche, 3. Protestantismus, by B. Lohse, 5, cols.
579-81.

I. "Ministry" in the Reformation Era

Brunotte, Wilhelm. *Das geistliche Amt bei Luther.* Berlin: Lutherisches Verlagshaus, 1959.

Brunstäd, F. *Theologie der Lutherischen Bekenntnissschriften.* Gütersloh: Ber-
telsmann, 1951.

Carlson, Edgar M. "The Doctrine of the Ministry in the Confessions." *LQ*
15 (1963): 118-31.

Elert, Werner. *The Structure of Lutheranism.* Volume 1. Translated by W. A.
Hansen. St. Louis: Concordia, 1962.

Fischer, Robert H. "Another Look at Luther's Doctrine of the Ministry." *LQ*
18 (1966): 260-71.

Gerrish, Brian. "Luther on Priesthood and Ministry." *Church History* 34
(1965): 404-22.

Goppelt, Leonhard. "The Ministry in the Lutheran Confessions and in the
New Testament." *LW* 11 (1964): 409-26.

Green, Lowell. "Change in Luther's Doctrine of the Ministry." *LQ* 18 (1966):
173-83.

Josefson, Ruben. "The Ministry as an Office in the Church." In *This Is the
Church,* Anders Nygren, editor; C. C. Rasmussen, translator. Philadelphia:
Muhlenberg, 1952, pp. 268-80.

Lieberg, Hellmut. *Amt und Ordination bei Luther und Melanchthon.* Götting-
en: Vandenhoeck und Ruprecht, 1962.

Münter, Wilhelm Otto. *Begriff und Wirklichkeit des geistlichen Amts.* Beiträge
zur evangelischen Theologie 21. Munich: Chr. Kaiser Verlag, 1955.

Schlink, Edmund. *Theology of the Lutheran Confessions.* Translated by Paul
F. Koehneke and Herbert J. A. Bouman. Philadelphia: Fortress, 1961.

Storck, Hans. *Das allgemeine Priestertum bei Luther.* Theologische Existenz
Heute, N.F. 37. Munich: Chr. Kaiser, 1953.

Tappert, Theodore G., et al. *The Book of Concord: The Confessions of the
Evangelical Lutheran Church.* Philadelphia: Fortress, 1959. The confessional writings are cited from this translation, by page, with reference to
document and section also being given.

II. Historical Development in Lutheranism

Askmark, Ragnar. *Ämbetet i den Svenska Kyrkan.* Lund: Gleerup, 1949. Summary in English by C. G. Carlfeldt in *LQ* 3 (1951): 318-19.

Bergendoff, Conrad. "Wanted: A Theory of the Laity in the Lutheran Church." *LQ* 3 (1951): 82-90.

————. *The Doctrine of the Church in American Lutheranism.* The Knubel-Miller Lectures 11. Philadelphia: Board of Publication of the United Lutheran Church in America, 1956. Especially pp. 19-36.

Drews, Paul. *Der evangelische Geistliche in der deutschen Vergangenheit.* Monographien zur deutschen Kulturgeschichte 12. Jena: Diederichs, 1905. One of a series on classes of people, lavishly illustrated with contemporary woodcuts and copper engravings, often on Evangelical and Catholic rivalry. Text describes aspects of the pastor's life in each period from Reformation to the Enlightenment about 1800.

Fagerberg, Holstein. *Bekenntnis: Kirche und Amt in der deutschen konfessionellen Theologie des 19. Jahrhunderts.* Uppsala, 1952.

Heubach, Joachim. *Die Ordination zum Amt der Kirche.* Arbeiten zur Geschichte und Theologie des Luthertums 2. Berlin: Lutherisches Verlagshaus, 1956.

Kalbhen, Walter C. "Holy Ordination and the Call in the First Hundred Years of Lutheranism. . . ." B. D. dissertation, Concordia Seminary, St. Louis (not available to me).

Lawson, Evald B. "The Ministry." In *Centennial Essays: Augustana Lutheran Church 1860–1960,* ed. E. Engberg, C. Bergendoff, E. M. Carlson. Rock Island: Augustana Press, 1960. Pp. 150-68. On pastors from Sweden, growth of theological education here, etc.

Mead, Sidney E. "The Rise of the Evangelical Conception of the Ministry in America (1607–1850)." In *The Ministry in Historical Perspective,* ed. H. Richard Niebuhr and Daniel Day Williams. New York: Harper, 1956, pp. 207-49.

Michaelsen, Robert. "The Protestant Ministry in America: 1850 to the Present." Ibid., pp. 250-88.

Muller, Arnold C. *The Ministry of the Lutheran Teacher: A Study to Determine the Position of the Lutheran Parish School Teacher within the Public Ministry of the Church.* Authorized by the Board of Parish Education of the Lutheran Church–Missouri Synod. St. Louis: Concordia, 1964. There is a summary at the close of each chapter. The chart on p. 10, of a tree with many branches, illustrates the thesis that from the roots and trunk (priesthood of all believers, the one divinely instituted public ministry) there are three main branches (synod, parish, and other ventures), each with many smaller branches.

Pauck, Wilhelm. "The Ministry in the Time of the Continental Reformation." In *The Ministry in Historical Perspective,* pp. 110-48.

Piepkorn, Arthur Carl. "What the Symbols Have to Say about the Church." *CTM* 26 (1955): 721-63.

Prenter, Regin. "Die göttliche Einsetzung des Predigtamtes und das allegemeine Priestertum bei Luther." *TLZ* 86 (1961): cols. 322-32.

Roloff, Jürgen. "The Question of the Church's Ministry in Our Generation." *LW* 11 (1964): 389-408. On developments in Sweden and Germany since 1918.

Schoch, Max. *Verbi Divini Ministerium.* Tübingen: J. C. B. Mohr (Paul Siebeck), 1968. Takes up the *Predigtamt* in Lutheranism and among the Reformed. Volume 1 introduces the problem of "the Word—speech and reality." Volume 2 (1969) deals with the office of service in the church that serves.

Schmid, Heinrich. *The Doctrinal Theology of the Evangelical Lutheran Church Verified from the Original Sources.* Translated by C. A. Hay and H. E. Jacobs. Philadelphia: Lutheran Publication Society. Third edition, revised, 1899. Reprinted, Minneapolis: Augsburg, 1961. A summary and compendium of opinions from the Lutheran scholastic theologians.

Tuchel, Klaus. "Luthers Auffassung vom geistlichen Amt." *Luther-Jahrbuch* (25) 1958. Berlin: Lutherisches Verlagshaus, 1958. Pp. 61-98.

Weidner, Revere Franklin. *The Doctrine of the Ministry: Outline Notes Based on Luthardt and Krauth.* Chicago: Wartburg Publishing House, 1907. Reflects the *Compendium der Dogmatik* by C. E. Luthardt (Leipzig, 1823–1902) and the manuscript lectures of Charles Porterfield Krauth (Philadelphia, 1823–1883).

Werdermann, Hermann. *Der evangelische Pfarrer in Geschichte und Gegenwart: Im Rückblick auf 400 Jahre evangelisches Pfarrhaus.* Wissenschaft und Bildung 216. Leipzig: Quelle and Meyer, 1925. Written at the 400th anniversary of the Lutheran parsonage, the book builds on earlier studies, like that of Drews and W. Baur on *Das evangelische Pfarrhaus* (1902[5]), proceeding by periods down to the end of World War I. No notes, but bibliography (pp. 145-49).

Wolf, Richard C., editor. *Documents of Lutheran Unity in America.* Philadelphia: Fortress, 1966.

SUPPLEMENTARY COMMENTS

This presentation to the dialogue on the history and varieties of the Lutheran position on "the office of public ministry fitted into the ministry of all Christians" went together with other Lutheran papers by Arthur Carl Piepkorn on

"The Sacred Ministry and Holy Ordination in the Symbolical Books of the Lutheran Church" (concerning what the Confessions say) and "A Lutheran View of the Validity of Lutheran Orders," and by Warren A. Quanbeck on "A Contemporary View of Apostolic Succession" (all reprinted in *Eucharist and Ministry,* pp. 101-19 [= *CTM* 40 (1969): 552-73], 209-26, and 178-88, respectively). The considerable work by Catholic colleagues, together with hours of discussion, enabled the dialogue to say in its "Common Observations on Eucharistic Ministry":

> 21. The Lutheran tradition has one order of ordained Ministers, usually called pastors, which combines features of the episcopate and the presbyterate. This Ministry is also conferred by a rite of ordination that includes the laying on of hands. The pastor who has received this Ministry possesses the fullness of that which ordination confers and in general he corresponds in his functions with the bishop in the Catholic tradition. In the Lutheran churches represented in this dialogue, the ordination of pastors is reserved to the district or synodical president or a pastor designated by him. The ordination of pastors in these churches goes back historically to priests ordained in the Catholic tradition who, on becoming Lutherans and lacking Catholic bishops who would impose hands on successors, themselves imposed hands for the ordination of co-workers and successors in the Ministry. From the Lutheran standpoint, such an ordination in presbyteral succession designates and qualifies the Lutheran pastor for all the functions that the Catholic priest (*presbyter*) exercises, including that of celebrating a eucharist which would be called (in Catholic terminology) valid. It is to be noted, however, that the Lutheran confessions indicate a preference for retaining the traditional episcopal order and discipline of the church, and express regret that no bishop was willing to ordain priests for evangelical congregations (pp. 14-15, footnotes omitted).

The Reflections of the Lutheran participants dealt primarily with traditional misgivings about the Roman Catholic church's ministry, many of them now deemed no longer problems, though other "barriers to eucharistic sharing" exist, matters "to be discussed before we can recommend pulpit and altar fellowship" (§§34, 33). The Roman Catholic Reflections were devoted chiefly to arguments, historical and theological, on how "our traditional objections to the Lutheran eucharistic Ministry," with its "presbyteral rather than an episcopal succession," can be "seen to be of less force today" (§36, 37). The parallel recommendations to respective church authorities said,

> As Lutherans, . . . we recommend . . . that . . . the participating Lutheran churches be urged to declare formally their judgment that the ordained Ministers of the Roman Catholic church are engaged in a valid Ministry of the gospel, announcing the gospel of Christ and administering the sacraments of faith. . . . (§35)

> As Roman Catholic theologians, . . . we see no persuasive reason to deny the possibility of the Roman Catholic church recognizing the validity of this [eucharistic] Ministry [of the Lutheran churches]. Accordingly, we ask the authorities

of the Roman Catholic church whether . . . ecumenical urgency . . . may not dictate that the Roman Catholic church recognize the validity of the Lutheran Ministry. . . . (§54)

Thus the affirmation by Lutherans about "the body and blood of our Lord Jesus Christ" being "truly present" in Roman Catholic "celebrations of the sacrament of the altar" and by Catholics about "the presence of the body and blood of Christ in the eucharistic celebrations of the Lutheran churches" (§§35 and 54)—already a conclusion in round three of the dialogue—was now extended in round four to an affirmation of each other's Ministers at the Eucharist. If we have "valid" sacraments, must not the Ministers at the altar be "valid" too?

Roman Catholic authorities, however, cannot be said to have found the arguments or urgency to be sufficient. Nor have Lutherans been quick to act either, though their confessions provide "no basis . . . for denying that Roman Catholic priests are competent Ministers of the gospel and the sacraments" and the question about whether "the Ministry of Roman Catholic clergymen is really a Ministry of the gospel" is allayed by the fact that "Vatican II has called the proclamation of the gospel of God to all a 'primary duty' of priests" (§30). To a great extent this Lutheran reticence comes from a desire for *mutual* recognition and a willingness not to act unilaterally or prematurely. Even the quite positive LCA response at its 1986 convention to the statement from round seven on "Justification by Faith" at best called for exploring "in appropriate ways with the Roman Catholic Church the feasibility of establishing some level of fellowship short of full communion" but allowing "limited eucharistic sharing."

The ordained Ministry thus remains a barrier that in the Lutheran–Catholic dialogue has not been overleapt. It must be remembered that at issue in the U.S. dialogue was the Ministry of male Lutheran clergy celebrating the sacraments in local parishes, not the questions of women's ordination, the role and status of bishops, or the place of laity in the church.

Bibliographically there has been an immense literature since my 1969 study on the Lutheran ministry. We shall note here some of the significant titles on a few selected aspects of the 97 sections above, and then conclude with subsequent Lutheran statements and the further topics that have been opened up.

Perhaps the volume that most parallels what is surveyed above is *Traditions of Ministry: A History of the Doctrine of the Ministry in Lutheran Theology,* by James H. Pragman (St. Louis: Concordia, 1983). It ranges from Luther, through the Confessions, Orthodoxy, Pietism, 19th-century debates and 20th-century issues, till about 1980. Unfortunately, Pragman stops short of reporting on the LCMS statement on "The Ministry" in 1981 that we shall take up below.

There is much to be learned from Pragman's pages, supplementing my study. He develops his account with only a single reference (p. 20, n. 27) to my essay (§11), that "the church is a priesthood, but it has an ordained ministry" (actually from Robert H. Fischer), so his can be termed an independent reading of the evidence. It is also one which allows for traditions (plural) within the Lutheran heritage. But it is a reading set within Missouri Synod debates and reflects a certain tendentiousness that is never fully articulated, namely, that in asking about "the universal priesthood of all believers" and "the pastoral ministry" and how they relate, Pragman favors universal priesthood and a "functional" view of the pastoral office. Neither emphasis is wrong in itself, but the book has the irritating habit of being "noncommittal" at crucial points. (Such criticisms are those also of H. Armin Moellering in a review in *Concordia Journal* 11 [1985]: 27-31, who speaks of the book's "apodictic insinuation.")

An example of the way Pragman reads evidence is to be seen in how he aligns positions in the 19th century (cf. §§44-48 and 59-60 above): Stahl, Loehe, and Vilmar are arranged on the side of "ministry as a divine institution," Höfling on the side of pastoral ministry and its foundation in universal priesthood as one ministry, so that a "middle ground" is thus created, to be occupied by the views of C. F. W. Walther. Walther is rightly viewed as reacting against hierarchical "Stephanism" (the effort of Martin Stephan to rule as bishop over the Saxon Lutheran settlers), but Walther's theses of 1852 are then quoted as "middle ground," principles that were to weigh heavily in subsequent Missouri Lutheran understanding, but reflecting a view that I would align more with Höfling's: "God transfers the public office through the congregation as the possessor of all church power" and, although "there is only one office of the public ministry in the church," this one office "is exercised by a variety of offices," deacon, almoner, cantor, teachers in a church school, etc. (Theses 6 and 8, as phrased by Pragman, pp. 144-46).

Pragman's underlying thesis is that Lutheranism has operated with both a "broad" sense of the ministry, one that includes the universal priesthood (so Luther, Pietism), and a "narrow" sense, where ministry is synonymous with the public, pastoral ministry of the church (so Melanchthon and the confessors, he says). His claim that the 20th century has not made universal priesthood "a topic of major interest" (p. 154) may be true of the Missouri Synod, but scarcely holds when one considers laity movements in other parts of Lutheranism and ecumenically.

Pragman is helpful for outsiders in understanding the complex LCMS debate over Christian day-school teachers, a matter which is even more complicated than I indicated above (§§65-66). Was Walther contradictory when he affirmed in 1856 that two men who had left the pastoral office to teach as professors at a church school were still participating in the one divine office (p. 146, though Walther did not seemingly term their new position "auxiliary offices," as successors have, n. 84)? A 1953 convention report denied that the phrase "pastors and teachers" at Eph. 4:11 refers to day-school teachers, but went on to affirm that such teachers are ministers of the Word, clergymen. Males in such roles are called and receive "tenure," whereas women are "contracted" for a specific time. (Pragman believes, however, that the committee "saw no essential difference between the ministries of male and female teachers," p. 173.) But ordination is to be reserved to pastors and would demand the same program of study and training as they receive—a fact not true of teachers. All this seems quite intricate, but never mind; the convention thanked the committee without voting the report and reaffirmed the traditional right of congregations to call "servants of the Word to conduct the activities of the ministry of the Word in their midst" and decided they should be identified as "ministers of the Word"—a valued decision for them in the face of selective service and the Korean War (pp. 172-74; *Proceedings,* 42nd Convention, 1953, pp. 285-326).

Pragman also notes a 1973 report from the LCMS Commission on Theology and Church Relations that shifts a bit: ordination need not be restricted to pastors, and women teachers can be ordained too; but ordination is an adiaphoron (peripheral matter), and "ordination to the teaching of the Word is to be distinguished from ordination to the pastoral ministry of the church" (p. 175; report on "The Ministry in Its Relation to the Christian Church"). Far more decisive and distinctive was to be the 1981 CTCR study, undiscussed by Pragman.

To many readers these last paragraphs may seem an arid digression into the (to them) uninteresting question of the ministerial status of parochial school teachers. Only Lutherans could get themselves into such a bind, other Christians might say. Only Missouri Synod Lutheran theology could get so convoluted, other Lutherans might exclaim. I confess to having felt something of the same emotions in working through a portion of the literature when preparing §§65 and 66 above. But in referring to the LCMS position in 1968 as "an exception to the usual division into ordained ministry and unordained laity," I confess I could not have foreseen what an issue this would become within the Commission for a New Lutheran Church in the 1980s. For the Association of Evangelical Lutheran Churches, in breaking away from the LCMS, took the step, oft debated in Missouri, of including its day-school teachers within the ranks of ordained ministers. See further, Chapter 5 below.

Besides Pragman, who should thus be read as a supplementary account but with awareness of certain tendencies in the book, we note more briefly some important titles on sections of the essay above. For the Reformer himself, Gert Haendler's *Luther on Ministerial Office and Congregational Function* (trans. Ruth C. Gritsch, ed. Eric W. Gritsch, Philadelphia: Fortress, 1981) shows, through a series of case studies, how Luther's view of the office of the ministry intertwines with his understanding of the local congregation as an active fellowship. Luther's answers may have differed from situation to situation, but he saw an active ministry to be required by "both 'officeholders' (*Amtsträger*) and congregations" (Gritsch, p. 12, who notes that for Luther "ordination is the call to function in the ministry as one Christian who has been chosen by other Christians to serve in public"; there is no "indelible character," and "the power of ordination ceases when there is no longer a call to work in the ministry of Word and sacraments"; for bibliography, see p. 10 n. 2, and pp. 17-20, 103-10). See also Mark Ellingsen, "Luther's Concept of the Ministry: The Creative Tension," *Word and World* 1 (1981): 338-46.

On the Lutheran Confessions, in addition to the literature already cited in my essay and Pragman, pp. 35-57, one will find a summary of the positions articulated by Arthur C. Piepkorn in the dialogue put succinctly in his *Profiles in Belief: The Religious Bodies of the United States and Canada*, vol. 2, *Protestant Denominations* (San Francisco: Harper and Row, 1978), pp. 85-88. In arguing for a middle ground between the elevated view of sacred ministry as "the contemporary form of the primitive apostolate and the incumbent as the personal representative of Christ" and the view that it is merely an activity the "universal royal priesthood" committed to some of its members for the sake of good order, he sees the ministry as service and an order but not hierarchical, unitary with one presbyterate-episcopate (the Confessions "call into question . . . grades within that ministry"; "separation of the presbyterate and the episcopate, along with the introduction of the initially lay office of deacon into the . . . sacred ministry they hold to be developed by human right," not divine). Ordination is as indispensable as good works are to faith. This sacred ministry is indeed a "mark" of the church. But in life-and-death emergencies laypersons can baptize and pronounce absolution, but the Confessions do not give them "authority to consecrate the eucharistic elements," for the Lord's Supper "is not as indispensably necessary" as the other two actions.

Perhaps the most widely used textbook on the Confessions in recent years is *Lutheranism: The Theological Movement and Its Confessional Writings*, by Eric W. Gritsch and Robert W. Jenson (Philadelphia: Fortress, 1976). Their section on "Ministry—Serving the Gospel" (pp. 110-23) stresses the Word-relatedness of this office by which God relates to us, the ministry that not only has the Word as its content to proclaim but that is also its agent. There is a "ministerial succession" to predecessors. The Reformation's understanding of ordained ministry is "functional," but ministers also specialize—in preaching, counseling, or teaching, for example—and so they are also "hierarchically differentiated" by special functions that are theirs. There is a cryptic warning that "the Reformation's functional understanding of ministry must compel us to rethink radically the whole question of leadership in the church" (p. 122; cf. 204-205).

Available now in translation from Swedish by Gene J. Lund is Holsten Fagerberg's *A New Look at the Lutheran Confessions (1529–1537)* (St. Louis: Concordia, 1972); see pp. 226-50 for his functional, evangelical view. Fagerberg discusses particularly the views of Scandinavian interpreters like Gustav Wingren, Per E. Persson, and Vilmos Vajta which connect with Höfling's analyses, though he himself is also critical at times of their interpretation of specific passages in the Confessions. In *Christian Dogmatics,* edited by Carl E. Braaten and Robert W. Jenson (Philadelphia: Fortress, 1984), ministry is treated under "The Church" (vol. 2, pp. 224-31) by Philip Hefner. He sees the role of the ordained as "to ensure that the church does not forget who it is and what its purpose is" (p. 224) and surfaces the tensions between ordained and the "priesthood of all believers"; between charism and office; and between ontology and function.

As can be seen from the secondary literature, Luther himself and the Confessions both agree and have different nuances on the ministry. Recent years have brought anniversary celebrations for each—1980, the 450th anniversary of the Augsburg Confession and the 400th of the Formula of Concord; 1983, the 500th of Luther's birth. As far as publications go, the anniversaries of the symbolical books probably produced more publications on the topic of ministry than did the Luther year. From the dialogue with Catholics may be noted the essay by Avery Dulles and George Lindbeck on "Bishops and the Ministry of the Gospel," in *Confessing One Faith: A Joint Commentary on the Augsburg Confession by Lutheran and Catholic Theologians,* trans. ed by George Wolfgang Forrell and James F. McCue (Minneapolis: Augsburg, 1982), pp. 148-72. More pertinent to Chapter 4, below, on bishops, it does also treat the theological foundation of Lutheranism's one single, functional office of the ministry and points of controversy over it in light of a hermeneutic that makes the CA itself the norm, not Luther, the Reformers' principles, or later developments (pp. 154-64, 166). Behind this approach on bishops and ministry looms Wilhelm Maurer's *Historical Commentary on the Augsburg Confession* (German, 2 vols., 1976 and 1978); trans. by H. George Anderson (Philadelphia: Fortress, 1986), especially pp. 188-204 in light of 59-85.

For the developments between the Reformation period and the shift to the American scene, Pragman's footnotes to pp. 58-126 provide a resource, often in the primary sources themselves. How the impact of Orthodoxy, Pietism, rationalism, and other forces came to be felt among Lutheran settlers in the United States and Canada can best be viewed within the frame of a general church history such as is now available in E. Clifford Nelson's *The Lutherans in North America* (Philadelphia: Fortress, 1975). The chapters by Theodore

G. Tappert on the period from 1650 to 1790, and by H. George Anderson for 1790–1840 take up the topic of clergy in particular (pp. 43-49, 87-88, 102-5, 125). Pragman's attention to Missouri Synod developments has already been characterized.

Useful for appreciating the experiences of many different ethnic groups from Europe that came to make up the ALC is the volume edited by Charles P. Lutz, *Church Roots: Stories of Nine Immigrant Groups That Became the American Lutheran Church* (Minneapolis: Augsburg, 1985). I am struck by the fact, in these accounts, of how, for even the most congregationally minded groups of pietists with their axiom of having only "converted" pastors, the person called was regularly ordained by another Lutheran clergyman—a frontier "presbyterial succession." Thus Elling Eielsen (above, §56) in 1843 "was ordained as the first Norwegian-American pastor," on call from a congregation of Haugean pietists at Fox River, Illinois, "by Pastor Francis A. Hoffmann of the German-background Michigan Synod" (p. 70); and the Dane, C. L. Clausen, who was to serve Norwegian immigrants, was ordained by a pastor, L. F. E. Krause, of the Buffalo Synod (with its "high" view of the ministry; see above, §54), also in 1843 (p. 55).

There is relatively little literature on the history of U.S. Lutheran laity in church life and serving in the world. But see Timothy L. Smith, "Lay Initiative in the Religious Life of American Immigrants, 1880–1950," *Anonymous Americans: Explorations in Nineteenth Century Social History,* ed. Tamara Hareven (Englewood Cliffs, N.J.: Prentice-Hall, 1971), pp. 214-49; Jerald C. Brauer, *The Role of Laity in the Life of the Congregation: A Report to the Lutheran World Federation Commission on Stewardship and Congregational Life* (Geneva, 1963); and, above all, Alan Graebner, *Uncertain Saints: The Laity in the Lutheran Church–Missouri Synod 1900–1970,* Contributions in American History 42 (Westport, Conn.: Greenwood Press, 1975; I know of no similar study on groups that made up the ALC or the LCA). Graebner unfolds "the gradual emergence of the laity in the Missouri Synod as immigrant laymen became more Americanized, more integrated into the culture and society surrounding them"; the search for "the most proper, meaningful, and complete role" for laity; and, rather dismayingly, "the synod's view of the world" as determinative factor (p. ix). (Studies of other Lutheran groups are desirable, to test if there has not often been something in Lutheran doctrine that so dichotomizes being "in but not of the world" that significant participation in much of national life is excluded.)

Early opportunities for lay involvement by Missouri Lutherans were, so it seems to us today, unbelievably limited, for clergy domination was extremely strong. The battle, for example, over whether church members could belong to Masonic lodges can be called "a cleric's quarrel over lay life" (p. 83). Laymen came more prominently into church life especially as money raisers (needed to cover deficits) and when there were demands for more efficiency in finances in church administration. Graebner sees certain crests of involvement in the periods of World Wars I and II and then in the 1960s. But "the 1954 *Lutheran Cyclopedia* . . . simply copied verbatim the entry from the *Concordia Cyclopedia* of 1927" for its article on "laity" (emphasizing the priesthood of all believers over against Roman Catholic sacerdotalism; Graebner, p. 165). There is little evidence presented that Missouri "congregationalism" led to significant lay leadership. But the repunctuation of Eph. 4:11-13 in the RSV to suggest that laity, not clergy, do "the work of ministry" (pp. 176-77, citing R. Caemmerer, "take out the commas" in v. 12), is held up as a significant new insight.

As for women, Missouri theologians argued in the 1890s that "women should not even appear at congregational meetings, for they had male relatives as their natural representatives" (p. 17). "Some St. Louis professors fought national female suffrage to the bitter end—and beyond," as "rule over men" and "contrary to the natural order" (p. 85). When in 1913 Franz Pieper presented his German essay on "The Lay Movement Ordered by God," most of it dealt with "the high and holy office of the ministry" (p. 23; trans. John Theodore Mueller, "The Layman's Movement in the Light of God's Word," in *What Is Christianity? and Other Essays* [St. Louis: Concordia, 1933]). With regard later to women's suffrage in congregations, the Lutheran Women's Missionary League was stifled in the late 1930s from even raising the question (p. 185). In the 1950s "Concordia Publishing House refused to print a manuscript by a Missourian clergyman, Russell C. Prohl, which challenged the customary exegesis of pertinent New Testament passages" (p. 186; see below, Chap. 2, note 7). How the role of women was involved in debates of the 1960s within Missouri and how laity played roles in the split when "the Missouri Synod finally came apart" (p. 187) are sketched on pp. 187-209.

While I have called attention in §85 of Chapter 1, above, specifically in note 126, to works of fiction about clergy, novels of course also often reveal portraits of the laity. Graebner, *Uncertain Saints,* p. 215, note 17, finds little of such chronicles from the German-American community but calls attention to Scandinavian-American examples: Ole E. Rølvaag not only for his *Giants in the Earth: A Saga of the Prairie,* trans. Lincoln Colcord (New York: Harper Torchbook, 1964), but also for his *Peder Victorious,* trans. Nora O. Solum (New York, 1929), and *Their Father's God,* trans. Trygve M. Ager (New York, 1931); and Wilhelm Moberg, *The Emigrants* (1951), *Unto a Good Land* (1954), and *The Last Letter Home* (1961), trans. Gustaf Lannestock (New York). Consider for Germans in Ohio "Reverend Wilme" and Lancaster Lutheran Church in George Dell's *The Earth Abideth* (Columbus: Ohio State University Press, 1986).

All sorts of updating might be done for the section of my essay on the ministry "in contemporary thinking," i.e., now since 1969. For example, in the exegetical reexamination of traditional views (§93) much more has been done, as can be seen by a glance at the "Concepts of Ministry" section in James D. G. Dunn's *Unity and Diversity in the New Testament: An Inquiry into the Character of Earliest Christianity* (Philadelphia: Westminster, 1977), pp. 103-23. He claims, rightly in my opinion, greater diversity "in the various concepts of ministry and community" in the New Testament than for any other doctrine or topic; here is "the 'spaghetti-junction' of first-century Christianity"—like the complex, multilevel turnpike interchanges, where all sorts of roads intertwine and twist around before leading out in different directions (pp. 121-22). The recent work of John H. Elliott, the one illustration I allowed myself in 1969 (see note 145, above), is reflective of a major trend in biblical studies, that of reading texts in light of their sociological setting. In *A Home for the Homeless: A Sociological Analysis of 1 Peter, Its Situation and Strategy* (Philadelphia: Fortress, 1981) Elliott views the epistle as presenting the image of a new household for people uprooted from their old religions and society; 2:4-10 is not so much cultic as societal, and the *oikos pneumatikos* not a "spiritual temple" but a house (community) where the Spirit resides (p. 169). Attention to social setting can, of course, also bring a much more realistic meaning to 20th-century views of ecclesiology and ministry.

Our attention here, however, is best directed to official church documents concerning the ministry. For the Lutheran Church–Missouri Synod (above, §§74-76), some developments have been noted in connection with Pragman's book, but the most significant statement is likely *The Ministry: Office, Procedures, and Nomenclature,* a report of the Commission on Theology and Church Relations of the LCMS (St. Louis, 1981). It clearly rejects the "transference theory" in its Thesis 1: "The office of the public ministry . . . is distinct from the universal priesthood of believers" and "is not derived from it"; there is rather a "divine constitution of the office," p. 25. A wider sense of "ministry of the laity" is mentioned, but the focus is on the "narrower" public sense (p. 11). The one Office of the Public Ministry "is equivalent to the pastoral office" with its multiple functions, and so the 18 categories in the synod's *Annual* under "Pastors of Missouri Synod" can include work beyond the local parish. The parochial school teacher performs "*that* function of the pastoral office" (i.e., teaching), but "the pastoral office is unique in that *all* the functions of the church's ministry belong to it" (p. 19). Those in "the teaching ministry" do not possess the oversight and accountability that pastors do, and "ordination" is "reserved for a man's entry into the office of the public ministry." Others hold "facilitating offices" and are "commissioned." Women may hold auxiliary offices but not the pastoral office.

The Lutheran Church in America (§§80-83, above) had before it a "Report of the Commission on the Comprehensive Study of the Ministry" at its 1970 convention. Its recommendations on the ordination of women and on the title *bishop* are considered in Chapters 2 and 3 below. It further affirmed that "all Christians are ministers" and described the ministry of the ordained as "representative" and "official." By these terms were meant one who "represents the Word," not "the representative of other Christians" or that the person " 're-represents' Christ in the Church," but that the person ". . . represents by life, word and activity God's act of reconciliation in Christ" so that the gospel is represented in a public way; and by "official," the public character of the ministry, "an official ministry" designated by the church, with authorization by the church in places for which the church accepts responsibility. The first aspect has to do with *function,* the second with *ordering* of ministry. The report was brief, the recommendations weighty (*Minutes,* Fifth Biennial Convention of the LCA, Minneapolis, June 25–July 2, 1970, pp. 428-50, especially 429-30).

"A Study of Ministry, 1980," from the LCA's Division for Professional Leadership, sought to deepen understanding of both "the ministry of the whole people of God" and "the office of Word and Sacraments," as well as the relationships between them. All sorts of recommendations followed, especially on matters like part-time service in a congregation and the case of ordained ministers doing graduate study. A series of "Expectations" of the LCA for its ordained ministers was subsequently spelled out. A 1984 report on "God's People in Ministry" dealt more fully with the roles of the non-ordained. None of these documents received convention approval, though specific recommendations based on them were acted on by the conventions, including a "Declaration of Ministry" about the "*laos,* people called by God" in 1984. The "Expectations" were approved by the LCA Executive Council. All these documents are printed together in a booklet, *Ministry in the Lutheran Church in America: Study Reports and Official Documents.*[158] For the 1986 convention a task force related to the Office of the Bishop produced a report entitled "God's People: Called, Empowered, Sent," asking for an intentional effort to get ministry in daily life into "the bloodstream of the church." This report was commended to the LCA and the New Lutheran Church, especially for its proposed study of the ministry (1988–1994).

The ALC (above, §§77-79) has been less active in producing statements of its own on ministry, though at its 1976 convention it added a definition of "ministry" to its *Handbook:* "the witness and service performed by this Church, its member congregations and their members in carrying out the mission given by Jesus Christ our Lord" (*1976 Reports and Actions,* Eighth General Convention, Washington, D.C., pp. 795-96, 986). Generally the ALC has preferred to work with other Lutherans on such matters. It requested the

Lutheran Council study on the ordination of women (Chapter 2, below) as part of a general treatment of ministry and ordination as early as 1967. This ALC request, carried out cooperatively, also led to the next document noted from LCUSA.

In 1974 the Division of Theological Studies of the Lutheran Council completed a report, published in its "Studies" series, on "The Ministry of the Church: A Lutheran Understanding." It treats the ordained ministry within ministry of the whole people of God, a pattern by now quite familiar, but introduces at least two different concepts. Ordained ministry is viewed as a series of significant moments (Greek, *kairoi*) on a time line in one's life. Ordination is such a "*kairos* on the continuum of ordained ministry," as would be each installation in a new field of labor. A pastor can resign from the ordained ministry and later resume this continuum. (Is it then a broken continuum?) A "covenant between individual, church, and God" is involved. A second novelty is the suggestion of "commissioned ministries," distinct from ordained or lay ministering. It suggests that a person could be called to the public ministry by and under the church for a form of ministry the church desires, as part of its mission. It is presumably not concerned with Word and sacraments but has its own continuum. Neither concept can as yet be said to be an idea whose time has come.

Finally there are documents involving U.S. Lutherans but from outside North America. The international Roman Catholic/Lutheran Joint Commission produced in 1981 a study on *The Ministry of the Church* (English, Geneva: LWF, 1982). It draws on many existing statements, as well as its own dialogue discussions, and illustrates ordination with a collection of Lutheran and Roman Catholic liturgies. The statement focuses on ordained ministry in light of God's saving act in Christ, with justification as "a joint starting point" (§9). The "one special ministry" (§§16-30) is spelled out in familiar terms, e.g., as "over against" as well as "within" the community, but there are efforts to deal with new issues like women's ordination. It can be agreed that "the church needs the special form of ministry which can be exercised by women just as it needs that exercised by men" (§25), but answers differ on their ordination, as a supplementary study makes clear (pp. 88-107). Bishops call for particular attention (§§40-58). The hope is for gradual, mutual recognition of ministries (§§81-86) so as to eliminate "the scandal of our separation at the Lord's Supper" (§81), and possible steps are suggested to this goal.

Some of these emphases can be duplicated in other bilateral dialogues, notably Lutheran–Anglican, and by multilateral dialogues as in Faith and Order (see Chapter 5).

A fruit of international Lutheran reflection upon all this ferment over ministry can be seen in a series of booklets from the Lutheran World Federation. In 1980 its Department of Studies produced *The Ministry of All Baptized*

Believers: Resource Materials for the Churches' Study in the Area of Ministry.
It reprints four Lutheran and seven ecumenical documents, including the 1974
LCUSA and 1980 LCA studies. In an introduction the ministry of the people
of God is described as "general" ministry and within it the Ministry (cap.)
as the "special" ministry of Word and Sacrament. Tied as it was to a Studies
Department project in worship, this presentation sees the clergy distinguished
especially by their "liturgical presidency" at the eucharist, i.e., they preside.
But the growing role of laity in planning and leading worship raises new
questions here.

LWF's contributions are especially to be seen in a trio of booklets in 1983.
Those on the ordination of women and on bishops will be discussed in subsequent chapters. *The Lutheran Understanding of Ministry* (LWF Studies,
Reports and Texts from the Department of Studies, Geneva, 1983) is basic.
While "episcopal office" is singled out for particular attention later (p. 5),
the foundation is the people of God (Part I) and the one ministry they all
carry out (Part II). But "ministry" threatens to be abstract; it becomes real
only in the ministries people carry out corporately and individually, in the
world and in the church. The ordained ministry (Part III) is then presented
as "a particular instance of the ministry to which all Christians have been
called," one of leadership, of Word and Sacrament, in interdependence with
all baptized believers (§18). The "essential task" of this ordained ministry
is "to assemble and build up the body of Christ by proclaiming and teaching
the Word of God" (§23). The authority of such ministers—the gospel—will
be discussed below in the Supplementary Comments on Chapter 4.

This LWF document wrestles with many issues, including "apostolic succession" in the apostolic faith and gospel, served and expressed by the ordained ministry (§§54-57). Ordination is stressed in a section (§§44-53) that
notes but does not develop "commissioning" for "other ministries" (§45).
It begins to face up also to the "mutual responsibility" of clergy and laity
"for common worship" and participation of both "in various liturgical ministries" (§§22 and 16). The document, while not shortchanging the ordained,
lifts up the ministries of the whole people of God in a way more balanced
than many statements.

Issues and topics that grow out of my essay in Chapter 1 have by now
become clear. Women and ordination, bishops, and ministerial authority will
be taken up in Chapters 2, 3, and 4, respectively. The status of those who
are unordained but who do various tasks within the church, often full-time,
will come out at several points—deaconesses, e.g., in Chapter 2, Christian
day-school teachers in 5. The question of papal ministry is not a matter of
Lutheran self-identity but has been treated elsewhere in Lutheran–Catholic

dialogue, notably rounds 5, 6, and 7, and we shall touch on it in Chapter 4 below.

In summary, on the subsequent literature concerning ministries of the ordained and the laity in Lutheranism since 1969, it can be claimed that the main points then in the dialogue have stood up well: a historical Lutheran emphasis on the one office of ordained ministry and its absolute necessity for gospel proclamation; a traditional but newly being discovered sense of the whole people of God as ministering; and a recurrent and ever fresh task of relating the two dynamically. It should not surprise Lutherans that, while the doctrine of the ministry is thus, on some points, firmly fixed, there is fluidity elsewhere. For so it was in the beginning. And any institution that has to do with the world and society and meeting needs within and without the church will inevitably require adjusting. The ministry of sinning saints must ever be reformed; *semper reformanda* applies more so here than almost anywhere else in Christendom.

2

The Ordination of Women: Exegesis, Experience, and Ecumenical Concern

A. THE SCRIPTURES ON THE ORDINATION OF WOMEN: AN EXEGETICAL ANALYSIS

Any decision about women functioning in the ordained Ministry of the church must rest, in the Lutheran tradition, on careful examination of the scriptural data, pro and con. The treatment that follows was written for an inter–Lutheran study of the topic in 1968–1969, as noted in the Introduction above and further described below in Section B. III. It was first published as "What in Scripture Speaks to the Ordination of Women?" in *CTM* 44, 1 (January 1973): 5-30.

I. Ordination[1]

"Ordination," it is well to remember, does not appear, full-blown and in our sense of the term,[2] in the Scriptures.

True, Judaism had ordinations, originally of pupils by a rabbi (by the end of the first century A.D.), and later limited to centralized officialdom and the patriarch (second to fifth centuries A.D.), modeled in the tradition after Moses' laying his hands on and commissioning Joshua as his successor (Num. 27:18, 23; Deut. 34:9).

Where such "laying on of hands" or ordinations appear in early Christianity (for example, 1 Tim. 4:14), the model was probably the contemporary Jewish one among rabbinic scholars, but it was filled with new content, in particular the imparting of the Spirit.[3] Hence Jewish and early Christian ordination have been termed not so much a "mother-daughter" relationship as that of two "half-brothers," descended from the Old Testament.[4]

Some references in the New Testament (for example, Acts 13:1-3; 6:6) refer more to a rite of blessing or sending forth of an empowered Christian or an installation than to an ordination. Moreover, there was considerable variation in New Testament practice, even according to our meager records: Paul (in his letters fully acknowledged by a variety of scholars)[5] and John know no rite of ordination; the Pastoral Epistles (treated by some as the work of "later Paulinism"), Acts, and probably Matthew suggest that ordination practices existed in their areas of the church.[6]

A uniform practice, however, akin to what we call ordination is not to be found in early Christianity, let alone a "theology of ordination."

II. The Old Testament[7]

In the Old Testament, priesthood and the Levitical offices were open to males only, and only those without physical blemish at that (Leviticus 21). Rabbinical ordination in Judaism did not involve women either.

While the faith of Israel can be said to have been marked by "exclusive masculinism"[8] (for example, circumcision as the rite of entry, no comparable initiation ceremony for women; women regarded as unworthy to study the Law), there were roles that women did play in Israel's life and religion, especially that of prophetess (for example, Miriam; Hulda in 2 Kings 22:14-20; cf. Anna, in Luke 2) and even judge (Deborah), and, according to some references, "ministering at the tent of meeting."[9] But Israel's cult employed no priestesses (in contrast to surrounding nations), and women held a subordinate place in life generally (as in many surrounding cultures).

Reasons have been sought to account for this attitude toward women: (1) the patriarchal society of the period; (2) the notion that women were a source of idolatry; (3) the view that woman's function was to bear sons, not to sacrifice or teach the Law.[10] These explanations hold only in varying degrees for the New Testament period, but do continue to be heard in later centuries.[11]

Probably most influential from the Old Testament in the long run have been the creation story in Genesis 2 (woman created after, out of, and as a "helper" for man) and the story of "the fall" in Genesis 3 (the woman tempted the man).

While attempts have been made to shape "an Old Testament doctrine of the ministry"[12] for Christians, it is by and large agreed that the New Testament ministry is no continuation of the Old Testament priesthood.[13] Israel provides no answer on the ordination of women to the ministry of the church of Jesus Christ.

III. The New Testament World and the Interpreter Today[14]

Early Christianity was influenced by many other factors in the world of the day besides the Old Testament witness and the practices of late Judaism—

for example, customs of the Greco-Roman world and philosophical and re-ligious currents of the period. We must remember there is a vast history-of-religions panorama in light of which New Testament Christianity develops. At times the New Testament reflects such factors positively (for example, Paul can use Stoic language and ideas), at times it reacts negatively (Paul rejects pagan practices). The attitude toward women in general is a case in point: at times the New Testament very much exhibits the general pattern of a day when women were not emancipated but in subjection; on other occasions early Christianity is quite epoch-making and liberating in its attitude toward women (she is an equal recipient of salvation with man, both receive the same baptism as the rite of entry, and so forth).

A perennial problem in this history-of-religions and cultural background for any interpreter of Scripture is to determine what is to be regarded as "time-conditioned" from the first-century environment (and therefore no longer binding on all Christians today), and what is permanent "word of the Lord." (For example, the admonition to long hair and a veil on the head for women in church, 1 Cor. 11:2-16, is scarcely regarded as normative for women today.)

A further problem is the frequent variety in emphases on an issue to be found in the New Testament writings. One passage taken by itself seems to say one thing; another by itself, something else. How is one to assess together what may have been said originally in differing situations? To what degree is it necessary to have a "theology of the gospel" from which the individual voices of the Gospels and Epistles can be assessed?

Finally, just as the New Testament writers faced problems that are no longer ours in the same way, under influences and environment that no longer hold in our world, so it is also worth noting we often raise questions with which the New Testament witness does not deal and may not be able to answer definitively.

IV. The New Testament Witness

Scriptural evidence regarded as pertinent to the question of the ordination of women has, in recent discussions, been employed in two chief ways: more general, theological arguments, pro and con; and specific passages, regarded as speaking a definitive word one way or the other. Of course, the theological arguments and specific passages often intertwine, and the New Testament passages cited often rest on Old Testament scripture in turn. The first three arguments here seek to deny ordination of women; the fourth is pivotal and has been used by both sides; the final two are presented in favor of ordaining women.

A. Theological Arguments

1. The "paternal" argument:[15] God is Father, and Jesus Christ, his Son, was incarnated as a male. Much is made of the fact that biblical theology rejects goddesses (Yahweh has no consort); the Son reveals the Father; the Incarnation was a theological principle, not social expediency. Therefore the divine analogy shows that the church's ministry must be male.

But, it is countered, this is to make too much of metaphors about God (Yahweh's love can also be described like "a mother's for her child," Deut. 32:18; Isa. 46:3; 51:1; Ps. 131:2). It is misused analogy that, if carried to logical conclusion, would exclude women even from membership in the church. And how else could God's promises to Israel have been fulfilled, in that milieu, than by sending a man? And he who came is the New Man who foreshadows a new humanity (men and women in Christ).

This "paternal" argument seems never invoked in the Bible or in the earliest centuries.

Occasionally encountered with this argument is one involving the Virgin Mary: while Jesus "had no human father, he has a human mother." Mary provides the model for Christian women: great as she was, she was excluded from priestly functions; it was by John, not Mary, that Jesus was baptized; Mary suggests the vocation of Christian women—to bear children who will be incorporated into the new humanity and thus replenish the body of Christ.[16]

This argument, however, depends on a typological and mariological outlook where the Virgin is regarded as a "female foundation" of the church. Yet in the New Testament picture she too is part of a fallen humanity, who must receive the Spirit, and she is not exemplified as the model here supposed.[17]

2. The "apostolicity" argument:[18] Jesus chose only males to be his apostles. From the facts that "the Twelve" were all men and Jesus designated no woman as an apostle, even though women followed him during his ministry and were witnesses to the resurrection (Mark 16:1-8, par.; and to be "a witness of his resurrection" was a requirement for being an apostle, Acts 1:22), it has been concluded that Jesus intended the ministry to be exclusively male, and, as God incarnate, "He knew what He was doing."[19]

Quite apart from all discussion of the meaning of "apostolicity" and whether historically *apostle* referred to the Twelve or to a larger group (perhaps even including women!),[20] it can be replied that this argument too never appears in the New Testament.[21] Further, how else but by men could Jesus' mission and the promises to Israel have been fulfilled in the first-century world? Can we be sure the historical Jesus deliberately excluded women and that he intended this stance to be determinative for all times? By the same kind of argument, in view of the fact that he apparently chose only Jews as disciples and apostles, it could be concluded that no Gentile ought to be a minister in his church!

Sometimes as part of the concatenation with these first two arguments there appears a related emphasis on the femininity of the church, in contrast to God the Father, who sent his Son, who, in turn, sent forth only a male apostolic ministry: the ministry must be male, but there are certain qualities of femininity that characterize the church. The picture is aided by New Testament descriptions of the church as the "bride" of Christ. Thus one can construct a series of equations: as Christ is to the church, his bride, so is the minister (Christ's representative) to the congregation, the householder to the household. Christ's representative must be male, like his Lord; a woman cannot rule the household. Indeed, she is incapable of receiving the indelible, sacramental character of holy orders, it is sometimes added by those who employ this argument.[22]

The "femininity" argument suffers from the weaknesses, noted above, of argument from metaphorical language and analogy. It depends on a view of "church" where clergy rule over a lower order, "congregation," and assumes a sacramentalist concept of ordination strange to the Lutheran tradition and apparently a notion of ontological incapacity in women (see 3 below) so that "apostolic succession" will not "take."

3. As already suggested, the "paternal" and "apostolicity" arguments sometimes are related to an assumed biological, spiritual, and even theological inferiority in women[23] compared with men, so that ontologically and in terms of sacramental receptiveness they are not up to "that eminence of degree that is signified by priesthood" (Aquinas). This view of women sometimes roots in Old Testament ordinances; it has been expressed by ecclesiastical canons in the patristic period and finds reflection in statements by theologians in contemporary discussion.

It must be asked, however, whether this assumed inferiority reflects an "order of creation"—or "the order of a particular economic and social system in one part of the world in one period of its history,"[24] a view no longer defensible in light of further biological and psychological knowledge and later sociological developments. The "church tradition" on the role of women in ministry may simply reflect the haphazard customs of the past and personal prejudices of patristic misogynists and their later heirs. Much of this line of argument was, long before the "post-Pill era," antiquated by modern emancipation, whereby women share educational and political rights with men. What is of theological significance in it is better expressed by the next argument, more deeply embedded in Scripture.

4. The most impressive general argument from biblical theology against the ordination of women is that of subordination:[25] by the very "orders of creation" and from the time of the very first man and woman, woman has been subject to man, and even the New Testament does not change this ordinance of creation; rather, Paul reiterates it, and early Christian ethics employ the theme "Be subject . . ." in addressing women.

Genesis 2 is often a starting point: man was created first (2:7), woman was created from man (2:22) and for man (2:18).[26] The narrative about the expulsion from the garden in Genesis 3 expresses woman's subordination more forcefully: because she gave the fruit of the forbidden tree to her husband, she was told, "Your husband . . . shall rule over you" (3:16). (Hence, some say, the inferior position of women in Israel, and even the claim that since the fall woman has had no direct relationship to God.) That this subordination of woman to man is not erased in the New Testament is seen in the type of hierarchy Paul sketches in 1 Corinthians 11 ("the head of every man is Christ, the head of a woman is her husband, and the head of Christ is God," v. 3; in vv. 8-9 he reflects Genesis 2, "man was not made from woman, but woman from man; neither was man created for woman, but woman for man"). Furthermore, the New Testament *Haustafeln* (tables of household duties) are built around the theme of "subordination," specifically, "Wives, be subject to your husbands, as to the Lord" (Eph. 5:22), though it is now emphasized that husbands are not merely to rule (as "the head of the wife") but are to love their wives "as Christ loved the church" (5:25). In 1 Timothy 2 it is the "submissiveness" of woman that underlies what is said about woman not teaching or having authority over men.

It is this argument of the biblical subordination of woman to man that has proven decisive in the opinion of many discussing the ordination of women; thus, among Lutherans, Peter Brunner (the reason behind Paul's position is "the express will of God who demands such subordination") and Fritz Zerbst (it is not the nature of the office of the ministry which excludes woman from ordination, but the nature of woman).[27]

Of course, it has been claimed that what the Old Testament says on subordination, and even the Pauline expressions of it, are simply reflections of an outmoded way of looking at women in an ancient, male-dominated society.[28] One can note that "subjection" (not only of wives to husbands, but of slaves to masters, subjects to the state, and so forth) was simply a commonplace in the ethics of the first century, non-Christian as well as Christian.

But the most important assault on this argument of "subordination" based on "orders of creation" in biblical theology has been launched not by repudiating biblical material as "the product of a past age" but by looking more fully at the biblical material itself, so that the "subordination" argument is turned to undergird the case for ordaining women. With regard to Genesis 2, it is pointed out that this chapter is really a second telling of the creation story, the initial account coming in Genesis 1,[29] where woman is not a subordinate derivative of man, but rather they both are created together by God ("male and female God created them," 1:27), and they are given dominion together over the earth (1:28-30). True, from Genesis 2–3 on, woman has been subordinate to man, but with the coming of Christ, there is now a new situation: man and woman have direct and equal access to God and salvation through Christ; man and woman enter a new relationship "in Christ," both by the same sacrament of baptism. There is a new creation, where man and woman fulfill the intent of God's original creation—in Genesis 1! Therefore, "in Christ" the subordination of Genesis 2–3 is reversed, and there is a change back to the situation of Genesis 1, where man and woman stand side by side, together. Admittedly, Paul may at times still, in specific, practical issues, reflect his rabbinical background or react to current conditions, but he more significantly envisions that "in Christ" (and that means, above all, in the body of Christ, the church) there is no longer "Jew or Greek," "slave or free," "male or female"—all are one, emancipated for freedom, in Jesus Christ (Gal. 3:28, cf. 5:1). The church is the place where, above all, man and woman should be equal before God.[30]

This pivotal argument on "subordination" has been presented in some detail precisely because it is the most significant theological one out of Scripture on both sides. And it has been variously interpreted.[31] If woman is irrevocably subordinate to man on the basis of what God established in creation, then it is hard to see how the church can consider ordaining women; if, on the other hand, the church of Christ is precisely where God's original will in creation breaks through afresh, then the church may have to draw implications about ministry that even Paul in his day never worked out. The question is not only, "What is the real 'ordinance of creation,' Genesis 1 or 2?" but eschatologically, "What is the relationship of the new situation in Christ to the 'old age'?"

Two things need to be added about "subordination":

(1) Paul plainly reflects a "theology of subordination" not only with regard to man and woman but also with regard to God and Christ (1 Cor. 11:3). It may be helpful to add that in his Christology this subordination is "functional," but it is subordination nonetheless (1 Cor. 15:24-28, at the end "the Son himself will also be subjected to [God]"). However, later, orthodox Christology did not hesitate to overlook this subordination of the Son to the Father, so as to declare him "of one substance with the Father," co-equal, and so forth. If Pauline subordinationalism has been reassessed in Christology, ought it not also be reassessed for anthropology "in Christ"?

(2) The New Testament texts taken to demonstrate the subordination of women to men seem in every case actually to refer not to women and men generally but to wives and their husbands. "Woman" means "wife," and sometimes before "man" (=husband) the adjective "one's own" appears; thus in 1 Corinthians 14, the command "the woman should keep silence in the churches" (v. 34) is explained by (v. 35) "let them ask their husbands at home." The references are thus not to society in general or to the church's ministry but to the home and family relation. This point has been recognized

as decisive in several recent studies on the ordination of women to the ministry.[32]

In opposition to the "paternal" and "apostolic" and "inferiority of women" arguments, two further arguments have been adduced by those who see the ordination of woman as not contradicting Scripture but actually according with it, both of them arguments to an extent involved in this discussion on "subordination."

5. The *"imago"* argument:[33] men and women are created in the image of God *(imago dei)* and are therefore of equal dignity and worth before God. An argument from creation is here involved ("God created man in his own image, in the image of God he created him; male and female he created them," Gen. 1:27). But it also involves the new creation since—a point not always recognized—in the Old Testament references (chiefly in the Priestly source) the image of God is not something lost after the fall (Gen. 5:1,3; 9:6) but something human beings retain, whereas in the New Testament only Jesus Christ is the image of God—people are conformed to this image only when they are created anew "in Christ" (cf. 2 Cor. 4:4; Col. 1:15, on Christ; 1 Cor. 15:49; Rom. 8:29). Here baptism renews them "after the image of the Creator" (Col. 3:9-10; Eph. 4:24), so that there is a new situation "in Christ" in the church, where accordingly "there cannot be Greek and Jew, circumcised and uncircumcised . . . slave, free man"—or, Gal. 3:28 adds, "male or female." Thus, in partaking of the *imago,* women acquire equal status before God, with men.

The objections by those who oppose the ordination of women to this use of the *"imago"* argument can take the form of denying that women received the *imago* as men did at creation (Genesis 2; only in a derived sense), or of holding that Christians have not yet eschatologically attained to the image of God, or of insisting that the image refers only to "spiritual" matters and not to equality in such things as the church's ministry.

6. The "all members are ministers" argument:[34] The whole body of Christ is called to witness to Christ and serve in his name; all members—male and female—have a ministry. Sometimes this argument invokes the "priesthood of all believers" theme: there is a "royal priesthood" of all baptized believers (1 Peter 2:9). This argument differs from the previous one in that it derives not from creation but, in *Heilsgeschichte,* from baptism, which is the ordination of each believer, no distinctions made because of sex, nationality, or condition of servitude (1 Cor. 12:13; Col. 3:9-11; Gal. 3:27-28). In thus admitting women fully to membership, early Christianity was doing something different than Israel had: women share in the ministry.

It may be replied, however, that from this general ministry or "priesthood of all believers," a special, ordained ministry is to be distinguished, and from that ministry women, for reasons noted above, are excluded.

B. Specific Passages

Against this background five prime passages frequently invoked in the
arguments above can now be noted. The first is the crucial New Testament
one cited for ordaining women; the other four are often cited to show the
New Testament forbids such ordinations. Then three more passages that concern a structure sometimes called "headship" will be taken up. Inevitably, a
great deal depends on how the verses are arranged and the assumptions with
which they are approached. The first five are here taken up in the most likely
chronological sequence in which they were written (a sequence that holds
whether or not some of the documents are assigned to Paul himself or his
helpers or pupils), and the effort is to examine the context, and not just set
forth isolated verses as "eternal laws."

1. Galatians 3:27-28

> For as many of you as were baptized into Christ have put on Christ. There is
> neither Jew nor Greek, there is neither slave nor free, there is neither male nor
> female; for you are all one in Christ Jesus.[35]

In his "Epistle of Freedom" against the Judaizers, Paul here holds that the
Law of Moses has been transcended in Christ at three crucial boundary lines:
those between Jews and Gentiles, between slaves and free persons, and between male and female. The thought is in sharp contrast to contemporary
prayers and maxims among Jews and Gentiles where men gave thanks that
they were not unbelievers or uncivilized, not a woman, not a slave.[36]

Here a new concept for women is set forth. The setting or basis is sacramental (baptism, to "put on" Christ). The implications drawn in the three
sets of terms ("neither . . . nor") are echoed in 1 Cor. 12:13; Rom. 10:12;
Col. 3:11, though only here is "male and female" specifically mentioned.[37]
That phrase, however, is a technical one, interrupting the flow of the Greek
and meant to recall Gen. 1:27. The "Christ event" means age-old barriers
are overcome; beyond even the division into male and female, God's original
will of "all one" in his image is reestablished "in Christ." Women, like men,
have experienced the gospel of grace.

Accordingly, this revolutionary insight has been hailed by more than one
writer on the ordination of women as "the breakthrough," setting forth the
possibility—which, however, the Pauline church, in his day, did not fully
realize—that women too are to witness to the gospel of grace and minister
in its name.

Those who oppose ordaining women seek to blunt the effect of Gal. 3:28
by maintaining it refers only to salvation, not to social life,[38] or that such an
"eschatological breakthrough" leads to Montanism, *Schwärmerei*, liberalism,
and so forth—such a "realized eschatology," it is said, ignores the unfulfilled

futurist aspects that are also part of Paul's views: believers are not yet fully "in Christ."

2. 1 Corinthians 11:2-16

I commend you because you remember me in everything and maintain the traditions even as I have delivered them to you. But I want you to understand that the head of every man is Christ, the head of a woman is her husband, and the head of Christ is God. Any man who prays or prophesies with his head covered dishonors his head. But any woman who prays or prophesies with her head unveiled dishonors her head—it is the same as if her head were shaven. For if a woman will not veil herself, then she should cut off her hair; but if it is disgraceful for a woman to be shorn or shaven, let her wear a veil. For a man ought not to cover his head, since he is the image and glory of God; but woman is the glory of man. (For man was not made from woman, but woman from man. Neither was man created for woman, but woman for man.) That is why a woman ought to have a veil [Greek: authority] on her head, because of the angels. (Nevertheless, in the Lord woman is not independent of man nor man of woman; for as woman was made from man, so man is now born of woman. And all things are from God.) Judge for yourselves; is it proper for a woman to pray to God with her head uncovered? Does not nature itself teach you that for a man to wear long hair is degrading to him, but if a woman has long hair, it is her pride? For her hair is given to her for a covering. If any one is disposed to be contentious, we recognize no other practice, nor do the churches of God.[39]

This somewhat obscure passage occurs in a section where Paul is correcting the Corinthian Christians about sacramental excesses (Chapters 8–10, their confidence in sacramental security when faced by the problem of "meats offered to idols"; 11:17-34, abuses at the Lord's Supper). The passage is also part of a discussion on problems in worship running on through Chapter 14. This section seems inserted here because in this matter Paul can praise the Corinthians somewhat (v. 2 "I commend you," cf. v. 17 "I do not commend you"). It is loosely tied to the context in that 10:31-33 ("all to the glory of God, giving no offense, trying to please all, that they may be saved") could stand over the discussion of veiling.

It is clear that in the congregation at Corinth women were prophesying and praying (vv. 5, 13),[40] presumably in public at the congregational assemblies (cf. v. 18; 14:26). Paul does not rebuke this expression of the gift of the Spirit they have received, but he does stress that women, in so doing, ought to have a veil on their head.

The arguments Paul uses to show it is wrong for a woman to pray to God with head uncovered come from a variety of sources: the "subordination" argument (v. 3, where the key word is "head"), subordinating, however, probably of wives to husbands, not women generally to men;[41] an argument from social custom (shorn hair is a disgrace), reenforced by an appeal to what nature teaches (vv. 14-15), and appeal to Genesis 2 (vv. 7, 18-23). There is also appeal to what has been dubbed "the ecumenical argument" (what the other "churches of God" do, v. 16).[42]

Many details remain obscure for us or at least debated ("the woman ought to have a veil on her head because of the angels").[43] The section has been termed a "limping argument."[44] Paul himself merely asks the Corinthians to "judge for yourselves" (v. 13) and scarcely dictates an answer, though his own preference—that Christian women have their head covered as in Judaism, so as to prevent slander against the Christian movement for libertinism and thus give no offense—is clear.

While the passage seeks to "maintain traditions," its most important emphasis, especially if a literal subordination of woman to man and of Christ to God is not made central (v. 3), is perhaps the aside in vv. 11-12, that "in the Lord" (that is, "in Christ" and the Christian community) man and woman are not independent, nor is it simply that woman is made for man, but there is an interdependence—perhaps one dare say, an equals-relationship. "In the Lord" is a new order—even women prophesy—though here too rules are needed.[45]

3. 1 Corinthians 14:33b-36

As in all the churches of the saints, the women should keep silence in the churches. For they are not permitted to speak, but should be subordinate, as even the law says. If there is anything they desire to know, let them ask their husbands at home. For it is shameful for a woman to speak in church. What! Did the word of God originate with you, or are you the only ones it has reached?[46]

In a long section of problems of worship at the congregational assembly at Corinth (11:2—14:40), particularly involving the gifts of the Spirit in which the Corinthians reveled, this unit comes between a larger passage on instructions about the congregation at worship (especially prophesying)—the emphasis is on order ("God is not a God of confusion but of peace," v. 32)— and a closing passage on prophets and those inspired (14:37-40; final emphasis: things done "decently and in order").

Paul's emphatic statement, "the women should keep silence in the churches" (v. 34), is presented as an "ecumenical" rule ("as in all the churches," 33b), undergirded by the subordination principle (v. 34) and appeal to the Law (evidently Gen. 3: 16, the man "shall rule over" the woman; Prohl, after considering Gen. 3:16 on the wives of the patriarchs; Num. 30:8; Eccl. 7:26, 28; Isa. 3:12; and so forth, decides for the Sixth Commandment, pp. 39-46). Women "are not permitted to speak"; anything they desire to know, "they should ask their husbands at home" (35a); for them to speak in church is "shameful" (35b). The unit concludes with a sober, almost ironic exclamation: "Did God's word go forth from you in Corinth?" (some feel the implication is, "No, it went forth from Jerusalem," but Paul certainly held that "Jerusalem could err too"); "Are you the only people God's word reached?" (No, there are other congregations; the "ecumenical" rule is to be followed, and not just Corinthian practice). Apparently, women were speaking at Corinthian assemblies. The passage seems to demand their silence.

On the basis of this apparently definitive ruling, *Mulier taceat in ecclesia* ("Let woman keep silent in church"), women have by some been forbidden ordination, the right to vote in congregation meetings, and even to teach in parochial schools.

Attempts have been made to brush the words aside as mere cultural accommodations to the day, no more valid for us than Paul's opinions on clothes or hairstyles.

However, for anyone who takes the passage seriously the exegetical difficulty is the relation to 11:2-16. There Paul allowed woman prophets to pray and prophesy; here he forbids them to speak. Although solutions have been sought by claiming that (1) Chapters 11 and 14 come from different letters, Paul having changed his mind in between, or that (2) Chapter 11 refers to a simple house meeting of a part of the congregation, while Chapter 14 has in mind liturgical gatherings of the entire community,[47] Barrett is probably correct that "only two possibilities are worthy of serious consideration": (3) that the verses incorporate a later insertion,[48] a marginal gloss made in the spirit of 1 Tim. 2:11-12—a view for which there is no manuscript evidence (though some manuscripts place vv. 34-35 after v. 40), but a view that has been supported by a number of exegetes on the basis primarily that Paul could not have thus contradicted Chapter 11; (4) that Paul, in seeking to regulate some of the feminist pressures at Corinth, was willing in Chapter 11 to allow women under the Spirit to speak, but in Chapter 14 he states his own preference, that women be silent.[49]

If the last-mentioned view is followed, one is then faced with an appeal here to the Law in a way that is not generally characteristic of Paul, and above all the probability that here "woman/women" does not refer to women in general but to wives (cf. v. 35, they are to ask their husbands: v. 34 therefore, "let your wives [*gynaikes* can be so translated; some manuscripts add 'your'] keep silence during service"). Wives are not to interrupt with questions but should ask their husbands at home.[50]

Because of this likely limitation to wives (not a general rule for women), the puzzling relation to 1 Corinthians 11 (and Gal. 3:28), and the possibility involved of interpolation (in the opinion of some), this verse today makes a much less certain basis for forbidding ordination of women than it often has seemed in past usage.[51]

4. Ephesians 5:22

Wives, be subject to your husbands, as to the Lord.

Cf. 1 Peter 3:1, "Likewise you wives, be submissive to your husbands. . . ."[52]

In each case, these verses are part of a "subjection" code of relationships: like slaves to master, wives are to submit to, be subject to their husbands. Ephesians 5:23 adds the sort of hierarchy already discussed: as Christ is the head of the church, the husband is head of the wife. The use of these verses in the debate has already been discussed above under the "subordination" argument.[53]

That some critics think Ephesians may not be by Paul himself but by some pupil is beside the point. Even if not Paul's own composition, Ephesians is still part of the New Testament.

But even if Ephesians is Paul's own letter, the material in this section is part of a *Haustafeln* type of morality, organized under the theme "be subject . . .," a morality found also in 1 Peter and elsewhere, indeed which could be a part of a catechetical form taken over by the early church from society of the day generally.

The most serious objection to the use of these verses in the discussion on ordination is the fact that they concern the marriage relationship, not the church's ministry.[54]

5. 1 Timothy 2:11-14

Let a woman learn in silence with all submissiveness. I permit no woman to teach or to have authority over men; she is to keep silent. For Adam was formed first, then Eve; and Adam was not deceived but the woman was deceived and became a transgressor.

Yet woman will be saved through bearing children, if she continues in faith and love and holiness, with modesty.[55]

The section from 2:8 to 2:15 mixes advice on prayer with general ethical admonitions. From the context about prayer (vv. 1, 8), it has been assumed that what is said about women refers to worship at church services; hence vv. 11-14 are often cited in discussions as forbidding the ordination of women.

At 2:8 the desire is expressed that "prayers should be said by the men of the congregation" (NEB), lifting up "holy hands" (cultic expression, here interpreted ethically, "without anger or quarreling"). It has been conjectured that the old Jewish custom, where only men recited prayers at synagogue, was breaking down by the time of 1 Timothy (hence the statement in vv. 11-14), as already it had been changed by "a new spirit of emancipation . . . spreading in the young Christian congregations," for example at Corinth (1 Cor. 11:2-22).[56] Verses 9-10 take what were apparently general rules of the day in Jewish and Christian ethical instruction ("women should adorn themselves modestly and sensibly, not with [jewels]" but with "good deeds"; cf. 1 Peter 3:3-4) and apply the admonitions especially to prayer meetings—the point, some think, so that female charms will not disturb the (male) worshipers.

Verses 11-12 then take up what may have been a "burning issue"[57] in congregations: the role of women at the church assemblies, against a Jewish synagogue background of traditional silence by women and a tendency for Christian women to pray and prophesy under the Spirit, at least in certain quarters.

The clear answer comes in two parallel sentences, the one of which helps interpret the other:

> let a woman learn in silence with all submissiveness;
> I permit no woman to teach or to have authority over men, she is to keep silent.

The chiastic order stresses that (1) woman is to be/learn "in silence"; (2) "submissiveness" *(hypotagē)* means subordination to what the men teach in the assembly, not domineering them.

Two reasons are advanced to support this position: (1) an argument from the chronological order of creation in Genesis 2—woman was the second, not the first, to be created; (2) Eve was the gullible one in Genesis 3; she, not Adam, was deceived and fell into sin—thus woman was first in sin and, the implication is, cannot be trusted to teach.[58] Here Genesis 3, the fall story, plays a part as in no previous reference.

Genesis 3:16 (pain in childbearing, the husband shall rule over the wife) seemingly stands behind the much-debated meaning of v. 15; woman, who was created second but fell first, nevertheless, though she is not to teach, has a proper role, motherhood, and will be saved, if she continues in the characteristic Christian virtues of faith and love and holiness (cf. v. 8), with modesty (v. 9), the "good deeds," such "as befits women who profess religion" (v. 10).[59]

The passage is sometimes "handled" by calling it "non-Pauline," but that scarcely solves the problem for anyone who makes the New Testament normative, for it is still in the canon.[60] If written by Paul himself, however, the section is usually placed late in his career and exhibits features of "early catholicism."[61]

Another approach is to point to the different environment from ours today found in this passage, and to argue that any literal application, as the author intended, would preclude any role for women in church: if 2:11-12 forbids their ordination, it also precludes their praying, prophesying, perhaps even singing or speaking liturgical responses and teaching males. At the least one must grant that the Jewish synagogal attitude toward women of the early Christian period, here imported into a "church order," has scarcely been universally observed in worship, church schools, and so forth.[62]

A more serious stumbling block to employing this passage to settle negatively the ordination-of-women question is the likelihood that, in the opinion of many exegetes, the verses refer to the relation of wife to husbands, not of women to men in general, something noted in other passages.[63] Only when read in the light of the traditionalist interpretation of 1 Cor. 14:34 does this verse clearly refer to the role of women in church, and the immediate context, especially v. 15, suggests the general place of women in nature and society, not in the "order of salvation."[64]

The acid test of the correctness of the view that any teaching ministry was apostolically forbidden to women in the early church is whether or not women did so teach. Apparently in gnostic Christian circles they did (perhaps in reaction to Jewish custom), and also among the opponents in the church against whom the Pastorals are addressed (cf. 2 Tim. 3:6); more important, in the later tradition about Paul, Thecla appears as a teacher and preacher; above all, quite apart from any "ordained prophetesses" at Corinth (1 Corinthians 11) or in Ephesus (hinted at in this passage), there is the reference in Acts 18:26 to how Priscilla and Aquila (note the order) took Apollos in hand at Ephesus and "expounded to him the way of God more accurately."[65] (See below, V.)

Finally, setting aside all debate over authorship, "early catholic" influences, Jewish customs, actual practice in the early church, and granting that 2 Tim. 2:11-12 applies to women in the church, one is still faced in Lutheran theology with the "canon within the canon" principle: shall these verses be read "evangelically" or "legally,"[66] shall they be appraised in relation to the gospel (with its implications of emancipation) or as on a par with every other verse and theme in the New Testament?

At the Lutheran Council consultation on "The Ordination of Women in Light of Church and Ministry," held at Dubuque, Iowa, September 20-22, 1969, it was requested that three additional passages be mentioned in connection with the New Testament evidence. All three concern the theme of "leaders" or "*kephalē* structure" [the Greek term for "head," therefore the man as possessing "headship" over women] and relate to the subordination argument (above, IV. A. 4). They do not seem usually to have been cited in articles and books on the subject.

6. Hebrews 13:7,17

Remember your leaders *(hēgoumenoi)*, those who spoke to you the word of God; consider the outcome of their life, and imitate their faith. . . . Obey your leaders *(hēgoumenoi)* and submit *(hypeikete)* to them; for they are keeping watch over your souls, as men who will have to give account. . . .

Cf. v. 24, "greet all your leaders."

These verses appear in the final chapter of admonitions in Hebrews (perhaps an appendage to an earlier homily). 13:7 and 17 fit closely together as the beginning and ending of a distinct section structured about obedience to, and imitation of, "leaders" (congregational founders, perhaps martyrs, now re-called by a second generation of Christians, v. 7; and present-day leaders who have authority as proclaimers of the word and as *Seelsorger* [those who care for souls], vv. 7, 17, 24). Such leaders stand in contrast to "strange teachings" that lead astray (v. 9). Especially stressed against such teachings are sound Christology (v. 8), suffering (of Jesus, v. 12), sacrifice (that is, confession of God's name, and praise for him), and sharing (doing good).

There is used here a term for "leaders" not found elsewhere in the New Testament (but cf. Luke 22:26 and Acts 15:22) but which occurs in 1 Clement and the Shepherd of Hermas. This term *hēgoumenos* derives from the Hellenistic political world, perhaps through Hellenistic Judaism, with possible Hebrew roots, but is vague in meaning. "Submit" is not the usual Greek word *hypotassomai* and is found in the New Testament only here. "As men who will have to give account . . ." is a masculine participle (which could cover a mixed group) and tells us nothing further definitive about the group. Recall, however, the suggestion that Priscilla (and Aquila) wrote Hebrews (an interesting though unlikely guess, which would make this the only New Testament document with a woman as authoress or coauthor—most recently advanced by Ruth Hoppin, *Priscilla: Author of the Epistle to the Hebrews, and Other Essays* [New York: Exposition Press, 1969]).

Who these leaders were we do not know (Michel, KEK, p. 488). The admonition to obey leaders is common in early Christian ethical instruction (1 Thess. 5:12; 1 Clem. 1:3; 21:6; Didache 4:1; 15:2), much like the attitude toward the teacher in the synagogue (Hans Windisch, *Der Hebräerbrief,* HNT 14 [Tübingen: J.C.B. Mohr (Paul Siebeck), 1931], pp. 119-20). In Hebrews, with its theme of the people of God in pilgrimage, there is no stress on human priesthood or hierarchy of offices (contrast 1 Clement); suffering and service characterize all God's people, every one of whom possesses the Spirit; there is a ministry of teaching, based on spiritual growth, and an orientation that "combats the institutional church" (E. Schweizer, *Church Order,* pp. 114-16).

While the passage is one with others in enjoining obedience to leaders whose proclamation, life, pastoral care, and witness rate due respect, we must be careful not to read into Hebrews other patterns of hierarchy or ministry (as Austin Farrer does, in *The Apostolic Ministry,* p. 156, who supposes Hebrews was addressed only to "elders," with "laity" thought of merely incidentally). The pilgrim people of God seems here more like a "charismatic democracy" than a body dominated by hierarchical orders.

7. 1 Peter 5:1,5

I exhort the elders *(presbyteroi)* among you, as a fellow elder. . ., tend the flock of God. . . . Likewise you that are younger, be subject to the elders *(hypotagete presbyterois)*. Clothe yourselves, all of you, with humility toward one another. . . .

In the concluding exhortations of this epistle Peter addresses first the elders (vv. 1-4), then the younger members of the church (v. 5*a*), then all members (5b-9) (cf. G. Bornkamm, *"presbys," TDNT,* 6:665-66). Some commentators have attempted to see a technical use of *presbyteroi* in v. 5, just as in v. 1, for office-bearers (so Moffatt, = *diakonoi;* Windisch, the younger = the "sheep" or laity), but most exegetes, while allowing an official connotation in v. 1, see v. 5 as merely a reference to those older in years (so Selwyn, Beare, E. Schweizer; cf. 1 Tim. 5:1; Acts 5:6, 10). Thus, William F. Beck renders, "you young people, submit to those who are older" (*The New Testament in the Language of Today* [St. Louis: Concordia, 1963]). On this interpretation, young people are being told to be subject to the older people, as wives are to husbands, slaves to masters, and so forth, a pattern in early Christian catechetical material (cf. Selwyn, *1 Peter,* pp. 435-37).

The term "elder" derives from the synagogue and from civil corporations in the Hellenistic world. It is undefined in 1 Peter, probably including "all who have any kind of authorized pastoral office and function" (Selwyn, p. 227). Envisioned is a college of presbyters, its exact scope not spelled out. Peter himself is described merely as a "fellow elder" (v. 1, *sympresbyteros,* a term coined for the occasion perhaps). There is no bishop in 1 Peter, Christ being *episkopos* (2:25). The presbyterate here has a "patriarchal character"; it shepherds, but is not in 1 Peter called "the guardian of the apostolic tradition against error" as in the Pastorals (Bornkamm). Like Hebrews, 1 Peter is oriented to the "people of God" theme, and Schweizer sees "no distinction between clergy and laity" in the epistle (*Church Order,* p. 112).

Results: here again is a passage urging due submission to pastoral leaders, but with no definition of office, no hierarchy, but a clear "people of God" emphasis.

8. 1 Timothy 3:1-5

The saying is sure: If any one aspires to the office of bishop, he desires a noble task. Now a bishop must be above reproach, the husband of one wife, temperate, sensible, dignified, hospitable, an apt teacher, no drunkard, not violent, but gentle, not quarrelsome, and no lover of money. He must manage his own household well, keeping his children submissive *(en hypotagē)* and respectful in every way; for if a man does not know how to manage his own household, how can he care for God's church?

This famous passage, introduced by the formula *pistos ho logos* (unless the reference to "the saying" points back to the previous section in 2:11-14, treated above; the formula also occurs at 1:15 and 4:9), lists qualifications for the office of *episkopos*. The section 3:8-13 goes on in a similar way, listing qualities needed in those who seek to be deacons. 1 Timothy (and the Pastorals generally) reflects a church "that has established itself in the world and is taking over ordinary Hellenistic ethics" (E. Schweizer, *Church Order,* p. 77). Structurally, the church of 1 Timothy has "the office of bishop" (3:1) and "deacons" (3:8), with presbyters also mentioned (5:17). Many exegetes, however, identify the *episkopoi* or overseers with the *presbyteroi* or "elders," the deacons being a second group distinct from them in the Pastorals. Here in 3:1-7 we have a list of qualifications for the *episkopos* (vv. 6-7 add that he ought not to be a recent convert, but a man well thought of by outsiders, and so forth).

It is well known that the 15 requisites for the *episkopos* in this list are remarkably mundane and negative (for example, "no drunkard"). One might assume that such minimal demands would hold for all church members. Further, some details are notoriously hard to define (does "the husband of one wife" mean he must be married, or that he not have two wives, or that he cannot remarry if his first wife dies?). It is also well known that the requirements are parallel in many ways to lists that circulated in the Hellenistic world of requirements for a good general, and so forth. Some think that 1 Timothy simply incorporates here such a list from the secular world, with a few "Christian touches" (B.S. Easton, Dibelius, and others; J. N. D. Kelly in his commentary admits the parallels but calls this history-of-religions aspect "greatly exaggerated," p. 74). The fact that such parallels do exist in secular lists may account for the variant reading in v. 1 in some Greek manuscripts: "this is a human (or 'popular') saying," as if the scribes recognized how prosaic it is.

At the Dubuque conference, this list of qualifications was taken up and emphasized by some participants in light of the *"kephalē principle,"* that man is the head of the woman, seen reflected in 1 Tim. 2:11, "Let a woman learn in silence with all submissiveness" (discussed above). This relation of man to woman was urged as an eternal and abiding feature (an "order of creation") especially incumbent on the church to preserve. At 3:4, the point was stressed that one requirement for a bishop (that is, pastor) is that he "manage his own household well, keeping his children submissive. . . ." The passage goes on, "If a man does not know how to manage his own household, how can he care for God's church?" The same point is urged for deacons, "Let them manage their children and their households well" (3:12), and there is clearly in the chapter a connection between "a man's household" (vv. 4, 5) and the household of God (v. 15), the church (vv. 5, 15). The conclusion drawn was that there is a parallel between ruling a family and ruling the church. "Rule" is involved in both, and just as man, the head of woman, must rule in the family, so also in the church. Ergo, no female clergy, who might rule over men.

To this position, exception was taken by others. Do we regard 1 Tim. 3:1-13 as a list of requirements for ordination for all time? (If so, how do we interpret "the husband of one wife"? Does "managing his own household well, keeping submissive his children" demand he be a married man, with children, who are properly obedient? *Cui bono?* [Who benefits by that?]) There was objection to absolutizing such a list. It was pointed out that a logical corollary to the "*kephalē* argument" is that the church should then today crusade for the subordination of women in society generally, not merely in the church, since this subordination to man, the head, comes from creation's structure and seemingly should apply to all of society. Our Christian duty would be to repeal the 19th Amendment.

Against such a view, exegetically, apart from the question of universalizing what may have been merely an ad hoc list of suggested minimums for local leaders in a particular situation, the chief difficulties are (1) the Hellenistic background to the list and (2) the reference to "the women" in v. 11. Addressing the first difficulty, if much of the list of requirements is but a commonplace in Hellenistic thought, should we make it eternal and abiding rules for the church? That point applies even to the analogy seen between the church and the family. To place family, city-state, and cosmos in parallel was common in Stoic thought (cf. Dibelius and Conzelmann). Is this argument from Stoic thought to be decisive for church structure today? (If so, can we determine a family pattern implicit in creation itself, unchanging, that applies to the church?) As to the second difficulty: both the requirements for the bishop and for the deacon include the stipulation "managing their children and their households well" (3:4-5, 12), but inserted into the section on deacons is a verse on "the women." We have already noted the possibility that, while this verse (3:11) might refer to the wives of the deacons, it may also (more likely) refer to deaconesses) wives of *episkopoi* are not singled out for similar mention; cf. section V above, note 4; Guthrie's commentary, in the Tyndale series (1957), p. 85, speaks of "a new class" here beside the deacons; Kelly translates, "women deacons"). If such is the reference, then the author of 1 Timothy rejected any connection between a "*kephalē*-structure" (which would prohibit women from such an office, apparently; the Pastorals never use *kephalē*) and his passing analogy involving home and church; perhaps he did not know the *kephalē*-structure as we term it. But he did know of a situation where women had some sort of ministry, and so the theological argument we have heard advanced may be contrary to actual practice in the Pastorals.

In short: if one assumes the *kephalē*-structure as abiding truth in biblical theology (so that woman is submissive to man as part of the God-given order of creation and cannot "rule" over him, which ministry would seem to involve) and hence that this *kephalē*-structure is something that it is the church's task to uphold, then such passages as those three just discussed do undergird the need for women to remain respectfully under their male leaders. But there seems too much evidence that the early church, with its eschatological consciousness of the Spirit's presence as a token of the New Age, did not opt just for retaining such structures, but at times—in spite of its historical circumstances, in a culture where the role of women in society was often severely limited—allowed women in ministry roles, as foretaste of the new creation "in Christ" or fulfillment of God's original will for male and female in Genesis, Chapter 1.

V. Women in the Ministry of the Early Church[67]

Quite apart from arguments over possible New Testament reasons permitting or forbidding the ordination of women to the ministry, there is the historical question of whether women engaged in types of ministry in the early church. Unfortunately, the picture suffers from the same paucity of evidence that makes discussions about the ministry of men in the early church often unclear, at least in detail.

Of course it can be argued, somewhat dogmatically, that "ordination of women would be incompatible with New Testament thought"[68] and therefore could not have happened except among heretics, but that already prejudices what should be a descriptive, historical question.[69]

The facts seem to be that women with Jesus are mentioned as ministering to him during his lifetime and at his death (for example, Luke 8:3; Mark 15:41), but they are not called disciples, let alone "apostles." "The Twelve" do not include any women, nor do the Lucan apostle lists, though in the broader sense of *apostle* the term may be applied to a woman once (Rom. 16:7).[70] Prophetesses have been mentioned (1 Corinthians 11; Acts 21:9), perhaps "ordained" (at Corinth), certainly speaking in the Lord's name under the Spirit to the community.

Originally a charismatic function, the "deaconess" type of ministry that Phoebe exercised (Rom. 16:1) probably only later became an office, but perhaps already by the time 1 Tim. 3:8-13 was written such "female deacons" existed (3:11, "the women" in parallel to "deacons" at 3:8, may refer to "deaconesses," as in the NEB note, or, as in RSV and NEB text, to the wives of deacons).[71] The same difficulty for interpretation that arises in this last passage also appears in later references to *presbytera, presbyterissa,* or *episcopa:* is a female presbyter or bishop involved, or the wife of a man holding that office?[72] There are also "consecrated widows" (1 Tim. 5:3-16), the exact status and function of whom, especially in relation to "official deaconesses" (as at 3:11), is debated. Finally, there are women mentioned by name who played leadership roles—Lydia (Acts 16), Priscilla (see above; conjectured by Harnack to have written Hebrews), or (outside the New Testament) Thecla.

The evidence is far from clear, falling somewhere between what partisans on both sides of the ordination-of-women question sometimes claim. It has been claimed, for example, that women in the New Testament period performed some offices of service but had nothing to do with sacraments[73]—but then, how much do we know about the administration of sacraments by any "clergy" in the New Testament period? On the other hand: a picture of three charismatic orders of women (deaconesses, "virgins," widows) alongside three ordained orders of men (deacons, elders, bishops),[74] set apart from the "laity," seems likewise to force the evidence into too smooth a composite picture.

It is worth noting that subsequent decrees and statements on ministry do not appeal, in many cases, to the New Testament texts prominent in modern debate which we have examined, to exclude ordination of women.[75]

VI. The Hermeneutical Question

The historical evidence being as incomplete as it is, and the exegesis of the individual verses and the force of the arguments from biblical theology being as controverted as we have seen, it is apparent that the whole question is basically one of hermeneutics:[76] how do you interpret and apply the Scripture?

If one argues by proof texts, certain individual verses seem to exclude women from ordination—and from engaging in many functions in which they commonly participate in our churches nowadays.

If a rigorous historical criticism is applied, some of these texts most frequently cited against ordaining women can be excluded (as glosses) or demoted in value (as deutero-Pauline).

If the entire mass of biblical evidence is considered, it is possible that there are seemingly conflicting views, even in the verses claiming to be from the same writer, Paul.[77]

Moreover, the biblical evidence, it must be added, is not the whole story on what the mind of the church has been on the subject through the ages. Inevitably, there was development—of ordination practice—and definition—of woman's role in the church—through later centuries. It must also be recognized that the later traditions obscure as well as develop New Testament insights on such questions. Today one finds oneself compelled to take into consideration also a host of other factors besides the biblical and historical factors.

For a church, however, that regards Scripture as normative, the real problem it faces in using Scripture, if that usage is to be serious but not simply literalistic, is hermeneutical. On a scriptural basis ordination of women has been both blocked and lifted up as an open possibility—depending on whether certain texts are read as determinative, forbidding the possibility, or others are made guiding expressions of the gospel overshadowing the others. Does a central gospel or do individual texts—and, if so, which ones and how interpreted—prevail in reaching a decision?[78]

VII. The Eschatological Question

At several points it has been suggested that the meaning of key texts depends on the eschatological stance involved. If the new age has come, then the old order is changed, and "in Christ" the new obtains. If, on the other hand, we are still in the old order or not fully in Christ in the new, then the orders of creation still hold, at least in some respects.

There is no question but that, for Paul and the New Testament, God was at work in Christ; the new has come; the old, passed away (2 Cor. 5:17— 6:2). But in spite of interpretations that stress this aspect of fulfillment or "realized eschatology," it is also true that, for Paul especially, all is not yet fulfilled; Christians have not fully entered into the new age, they have not yet completely arrived. At Corinth it may precisely have been the eschatological miscalculation of the gnostic opponents to have assumed they "already reigned" with Christ (1 Cor. 4:8). Paul himself had eschatological reservations, all has not yet come.

In the church today, therefore, with regard to its preaching and worship life, with regard to the ministry, is the situation to be seen fundamentally in terms of the new and fulfillment, or by reference to the old and creation? Paul's use of Genesis categories scarcely answers that question in unambiguous terms: he sees a "new creation" in Christ, yet he can invoke the order of the original creation as a restraint on going too far too fast.

First Corinthians 11, on this reading, turns out to be the key passage: Paul allows women to pray and prophesy in church, because it is a prompting of the Spirit that moves them; this overcomes all the inclinations from his Jewish heritage; at the same time he regulates this ministry, like all gifts of the Spirit, so that it will really build up the body of Christ, the people of God, and not cause offense at the wrong points. That in Paul's day and environment!

It follows that in our vastly changed day and generation the ordination of women is often culturally more easy and obvious than in Paul's, and that biblically there is a case for allowing it.[79] Church leaders must ask whether the movement toward it is a prompting of the Spirit or whether one should continue to cling to the old and to the traditions long established. If they conclude for the work of the Spirit in drawing women into the ministry, these leaders still have the duty of regulating it, for the edification of the church and its mission, for the sake of good order, and to show that, while the new has dawned for believers, all is not yet the fullness of the kingdom.

It remains to add that if this eschatological argument is given proper weight, it should provide an answer to the proposal sometimes made that women ought to have a fuller ministry in the church but not at the eucharist. The answer is to reject such a solution, for if there is any one place where the church most perceives the presence of the new age, the forgiveness, the eschatological rejoicing the Lord has brought, it is at the Lord's Supper. It follows that here, if anywhere, there should be neither Jew nor Greek, slave nor free, male nor female, but "all in one—in Christ."[80]

B. ECCLESIAL RECOGNITION OF THE MINISTRY OF WOMEN: LUTHERAN EXPERIENCE AND AN ECUMENICAL IMPASSE

Exegetical results, in light of a hermeneutic for using Scripture, must be put together coherently so as to find, if possible, an overall biblical view on a topic like women in ministry.

Further factors are also involved, beyond the Bible, from the subsequent centuries of church history. Here various confessional groups and denominations have emerged, with various experiences, and by now take different views on the subject, often in sharp opposition to the position of other Christians. The firm stance of the Roman Catholic church and the Eastern Orthodox against the ordination of women is, for example, poles apart from that of some Protestant groups that have ordained women for much of the 20th century. Some Conservative Evangelicals and Pentecostals, however, hold, on biblical grounds, a view against women in the ordained Ministry as adamant as that of Catholic groups. Lutherans and Anglicans have until recently not ordained women but in the 1970s began to admit them to the ranks of the clergy (though not in every Lutheran or Episcopal church throughout the world).

In addition there is the fact to be reckoned with that to recognize the ordained Ministry of another church, let alone regard it as coequal and interchangeable with one's own, has always been a thorny problem. Rome, for example, has historically rejected Anglican orders (as "null and utterly void," according to an encyclical of Pope Leo XIII in 1896) and has never formally recognized Lutheran or other Protestant clergy as validly ordained—all this quite apart from the question of women clergy in these groups, a point that may only exacerbate the matter. For one church to allow women into its clergy can be divisive within that confessional family, to say nothing of its relations with great parts of the rest of Christendom. The ordination of women is therefore an ecumenical problem because of centuries of ministry in most churches without it and because of vigorous voices today objecting to it.

The pages which follow were originally presented during the 1977 Theology Institute of Villanova University on "Ministering in a Servant Church." The audience was ecumenical but chiefly Roman Catholic. The address was published as "Ecclesial Recognition of the Ministry of Women: New Testament Perspectives and Contemporary Applications" in the Proceedings of the Institute, *Ministering in a Servant Church* (Villanova, Pa.: The Villanova University Press, 1978), pp. 99-149. Some references to other papers at the Institute and a review of the material given in Part A, above, have been omitted here.

From the overall theme of "Ministering in a Servant Church," we shall assume (1) that the ministry belongs within the context of ecclesiology, and ecclesiology is to be understood in light of Christology; and (2) that christologically "the Son of man came not to be served, but to serve." These words of Mark 10:45 shape ecclesiology and inform all its ministerial functions.[81]

(3) It is further assumed that, in speaking of "ministry," we encompass the various tasks of ministering, those to be carried out by "laity" and those by "clergy." At times I shall, following volume 4 of Lutherans and Catholics in Dialogue in the U.S.A., distinguish within "the ministry [lower case *m*, *diakonia* in Greek] of all believers" a Ministry (with a capital *M*), also characterized by serving, that is specifically set aside within the whole community to function for "the equipping of the saints for the work of ministry (lower case *m*), for the building up of the body of Christ" (Eph. 4:12).[82] With regard to the "ministry of women," we shall focus on the inner of these two concentric circles of the ministerings of the people of God, i.e., the ordained Ministry (capital *M*).[83]

(4) By "ecclesial recognition" will be meant acknowledgment through declaration and praxis of a church that its ordained Ministry officially can include women. Current practice varies greatly.[84]

(5) Finally, we note that in between the needs of today and New Testament origins of Christian ministry, the ancient Christian developments of office and structure need to be respected, but not absolutized. In the New Testament we deal with that segment of the tradition which is most decisive, foundational, and provides indeed the norm. But it too must be—and has been[85]—interpreted through historical study in seeking perspectives for today.

As we consider the theological arguments[86] and the biblical data, we shall pay particular attention to the Declaration of the Sacred Congregation for the

Doctrine of the Faith on January 27, 1977, "On the Question of the Admission of Women to the Ministerial Priesthood."[87] There the "subordination" argument is set aside. Instead, the argument that there must be a "natural resemblance" between priests and Christ, and that "Christ is a man," seems the decisive one in the document. In surveying the biblical materials we shall now venture a different approach, beyond exegesis but dependent on it, of arranging the data.

I. The Biblical "Trajectory": New Testament Perspectives

Recent scripture study has made a good deal of use of the term "trajectory" to describe how a topic moves through early Christianity, for example, the "Petrine trajectory" for images about Simon Peter in the New Testament.[88] The endeavor tries to avoid the notion of "static concepts" against a mere "background" and seeks instead to show the course of movement from one ascertainable point in history and the documents to another, interfaced with other trajectories of the day.

Elsewhere I have indicated my own objections to the conceptualization involved and suggested a moratorium on the term until better defined.[89] For, "trajectory" suggests *(a)* a smooth, upward flight, toward a targeted goal, an evolutionary path, whereas the historical data often indicate a series of ups and downs, with outcomes yet to be determined. A trajectory *(b)* suggests *one* target path, whereas in reality the evidence may suggest a series of competing launchings, even in the same period. *(c)* Trajectories suggest a divine hand has given aim and directs the course, *jure divino,* whereas sometimes the evidence appears to us to suggest a course directed and redirected by many human, cultural, or social factors—and even by the hand of the exegete! My own preference is to speak of "lines of development" instead, and leave open many of these questions until we see what the evidence shows.

With few topics is this caution about tracing a "trajectory" more in order than with "women and ministry" in the Bible. For one thing, we must be precise about what we are after, for there are perhaps three lines of development which can interwine. The first is the course of social-cultural attitudes toward women in the ancient Near East and the Greco-Roman world generally, in light of which anything Israel, or Jesus, or Paul says about women needs to be assessed, as reflection or contrast. The second line of development has to do with the roles and place of women generally in the community of Israel, among the disciples of Jesus, and in the early church. The third, and most important for our purposes, concerns the participation of women in various ministries, above all, the kerygmatic-cultic in Israel and in Jesus Christ's. Yet, the evidence is often so limited, and the problems so interrelated, that we shall find we must pay attention to all three possible courses of development. Indeed, the data are so sparse that we may have to ask whether there *is* a trajectory or only hints of developments. Finally, by way of introduction, we must note that here, as with few other trajectories, the course will often change, move in new ways, divide or bifurcate; we may even see contrasting lines of evidence.

A. The Old Testament

One is tempted to hasten through the Old Testament picture with three simple observations. Let us concede that (1) ancient Israel allowed no role for priestesses in its worship and ministrations. (2) This was likely due to a reaction against Israel's environment, where nature religions and fertility roles for women at temple worship prevailed. Israel rejected this as contrary to Yahweh's will and revelation. But, (3) all this is of little or no importance for the *Christian* ministry, since Israel's temple and priesthood did not provide the basic pattern for the early church.

That third point may require some amplification, since often concepts of "the Christian priest" have been developed on the basis of the Old Testament. It is probably significant, and helpful in my opinion, that the 1977 Vatican Declaration and the commentary on it make no reference to Old Testament praxis as a basis for maintaining that the church "does not consider herself authorized to admit women to priestly ordination." With this position that Christian ministry does not rest on priesthood, Old Testament style, most recent biblical scholarship is in agreement,[90] and those attempts to find, or read in, priests in the New Testament are scarcely convincing.[91] When, in fact, according to Acts 6:7, "a great number of the priests" (from the Jerusalem temple or possibly Qumran) became obedient to the Christian faith, they "lost their priestly identity on entering a community in which the ministers were definitely not *hiereis* [priests]."[92] And, when—and if—we have any "neo-Levitical codes" in the New Testament, as at 1 Peter 1:16 (= Lev. 11:44-45), the reference is to the whole people of God and not to a special group. So, Old Testament priesthood is no launching pad for the trajectory about or against the Christian ministry of women.

Such a position seemingly removes the Old Testament from being any part of a relevant trajectory. Yet, recent studies of the Hebrew Scriptures, often by women themselves, have raised questions over whether there may not be some *positive* insights favoring women in this material. For example, in the ancient Near East, while life had a uniformly patriarchal structure, there were times when women enjoyed greater margins of freedom (e.g., in the Old Babylonian period).[93] Moreover, their role in cult life as priestesses may be overdone in the view we sketched above, for women played "only a minor role in the cultic life" in the ancient Near East, and then chiefly in "the lower echelons" or as prophets.[94] Turning to the Old Testament itself, we find that the image of women in Israel both mirrors and challenges this picture. In a male society, "women were . . . participants," although be it inferior ones in Israelite cult.[95] Even so, there were exceptions in certain individual cases involving the judge Deborah, and charismatic figures like Miriam, and the other prophetesses like Huldah, and Noadiah (Neh. 6:14), who plotted against Nehemiah and whom the Septuagint interpretatively makes into a man(!).

While it may seem snatching at straws, proponents of the women's movement have pointed to such figures as well as to the "enlightened" attitudes of such prophets as the bachelor Jeremiah,[96] or to the fact that Israelite women were not kept in *purdah* as in later Moslem lands.[97] More impressive, but inconclusive, are the attempts to argue that women played some minor role in worship or had a share in sacrificial meals. Cf., e.g., 1 Sam. 2:22, and Exod. 38:8 ("women who served at the entrance to the tent of meeting"), Num. 6:2, 13-21 (a woman may make a Nazarite vow and peace offering), and Prov. 7:14 (a harlot offers sacrifices).[98] But, such shreds of evidence prove little more than that the truth was less monochromic than our traditional impressions.

Finally, there are bold attempts to show that the evidence reflects a variety of Israelite traditions. Fr. George H. Tavard[99] has argued that behind Gen. 2:18-25 and 1:26-27 lurk two traditions, according to one of which woman was originally the higher and better part of humankind; in this prelapsarian state she brought perfection and completion to man; after the fall she became subordinate and inferior. These two traditions continued, with Christ affirming full equality and Paul allowing the tension of the two beliefs to assert itself. So, Tavard. More remarkable is the claim for a "counter culture"[100] within Israel, exalting woman as the climax of creation (Gen. 2:23) and the "helper fit for man" (2:18), i.e., his equality. The Yahwist, certain prophets, and the Song of Songs are claimed as representatives of this more liberating view. If Phyllis Trible is correct, there was a "de-patriarchalizing principle" at work from about the ninth to the sixth centuries B.C., but, then, during and after the exile, a reaction opposed to womankind set in, through Ezekiel, the Priestly writer, and Ezra, ending in the misogyny of the rabbis. As they said, "Better to burn the Torah than teach it to women."[101] Such a sketch comes closest to a "trajectory," but it would be at best a counter line-of-development that had its day and then vanished in the face of general ancient Near Eastern patriarchal attitudes. Perhaps the most sensitizing thing these new exegetes have done for us is to point out how certain facets of the Old Testament picture of God are "feminine" in imagery.[102] The Scriptures appropriate both andro- and gynomorphic details to describe a God who ought not be described just as "a male deity."

But, women in Israel's ministry? The picture is of general conformity to the world cultures of the day, with some protest against pagan practices and occasionally a hint of a counterculture view of woman as more than a subordinate to man. If eschatology did not always promise much here (but cf. Mark 12:25 as typically Jewish, "in heaven people do not marry, nor are they given in marriage"), hints of what creation had been did. Remember Genesis 1–2! If only the lapse of Adam and Eve were somehow reversed!

The last centuries prior to the appearance of Jesus of Nazareth do little but reinforce this view of the denigration of women in the Jewish world. The apocryphal or deuterocanonical books present some of the most notorious antifeminist statements: woman is seen only in relation to man, as an object for his will and wishes; "from a woman sin had its beginning, and because of her we all die" (Sirach 25:24).[103] Not only did the rabbis not ordain women; to teach them Torah was like teaching them lechery.[104] The judgment is correct that opinion had moved radically away from whatever freedom had been enjoyed by women in the Old Testament period, especially before the exile.[105] I am not therefore impressed with efforts to make something out of female skeletons in the cemetery at Qumran or the fact that Philo's ascetic sect of the Therapeutae included women.[106] That in diaspora Judaism women might have some participation in liturgical life[107] seems to show cultural influences of the Greco-Roman world, where the status of women was higher at points than in Judaism, though I would not overdo the notion of pervasive pagan priestesses everywhere.[108] If early Christianity made no priestesses, it had no priests either, except that all members in Christ belong to a "priesthood of the kingdom" (1 Peter 2:9) for missionizing purposes.[109] The modern judgment, on the basis of Jewish views of women, that, if they should be ordained, the precondition ought to be that women first be married, as Raphael Loewe suggests,[110] may be called a reflection of Jewish realism or a final bastion of male chauvinism!

B. Jesus of Nazareth

Against this background of broken trajectories in Israel and a dominant and even growing attitude of patriarchalism and male superiority, the stance of Jesus is little short of revolutionary: he gives women a new place of equality, even though, in line with customs of the day, he does not call any women to a clear leadership role in his group. In so doing, he creates the possibility of a new trajectory or line of development, in light of the gospel, unheard-of since those few tendencies we noted in preexilic Israel or in creation references.

Of course, we are dealing here with the most difficult part of any New Testament course of development. For, to get at the historical Jesus we run the danger of confusing what took place during his earthly ministry with attitudes of the later church and post-Easter practices, as form and redaction criticisms point out. Furthermore, we are here looking at the materials in a way that is contrary to a great deal of the traditional Christian view about Jesus over the centuries. All too often he has been looked upon simply as a Jewish man who chose 12 men (and then 70 men) to carry on a mission which carried over all the strictures of the Old Testament about females.[111]

Yet nowadays there is wide agreement that Jesus' own attitude and practices showed a certain openness toward women. Typical is the 1977 Vatican declaration, " . . . his attitude towards women was quite different from that of his milieu, for he deliberately and courageously broke with it."[112] Among the bits of evidence then cited are public conversation with a woman (John 4:27; cf. 4:9), rejection of legal taboos about women (Matt. 9:20-22; Luke 7:37-50), pardon for a woman accused of adultery under rules which favored the males (John 8:11), and Jesus' return to God's original will in creation in place of the Mosiac law about divorce (Mark 10:2-11). As with many other developments in the later church, so here, the impulse, it is argued, must stem from what actually was characteristic of the earthly Jesus. Some would go so far as to call Jesus a feminist.[113]

Oddly enough, in my exegetical discussion for the Lutheran Council, such passages about the historical Jesus played no role. This is generally so in many debates about the ordination of women, an attitude stemming from the reticence of many biblical scholars to be too certain about results from any "quest for the historical Jesus" and a reluctance to put too much stress on an *imitatio Jesu* (instead of *Christi*). Briefly, however, there are enough solid exegetical efforts to make the following arguments plausible and impressive.

(1) Women played a role in the entourage that accompanied Jesus' ministry (Luke 8:1-3—they "minister" to the other disciples). These women (alone) remained constant at the cross, went to help bury Jesus properly (Mark 15:40-41,47; 16:1), and were the first witnesses to the empty tomb (16:2-8) and risen Christ (Matt. 28:9-10; John 20:11-18). If other traditions do not give them pride of place in attesting that he is risen, it is presumably because women were not readily accepted, especially in Judaism, as legal witnesses.[114]

(2) Certain stories, like John 4 and the Samaritan woman, or Luke 10:38-42, suggest a remembered concern on the part of Jesus for women of varying sorts.[115]

(3) The place of his mother Mary in the story of Jesus has been variously assessed. Traditionally, it is said she was not entrusted with ministry, even though she exceeds the apostles in dignity, because women simply cannot receive the office of the keys or apostolic ministry.[116] But detailed discussion of the Marian material, such as in the ecumenical task force on "Mary in the New Testament," suggests: *(a)* Mary once may have shared family doubts

about Jesus, such as his brothers show, especially in Mark (cf. 6:3; 3:21, 31-35); and *(b)* even in Luke, where the infancy material gives her special place, Mary must learn there is no special claim on Jesus, even for family, but only "hearing the word of God and doing it" mattered (8:19-21); indeed, the realization of this may be "the sword which had to pierce her heart" (cf. 2:35).[117] In short, Mary is like other members of the believing community—they must believe (cf. Acts 1:14). If she holds no office in the Jerusalem community, that is a reflection of general conditions in the Jerusalem church, including sociocultural ones, and not a Lucan way of honoring Mary as supreme model for women while excluding women from church offices.[118]

(4) The most sure thing which emerges from study of the historical Jesus is the fact that his good news was, above all, about the acceptance of outcasts.[119] God accepts the lost, so does Jesus, in forgiveness and table fellowship. "This man receives sinners—taxgatherers and prostitutes" is bed-rock history of Jesus (cf. Matt. 21:31-32; Luke 15:1; 7:36-50). And, women fit this category of outcasts. If there were none at the Passover table in Jerusalem, at least the records suggest women were included in the crowds at the miraculous meals in Galilee which are, like the last supper in the upper room, roots of the Lord's Supper in the church.[120]

Jesus thus begins a new course in the line of development about equality and openness toward women, far beyond the cultures of his day. If he does not appoint them to "office," that is both reflection of the conditions of the day and of the fact we must be chary about seeing anything much of "office," during the lifetime of Jesus. Indeed, we may say historically with more confidence that Jesus gave women a role in his ministering than we can claim Jesus, prior to Easter, instituted a Ministry with a capital *M*.

C. The Early Church

After Easter, when the Jesus-movement developed into a church centered on the confession that "God has raised Jesus from the dead and made him Lord," the good news of Jesus began to spread beyond Galilee and Jerusalem and came eventually into the Gentile world. We must be careful not to structure the stages of this development too simply or to remove issues from the world and cultures of the day. There will be eschatology involved, but not simply a progression through three levels, such as W. E. Hull has proposed: an old age of subservience for women, the messianic age, and an age to come.[121] There will be cultural factors, but not simply a contrast between the Jewish and the Greco-Roman worlds.

The eschatology we shall note at various, different points. The cultural context, which has been an object of increasing study in the New Testament research, can be described something like this. Generally, women were suppressed. They had the greatest relative independence in Egypt and at Rome, the least in Palestinian Judaism, with the Greek world somewhere in between. Among the Greeks, men had once established their very identity over against women; Thales and Plato are said to have prayed with gratitude to have been "born a human being and not a beast, next, a man and not a woman, thirdly, a Greek and not a barbarian," long before such a sentiment found its way into the synagogue liturgy![122] The Hellenistic period eroded many such sex differentiations, but by New Testament times, while the status of women had often improved, there was also "a bitter reaction in the form of misogyny," with many advocating preservation of the status quo.[123] In the Gentile world, the place of women was an explosive issue.

In exploring developments between Jesus' resurrection and the time of Paul in the 50s, or of the evangelists ca. 65-90, we must try to follow the historical stages of development which have been so helpful in tracing the rise of Christology, as in the approach of Reginald H. Fuller,[124] and distinguish, when possible, among (1) Palestinian Christianity, often Aramaic-speaking; (2) Hellenistic Jewish-Christianity, i.e., the Greek-speaking Jewish church, in Palestine and as it advanced into the diaspora; (3) the Hellenistic Gentile mission, i.e., Christianity among converts who had not first been Jews or proselytes. All this, *before* looking at Paul. Only so is it possible to ascertain any trajectory.

For the oldest Palestinian Christianity, Aramaic-speaking, rooted in Judaism and the Old Testament, the records are even more sparse on this topic than on most. If we accept Acts at face value, Mary and "the women," and Sapphira along with her husband Ananias (5:1-11), were active in the Jerusalem community. Later, there is reference at Caesarea to the four unmarried daughters of Philip the evangelist, one of "the seven" in Jerusalem (21:8; cf. 6:1-6). The daughters prophesied. Their father might be called, not a deacon, but a kind of "bishop" for the "Hellenists" of Jerusalem[125]—but that may already advance us into Hellenistic Jewish Christianity. About Palestinian Christianity in Galilee we know little, but rules for women may have been more relaxed there than in Jerusalem. Our best testimony for this earliest Jewish Christianity in its attitude toward women may be the simple fact that it transmitted the materials about Jesus and women noted above. Jewish Christians in Palestine passed along such stories and sayings in spite of the religio-cultural environment which surrounded them. Elisabeth Schüssler Fiorenza concludes from these details that women "played an important role in the Christian movement in Palestine."[126]

Hellenistic Jewish Christianity would have carried these currents into the world of the diaspora and into contact with the trends and countertrends of the Greek world. Here, women are mentioned in inscriptions as patronesses of a synagogue, probably because of their financial support. Were they more apt, in the diaspora, to be allowed to read one of the synagogue lessons, which the rabbis allowed?[127] Who led worship at the Jewish "place of prayer" outside Philippi which Lydia and "the women" attended? We do not know, but seeds were there for greater involvement of women in Hellenistic Jewish Christianity.

It is, of course, in pre-Pauline Hellenistic Gentile Christianity that the greatest involvement of women is to be expected, under the impact of the cultural-social mores of the Greek world. That is exactly what happens, in that kind of enthusiastic, Christ-the-Lord-centered type of Christianity which is now recognized to have given us so much in the way of Christology, hymnody, sacramental life, and ethical development, as reflected in the Pauline and other, later epistles.[128] We sketch the general picture and explore one set of texts.

In the Christian conventicles of Jews and Greeks scattered throughout Asia Minor, Macedonia, and Achaia, the message of Jesus burst upon people with radical newness, liberating them from fate, demonic-cosmic powers, death, and sin. In turn, converts burst forth in paeans about the lordship of Jesus Christ over all the world (e.g., Col. 1:15-20; 1 Tim. 3:16). Salvation was seen as a cosmic drama, in mythological terms, of Christ's preexistence, humiliation, and enthronement (Phil. 2:6-11). He was confessed as mediator of creation, too (1 Cor. 8:6). All this led, from baptism on, to applications to humankind's condition, in light of the experience that a great reversal had taken place through Christ, eschatologically. The original will of God at the beginning of things was now being realized, drawing together in a new community in Christ those who accepted his lordship.

The paradigm text for all this is Gal. 3:28, recognized as a fragment of an early Christian baptismal liturgy.[129] Subsequent work by Robin Scroggs and Wayne Meeks encourages us to hear in it a "baptismal formula of equality" or a "baptismal reunification formula."[130] After reference to the ritual action of "putting on" Christ (v. 28, a reference to donning [white] robes after putting off one's clothes and descending into the waters of baptism), there is assertion of "oneness" now "in Christ," with the following old lines of distinction obliterated: in Christ,

> there is neither Jew nor Greek,
> there is neither slave nor free man,
> there is not "male and female"—a reference to Gen. 1:27.[131]

We can hear reflections of this same formula in 1 Cor. 12:13; Col. 3:10-11; and elsewhere.[132] Perhaps there is rebuttal in this formula of the old Greek prayer and rabbinic *berakah,* blessing God "because he did not make me a Gentile, a peasant, or a woman."[133] The Christian assertion transcends all of these—there is a "third race," beyond the old economic, sexual, social value judgments. To be in the Son of God makes us all "sons of God" (3:26).

One may or may not want to follow Meeks in suggesting that a myth of the androgyne or bisexual progenitor of the human race lies behind this imagery.[134] There is evidence for such speculations in the Greek world and the rabbis. The notion is harder to document for the New Testament than it is for gnostic forms of Christianity later on.[135] The same is true of rituals which develop to express this—it is gnostics who stress these.[136]

The real question is whether this radical attitude towards equality of men and women shows up at all in Christian life and practice in these communities. The answer which Scroggs and Meeks and others give is yes, because the appearance of such an attitude toward women in pre-Pauline Christianity is the best explanation for the approach of Paul to certain phenomena involving women in congregational situations with which he deals.[137] The trajectory begins, then, not simply from pagan cultural conditions, but from Jesus, and runs through the early church, for Paul to accept or modify. The prophetesses and other female leaders in Corinth and elsewhere are not results of "the Greek spirit" imposed on the Christian movement, akin to the slave girl of Pythian Apollo (Acts 16:16), but genuine manifestations of a type of charismatic Christianity in the 40s and 50s A.D.

I add three comments:

(1) I have placed this development primarily within Hellenistic Gentile Christianity. But reference to the Jew/Gentile division (Gal. 3:28, etc.) may suggest it goes back to Hellenistic *Jewish* Christianity. The milieu of the hymns and liturgies of this period is notoriously hard to pin down.

(2) A great deal of this line of development leads into gnosticizing, or downright gnostic perversions of, Christianity. But then, legitimate early Christian emphasis on the Spirit or the law could also lead to perversions. *Abusus non tollit usum* (abuse does not take away use).

(3) I am impressed with early Christian use of the Old Testament during these crucial days as a clue to what is characteristic and indicative of normative Christianity. Gal. 3:28, after all, reflects Genesis 1. Acts 2:17-18 quotes Joel 2:28-29, where "sons *and daughters*," "manservants *and maidservants*," are both given a role in the fulfillment theme for these "last days." The worst antifeminist passages of the Old Testament are conspicuously omitted from New Testament use of the Old. Is that a reflection of this attitude of baptismal equality, and a hint it came from an earlier stage than just Hellenistic Gentile Christianity?

D. Paul

The letters of the Pauline school occupy a pivotal place in reconstructing the line of development concerning women and their ministry in early Christianity. Just as we have distinguished pre-Pauline elements quoted in the epistles, so must we distinguish Paul's own writings from those of his followers in his name, i.e., the deutero-Paulines and the Pastorals.

The starting point is to appreciate that Paul, at least in the Hellenistic churches, inherited a view from earlier Christianity whereby women had the right to take part in the mission of the church and in local congregational activity. Female leaders were accepted.[138] For Paul, the place of women in the church was not a battle to be won but functions to be worked out. The surprising thing is that he overcame the views with which he grew up—he might have continued to hold, as Josephus is said to have, "Woman, says the Law, is inferior to man in all things. Let her accordingly be submissive . . . for God gave the authority (*to kratos*) to man."[139] Instead, Paul accepted the radical implications of Christian baptism.

In Galatians, where Paul fights not only against legalist Jewish Christianity but also probably against a libertinistic, gnosticizing tendency,[140] it is significant he accents the baptismal formula (3:28) and applies it to Jew and Greek, the relationship which was under dispute. Apparently male-female equality was not an issue. Here, we see both how the gospel can cross cultural frontiers, taking root in a new situation, and how there may need to be limits to contextualization in Galatia.[141] The same stance is maintained by Paul in Corinth and elsewhere, though at Corinth the question of limits will more clearly arise.

We see the Gentile attitude at work in a number of references to women. Paul's letters refer to women who are "patronesses" of local congregations, like Phoebe (*prostatis,* Rom. 16:2) and Mary, mother of Rufus (16:13), as those who have church assemblies in their houses (16:5; 1 Cor 16:19; Col. 4:15; Lydia, in Acts 16).[142] Phoebe as *diakonos* may simply "serve" in general, or she may be like the congregational leaders in Phil. 1:1.[143] Women labor, with Paul, for the gospel.[144] The possibility of female *apostoloi* may also be mentioned (Rom. 16:7).[145] The evidence need not be repeated here.

Of course, it has been objected that Paul never designates these women with clerical terms referring to their administration of the sacraments. But then, whom does he mention as officiating at the Lord's Supper or baptism? He did not baptize much himself (1 Cor. 1:14-16), for people may have baptized themselves (1 Cor. 6:11, middle voice).[146] There is no complaint in 1 Corinthians 11 that women may have been involved in the Lord's Supper celebrations.[147]

The Vatican "Declaration" of 1977 seeks to reject this picture by claiming a distinction in Paul's references to co-workers. According to this argument, Paul called men and women who helped him "my fellow workers" (Rom. 16:3; Phil. 4:2-3), but reserved the phrase "*God's* fellow workers" for males like Apollos, Timothy, and himself in the apostolic ministry (1 Cor. 3:9; 1 Thess. 3:2).[148] Quite apart from the textual uncertainty of the last reference[149] and the likelihood that 1 Cor. 3:9 may mean "fellow workers *for* God" (so RSV), the fact is that each verse relates *synergos* or fellow worker with *diakonos* (1 Cor. 3:5), a term which we saw could be applied to women. Moreover, in 1 Cor. 3:9, the emphasis on "God" seems set by the phrases which follow, "God's field, God's building," which apply to *all* the Corinthians. Even more important, women are called "fellow workers *in Christ Jesus*" (Prisca, Rom. 16:3) or "in the gospel" (Phil. 4:3). It is a strange argument which allows women to be *synergoi* "in Christ," but not "of or for God"! Moreover, it may concede too much, if women are "fellow workers" at all, for 1 Cor. 16:16 refers to the "household of Stephanas" (women included?) and says, "Be subject to such people and to every *synergos* and laborer," cf. Hebrew ᶜ*bd* and ᶜ*ml;* ᶜ*bd* and *ygᶜ* in Isa. 43:24, where it refers to God's own work.[150] The contention stands that Pauline churches included women who were fellow workers with Paul, in Christ, for God.

What, then, of the "difficult" passages? First Corinthians 11:2-16 proves precisely that women were functioning as prophets in the congregational assemblies at Corinth. What Paul is concerned with is *regulating* this charismatic activity to prevent offense against the young Christian movement. Verse 3 is no charter for the ontological subordination of women, but a midrash on Genesis 2: the source or origin, chronologically, for woman is Adam.[151] Verses 4 and 5 lay down rules for both men and women in prophesying. Verses 7-9 attempt to buttress the rule for men, and v. 10 the rule for women, with arguments which wheeze, at least for us today. The "authority" *(exousia)* on the woman's head is really meant to be a sign that she is in the new age.[152] Finally, vv. 11-12 sum up the reapplied creation story with a mutuality of man and woman, neither without the other, under God, of course.[153]

If that is Paul's stance in 1 Corinthians 11, then 14:33*b*-36 is a later gloss which we place in the trajectory at the same point where 2 Tim. 2:11-12 arises.[154] For later, even in the Pauline school, a reaction set in, in light of the bourgeois views of the Greco-Roman world, and a toning down of the robust Pauline eschatology. These verses in the Pastorals, reflecting synagogue praxis and the view that Eve was second in creation but the first to sin, enjoin wives at least, not to teach or have authority over males, but to be silent and submissive. This act of church order could forbid almost any involvement of women in church life, and has seldom been followed literally.[155] The Vatican "Declaration" limits the restriction on women to "the official function of teaching in the Christian assembly."[156] Someone, long ago, must have felt it applied to prophesying too, and added 14:33*b*-36 to 1 Corinthians.

Before we sum up on Paul, there is just one other area at which to look, the sphere of ethics and morality. Does not Paul put women in a subordinate position here? No. Actually, in 1 Corinthians 7 there is a surprisingly parallel effort to address himself first to men, then to women, with equality, on each point.[157] His own preference for the single state is not just a matter of auto-biography or an imminent parousia, but, as Scroggs puts it, a "preference for the larger community of the church over the smaller community of the family."[158] His eschatology is not controlled solely by an expected end to history, but primarily by the new life and situation which has come about by being baptized into Christ.[159] And finally, while Paul himself takes over from the world of the day catalogs of virtues and vices to guide the believer between his or her baptism and the parousia, Paul's acknowledged letters never use the *Haustafeln* form with its subordination code; that remained for the deutero-Paulines to do.[160]

Thus Paul, building on what Jesus did and the theology and practice of the church he knew, emerges, not as a chauvinist, but as a rare champion of the place of women as equals of men, in Christ, in the church. But the vision succumbed to the heritage of centuries in the Jewish and Greek worlds, swallowed up in the watchwords of submissiveness, silence, and subordination for women as the will of God for them. The line of development which ran through the pre-Pauline and Pauline church was submerged by the stronger, older patriarchal trajectory and the "reactions of the mainstream church."[161]

E. John

If openness toward a ministry for women flourished especially where there was an eschatological sense of the newness of the gospel, what about John and the Johannine community? If the Johannine literature is strong on "realized eschatology," it is far from rigid on ecclesiology and almost devoid of emphasis on specialized ministries.[162] Community, yes; hierarchy, no.

While it may, therefore, seem a surprise to find any evidence in John on our subject, the following points have been adduced:

(1) A woman, Martha, serves *(diakonein)* at table (John 12:2); does that mean, as Raymond Brown suggests, that "in the Johannine community a woman . . . [exercised] a function which in other churches was the function of an 'ordained' person"?[163]

(2) The Samaritan woman (Chap. 4) not only speaks with Jesus, to his disciples' surprise (4:27), but also brings Samaritans to believe in Christ "because of the woman's testimony" (4:39; cf. 42). She sows the seeds, for an apostolic harvest (4:38).[164]

(3) In Chapter 20 Mary Magdalene not only is the first to see Jesus but tells his brethren, the disciples, the good news (20:17-18). She is a counterpart to Peter elsewhere as first witness to the resurrection.[165]

(4) A confession very close to that of Peter in Matt. 16:16 is placed on the lips of a woman, Mary, in John 11:27, "You are the Christ, the Son of God."[166]

(5) In the Fourth Gospel there is a disciple "whom Jesus loved." That phrase is used of only one man who is named, i.e., Lazarus. But, 11:5 says

"Jesus loved Martha and her sister," Mary, as well as Lazarus. Whether Lazarus is "the disciple whom Jesus loved" or simply a model disciple of whom the same phrase is used, the description is also applied to two women.[167]

(6) The mother of Jesus learns, according to John, as in Luke, that it is by hearing and doing the word of God she is truly a disciple, and in 19:25-27 symbolizes, along with the beloved disciple, true discipleship.[168]

Thus, in the Fourth Gospel, women stand among Jesus' "own," on an equal plane with men beneath the cross, serving. Indeed, Brown suggests, the Johannine community may have been a place where the dream of Gal. 3:28 was more fully realized—no differences between male and female.[169]

F. Other References

The other gospels tell us little more about roles, let alone prominence, for women in early Christianity, especially if we credit pericopes describing women's involvements during Jesus' ministry or at his burial and resurrection as stemming from the historical-Jesus level or the oral period in Jewish or Hellenistic Christianity.[170] The most we can say is that the evangelist-editors accepted such testimonies to the place of women and built them into their gospels. The significance of the three women in Mark 15:42, 47 and 16:1-8 has been so variously interpreted in recent scholarship that I hesitate to draw any conclusions from it.[171]

The Matthean church is harder to assess; its proximity to rabbinic Judaism and its stress on "Christian scribes" (13:52; 23:34) might indicate a quite minimal role for women. On the other hand, the Matthean church, for all its Petrine emphasis, is notoriously nonhierarchal. It opposes earthly titles like "father" or "master" or "rabbi" (cf. 23:8-12), and as a *corpus permixtum* (a "mixed body" of "good" and "bad") (13:36-43; 22:1-14) was open to "sinners"—taxgatherers, harlots, outcasts; ought we emphasize women?— as Jesus had been. Yet to expand 23:8, ". . . you are all brethren," to read "brothers (and sisters),"[172] goes further than Matthew ever does. Luke's emphasis on women, as on Samaritans, in his two volumes, is well known, and he reflects far more the Greco-Roman world. Yet, that was a world of reaction against women as well as of greater rights for them, and Luke's church may also have been affected by the tendencies seen in the deutero-Paulines and Pastoral Epistles, which would subordinate women. In any case, texts about their direct leadership roles are scarce in Luke-Acts.[173]

Other passages which have been brought forth as settling the issue against the ordination of women, seem to me to add little additional insight. Hebrews 13:7, 17 calls for submitting to leaders, perhaps a group of charismatic elders.[174] First Peter 5:1,5 is likewise an exhortation to be subject to elders; 1 Tim. 3:1-5, to an *episkopos*. I continue to find unconvincing an appeal here to a *"kephalē* principle," whereby males must always rule over females as their head, imported from assumed orders of creation. In the "people of God" context in all these documents, there is scarcely the hierarchalization being assumed by this argument; the reference is seemingly to *wives* in relation to husbands (cf. 1 Peter 3:1), not to all women; and, is eternal theological truth involved or cultural reflection of the day? If to be a bishop one must manage his household and children well (1 Timothy 3), in today's world do not women often meet that requirement, more than men? If celebrating eucharist in the church of that day depended on a charism and consent of the community," [175] then it is hard to insist some types of early Christianity did not allow women so to function here.

Summary

The biblical lines of development turn out to run like this. Overall, there is a "patriarchal trajectory," where women submit to men, throughout the ancient Near East and, with exceptions, in Greco-Roman civilization. It is culturally and sociologically dominant, and religiously and theologically as well. Within the Bible, alternative trajectories appear in Israel, ninth to sixth centuries B.C., and beginning with Jesus on through the early church, especially in (Jewish) Hellenistic Christianity, Paul, and John. In the later New Testament, and the patristic church, the dominant, patriarchal line comes to control. There are enough hints and data here to raise questions about traditional views, but no conclusive evidence that women regularly engaged in the tasks later recognized as marking the ordained Ministry in the New Testament period. But then, as we said at the outset, "ordained Ministry" has had a history of development too.

II. "Ecclesial Recognition"
or "Validity" of Women's Ministry

We turn now to the opening words in our topic, concerning "ecclesial recognition" of women in ministry. An earlier version of the title talked about "validating the ministry of women." In many traditions, including my own, that latter term is strange, and even in circles where it is used, today the talk is less and less about attempting the route of "validating" the orders of some other church, as if an airlines ticket were involved or the Immigration Service were stamping a visa to sojourn in our land. Indeed, I have found myself increasingly asking how the New Testament would go about even "recognizing" the ministry of some Christian who appears from elsewhere.

Suppose, for instance, an elder from a church in Galilee or Syria had turned up in Ephesus in A.D. 60 or so, or a *diakonos* or one of the *episkopoi* from Philippi arrived in Rome in time for a Sunday service, or, more difficult, an

Alexandrian Christian happened in on one of the churches on Crete reflected in the Epistle to Titus. How, if at all, would they have proceeded to check out this visitor, to let him or her participate in their worship, to pray, preach, or help in the meal?

Perhaps our hypothetical visitor would have brought a letter of recommendation, such as Phoebe carried (Rom. 16:1-2). But then, false apostles carried letters like this, even in Paul's day (2 Cor. 3:1). Or, our wandering Christian might have been asked about his profession of faith—do they share the same creed with each other (cf. 1 John 4:2)? Or, the question might be about who his teachers were, or with whom he and his home community shared fellowship. A minimal question might be, "Do you love the Lord Jesus?" (1 Cor. 16:22). The sign of a fish, the sharing of a story about Jesus as one's testimony, an acclamation of Christ as Lord, might suffice. In the *Didache,* more elaborate tests are provided, but these have to do with how long an "apostle" should stay: if he sponges on the congregation for more than two days, "he is a false prophet" (11:5). In general, the advice is, "Receive them" (11:1,4; 12:1) and even let such prophets take part in the eucharist, with the length of prayers "as they desire" (10:7). There is remarkably little in these early Christian writings about modes of "ecclesial recognition," and one gets the impression it was not the problem which it is for us today.[176]

It is, therefore, our thesis, in light of this situation in the New Testament, that a church today may, and, indeed, has the task and the right to recognize ministries, or, if it chooses to use the term, to "validate" them, on the basis of whatever New Testament standards, developed traditions, sense of order and implications of reason, or current needs, it chooses. Recognition lies within the frame of reference of each church. A Christian group has the right so to do, assessing other ministries in light of its standards. But, in today's ecumenical world it owes explanations to others of the criteria employed and ought to be very wary about maximalizing its standards as "God's known will," so as to exclude others arbitrarily.

If this seems an imprecise or even sloppy way of certifying ministries, it is in part because the New Testament offers us little to go on here. As noted before, even "ordination" is not a developed term in the Scriptures, nor is "ordained Ministry." Such a stance is also necessitated by our assumption that ecclesiology shapes ministry. The church group has the right to determine its own ministry, "giving reason for the faith that is in it" on that point.

Very well, how have Christian groups gone about giving recognition to ministries, theirs and other groups'? At least the following six ways occur to me, though likely several of the approaches have often been intertwined in a given church body.

A. Some Christian groups or churches have rested recognition of Ministries mainly or exclusively (they thought) on biblical evidence. How complicated that evidence can be we have seen above. How confusing the hermeneutics, modern discussion has shown.[177] How contradictory the conclusions can be is also apparent.

To begin with the Old Testament, with 1 Corinthians 14, or 1 Timothy 2, can lead only to the exclusion of women from ordained Ministry (and also from a number of other functions they actually fulfill in almost all Christian groups). Both conservative Protestants and Anglo-Catholics end up in agreement that the Bible excludes ordination of women. On the other hand, if one begins from Gal. 3:27-28, a case is possible that women should share equally with men in the church's Ministry, especially at the eucharist. Many Lutherans, Catholics, and others agree on this point.

But the biblical evidence thus does not settle it. Often, for a passage on one side, another can be cited on the opposite side of things.[178] The U.S. Lutheran study in 1970 reached the conclusion that, in light of the biblical material, "the case both against and for ordination [of women] is found to be inconclusive"[179]—possible, but not demanded. But even that conclusion was gain, compared with the view held over the centuries that women may not be ministers, on the basis of Scripture.

B. A second line of solution for validating ministries or deciding which a church shall recognize lies in the area of ecclesial tradition. A church selects out of its heritage what it holds dear and dominant on a point. Under this approach there is no question but that the conclusion has generally been "No women may apply" for ordained Ministry.[180] Yet, recent research on many aspects of the traditions over the centuries has raised questions, if not found loopholes, as to what these traditions have actually been. The studies by Haye van der Meer and Joan Morris, to mention just two, demonstrate that the Western Catholic tradition has been far from unanimous, and cases can be raised where women apparently ordained or were ordained even in the Middle Ages.[181] But, are the loopholes big enough to justify such ordinations now? Was the dominant practice of centuries God's will or cultural conditioning? Is it, as with use of the Bible, that we can choose cases so that one balances out the other? Ecclesial tradition does not settle the matter fully.

C. A third way involves institutional authority. A church may, with or without appeal to a biblical or ecclesial tradition, make its own pronouncements as to who may be a Minister, on the basis of its claim to institutional authority or specific revelation or divine sanction. Such a basis may be quite theological or purely sociological, or a combination of the two. Involved may be a hierarchy, a council or convention, or a local congregation. The Roman Catholic church, the Church of Jesus Christ of Latter Day Saints, or a storefront Pentecostal group can each decide who shall minister, on the basis of the authority in that church. To an extent every group partakes to a degree of this approach. At the least, ordination is recognized or validated intra-systematically, i.e., within the system of thought and authority of the group concerned. At issue is what that group claims as its authority (which generally takes us back to Bible and tradition) and whether and how it imposes its standards and system on other ministries in recognizing them or not. Women's Ministries fare variously under this approach, depending on the system of the institution.

D. Turning from the past and whatever Scripture or tradition or institutional churches do or do not say, we may appeal, next, as a basis for what ministries to recognize, to cultural, social, and psychological factors. These may be insights from research into our own day or study of needs today. For example, it is said, "Women have shown proven abilities in other professions, they would bring qualities needed nowadays for ministry." Or, it may be that these cultural, social, or psychological insights at which we have arrived can be applied to biblical or traditional statements in the past, neutralizing them. Thus, the argument, already obvious in Part I of this paper, but never allowed to be fully determinative there, that culture of the day shaped what Israel, Paul, or medieval theologians said about women. Or, the judgment that Paul affirmed women's ordination theologically, but not sociologically in his day.[182] Few theologians make such factors as the sociological, cultural, or psychological decisive, but they are important, increasingly so.

One implication is the possibility that a worldwide church might want to allow ordination of women in some countries or cultures or at certain times, but not in other places, societies, and times. The nations of the North Atlantic Alliance are one thing; India or Latin America may be quite different. Dare one even speak of possible ethnic differences and needs on a point like this? I have heard black Lutherans in America argue, for example, that black women should not be ordained as yet—in a matriarchal society black urban youth first need male models, black clergy*men,* with whom to identify.

E. A sure and certain way for some groups to determine whether a ministry is valid involves the charismatic test—does the person have the Spirit and the gifts and the call direct from God? One suspects the approach was congenial to some Corinthians in Paul's day, and existed in the time of the *Didache.* Acts 13:1-2, with prophets and teachers leading worship at Antioch, provides another example. Possibly such ministries existed side by side with more "official" ones from the outset of Christianity.[183] This method of recognizing a proper minister has never gone away, for all our institutional development, and is again a lively option in our day. The gist of the position is simply that God chooses whom God will, whenever and wherever. Obviously, women are included in such ministries, validated by God and by the charismata given them. Some would suggest we rediscover this means as a way of validation for our day—it could solve the ordination-of-women issue, as well as some other ecumenical problems.[184]

Oddly enough, such a procedure gives a Lutheran almost as much trouble as it does a Catholic orthodoxist. For, what are the criteria? Pneumatics offer little in the way of standards outside themselves and their experiences. It is as in the days in Israel when there was no king: "each one does what is right in his own eyes" (cf. Judg. 17:6). Paul himself had to invoke gospel and church criteria in Corinth, namely, conformity to the crucified Jesus as Lord, and edification of the community. To determine ministries charismatically raises problems as well as solves them.

F. A final possibility to determine whether to recognize or declare valid a ministry: does it express and conform to the gospel? Here, the standard is whether or not it advances the authentic good news of Jesus Christ. The sequence runs: gospel-church-ministry. Those ordained are set apart to proclaim the glad tidings for the community. Functional fulfillment of that task legitimates a ministry. Of course, we must have some agreement on what the biblical gospel is, in light of which all subsequent ministry is to be done, but I assume modern study of the Bible and ecumenical dialogue allow some basic agreements here.

Here, it is usually to be assumed that a woman can proclaim this gospel to others, to women, to children, and to men. She can proclaim it by behavior (1 Peter 3:1), by what she says (John 4:39), and sacramentally—we allow it in baptism, at least in emergencies; the Lutheran experience has been it can happen too in the celebration of the Lord's Supper. Here, then, is what the Lutheran experience finds determinative: with full respect for the biblical data, which neither directly enjoin nor seem to us to forbid ordination of women, with awareness of the tug of tradition (and all its variety), impressed by cultural influences and the need to be open to workings of the Spirit and the charismata, but not to rest the case on new pneumatic manifestations beyond the old criteria, we find ultimately persuasive the gospel as legitimating factor for all churches and ministries. Where the gospel is rightly preached, and the sacraments administered in accord with the gospel (Augsburg Confession, Article 7), there is the church, and it is to further the gospel that Ministry has been instituted.[185] Ordained Ministry is thus validated by the gospel. We should, therefore, recognize priests, presbyters, evangelists, and leaders of other groups to be engaged in the valid Ministry when they are engaged in proclamation of the true gospel.[186]

There must, however, be a freedom here to let other churches decide, in their situation, whether they want to ordain women as yet or not. Our testimony is that in the 1970s in the United States ordination of women conforms to the gospel.

At this point, it is necessary to meet, on Lutheran grounds, one counter-argument which seems to me most serious. It has been noted that roles for women in ministry have been most readily apparent where "realized eschatology" flourished (e.g., Paul and John). Yet, there is a kind of "eschatological reservation" in these biblical writers which Lutherans especially cherish, i.e., the understanding that we have not as yet fully arrived in the kingdom or attained to perfection. Because of this future reservation, it has been argued, Lutherans above all should recognize that we remain under the law, within creation, and do not structure church life by the gospel alone or what may be some day eschatologically fulfilled. "Let women be emancipated in the world," the argument runs (usually with a wistful sigh that the world has gone mad in letting them vote, be judges, or hold political office); "at least the church should hold the line with its Ministry, and cleave to the will of God." [187] Such a line of argument seems to me precisely to invert the point of Gal. 3:28. It is in Christ, at worship, above all in the celebration of the eucharist, that eschatological reunification and baptismal equality should be realized, whatever the world does.

If we recognize Ministries on the basis of the gospel, ordination of women is allowable, even ultimately called for, but it must be decided, I am suggesting, in the case of each church, land, and time with reference to that church's situation, including cultural and social factors.

III.
The Lutheran Experience:
A Contemporary Application

There is considerable agreement that decisions to ordain women, taken by a number of Lutheran churches, in Europe (particularly Sweden) and the United States (first by the Lutheran Church in America), have been influential in bringing to the fore the question of ecclesial recognition of the Ministry of women. [188] There are several reasons a case study of this Lutheran experience is of special significance for consideration of the issue by Roman Catholics and others.

(1) The step was taken by a confessional church, in the Western tradition, with strong biblical, doctrinal, liturgical emphasis, in some cases even a "high church caste." These Lutheran churches had long included deaconesses or sisters, but "consecrated" rather than "ordained" them. So, it was no longer a matter of the Salvation Army, Congregationalists, or others taking the step where "the community is considered the unrestricted bearer of all authority." [189]

(2) The step was taken after careful, open debate, which, especially on the scriptural passages, was quite thorough, and with awareness of the Western traditions and the broad ecumenical arguments. [190]

(3) The step was taken, by and large, without rancor and factiousness. In the United States one need only compare the almost effortless transition to

the ordination of women among Lutherans who have decided for the step, in comparison to the high feeling among Episcopalians over the "Philadelphia eleven" and subsequent events.[191]

(4) Precisely because of these analogies, the exploration of the theological questions, and the generally successful course of women into the ministry, the Lutheran experience is worth pondering for some questions it raises for all of us and the possible cost to a denomination when such a step is taken. For, it can be argued that "the women's issue" has been a key factor in what has been termed "the civil war" within the Lutheran Church–Missouri Synod.[192]

Statistically, national Lutheran churches in Denmark (including Greenland), Norway, and Sweden, as well as territorial churches in Germany, France, Holland, and Czechoslovakia, have authorized the ordination of women.[193] The Swedish decision in 1958 was a turning point, as was the U.S. action in 1970. This is not to say that discussion does not continue, as in Norway where the Independent Theological Faculty in Oslo has been debating whether to train women for ordination in its practical seminars, in Sweden where a bishop may refuse to ordain a woman in his diocese, and Finland where opinion varies on whether women should be ordained. But the fact is that ordination of women has come to pass without, even in Sweden, the divisiveness predicted by some (from 1958 to 1974, 130 women were ordained in that country), and the practice has spread, e.g., to Brazil (1971) and Japan. Worldwide, there are said to be 556 women Lutheran pastors, as of summer 1977.[194]

For our case study I shall concentrate on the Lutheran Church in America, a national body of more than three million members in the United States and Canada, commonly conceded to be the most "Americanized" and ecumenically minded of the Lutheran bodies in America.[195] By 1960, its ranks (actually those of its predecessor bodies, for the LCA was formed only in 1962 by merger of the United Lutheran Church in America, the Augustana Synod, and some smaller ethnic churches) included some 50 women who had been graduated from seminary but not ordained.[196] While there were some 220 deaconesses in 1963, pressure for the ordination of women did not particularly come from that quarter (for the diaconate was undergoing its own identity crises in that period). Rather, it was an in-depth study, inaugurated in the late 60s by Lutheran Church Women, an official auxiliary for laywomen, plus a series of reports to the national convention by commissions on the Ministry in 1952, 1966, and 1970, and the leadership of certain theologians and pastors, which raised the issues.[197]

The climate in the LCA by 1966 was clearly toward favoring admission of women to its Ministry. In addition to its own study process, the LCA, therefore, gladly joined in a study which the ALC requested in 1967 of the Division of Theological Studies of the then newly formed Lutheran Council in the

U.S.A., which included the Missouri Synod. At the LCA's 1968 convention, Professor T. A. Kantonen persuaded the church to delay action in the hopes that other Lutheran bodies could concur. Accordingly, LCUSA's Division of Theological Studies appointed a four-person subcommittee which in 1968–1969 examined prior studies, listened to consultants, and generated papers on women's ordination in light of Scripture, the Confessions and Lutheran theological tradition, practices in other Lutheran churches and in the *oikoumēnē*, plus social, psychological, and theological reasons pro and con.[198]

The conclusion of the LCUSA study, reached by March 1969, was that "there are no conclusive grounds for forbidding the ordination of women and no definitive ones for demanding it," so that "a variety of practices at any given time remains possible amid common confession." The statement of findings and the study papers went to the churches involved later that spring, but the results were also tested in a larger conference on the Ministry at Dubuque, Iowa, September 20-22, 1969. Here, again, the exegetical results withstood the challenge, Dr. Martin Scharlemann, of the Missouri Synod, making his opposition chiefly on the basis of the so-called "orders of creation."[199]

The next step came when all these results were reported at the annual meeting of the Lutheran Council, February 3, 1970. In what can only be described as a charismatic moment, the counselors present, including the church body presidents, seemed totally inclined to vote approval, but it had been decided to request only transmission of the DTS report to member churches for "study and consideration."[200] It was also voted, however, to transmit a popularized summary of the study to all clergymen in the three bodies; hence, the booklet, *The Ordination of Women,* condensed by Raymond Tiemeyer.[201] But, even the popularization process became a bone of contention. President J. A. O. Preuss of the Missouri Synod felt that the style was "flippant" and did "not reflect the seriousness which the question of the ordination of women requires."[202]

The actual legal step in the LCA permitting the ordination of women was quite simple. At the biennial convention at Minneapolis, as part of the report of the Commission on the Comprehensive Study of the Doctrine of the Ministry, it was recommended that in church bylaws the word "man" in defining "a minister of this church" be changed to "person." Shortly after 10 P.M. on June 29, 1970, the item was adopted "with a resounding voice vote," one delegate (a woman) asking to have her negative recorded.[203] Appropriate changes were made in other church documents, and the first woman ordained, a campus pastor, on November 22, 1970.[204] The ALC took similar action that same year. The closest the Missouri Synod came was a 1969 convention action which allowed women to vote in congregational or synodical assemblies and to serve on boards or commissions, provided there was no "violation of the order of creation," while forbidding them on scriptural grounds from holding "the pastoral office" or exercising "authority over men." [205] By 1971, the Missouri Synod, which had established fellowship with the ALC (but not the LCA), requested the American Lutheran Church to refrain from further ordinations of women and to reconsider its decision—something the ALC refused to do.

Since then, the ordination-of-women issue can be said to have become increasingly important in the eyes of LCMS leaders. To oppose it was a mark of orthodoxy. The issue has contributed to the split between the Missouri Synod and most other Lutherans. At its 1977 convention the LCMS created a unique category of "fellowship in protest" to describe its rupturing relation with the ALC. That the ALC continues the ordination of women is a big factor in this rupture. The issue was also among the points of dispute leading to the exodus of Seminex from Concordia Seminary, St. Louis, and the formation of "Evangelical Lutherans in Mission" (ELIM movement), and in 1977, of the Association of Evangelical Lutheran Churches (AELC). In the fall of 1977, the Pacific Regional Synod of the AELC ordained its first woman. Inasmuch as Bishop James S. Rausch has declared that, for Roman Catholics, to ordain women would cause "the biggest schism in the history of the church," [206] it is worth pondering the cost to American Lutheran unity of events since 1970. For two of the three bodies to have ordained women has been made a reason to impede further unity. Yet Missouri did not withdraw from the Lutheran Council and has not [as of 1977] ended fellowship with the ALC, and if these steps come, other factors will be involved. In fact, if not the ordination of women, then some other issue would likely have become a focal point of differences. [For subsequent events, see below, pp. 132f.]

But what has been the experience among the majority of U.S. Lutherans who have been ordaining women since 1970? Statistically, the LCA has 54 ordained women, as of October 1977, out of some 7600 ordained ministers. Of the 54, more than half (29) are pastors of congregations, 6 more are associates and 4 assistants in parishes; one is developing a new congregation, 4 work with students on campuses, 4 are institutional chaplains, and 2 are on seminary faculties. [207] The number will rise sharply for a time. As of 1974-1975, 75 women were studying for ordination. In seminaries such as those in Philadelphia and Chicago, the percent of women in the student body is almost 30%.

A 1976 report by a woman for the LCA's Division for Professional Leadership[208] predicts this number will level off in a few years, and stresses the variety among women as persons studying for the ministry. A frank listing of their problems and complaints includes the way (male) officials and committees quiz them about their aims; financial problems, in part reflecting the way society treats women generally; the lack of models in faculty and ministry; prejudices, especially in field education, but also in the classroom, including use of "male language"; attitudes of male students, which move from humor to hostility to fear over these new creatures in their midst; problems in placement after studies; the trials of getting clergy shirts and garb which fit and are appropriate; and, one doubtless strange for Catholics, dating and marriage patterns.

The same report begins to recount some of the experiences of women in congregational ministries.[209] Support seems to come especially from men and women over 55 and some young people. Middle-aged women are most resistant. Relationships with fellow pastors present all the problems newly ordained clergy always have, and then some. False assumptions have been challenged, however, such as that women, when ordained, will all be warm and open or that they will not take to business management details. An attempt to list the special contributions of women pastors includes the following: "a humanizing and liberating effect on the congregation"; energy and scholarly ability in seminary which brings new standards and resources to study; a feeling they are "part of the laity," even when ordained, identifying with lay-people, who respond to them with enthusiasm; greater flexibility than men exhibit; more sensitivity to feelings; an orientation to people more than to programs, including the judgment that women pastors are "great in visitation." The study also speaks of the reaction of some parishioners that women pastors have a "motherly way" in pastoral acts; they "bring the other half of humanity to the Lord's Table in a new way."[210]

I could add my own observations to this list. Women students vary quite as much as male students do, and should not really be looked on as a "distinct group." They bring excellence and new insights to the campus of a school. Their problem lies in getting parish placement and then, the bane in churches which have longer ordained women, securing advancement in keeping with their abilities.[211] An increasing phenomenon is the proportion of women divorced but with children, who seek to enter the Ministry; they are often most difficult for a bishop to place in a system where the local congregation must vote to call a person. Finally, I think, admission of women to ordination cannot help but reshape the ministry itself and ultimately theology. But then, these things have long been undergoing change, and our only alternative is to disenfranchise women, bar all recent cultural, social change, canonize the patriarchal society of ages past, and let the "orders of the fall"[212] ride sovereign over God's original will at creation and the redemptive impulses in the earliest church.

The Lutheran experience, however, suggests that transition to an ordained Ministry for women is possible, while keeping much of the traditions of the past, but adapting, in conformity with the gospel. In all this we must recognize such diversity of views and practice which conditions may make desirable, even in the same confessional church.

IV. Our Impasse and the Divine Economy

If it is at all true that the witness of the biblical revelation at times points to the possibility of equal roles for women in all Ministries for the people of God, but does not demand their ordination; and if ecclesial recognition of women in Ministry derives from a number of factors—Scripture, tradition, church and cultural setting, actual charismatic gifts, and, above all, the gospel itself; and if, finally, the Lutheran experience gives some clues as to what can happen, then an argument is needed which will be persuasive in those communities which as yet do not find themselves "authorized to admit women to priestly ordination."[213]

We have already admitted that a great deal depends on cultural, social, and psychological factors. It is probably no accident that among Anglicans ordinations of women first occurred in Hong Kong, since, as a bishop there expressed it, "Chinese civilization has always given a higher place to women both in culture and social life than any civilization apart from Christianity."[214] But, our argument dare not rest simply on cultural factors, even though these may have been an important element in shaping the biblical testimony itself.

We have allowed, especially on the basis of varied cultural and other factors, that even a national or universal church need not act uniformly at the same time in every diocese or region on an issue like this. Thus, U.S. Lutherans have respected the right of the Missouri Synod to take only the step of women's suffrage at this time.[215] Swedish Lutherans have allowed the right of individual bishops not to ordain women in a particular diocese, like Gothenberg. Anglicans are obviously faced with differences in various provinces and even within the Episcopal Church in the U.S.A. The "principle of subsidiarity" here applies.[216] Where there is not clear dominical command to do it, and cultural factors are involved, proponents of ordination for women must allow some flexibility.

Such flexibility could take various forms, but I am not inclined to some of the suggestions which have been made. For example, that "*older* women workers" ought to be ordained to the priesthood, on the grounds that, in the New Testament, age carries more authority than sex.[217] Or that, for the Church of England, women should function always in *teams* of presbyters, replacing the traditional one-man vicarages.[218] Or, women should "demand ordination as *bishops* first," before they can afford to be ordained as deacons and priests, and furthermore, that the step should not involve simply "some nuns who evidence a great dependency on church authority," lest the last state of clericalization and hierarchicizing will be worse than the first.[219] Finally, it is but a step to the position that women should refuse any ordination into the present structures of ministry because these are patriarchal and male-dominated.[220] On this view the system is so bad it must be replaced, not reformed.

My own inclination, in terms of conservative reformation, is that ecclesial recognition of women in Ministry will involve *existing* structures, which will then change *later on,* as they always have been changing anyway, and that women should be accepted from the outset as eligible for *all* forms of Ministry, all ranks and offices.

One final caveat before advancing to our argument: in spite of the theme for this Theology Institute, "Ministering in a Servant Church," I do not believe that "servanthood" is currently the right way for women out of their dilemma. Yes, the church is, or should be, servant of the word and is to serve people and their needs. "Ministry *is* servanthood," as Matt. 23:8-12 and a number of recent writers forcefully remind us.[221] Authority in the church ought to reflect servanthood, not power, and perhaps "servanthood is more characteristically female than male.[222] But, the splendid biblical theme of *diakonia* has been used, I fear, as part of a traditional put-down of women: they may minister as Martha and the women about Jesus did (Luke 10:38-42; 8:3), but that was taken to mean simply domestic toil. Women might be deaconesses, but not ordained. Institutionalized servanthood served to exclude women from "higher" forms of Ministry. The following remarks from a Lutheran woman pastor have made an impression on me. In the dynamics of servanthood, she writes:

> males were called into positions of authority, with the role of pastor being at the top of the ladder, and in administering with authority, were quite sure they were serving Christ. Women were called into lay or commissioned roles of servanthood (as deaconesses or parish workers) or within the life of the congregation as those who cooked, sewed, or cleaned. . . . Both thought they were serving, and of course, both were. But in the process the serving being done by the women was deemed less valuable; it was worth less pay, commanded less prestige, and eventually produced self-images of less worth. Inasmuch as the whole concept of servanthood is important in the Christian faith, it will probably need to be reexamined as it is separated from masculine and feminine limitations.[223]

I agree, and hence the route of servanthood, important as it is, cannot be the right one now.

The roots for the argument I want rather to advance lie in the "Declaration" from Rome on "the Admission of Women to the Ministerial Priesthood." They lie in the phrase "God's plan," "God's plan for his church," or "the economy of salvation."[224] The declaration makes a great deal of this important theme, for, while possible cultural conditioning in past views about women is admitted, it is "from the economy of the mystery of Christ and of the church" that priesthood stems. Citing *Gaudium et Spes* ("Joys and Hopes," the decree from the Second Vatican Council in 1965 on "The Church in the Modern World"), the declaration says "discrimination based on sex" must be eliminated in our world precisely because it is "contrary to God's plan." [225]

The "plan of God" here will be recognized as an important Vatican II theme. Its classical expression has been the phrase, "the economy of God," in Greek, *oikonomia tou theou*. In German, this has been expressed by the word *Heilsgeschichte*, "salvation history." Among modern theologians, Oscar Cullmann, that Protestant professor of New Testament at Basle and Paris who became a kind of Vatican II *peritus* (expert consultant) for the *una sancta* (one church), is the great champion of *Heilsgeschichte*. [226] His influence among Catholics with regard to "the mystery of salvation" has been enormous. And if we look at the Greek word he claims as the early Christian term for salvation history or the "plan of God," namely, *oikonomia*, we find a rich host of connotations in the church fathers. [227]

In Cullmann's thought, as is well-known, *oikonomia* stands for the saving plan of God and its history as it stretches from creation, through all humankind and Israel and the remnant, to the One who is the center of history, Jesus Christ, and then in expanding stages (which match those of the narrowing advance in the Old Testament), from Christ to the apostles through the church to all humankind and finally to the new creation. It may be observed that this *heilsgeschichtlich* sweep from creation to new creation serves as a significant backdrop for the lines of development we have found in the Bible regarding the roles of women. There, we found particularly an appeal, in ancient Israel, to the original place of woman, with man, *at the creation*, and hints of a concern at times to preserve this equality, all cultural patriarchal conditions to the contrary. Only *in Christ* and the eschatological fulfillment which he brings could this eventually come to pass, above all, in early Christian worship.

Turning to the church fathers as a second example of salvation-history thinking, we note that our word in Greek, *oikonomia*, was used especially for God's management or arrangement of the plan of salvation, within God's administration of the universe; then, more specifically, for particular events within that plan of salvation, like the cross, resurrection, or exaltation, but, above all, for the incarnation. In fact, in patristic Greek *oikonomia* especially denotes the incarnation of Christ, his becoming flesh (*enanthrōpēsis, ensarkos oikonomia*). We could pause to note how *oikonomia* was used to refer to this arrangement or that event in Jesus' ministry, or how the term continued to be applied to God's interpositions, interventions, mercies, and providences for his people in the church, but the evidence is readily available elsewhere. [228] We add simply that this same word, *oikonomia*, could also refer to the inner arrangement within the Godhead, and, thus, to the Trinity, and to the "administration" of the Lord's Supper. Its central use, however, has been for Christ's incarnation, as focal point for the plan of God. I remind you, also, regarding women, of the trajectory we saw in Jesus' attitude toward women which carried over into the earliest church, as a result of the ministry of the Incarnate One. Indeed, a current tendency in biblical studies is to read the course of *Heilsgeschichte* more positively towards women.[229]

If the basic appeal in theology is to the plan or economy of God as grounds for overcoming discrimination based on sex (as in *Gaudium et Spes*), then it is hard to exclude the role of women in Ministry from the implications of salvation history for the church.

But there are two final turns to give to our argument, to lock it into place. The first has to do with the fact that this same Greek term, *oikonomia*, came to be used in the sense of an arrangement, often canonically in church law, which prudently handled some difficult matter where the legal evidence pointed to one conclusion, but justice or love pointed in another direction. This principle of economy, well known in Greek Orthodox thought and practice and reflected in Latin as *dispensatio*, a "dispensation," has traditionally implied a certain "elasticity in the interest of the Christian community."[230] When something is done *kat' oikonomian* (according to the 'economy' or by arrangement), there is consideration for the special circumstances involved: concession, accommodation, reserve, diplomacy, stratagem, to cite some of the appropriate renderings suggested in the Oxford *Patristic Greek Lexicon*.[231] In Byzantine practice, *oikonomia* was employed especially in matters regarding the general well-being of the whole church, particularly in relationships with clergy and Christians of other sorts. Thus, Orthodox writers in the 12th century, for example, who wished to remain in some sort of fellowship with the Latin Church, applied the concept to the Latins.[232] In our own day, Greek theologians have invoked the principle of *oikonomia* as the basis for Orthodox involvement in the ecumenical movement.[233]

It has already been suggested that this principle of economy might be a way of validating ministries of other groups within a divided church.[234] I am suggesting that it also bears examination as a means for some churches to recognize the Ministry of women where, strictly speaking, their own tradition might seem to preclude it entirely. The doctrine of the economy enables one to take another look at the matter and reach a different conclusion, with some elasticity, for the good of the whole Christian community, in the face of the circumstances involved. There has, as mentioned, been appeal to the principle of economy for validating ministries, but not, I think, with an awareness that the concept relates historically, terminologically, and theologically with the plan or economy of God.

The final twist to our argument has to do with the fact that this Greek term *oikonomia*, which refers to salvation history, the incarnation, and a dozen other things, also came to have a meaning of "accommodation" or "arrangement," whereby a thing arranged might have a different meaning from that which appears on the surface. To cite a famous example, Basil the Great was reticent to speak about the deity of the Holy Spirit and so was suspect in the eyes of monks of the day because of this reserve; but Athanasius wrote in his support, urging them to obey Basil, considering his intent and purpose (*oikonomia*).[235] Basil himself referred to our frequent inabilities to see "the economies of God" in life, events which in the wisdom of "God who administers all things" may turn out differently from the way we suppose.[236] Thus, there arose the notion of "economical conduct," on the part of church leaders or even Christ or God, when something is done for the sake of the economy, i.e., God's plan, salvation, for a purpose not discerned at the moment. Numerous examples could be cited of what amounts to "condescension" or "economical conduct," when someone acts in an accommodating fashion or arranges a matter economically.[237]

Of particular interest is the way the church fathers apply this notion to certain events or statements in Scripture. A famous example concerns the quarrel Peter and Paul had at Antioch (Galatians 2); some church fathers claim it was a sham fight, staged to flush out the Judaizers, the opponents of Paul and the gospel in Galatia.[238] Chrysostom similarly explains Paul's conduct in Acts 21:20-21, when he joins in a Nazirite vow at the temple; according to Chrysostom, the apostle "judaized because he was compelled to condescend, but not from his real opinion, but what happened was 'by arrangement.' "[239] The same father has a list of passages where God or Christ says something, not out of ignorance, but "arranging things fittingly"—e.g., Gen. 3:9, to Adam, "Where are you?"; Gen. 18:20-21, "I will go down to see what's going on at Sodom and Gomorrah"; John 21:15, "Simon Peter, do you love me?"; John 11:34, when Jesus asks where Lazarus had been buried; Luke 20:13, the owner of the vineyard (God) said, "What shall I do?"; and that passage on which many fathers comment, Matt. 24:36, about Jesus' supposed ignorance of the date of the parousia, "Of that day and hour no one knows. . . ."[240] As John of Damascus remarked, "Even though Jesus very often conducted himself in an accommodating fashion, he was not ignorant of the time."[241] One final citation from Photius illustrates the technique: Christ employed "the method of philanthropic providence," assuming ignorance out of an economy, rather than teach his disciples something it was not expedient for them to learn as yet.[242]

Our final suggestion, therefore, is to ask whether a great deal of the seeming acceptance in the Bible of customs and cultures of the day ought not be explained as an accommodation, by Christ and God, to the situation then, especially involving women and their roles. If the church fathers had shared the view of the Vatican "Declaration" that "discrimination based on sex" is "contrary to God's plan," I am sure they would have explained apparent instances of discrimination in the Scriptures as things allowed to happen "economically," "by arrangement," under the *oikonomia* of God.

As to the fact that Jesus chose 12, all males, to spread his message, social conditions could hardly have allowed it to be otherwise in Jewish Palestine. No rabbi, no prophet, no charismatic could do otherwise and expect a hearing. The wonder is that Jesus did as much as the Gospels record in expressing his "different attitude toward women." It is similar with the fact Jesus was male. Could the one who was to fulfill messianic promises be otherwise? And did not the Davidic line of rulers necessarily envision a coming king, rather than a future queen? As for the incarnation itself, the patristic emphasis is upon "becoming flesh" (*ensarkos oikonomia*), not on "becoming male." *Enanthrōpēsis* means becoming human, not specifically "being masculine" as over against "female." The *oikonomia* or incarnation here involved refers to Christ's human nature, in contrast to his *theologia* or divine nature.

Our final suggestion thus implies that God, in revealing the divine will regarding the sexes, did so most clearly at creation prior to the fall (Genesis 1–2) and in the incarnate ministry of Jesus Christ and its immediate impact in the early church. At many other points this will was subject to the necessary cultural, social patterns of the times, i.e., to patriarchy. That ancient Israel rejected much of a role for women in worship because of nature-god rites in surrounding civilizations; that Jesus was male; that his message was spread publicly primarily by men, including 12 he chose during his lifetime—all these and many other details are part of the economy in the sense of God's condescending and accommodating the divine self to the modes of the time. They are no more determinative for future structures in Ministry than the use of Hebrew and Aramaic or the wearing of sandals and beards. Neither circumcision nor uncircumcision, neither being a free citizen nor a slave, neither maleness nor femaleness is determinative, but being in Christ (Gal. 3:28; 1 Cor. 7:19-24).

Chrysostom has a comment on the Canaanite woman in Matt. 15:22 who says to Jesus, "Have mercy on me, O Lord, son of David." This woman, he wrote, "is a preacher of the gospel (*euangelistria*), she is confessing both the divinity and the economy (*oikonomia*)" of Christ, that is, his deity and incarnation, as Chrysostom explains, "the assumption of flesh."[243]

It took some years for other non-Jews like this Syro-Phoenician to be recognized as valid ministers of the gospel, and that battle may not yet be fully won for racial minorities in some churches. It took 18 centuries more for many Christians, including those in the United States, to transcend the ancient socio-cultural distinctions between slaves and freeborn persons. Some of the ancient patterns of subordination to the state (cf. Romans 13) are still being worked through, but for Catholics, the Second Vatican Council has brought freedom of conscience and democracy to the fore in ways not previously recognized.[244]

And now, in this decade, the social, cultural milieu, at least in the United States and Europe, has brought the question of the place of women in society and church to our agenda as never before. The Vatican "Declaration" rightly recognizes the fuller rights of women based on God's plan, and a resulting equality. The question before all the churches is the extent to which the official Ministries of women shall now be recognized. They already have ministering functions; they are proving ready and capable of far more, in all churches. The challenge is to recognize and order the phenomena.

The argument above is that the biblical data give us encouragement to proceed; the argument from the economy of God offers an opening through seeming barriers about ordination. The Lutheran experience is positive testimony to the rightness of the step that we should ordain, support, learn with and from, and help women to grow, even as we are helped by them, to all grow together in the oneness of that new humanity which is the church of Jesus Christ (Eph. 2:15). We are challenged to implement more of the impact of our own gospel, that in Christ God's original will is being restored for humankind.

SUPPLEMENTARY COMMENTS

The outcome of the study that makes up Part A of this chapter has already been recounted. My essay, as part of the Division of Theological Studies process, had effects first within the Lutheran Council in the U.S.A. (see the Introduction to this book). It helped show there are no conclusive grounds in Scripture against ordaining women, a decisive matter for Lutherans in deciding such an issue. The view that women could be ordained prevailed, though challenged by Missouri Synod representatives at a DTS consultation, on the grounds of the "orders of creation." The DTS position held up within the Council, indeed was received with enthusiasm, at its annual meeting. Eventually, however, this exegetical finding and its implications became a dividing line between the Lutheran Church–Missouri Synod and other Lutheran bodies in the Council (see above, Part B, III).

The essay, secondly, played some role, as part of the LCUSA study, in gaining convention approval in the LCA and ALC and a smooth transition in those bodies to having *persons* in the ordained ministry and not just men, as described in B, III, and the Introduction chapter. The AELC, when formed, took a similar position. The Evangelical Lutheran Church in America, without any real questioning of the practice, begins its life with ordained women and will continue ordaining qualified persons.

This common stance of ALC, LCA, and AELC on the ordination of women has also played a role in their reactions ecumenically, as to the *BEM* statement (see Chap. 5). Each church has vigorously affirmed commitment to this step.

The deleterious impact of the ordination of women by the ALC on its relationship with the Missouri Synod (one of "fellowship," declared at the 1969 LCMS convention) can be seen, however, in the 1972 report of the ALC Inter-Church Relations Committee. The ordination-of-women issue was made the "special concern" that caused Missouri to defer further implementation of fellowship in 1971. When the ALC was asked to "reconsider" its action, the President of that body, Dr. Kent S. Knutson, asked all three seminary faculties of the ALC to respond on two questions:

(1) Do you find that the Scriptures forbid the ordination or service of women in the ministry of Word and sacrament?
(2) Do you find in the Scriptures, orders of creation which enunciate a principle of women being subordinate to men which then pertains directly to the role women should serve in the ministry?

The faculties of Luther, Wartburg, and Columbus answered no on each count. Their reports plus papers by Joseph A. Burgess on "What Do the Scriptures Say . . .?" and by Duane A. Priebe on the *kephalē* principle, headship and the orders of creation, are found in the *1972 Reports and Actions, Sixth General Convention of The American Lutheran Church,* Minneapolis, pp. 459-60, 465-86. Eventually the LCMS relationship with the ALC became suspended—fellowship in protest—and then ended. The 1986 LCMS convention reaffirmed its rejection of women's ordination, but also reiterated its decision to allow women to vote and to hold certain offices (78% of LCMS congregations permit women to vote in congregational assemblies).

Part B of the chapter, of course, proves harder to assess in influence. For those present at Villanova or who read the paper, its arguments have probably contributed to the overall case in their minds for ordaining women. Leopold Sabourin, s.j., in a survey on "Questions of Christian Priesthood," featured the two articles in moving toward the conclusion that "women cannot be barred from ordination for reasons based on divine law" (*Religious Studies Bulletin* [University of Sudbury, Canada] 2,1 [January 1982]: 11-14). My argument invoking "the economy" has, of course, not been put into play, but in churches that hold firmly to the traditional arguments for a male priesthood it is perhaps the only line along which accommodation could be sought with those churches that do accept both genders into their clergy. Some churches might not wish to ordain women for themselves but could relate to churches that do *kat' oikonomian.*

The literature on the ordination of women has, if anything, grown over the years since 1969, and while Part B updates bibliography till 1977, the past decade has not seen much abatement in the flow of books and articles. Often, however, in this period the ordination issue has become related to the role of women generally in the church, the feminist movement, and "inclusive language." On ordination as an issue, Lutherans in America have not felt much need to continue writing, for the issue is deemed settled (in LCMS as well as in those churches that do ordain "persons"). Opponents go underground. Arguments pro and con are probably less widely known than 15 to 20 years ago. Nonetheless, we may cite some pertinent items.

One exception among Lutherans is the book by Walter Freitag, *The Ordination of Women: Challenge for Canadian Lutheran Unity* (privately printed, Saskatoon, Canada). In a pending all-Lutheran merger things came apart between the Missouri Synod districts in Canada and the other Lutheran groups (LCA and The Evangelical Lutheran Church of Canada, a denomination developed from the ALC north of the border) especially over the ordination-of-women issue. Professor Freitag, a New Testament scholar, came to a different conclusion than he expected when he began his work, for he stated at the end, "The answer has to be affirmative" (p. 103). His "epilog" (pp. 106-13) helps one to see how the formation of the Evangelical Lutheran Church in Canada took place eventually without Missouri, especially because of the issue that helped cause a split in the United States also.

Missourian debate is reflected in the position papers on "The Question of the Ordination of Women" by Theodore Jungkuntz (con) and Walter E. Keller (pro) in *The Cresset* (Valparaiso University, Indiana) 42/2 (December 1978): 16-20, and 42/3 (January 1979): 16-19 (subsequently reprinted). In the same journal 45/2 (December 1981): 29-30, Stephen B. Clark reviewed Paul Jewett's *The Ordination of Women*, and Richard John Neuhaus reviewed Clark's *Man and Woman in Christ* (44/5 [March 1981]: 24-31), warning that, since "only a male can symbolically represent Christ," the church today "continues to slide into a parody of its mission" (p. 31).

The 10th anniversary of women's ordination in the LCA and ALC in 1980 provided an occasion for some further assessment. In that year the LCA reported 165 women clergy on its roll of ordained ministers (out of 6,876 active clergy). Eighty were "solo" pastors, 18 worked with husbands in team ministry, 15 were associate pastors, 9 assistants. Two were on seminary faculties in Philadelphia and Chicago. One was retired, 10 awaiting new calls or on leave. Seventy-one were married, though others were widowed or divorced. Because of family schedules, part-time ministry was the choice of some, especially when raising children. In that same year the ALC had 61 women clergy. For comparison: the Episcopal Church (since 1977) had ordained 286 women; the United Methodist Church had 1,082 women clergy; the United Church of Christ, 600; statistics in *The Lutheran* 18, 22 (December 17, 1980): 10-12.

At a 1985 conference at Stony Point, New York, marking the 15th anniversary of the first ordinations of women by American Lutherans, the three churches so doing were able to report a total of 664 active ordained women, 4.8% of all active clergy. The percentage was highest in the LCA (408 women, 5.8%). But women, the statistics show, wait longer for first call, are more likely to go as assistants or to places other than congregations, and to smaller congregations (LCUSA press release 85-40, 11/4/85). Figures for 1986 are 426 ordained women in the LCA, 249 in the ALC, and 30 AELC, for a total of 705 (LCUSA press release 86-31, July 30, 1986). For the LCA in June 1987, the figure rose to 510 ordained women, 348 of whom were full-time pastors. On the average, 7% of those on the roll of active clergy in an LCA synod were women, 8 out of 30 synods being over 10%. The highest concentration of women clergy in the LCA were in the Northeast, Illinois, and Minnesota. The Upper New York Synod led the LCA in percentage of women clergy, 15% (25 out of 168) (LCA press release 7-20-87-15-DM-67).

An examination into what happened since the (Lutheran) Church of Sweden decided in 1958 to receive women into the priesthood—the first church with a claim to apostolic succession so to do—has been examined by Brita Stendahl (*The Force of Tradition: A Case Study of Women Priests in Sweden* [Philadelphia: Fortress, 1985]). The path has by no means been easy. Clear polarization resulted as High Churchmen and Evangelical biblicists joined together against women clergy. But women constitute by now one-tenth of the ordained, and have adjusted well to roles and duties; Mrs. Stendahl sees "tradition" as also a force *for* change and an increasingly lay leadership as a hope for a new vision of the church (pp. 121-24).

Statistically, more countries and churches have approved the ordination of women as the years went by. The Church of Finland, for example, did so in 1986, after 30 years of debate; a hundred qualified women are expected to apply in 1988 when the law takes effect. Some European Lutheran churches have in 1986 moved to ordain women *prior to* their receiving a congregational call (an unusual practice in Lutheranism) because placement is often slow for women. But the large Evangelical Lutheran Church in Tanzania is typical of a number of churches that have not yet approved women pastors. On the other hand, women sometimes find new acceptance when ordained, as did the Rev. Janice M. Erickson-Pearson, of the LCA, in becoming "the first woman to celebrate the Eucharist in a Russian Orthodox church" (LCUSA press release 85-30, 7/24/1985).

Endless examples of this and that could be cited as cases within "the Lutheran experience." Objectively, church statements may be more important. The *Report from the LWF Workshop on "Women in the Ministries of the Church"* in 1983 (in the "LWF Studies" series, Geneva) does not so much have to argue for women's ordination but rather analyzes the situation where "most of the large Lutheran churches have decided to ordain women to the pastoral ministry during the last two decades" (p. 13). (The brief understanding of ministry which begins the report speaks of the "priestly ministry" of all believers, not clerical or cultic but ethical, and the "pastoral ministry" of the ordained, functionally understood.) Most of the document takes up factors like socialization and feminization that affect women in all sorts of church ministries and issues like leadership and power.

The way in which "the new practice of ordination of women is spreading in the Lutheran churches" was not overlooked in the international Lutheran-Roman Catholic dialogue. Together, both sides could speak of the church as "a society molded by God's recreating Spirit," in the form of a "community of men and women," who can both make "a specific contribution within the ministry of the people of God." But different answers are then given about women entering into ordained ministry, the answer yes usually for Lutherans, and no for Catholics (*The Ministry in the Church,* §21).

While Lutheran churches take a varied attitude, mostly in favor, an official document of the Roman Catholic church, *Inter Insigniores* ("Declaration on the Question of the Admission of Women to the Ministerial Priesthood"), from the Congregation for the Doctrine of the Faith in 1976, states unequivocally, "The Church, in fidelity to the example of the Lord, does not consider herself authorized to admit women to priestly ordination" (see above, n. 87, and below). Anyone in doubt about how difficult the ecumenical question is should read the supplementary study by Hervé Legrand and John Vikström on "Admission of Women to the Ministry" in *The Ministry of the Church,* pp. 88-107. The divergence, they write, "will continue for a long time," so each side must ask whether "its theological justification is irreversible." Lutherans too. In the unlikely possibility that Rome could change, the consensus of a universal council would be required, including "consultation with the Orthodox sister church" (p. 105).

Ecumenically, perhaps the most revealing overview comes from the pen of the Rev. Constance F. Parvey, an LCA pastor who served as director of the "Community of Women and Men in the Church" project for the World Council of Churches in Geneva. Her account, "Stir in the Ecumenical Movement: The Ordination of Women," appears in the Brita Stendahl book as an Appendix (pp. 139-74, 192-200). It must be remembered that the ecumenical movement long ago noted that "the right place of women in the church and in the councils of the Church is one of grave moment" (so at Lausanne, Faith and Order, 1927, where only 7 of some 400 delegates were women). But typical is the comment of William Temple, Archbishop of Canterbury to be, an advocate of women's rights: "reunion [of the churches] is more important" (p. 140).

The Parvey article traces attempts, after the early years, to find "the right place" for women and how by about 1970 their ordination began to be raised in discussions. Then came "the turbulent years." By 1975 some Roman Catholic theologians spoke favorably of the possibility of ordaining women, but *Inter Insigniores* sought to clamp down on such opinions. In various parts of the Anglican world women were beginning to be ordained as priests (1974 in the United States), but the Joint Orthodox–Anglican Consultation in 1976 concluded that "biblical, conciliar, patristic, and canonical evidence"—and that, "reflecting and protecting the order of creation"—"affirms that only men, and only some men, are eligible for the offices of priest and bishop" (p. 159). Among Conservative Evangelicals similar debates arose. In the Southern Baptist Convention a woman was ordained for the first time in 1964, but "ordination does not remove subordination," especially in practice (p. 164).

"Tradition and Equality in Confrontation" is the title given to the years since 1978. The WCC consultation at Klingenthal, France, in 1979, on "Ordination of Women in Ecumenical Perspective," gives some insight into how, very gingerly, the maleness of the historical Jesus is to be related to the incarnation and the eternal high priesthood of Christ and the gender of clergy. The Sheffield consultation in 1981 not only asked whether churches could not be "in Communion with each other when they have different policies with regard to the ordination of women" but stirred up a hornets' nest by asking how "fundamental human rights" relate "to the calling of women and men to the ordained ministry" and that 50% of elected members in WCC subunits and committees be women (cf. Constance F. Parvey, editor, *The Community of Women and Men in the Church: The Sheffield Report* [Philadelphia: Fortress, 1983]). One could anticipate that the Faith and Order statement on Ministry at Lima in 1982 would not avoid mentioning women's ordination, but scarcely could expect to achieve much agreement.

The analysis by Constance Parvey concludes that, while obviously more women are now involved in ecumenical leadership and the churches are openly discussing women's ordination, none of this has brought unity endeavors to an end. Indeed, in the years since 1958 when the Church of Sweden and the Church of England differed over women priests, they have nonetheless managed to remain in communion. The issue did not prevent church unions in South and North India (though temporary compromise was necessary by Methodists in joining the CSI, for they had to give up ordaining women to fit Anglican practice then); today both united churches in India do ordain women. (This listing seems to me to pass over too easily the disruption *within* a church like the Episcopal Church or within a denominational family, like U.S. Lutherans, that has occurred.) The dialogue has come a long way since Karl Barth at the WCC's Amsterdam Assembly in 1954 stressed the importance of the tradition that women be subordinate to males (pp. 141, 173). But there are many vexing questions still unresolved over "equal partnership versus male hierarchy" (really an issue of authority). If one regards male hierarchy as "truth," can there ever be unity with those who do not? If an egalitarian community and women ministers are part of "truth," can it be sacrificed for Christian unity? So the debate goes on, ecumenically and in almost all churches.

For a briefer, even more recent overview, see Shannon Clarkson's article, "Steps Toward Unity—A Mutual Recognition of Ordained Ministries," in the *Journal of Ecumenical Studies* 23 (1986): 489-91, and, of broader scope, "The Graymoor Papers VII—Women and Religion: Scripture-Tradition-Institution," in the same journal, 20 (1983): 531-84.

For Roman Catholic discussion, see *Women Priests: A Catholic Commentary on the Vatican Declaration,* ed. Leonard Swidler and Arlene Swidler (New York: Paulist, 1977), where the English text of *Inter Insigniores* is printed with some 46 critical commentaries on it. Reflective also of pro-ordination sentiments are *Women and Priesthood: Future Directions, A Call to Dialogue from the Faculty of the Catholic Theological Union at Chicago,* ed. Carroll Stuhlmueller (Collegeville, Minn.: Liturgical Press, 1978); and *Women, Ministry and the Church,* by Joan Chittister (Ramsey: Paulist, 1983), where the vision is of women in the diaconate.

The agony of Anglicans over the question may be seen in *The Ordination of Women: Pro and Con,* ed. Michael P. Hamilton and Nancy S. Montgomery (New York: Morehouse-Barlow, 1975); it includes articles by persons involved in the first ordinations in Philadelphia, on July 29 (Sts. Mary and Martha Feastday), 1974. The case against women in ministry is put by the essays in *Man, Woman, and Priesthood,* ed. Peter Moore (London: SPCK, 1978); Bertil E. Gärtner and another Swedish Lutheran there paint a picture, in what they term "very dark and frightening colours," of "The Experience of the Church of Sweden" since women were ordained (pp. 123-33), though they are not without hope, as "loyal opposition," of reversing the situation.

Noteworthy among treatments of the issue in Protestantism is *Presbyterian Women in America: Two Centuries of a Quest for Status,* by Louis A. Boyd and R. Douglas Brackenridge (Westport, Conn.: Greenwood Press, 1983). In the United Presbyterian Church, which voted to ordain women in 1956, the number rose slowly to just over 160 in 1975 but by 1985 was over 1000. Between 1956 and 1977 Methodists and National Baptists and Southern Baptists, among large bodies, shifted their position, allowing women to be ordained.

Some of the best recent discussion has taken place in Conservative Evangelical circles. The most able of the negative volumes may be Stephen B. Clark's *Man and Woman in Christ: An Examination of the Roles of Men and Women in Light of Scripture and the Social Sciences* (Ann Arbor: Servant Books, 1980). For a positive response, see *The Ordination of Women: An*

Essay on the Office of Christian Ministry, by Paul K. Jewett, of Fuller Theological Seminary (Grand Rapids: Eerdmans, 1980), or *Women, Authority, and the Bible,* ed. Alvera Mickelsen (Downers Grove, Ill.: InterVarsity Press, 1986). Parvey cites as a recent example of a switch in position Kenneth S. Kantzer ("Proceed with Care," in *Christianity Today* 30, 14 [October 3, 1986]: 14-I to 15-I). From an earlier view that in a family the husband is "chairman of a committee of two," he now holds "that the subservience of women is part of the curse from which the gospel seeks to free us." In his words, "For centuries the church has allowed its view to be warped by the society around it."

The Eastern Orthodox position against other than males in ministry has been reiterated in *Women and the Priesthood,* ed. Thomas Hopko (Crestwood, N.Y.: St. Vladimir's Seminary Press, 1983).

Changes in image that have developed as women entered the ordained ministry are analyzed in *Women of the Cloth: A New Opportunity for the Churches,* by Jackson W. Carroll, Barbara Hargrove, and Adair T. Lummis (San Francisco: Harper and Row, 1983). The good news, they say, is about women meeting with acceptance and functioning well in ministry; but along with the "milk and honey" of the "promised land" goes bad news too: there are still "giants to be met," in placement, or acceptance in rural areas and small towns. Further, see Judith Weidman, *Women Ministers: How Women Are Redefining Their Roles* (New York: Harper and Row, 1981) and Edward C. Lehman Jr., *Women Clergy: Breaking Through Gender Barriers* (New Brunswick: Transaction Books, 1985).

In the extensive exegetical literature since 1978 I reckon Elisabeth Schüssler Fiorenza's book *In Memory of Her: A Feminist Theological Reconstruction of Christian Origins* (New York: Crossroad, 1983) to be the most significant volume, backed as it now is by the hermeneutical undergirdings in her *Bread Not Stone: The Challenge of Feminist Biblical Interpretation* (Boston: Beacon Press, 1984). Compare the detailed reactions in *Religious Studies Review* 11 (1985): 1-9 and 12 (1986): 197-202. The review article in *RSR* 11 (1985): 217-23 by Barbara Hilkert Andolsen on "Gender and Sex Roles in Recent Religious Ethics Literature" shows how the ordination question (see her bibliography) is now related to (and takes a back seat to) a host of other issues.

A minor point: on consecrated sisters in the Lutheran churches in America, to whom my articles made passing reference, as in B. III, above, see Frederick S. Weiser's *1884–1984: To Serve the Lord and His People, Celebrating the Heritage of a Century of Lutheran Deaconesses in America* (Gladwyn, Pa.: The Deaconess Community of the Lutheran Church in America, 1984). This book updates his earlier and broader portrait, *Love's Response: A Story of Lutheran Deaconesses in America* (Philadelphia: LCA Board of Publication, 1962). The deaconesses have in the 1980s developed a clearer perspective of their identity in various serving roles within the church, a role that does not call for ordination or even the making of "deaconess" a "minor order" in the ordained ministry. See Weiser's *1884–1984*, pp. 20-24, on, as it was termed in an issue paper, "The Crisis in the Diaconate," and its resolution (DPL report to the 1978 LCA Convention, *Minutes*, pp. 292-310).

The future issues for discussion growing out of the ordination of women in so many Lutheran and other churches are obvious: deepened re-examination of the reasons, pro and con; once women can be ordained, to provide proper opportunities for their talents, including initial placement and upward mobility, where recognition often lags; healing of tensions within a church and between churches over the issues; and, above all, continued ecumenical consideration of how there can be a meeting of minds, practices, and persons here.

3

The Title *Bishop*

Along with how one understands the ordained Ministry within the ministering of the whole people of God (Chapter 1) and the question of whether women may be ordained to the Ministry of Word and Sacraments (Chapter 2) has also come—and increasingly in recent years among American Lutherans—the question of the title and role of the person who is the focal point of leadership in a church within a particular geographical area. Shall the clergyperson, usually of considerable experience and maturity, who is chosen to lead the church as a whole in a region that includes dozens or hundreds of congregations or in an entire nation be called "president" or "bishop"?

Lutherans in the United States and Canada regularly used the former term until 1970. Then the American Lutheran Church voted to employ the titles *bishop* and *supervising bishop,* but without making formal constitutional changes in nomenclature. A similar proposal in the Lutheran Church in America, made in 1970, failed at conventions in 1972 and 1974 to obtain the necessary two-thirds vote of approval by delegates. The 1978 convention approved the title *bishop* at a first reading, decisive action to be taken at the 1980 convention in Seattle.

To aid delegates to the 1980 convention, a paper was requested, analyzing the issue, pro and con. It was printed as "A Further Report on the Title and Office of Bishop in the Lutheran Church in America" in the Convention Workbook of the Tenth Biennial Convention of the LCA, Section L, pp. L-15 through L-27. The convention voted the change in terminology by a count of 464 to 177 (more than 72%, 428 votes required). The report was included in the 1980 *Minutes,* pp. 685-96 and was also separately published by the LCA Division for Professional Leadership in 1980, with a Preface by Dr. Lloyd E. Sheneman, Executive Director of DPL. The first part of the paper is necessarily concerned with parliamentary background and the rest with historical, biblical, and other data.

I. Background and Actions in the Lutheran Church in America

The Report of the Commission on the Comprehensive Study of the Doctrine of the Ministry recommended to the 1970 convention of the Lutheran Church in America that the church look with favor on changing the title of Synod President to Bishop, and that the Executive Council be instructed to take the necessary steps toward the adoption of the title and to define the duties of the office resulting from that change (1970 *Lutheran Church in America Minutes* [= *LCAM*], Fifth Biennial Convention, Minneapolis, p. 440).

The 1970 convention, which approved the ordination of women among other items in the report, referred to the Executive Council for consideration and action [this] and other matters on which, because of time limitations, "the convention was unable to take final action" (1970 *LCAM*, p. 649). The Executive Council then appointed a committee of five to study the recommendation.

The Report of the Committee to Study the Office of Bishop, dated December 30, 1970 (published separately and in the 1972 *LCAM*, pp. 183-88), viewed the matter of "how the question comes before us" not simply as a Commission recommendation but as a reflection of concern for "pastoral oversight" in contrast to "too large a component of organizational and promotional responsibilities" on the part of synodical presidents, as reflecting need for local congregational awareness of "the larger church," and as a reflection of ecumenical involvements: the Lutheran World Federation had recently completed a survey volume, *Episcopacy in the Lutheran Church?* (cited below, note 4); the Consultation on Church Unity envisioned use of the title *bishop* in a united church; and Roman Catholic dialogue was deemed to make the question pertinent also.

The 1970 Report distinguished three types of issues involved (actually, four are then listed):

(1) *utility*—the committee considered the title helpful for "effectiveness of the church's witness" and for "pastoral connotations";

(2) *interpretation* which people would make *of the change*—it might appear trivial to some and counter to greater participation by members in church governance, but, on the other hand, to others, quite positive in terms of better religious identification;

(3) *historically, why now?* Here the answer was given that the contemporary situation no longer is counterpart to past reactions against experiences with state churches in Europe or with one-time Anglican-Lutheran competition for Lutheran immigrants—"even though we would not be able to accept the full implications of that title (bishop) as affirmed by the Anglican church."

(4) The inclusion of the Orthodox churches and the Roman Catholic church in *ecumenism* suggests it would be simpler if Lutheran counterparts were designated "bishops," while at the same time definition and distinction of the concept in the Lutheran view would be necessitated.

In setting forth therefore "A Lutheran Concept of the Office of Bishop," the Report, against the background of the 1970 Commission Report, affirmed the office of the ministry as "representative" and "official," as one of Word and sacraments, certified by the believing community; it then regarded "the bishop of a synod . . . as a special instance of the office of pastor," though not necessarily located in a specific church as its chief pastor. The ordained clergyperson who is elected as bishop is thus "certified" for this particular ministry by the elective process involved. Generally, it was said, there is "agreement between definitions of functions for the presidents of synod and those which are implied in the term bishop," but the Report urged emphasis on being "a pastor to pastors" and on "congregational contacts . . . on a more regular basis." The change in nomenclature would not imply for a bishop, it was stated, any "grant of authority transmitted through historical episcopacy," any increased power in assigning pastors, or "tenure in office except for the period covered by the election." A bishop "should have deep concern for . . . preaching and teaching," but responsibility for determining what is "faithful preaching does not inhere uniquely" in his office, for he shares that "responsibility with others who also enjoy the confidence of the church, such as Biblical and theological experts and dedicated and competent laymen."

In urging changes in the official documents, the Report insisted that "change in title . . . must be accompanied by the removal of certain other duties from the president's responsibility," in synods and for the president of the church, so that the "administrative or managerial" might be separated from the greater, hoped-for pastoral concern. As title for the LCA president, "presiding bishop" or "bishop of the church" might be used.

The Conference of Synodical Presidents observed at its February 1971, meeting that change of the title would not change the church's polity; "'supervision' of congregations and ministers has both biblically and historically been an integral part of the responsibility of bishops," and "it would be unrealistic for the congregations and ministers of the LCA to expect any unusual expansion of the pastoral functions of the synodical president merely because of the change of title" (1972 *LCAM*, p. 188).

The Executive Council then voted to "concur with the Conference of Synodical Presidents in regard to favoring the title of bishop as a substitute for the title of president of a synod" and to "look with favor on . . . presiding bishop for the . . . president of the church" (ibid.). Proposals for constitutional changes were accordingly drawn up (pp. 357-59).

At the 1972 convention these recommendations of the Executive Council for amendments to the LCA Constitution, first reading, were moved and voted upon. A two-thirds vote was required to pass them. The result was 286 in favor, 218 against (57% affirmative; 1972 *LCAM*, p. 734).

At the 1974 convention, memorials to reconsider the question were received from the Pacific Southwest and Upper New York Synods (1974 *LCAM*, p. 49). Under the report of the Executive Council the 1972 proposed amendments (changed only as necessitated by other amendments) were presented for approval, as first reading. (Technically, the amendments had been introduced to the convention by signatures from the required number of delegates and presented then by the Executive Council.) The vote on Article VI, Section 5 of the Constitution, to change "president of the synod" to "bishop of the synod," received 321 yes votes, 300 no (52% affirmative; two-thirds needed) (1974 *LCAM*, pp. 364-66, 581-82). A motion at the Tuesday morning session to reconsider the Monday afternoon vote lost (p. 680).

At the 1978 convention a memorial from the Michigan Synod to reconsider changing "president" to "bishop" was received as information, since "the only way to introduce the title . . . is through the process of amendment to the LCA Constitution" (1978 *LCAM*, pp. 60-61, 104). Proposals so to amend were received from the required number of delegates and the matter was referred to the Executive Council (p. 112), which presented to the convention the proposed amendments to make the change. An Executive Council motion to delete "presiding" before "bishop of this church" was adopted, and then all the amendments were approved (first action) (p. 314).

It is in this form (1978 *LCAM*, pp. 311-13) that the matter concerning "bishop of the synod" and "bishop of the church" (the LCA) will be before the 1980 convention for second and final action.

Arguments as presented at the 1978 convention included:

pro—increasing use by Lutherans, including the ALC;

    ecclesial significance among churches and the general public;

con—Lutherans when they came to America intentionally used other terms;

    the title implies earthly power, pomp, elaborate liturgies.

It was agreed by all that unlimited power over clergy placement and life-long tenure for the bishop are not involved, and that the powers to ordain and make parish visitations already belong to synodical presidents (p. 314).

If the 1980 convention acts favorably on the second reading of the nomenclature changes before it in the Constitution, similar changes will have to be made in due time in Bylaws, synodical constitutions, and the Approved Constitution for Congregations. If the 1980 convention fails to approve the changes by a two-thirds vote, the matter drops until such time as it is again proposed. An alternative is to introduce less-than-official use, possibly for a specified trial period, such as The American Lutheran Church did in 1970 (see below).

II. Actions in Other Lutheran Churches

1. At the 1970 convention in San Antonio of The American Lutheran Church the report of the then-retiring President, the Rev. Dr. Fredrik A. Schiotz, noting that the Southwestern Minnesota District had several times requested

consideration for the title *bishop* for the president of the church and for district presidents, commented favorably on the proposed change. Dr. Schiotz called it "biblical" rather than "secular" nomenclature; it "identifies the person as a servant of the church rather than some industrial corporation" (1970 ALC Reports and Actions, pp. 141-42).

Upon recommendation of the general convention committee it was voted to "encourage" use of the terms *bishop* and *supervising bishop* "both formally and informally" and to submit future Constitution and Bylaw changes to reflect the practice "when the practice is sufficiently accepted to warrant such change" (p. 145).

At the 1972 convention a memorial from its Southern District asked The American Lutheran Church "to consider adopting officially" the titles. The Church Council recommended that the trial period using the title be continued, "except in the Handbook, or in legal documents" (1972 Reports and Actions, pp. 661-62). An amendment from the convention floor to delete reference to "the trial period" (so that the use would simply continue) was defeated, and the Council recommendation was adopted (p. 921).

The reasons cited in The American Lutheran Church action of 1970 refer to the biblical and long historical usage of the term, the practice in other Christian bodies, and the aspect of ecclesiastical identification, plus the fact that titles are not "of the essence of the doctrines of the Lutheran Church"; adoption does not imply, it was stated, "support for the concept of apostolic succession or life-long tenure in the office" (1970, p. 145).

2. The issue has not been before the Lutheran Church–Missouri Synod in the last decade.

3. The Association of Evangelical Lutheran Churches uses the title *bishop* in some cases for the presidents of its regional synods.

4. Of other Lutheran church bodies in North America, only the Estonian Evangelical Lutheran Church lists a "bishop" instead of a "president" (1980 *LCA Yearbook*, p. 65).

5. Statistics for world Lutheranism are misleading, because one is often comparing quite small churches with very large ones, but a brief perusal of "Lutheran Churches of the World: A Handbook," by E. Theodore Bachmann (in *Lutheran World* 24, 2-3 [1977]) reveals the following statistics (some necessary interpretative comments follow):

Lutheran churches in	*using "President"*	*"Bishop"*	*other titles*
Africa	16	7	6
Asia/Australasia	25	7	8
Europe	6	26	5
The Americas, except USA	19	1	9
Totals	66	41	28

a. For Africa, *president* appears in all churches of French-language background, Ethiopia, and many churches in South Africa. "Other" titles include *superintendent, Landespropst, dean, general secretary* (for a federation), and *chairman. Bishop* is the term in Tanzania and the Evangelical Lutheran Church in Southern Africa, among others. The figures above are misleading in that they include among the 16 using *president* small churches like Eritrea (7400 Lutherans) and Kenya (15,000), while Tanzania (758,000) and the ELC in Southern Africa (456,000), each with a bishop in 13 and 5 dioceses, respectively, are counted but once. Often the church today reflects nomenclature from the country whence its missionaries came; in Namibia, e.g., the Evangelical Lutheran Church in Southwest Africa (Rhenish Mission Church) of 115,000 members has a *president;* the Evangelical Lutheran Ovambokavango Church (244,000), a *bishop* (work initiated from Finland). The Lutheran Church in Liberia (of American missionary background) has shifted from *president* to *bishop.* With some exceptions, such comments on Africa apply to other parts of the world too.

b. Asia/Australasia—Other titles include *(general) superintendent, chairman,* and *ephorus* (Indonesia). *Bishop* appears in Malaysia-Singapore, Papua New Guinea, Jordan (1979), and some Indian churches. Generally in India (including the Andhra Church), Hong Kong, and Japan, *president* continues to be used.

c. In Europe *bishop* is overwhelmingly the title in the Federal Republic of Germany, the German Democratic Republic, Scandinavia, and eastern Europe. Each German *Landeskirche* is counted separately above, but each Scandinavian country only once. Denmark, Norway, and Iceland term one bishop *primate,* Sweden and Finland *archbishop.* Where *president* is used, the church may be a smaller one (e.g., Netherlands, 36,000). *Superintendent, dean,* and *senior pastor* also occur as titles.

d. The Americas—*President* has been the overwhelmingly common title in Latin America (and Canada). The only exception listed in 1977 was the 23,000-member Iglesia Luterana en Chile, a conservatively oriented body which arose out of the political tensions of 1973 and succeeding years; its one pastor is termed *bishop.* To that list one may add reports on usage of the title by a small number of moderates leaving the Missouri Synod–related Council of Lutheran Churches in Central America and Panama. The political climate in much of Latin America, as well as past history (where "the bishop" has often been seen allied with governmental forces of repression), is no doubt a factor in nomenclature; but note exceptions like Archbishop Dom Helder Camara of Recife, Brazil, as a different sort of example.

Conclusions: In world Lutheranism the trend toward the use of the title *bishop* exists but may not be so strong as some have suggested, certainly not in Latin America. The European churches, historically in Scandinavia and after 1918 in Germany, have regularly used the title with an evangelical understanding of the office. Mission churches tend to use the terminology of their parent bodies. But in ecumenical mergers (North and South India, for example) the tendency is to adopt the office of bishop, and neighboring Lutheran churches, even if not a part of the merger, may take up the name too (e.g., the Jeypore and Tamil Evangelical Lutheran Churches in India). Biblical influence is also one of many factors in Third World adoption of the office and title of bishop. No title other than *bishop* or *president* has much parlance today.

6. Examination of the rest of world Christianity would probably produce little of additional help in reaching a decision on the title. Roman Catholics, the Orthodox, and Anglicans, among others, use the term *bishop* in a traditional historical and doctrinal framework of governance. Many other groups, including Methodists, Moravians, Mennonites, and the Church of the Brethren employ it in a different sense. Especially if Pentecostal groups worldwide be counted, there are also large numbers of Christians who do not use *bishop* as a title. The figure is often given that two-thirds of world Christianity lives under some form of episcopacy.

III. Clarity on Terminology

The LCA proposal is for the title and office of bishop according to "a Lutheran concept" (1972 *LCAM,* pp. 185-87). The constitutional changes before the 1980 convention call for a change in nomenclature only, all other aspects continuing as they have been for the election and functions of a synod (or church) president. But in the extensive literature on the subject and discussion pro and con, certain terms have been used on which it is helpful to have clarity.

A. "Apostolic succession" refers for many to the view that the church's ministry derives from the original (12) apostles, in a continuing succession transmitted by ordination. The view has often been tied to the further assumption that bishops were the successors of the apostles, and therefore that clergy are validly and rightly ordained only when the act is performed by a bishop or bishops in apostolic succession.

Quite apart from historical questions which can be raised about the view, Lutherans have held that such succession through an unbroken line of bishops is unnecessary for a "valid" ministry of Word and sacraments. Faced at the Reformation with a choice between remaining within the validating structures of the medieval church and the gospel as they had come to understand God's good news on the basis of Scripture, they chose the latter, preserving, however, a continuity with the past in terms of the apostolic gospel and faith and the practice of having clergy (priests, presbyters, ministers) ordain clergy (at times also with the involvement of lay people in the believing community).

The Lutheran–Catholic dialogue in 1970, noting the historical facts of the 16th century, recognized the Lutheran way of structuring the Ministry without episcopal order as "consonant with apostolic teaching and practice." For "succession to the apostles" may, in the patristic period, have involved "succession in the episcopal office" *or* "doctrinal succession."[1] Lutherans can claim in Sweden an apostolic succession through bishops, but traditionally have made nothing of it. It is succession to the apostles' teaching which has been determinative in a confession for which the church is "the assembly of all believers among whom the gospel is preached in its purity and the holy sacraments are administered according to the Gospel" (Augsburg Confession, Article 7).

Therefore, in introducing the title and office of bishop, as proposed in the LCA, Lutherans are making no change in their characteristic understanding of "apostolic succession."

B. "The historic episcopate" is a term sometimes employed to suggest that bishops have been the time-honored, necessary, and, for some, only prior form of church governance; it is often added that such an episcopate is the pinnacle of a threefold order of ministry, i.e., deacon, priest, and bishop.

Again, there are historical problems with this view. The threefold ministry is a post–New Testament development. Each term—*bishop, priest,* and *deacon*—has had a history of its own. The episcopate as a system of church government has by no means been the only one, even in patristic times. The term *bishop* today covers a wide range of types of church leadership, legally, doctrinally, and in terms of style and methods. Even in any one church, such as the Roman Catholic or the Anglican communion, the meaning, power, and functioning of the office have varied over the years.

Moreover, Lutherans have been accustomed to speak of one office of the ministry, that of pastor,[2] and indeed the 1970 Report on the Office of Bishop places the proposed use of that title within the framework of the church's "official" and "representative" ministry.

Therefore it is important to be clear that in adding the title *bishop* to its present structures, the LCA, like other Lutherans who have employed it, is not assuming what some have claimed for the episcopate, namely, that it is divinely instituted as *the* method of church governance (to use traditional terms, *iuro divino,* "by divine law") or that it entails a threefold order of ministry.

IV. Arguments and Evidence in the Last Decade

A. Biblical

In many cases, as in The American Lutheran Church, appeal to biblical as opposed to secular nomenclature has been an important item in the discussion. While some have tended to read the New Testament evidence in light of later patristic practice[3] and others in view of particularly Lutheran questions,[4] the comparatively few relevant references in the New Testament ought to be heard in their own right.

1. Modern scholarship has taught us a great deal about "church order" in the New Testament, above all its tremendous variety.[5] One simply cannot speak of *the* New Testament way of structuring a church. Lutherans have always reflected this variety in later, practical situations and have refused to endorse exclusively episcopal, presbyterian, or congregational government. Without going into details, it has become apparent from biblical studies that the concept of apostle is one thing in Luke-Acts and another in Paul; that the term *elder (presbyteros)* for a Christian leader occurs only in Acts, James 5:14, 2 and 3 John, and the Pastoral Epistles, never in Paul's undisputed letters; that *priest* never occurs anywhere in the New Testament for Christian "clergy," that *diakonos* (literally "servant, minister") has a variety of senses and is used of both men and women, and that the type of church structures in Matthew's and John's communities differ from those of Paul or that which Luke knows of in Acts. How do bishops fit into this variety?

2. A word which has been brought to wider attention in the Lutheran–Episcopal Dialogue Report of 1973[6] is *episcopē*, meaning "visitation" (Luke 19:44, 1 Peter 2:12) and "(office or position of) oversight" (1 Tim. 3:1 is the significant reference; cf. also Acts 1:20).

The related noun *episkopos* ("overseer"; traditional rendering, "bishop") occurs five times. While the term has a long history in Greek usage for overseers or inspectors in all sorts of political and religious groups, a possible Semitic background has been pointed out in the Dead Sea scrolls: Qumran had an overseer or inspector *(mᵉbaqqer)*, a layman in some texts, a priest in others, who knew the Law and made decisions, doctrinally and administratively. Attractive as such a background is, caution is called for, since *episkopos* seems not to have been employed in Palestinian-Jewish Christianity; it makes its appearance in the Greek-speaking Hellenistic churches.[7] Christian use of *bishop* as a title is clearly taken from the world of the day, perhaps ad hoc from Greek usage.

3. Applied a single time to Christ as "Shepherd and Guardian *(episkopos)*" of our souls in 1 Peter 2:25, the noun seems to have its earliest New Testament occurrence for Christian leaders in Phil. 1:1 and then later in the Pastoral

Epistles. Acts 20:28 is harder to determine, when Paul addresses the elders *(presbyteroi)* of the church at Ephesus (Acts 20:17) as "guardians" (RSV; Greek *episkopoi*) placed by the Holy Spirit to "shepherd" or "pasture" the flock (church) of the Lord. The noun (note the plural) is as yet nontechnical, it is synonymous with "elders" and clearly pastoral in function.

Philippians 1:1 addresses "all the saints in Christ Jesus who are at Philippi with the bishops and deacons" *(episkopois kai diakonois;* RSV alternate reading, "overseers"). In spite of the heritage from the 1611 King James Bible to use "bishops" here and the tendency to see two groups of officials, some recent commentators incline to a rendering "overseers and attendants" and even toward seeing just one group, *"episkopoi*-who-are-persons-who-serve" (cf. Did. 15:1, 1 Clem. 42.4-5, and the Shepherd of Hermas, Visions 3.5.1), unless Paul himself added the words *kai diakonois* to emphasize the servant function of the overseers.[8] In any case, the overseers at Philippi were plural in number, not a "monarchical bishop" and likely equivalent to "elders" in Acts. They exemplify a way of fulfilling the leadership task which was always present in the Christian community (cf. 1 Thess. 5:12, "those who labor among you and are over you in the Lord and admonish you").

In the Pastoral Epistles, 1 Timothy 3 gives a list of rather minimal personal qualities which ought to characterize the *episkopos,* one who desires the "office of oversight" (3:1-7, including that he be "an apt teacher" and "able to manage his own household"), and another list to characterize the *diakonos* (3:8-14), but none on "elders" (cf. 5:17, 19, however). Some think that in these letters "elder" and "bishop" are used synonymously (cf. Titus 1:5 and 7). Titus 1:7 also provides a list of qualities for such a (presbyter-)bishop, including again ability to "give instruction in sound doctrine." The function of church leaders in presenting and defending the word of God against alternative views in church and world is here coming to the fore; bishops were to be a bulwark against heresy.[9]

4. The modest findings from these references indicate that there were *episkopoi* carrying out leadership functions in the New Testament church, functions of teaching, managing, admonishing, and generally serving in the life and mission of the church. From this background there arose in later times the concept of the single bishop in each community, standing in succession to the apostles, as a defender of orthodox Christian faith. Lutherans had traditionally been willing to see episcopacy as a fortuitous development in church history, though not automatically an unmixed blessing, and their reluctance to view episcopacy as willed by God according to the New Testament seems supported again and again by recent critical studies on the early church.

5. Before leaving the New Testament period it is probably worth observing that modern analysis by Roman Catholic scholars of the New Testament data underscores much of what has been said above. Though bishops have often

been spoken of as "the successors of the apostles," one can no longer assume that the original apostles "ordained" bishops to succeed them, precisely because of the lack of evidence for such a thing and the variety of views about apostleship in the New Testament and other early Christian literature,[10] plus the difference between the Lucan picture of "12 apostles" and the Pauline of a larger group of missionary apostles. The "functional succession" to tasks of these varied apostles was not simply and solely picked up by "bishops."[11]

The New Testament variety extends even to the sort of church community depicted in the Johannine literature where, according to some recent analyses, the Paraclete himself and the Beloved Disciple were the teachers of the group, there were no "bishops" and seemingly no apostles (except Christ) or even a ministry in the sense of "clergy." Only in time, when faced by false teachers and secession (those who "went out from us," 1 John 2:19) did Johannine Christianity eventually accept the pattern which had arisen elsewhere of presbyter-bishops.[12]

Awareness of such New Testament pluralism has always kept Lutherans from being too dogmatic about church order, yet they have always acknowledged that *episkopoi* were part of the New Testament church and have played an important, developing role in later church history.

B. Historical

A profound awareness of the realities of history has always marked Lutheran attitudes toward church order and governance. The Augsburg Confession, Article 28, goes into considerable detail about "the power of bishops," both as it has been "improperly confused" with temporal power and how it ought to be "a power and command of God to preach the Gospel, to forgive and retain sins, and to admonish and distribute the sacraments" (28, 5).

1. For the centuries between the New Testament era and the Reformation period, the Reformers were aware both of the rise of a particular form of bishop's office, the monarchical episcopate, together with the threefold order of ministry, and of the fact there often had been considerable variety in practices (i.e., the pattern in the writings of Ignatius of Antioch did not hold everywhere; Alexandria in particular long maintained a more collegiate type of church government; cf., e.g., the "Treatise on the Power and Primacy of the Pope," §§60-82). Such variations in the patristic period modern scholarship has often further underscored, and contemporary ecumenical dialogue has sometimes pointed to these variations to account for and to seek solutions for long-standing differences among churches by means of convergences today and recognition of the legitimate pluralism which has and may exist in the church.[13]

2. Where they could not simply carry over existing church structures as part of their conservative Reformation, Lutherans often have reflected in

church polity the political tenor of the land in which they lived. Thus, settlers in North America from Germany, Scandinavia, and elsewhere in Europe, in light of democratic practices here, generally have adopted the title *president* for the elected leader of a synod. Sometimes a German equivalent like *Praesis* was employed. In part this reflected, at least in the colonial period, objection to the very title *bishop* (and of the authority of Parliament) and reaction to experiences in the Old World. At times titles like *senior* were used (Henry Melchior Muhlenberg), *overseer* (Ministerium of Pennsylvania, 1750; next year, *president* or *overseer*), *provost* or *dean* (the Swedish mission on the Delaware).

In the Missouri Synod the unhappy experience with the Rev. Martin Stephan as "bishop" led to a strong reaction against the title and office. The Buffalo Synod, under the Rev. J. A. A. Grabau, used the titles *senior* and *superin-tendent,* and the Iowa Synod *president* or *senior,* in each case with bishoplike powers. The Church of Norway in America in 1849 wrote into its constitution that "so long as the Church has no bishop, the convention shall elect a Superintendent. . . ." Occasionally in the 19th century and since the 1930s there have been voices calling for the introduction of bishops.

Almost uniformly, however, the title *president* has prevailed, reminding Lutherans that all church organization is, as Luther put it, a "worldly thing," and that church unity does not require uniform polity (Augsburg Confession, Article 7).[14]

3. Both the current ecumenical dialogues and the celebration in 1980 of anniversaries for the Augsburg Confession and the *Book of Concord* have given Lutherans occasion to renew and reclaim the positions of their Refor-mation forebears. For example, in the Lutheran–Catholic dialogue, the joint statement in 1970 noted,

> the Lutheran confessions indicate a preference for retaining the traditional epis-copal order and discipline of the church (vol. 4, p. 15),

citing Augsburg Confession, Article 14, which states that a person must not publicly teach or preach or administer the sacraments in the church without being regularly called. That last phrase, in Latin *rite vocatus,* has even been interpreted to imply that the confessors at Augsburg meant to suggest, "rightly called and ordained by a bishop."[15] Lutherans, in their reflections on the 1970 statement, affirmed for their constituencies:

> The episcopal structure and polity of the Roman Catholic Church does not in itself constitute a problem for Lutherans. Indeed the Book of Concord itself affirms the desire of the Lutheran reformers to preserve, if possible, the episcopal polity that they had inherited from the past [cf. Apology 14, 1, 5]. As long as the ordained Ministry is retained, any form of polity which services the proclamation of the gospel is acceptable (vol. 4, p. 19).

A Lutheran essayist in the same dialogue, Arthur Carl Piepkorn, included as part of his description of the sacred ministry in the Lutheran confessions a "preference for episcopal polity" where bishops hold an authority under the gospel in the governance of the church (vol. 4, pp. 110, 116-17; cf. 212-13). Similar statements have been made in thae Lutheran–Episcopal dialogue.[16]

The net effect of recent historical studies, often in the context of ecumenical dialogue, has been to remind Lutherans of the reluctance with which the Reformation broke with episcopal structures for the sake of the gospel, and their willingness to allow for bishops who put themselves under the gospel and furthered its proclamation.

C. Ecumenical Dialogues and Relationships

The 1970 LCA Report emphasized the ecumenical factor in the case for use of the title *bishop*. In the last decade bilateral dialogues and other contacts have sometimes touched on the question of episcopacy.

1. Frequent reference has already been made to Lutherans and Catholics in Dialogue in the U.S.A., especially volume 4. Lutherans have here sought to show their dialogue partners how the choice was made in the 16th century between episcopal structures and the gospel, the ways in which Lutherans have retained and sometimes restored the office of bishop, and the Lutheran concern for an evangelical understanding of episcopacy and even of papacy (see vols. 5 and 6). The Catholic theologians in the dialogue have replied that, in their judgment, "despite the lack of episcopal succession, the Lutheran church by its devotion to gospel, creed, and sacrament has preserved a form of doctrinal apostolicity" and they see "no pervasive reason to deny the possibility of the Roman Catholic Church recognizing the validity" of "the eucharistic Ministry of the Lutheran churches." They add: "We would rejoice if episcopacy in apostolic succession, functioning as the effective sign of church unity, were acceptable to all; but we have envisioned a practical and immediate solution in a *de facto* situation where episcopacy is not yet seen in that light" (4, pp. 27, 32-33).

The international Joint Lutheran–Roman Catholic Study Commission report on "The Gospel and the Church" (1972), especially §§55-64, reflects many of the same views, without going further and specifically into the office of "bishop."[17]

In light of Lutheran–Catholic dialogue it may be said that LCA adoption of the title *bishop* would be consonant with the confessional heritage of Lutherans but of no direct value in the dialogue itself, except as Lutheran presidents meet with Catholic bishops, congregations, and audiences, as a means of ecclesiastical identity.

2. Lutheran–Episcopal dialogue in the U.S.A. has stressed *episcopē* (ov-

ersight) as a means, along with common confession of faith, of guarding the church's apostolicity; ". . . both the Anglican continuity of the episcopal order, and the Lutheran concentration on doctrine, have been means of preserving the apostolicity of the one church." The report admits that "the functional reality of *episcopē* is in flux in both our communions" and hopes for exploration together of "future common forms of ordered ministry and *episcopē*" *(Report,* pp. 20, 22, 24). Subsequent discussions, testing such agreements, have not as yet been publicly reported upon.

Anglican-Lutheran International Conversations[18] reported in 1972 on how *episcopē* or oversight in doctrine, ordination, and pastoral care has been exercised in each communion, sometimes for Lutherans episcopally, regularly so for Anglicans. Each communion is "open to new forms in which *episcopē* may find" appropriate expression.

Adoption of the title *bishop* would be a step toward commonality of nomenclature with Anglicans but not, it is clear, agreement on polity.

3. Lutheran–Reformed, Lutheran–Methodist, and Lutheran–Orthodox dialogues have not dealt with the topic of bishops to date.

4. The evaluation of all these dialogues as of 1976 by a special task force of Lutheran churches and agencies in the United States concluded generally that "positions taken by Lutherans in the various dialogues do not in any overt way contradict one another, but whether they are fully consistent in every sense would be hard to demonstrate"; this evaluation commented of the Episcopal dialogue, ". . . much more discussion will be needed to resolve the question of episcopal succession and of the threefold ministry."[19]

5. A major document in the area of ministry was the agreed statement completed by the Faith and Order Commission of the World Council of Churches in 1974. It views *episcopē* (oversight) and the presbyteral function of proclaiming the gospel as part of the overall *diakonia* (service) in the church. The sort of historical variety sketched above in the rise of the episcopacy is mentioned, without devaluing or diminishing, it is said, the importance of the historical episcopacy. Steps toward mutual recognition of ministries by churches with and without episcopal succession are suggested. Adoption of the title *bishop* is not mentioned as one of these steps, but recovery of "the fullness of the *sign* of apostolic succession," i.e., episcopal succession, is listed as part of full unity.[20]

The LCA's response (in 1978 *LCAM,* p. 761) states the traditional Lutheran view that there is "no need to consider recovering what is referred to in paragraph 104 [the one cited above] as 'the fullness of the sign of apostolic succession,'" for "the primary manifestation of apostolic succession" occurs "in the life of the Church as a whole" and "as a succession in the apostolic gospel and faith"; for "no human authority in the church, including bishops, are free from the temptations of heresy and apostacy" (Augsburg Confession 28).

6. The Plan of Union[21] for the "Churches of Christ Uniting (COCU) in the U.S.A." envisions a threefold pattern of ministry—bishop, presbyter, deacon—but the terms are either not precisely defined or vary from traditional understandings of the threefold ministry.

In summary, the ecumenical discussions in themselves over the last decade cannot be said to have placed a demand on Lutherans to adopt the title *bishop*. Greater congruity in nomenclature would result with many churches, however, if Lutherans employed the term.

V. Conclusions

A survey of the past 10 years leaves the arguments pretty much where they have previously been, but does allow us to see the significance perhaps more clearly. Some pressures foreseen in 1970, such as ecumenical ties with COCU or Roman Catholics as an argument for the title, or fears about loss of democracy or increase of earthly pomp as arguments against it cannot be said to have proven more real in the past decade. Celebration of the U.S. bicentennial in 1976 scarcely heightened anyone's emotions over past feelings against "Old World episcopacy."

Lutherans remain free to adopt the title *bishop*, especially if they are clear what a Lutheran concept of episcopacy excludes, namely, lifelong tenure of office and title, new power in placing clergy not now given to synodical presidents, hierarchical status, ontological change, apostolic succession in the sense of transmission of grace by office from a chain of predecessors, or a threefold ministry and historic episcopate. LCA constitutional statements about synodical presidents still apply for proposed bishops.

Against the change stand the following points:

(1) more than two hundred years of American experience which has thus far rejected the title, often knowingly and deliberately;

(2) fear that the term, no matter how carefully powers are defined, will inevitably carry with it un-Lutheran concepts;

(3) awareness that having bishops has never necessarily meant greater efficiency, pastoral care of clergy and people, or fidelity to the gospel and sound preaching;

(4) the fear in a democratic society that the title will lead to a hierarchical structure and fewer (lay) persons involved in church decision-making;

(5) the feeling, possibly by some, that calling synodical presidents "bishops" would really not make them such in the Anglican or Roman Catholic sense, so "Why do it?"

For the title *bishop* are these factors:

(1) biblical background and long historical usage;

(2) the expectation it will identify a church leader more specifically as such to the world and to other churches, in a way *president* does not, while making Lutherans define more clearly what the office of leadership in the church is;

(3) the hope the title will convey an even greater pastoral concern to incumbents, though administrative tasks can scarcely be omitted or readily shifted from the work of a bishop;

(4) congruity at last with the term used by a majority of world Christians and a growing number of Lutheran churches;

(5) recovery of a Reformation hope or at least a view to which the confessions were open, of "our deep desire to maintain the church polity and various ranks of the ecclesiastical hierarchy, although they were created by human authority" (Apology 14, 1). For "true bishops . . . concerned about the church and the Gospel . . . might be permitted (for the sake of love and unity, but not of necessity) . . . provided this would be done without pretense, humbug, and unchristian ostentation" (Smalcald Articles 3, 10, 1).

In the anniversary year of 1980, the question may well be not "Why?" but "Why not?"[22]

SUPPLEMENTARY COMMENTS

This paper was part of an LCA debate, and so any influences are to be expected primarily within the Lutheran Church of America. My oral presentation to the convention at Seattle on July 1, 1980, highlighted the pros and cons in the report itself and sought to indicate how, in a time when the experience with women in the ordained ministry was already reshaping churches, Lutherans had the right to use this time-honored term *bishop,* which has so many senses, but to give it the meaning they wished. The authority of the office would be what conventions grant to it. One must distinguish between democratic process (which we affirm in the church) and democratic titles (which we do not necessarily employ, for we speak of the "royal priesthood" and "the pastor"). Decisive in the voting is not just what I (or any theologian) thinks or what the president of this church fears but what delegates believe the Augsburg Confession and other standards say.

The discussion from the floor touched on many of the arguments from both sides. Some noted the scriptural and confessional evidence and invoked the pastoral image that the term would bring and the fact it is not a political term like *president.* Those against *bishop* spoke of its "European" connotations in the eyes of the "common people" or the mixed response one pastor received in polling his congregation. Synod presidents, it should be noted, were not necessarily for the change in nomenclature. One spoke of sticking with the choice of *president* that our forebears had made and of the expectations *bishop* stirred up like "historic episcopacy." The "fear and trembling" that the President of the LCA felt about the change was invoked. Another synod president felt the statement in the report's "Conclusions" (second paragraph), about what a Lutheran concept of episcopacy excludes, had "denuded" the term of meaning and caused problems in explaining what is meant. One parish pastor, favoring the change, called attention to the closing arguments for the title in the paper, especially the citation from the Smalcald Articles, that "true bishops . . . might be permitted . . . provided this would be done without pretense, humbug, and unchristian ostentation."

The actual vote was not on the report but on a series of motions framed by the LCA Executive Council, the heart of which was that "the term 'bishop' be substituted for 'president'" in a whole series of amendments to the LCA Constitution and Bylaws; these had been passed on first reading at the 1978 convention in order to make this test possible. The Rev. G. W. (Lee) Luetkehoelter, President of the Central Canada Synod, moved to substitute *pastor* for *bishop*. This was defeated. In the vote on the main motion a two-thirds majority was needed of the 641 delegates voting, i.e., 427 in favor. The count as announced was 464 "for" (applause—ruled out of order), 177 opposed. A shift of 36 persons from the yes to the no column would have been necessary to change the result. A motion that was prepared in case of a negative vote— that use of the title be encouraged informally, as in the ALC, with the Executive Council bringing constitutional changes to the convention at a future date "when the practice is sufficiently accepted"—proved unnecessary. (The official account in the *Minutes, Tenth Biennial Convention* of the LCA, 1980, at Seattle, pp. 256-58, 685-96, is amplified above from my notes on the session.)

President James R. Crumley Jr., who, it was known, did not favor the change in title, then spoke, making it clear "that the changes which have been made in no way change the function or tenure of the chief executive officers of the church and synods" (*Minutes,* p. 258). As Lloyd E. Sheneman, Executive Director of DPL, commented in his foreword to the reprinting of my study for broader distribution, "That interpretation appears to be consistent with the conclusions reached by Dr. Reumann in his paper" (p. 1)—of course, for such was the shape of the parliamentary proposals, going back to 1970.

I confess that I was never quite clear, however, on what the 1970 "Report of the Commission on the Comprehensive Study of the Doctrine of the Ministry" meant when it recommended "that the Executive Council be instructed to take the necessary steps toward adoption of the title [*bishop*] and to *define the duties of the office resulting from that change*" (1970 *Minutes,* p. 440, italics added). All the 1970 Commission Report had said in looking favorably on the change in title was that our Lutheran heritage and other Christian bodies use *bishop* for "that official who serves as pastor to pastors" and that it "does not imply the preoccupation with administration that 'president' conveys" (p. 431). (Perhaps so—unless one knows the working schedule, with its administrative load, that a Roman Catholic, Anglican, or Methodist bishop bears.) What the subsequent 1970 report (for the 1972 LCA convention) said is spelled out in my paper. Very clearly, though, the proposals before the 1980 LCA convention called for no changes in authority, duties, or anything else for presidents/bishops. I sought to make this point several times in what was written for the convention and regard it as entirely "Lutheran" to be able to use a title so multifaceted and polyvalent in its long history with a sense that Lutherans in America at this stage wished to give it.

Perhaps a fear was that "pastoral-episcopal" concerns would be added on top of an already crowded workload, but I suspect most synod presidents welcomed the surcease that the title gave, allowing them in good conscience to devote more time and effort to what they know to be crucial, being pastoral with pastors and professional leaders and their families. I confess also to uneasiness about describing synod presidents as "chief executive officers." Certainly, some at the convention feared the trappings that can go with a title like "bishop"—Rome has too, trying since the Second Vatican Council to degrandeurize the style of its bishops. Again, my paper sought to make clear that no such changes toward pomp and power were intended (with the implication that the church might need to watch this aspect of its life in the future, as it must keep watch on all aspects of the ecclesial institution). Dr. Crumley's comments, in 1980 and subsequently, arose, I suspect, both from honest concerns about expectations that a nomenclature change might bring and, from contacts ecumenically with bishops in churches that define the term in their own ecclesiological systems, a wondering about what *bishop* ought to imply for the LCA in such a world. We shall hear more about the title and its implications in both *BEM* and CNLC discussions.

The focus thus far has been on results from this paper in the LCA. There were no real results of the 1980 vote within the other U.S. Lutheran bodies. The ALC and AELC continued their existing uses of the term, informally and otherwise. But now they felt the LCA was moving in the same direction. The fact that it had been done constitutionally probably helped diminish any real battles about the title as the Commission for a New Lutheran Church worked over its plans for the ELCA. There the discussion was over the powers of the judicatory heads to be called bishops, not the title itself (see Chapter 5, below).

The not-inconsiderable literature on bishops since 1980, in New Testament exegesis, historical study, and ecumenical discussions, can be kept within reasonable bounds for our purposes by noting only a few publications, some of them already mentioned in connection with "ministry" in the Supplementary Comments to Chapter 1.

The Gritsch-Jenson volume, *Lutheranism,* for example, takes up episcopacy (pp. 123, 198-200, 204-5) under "adiaphora" (from the Greek for "things that make no difference," really "things not mandated in Scripture"). Luther and the Confessions are held to have "reaffirmed the ecumenical office of bishop or 'superintendent' " but to have "rejected the medieval fusion of 'jurisdictional power' and 'teaching authority' (*magisterium*)." A long history with a variety of titles and the German experience with a *Reichsbischof* in the Hitler period have caused reiterated rejection of any apostolic succession of bishops and of episcopacy as "divine law" in European Lutheran churches (pp. 198-99). But the dismal U.S. history of "managerial" methods in church governance—" 'bishops' and 'presidents' with their multitudinous staffs"—is severely castigated (p. 205). A. C. Piepkorn's brief description of ministry takes up the Confessions' claims about bishops, among them that "when bishops become heretics or refuse to ordain fit persons, 'the churches are compelled by divine right to ordain pastors and ministers, using their own pastors for this purpose' " (*Profiles in Belief,* 2:87-88, citing "Treatise on the Power and Primacy of the Pope," §72).

Out of Lutheran–Catholic ecumenical discussions of the Augsburg Confession for the anniversary year of 1980 has come what may be the most striking essay, "Bishops and the Ministry of the Gospel" by the Jesuit theologian Avery Dulles and George Lindbeck, Lutheran layman and professor at Yale (cited in note 15 for this chapter; as indicated there and in the Supplementary Comments on Chapter 1, the argumentation has behind it the historical work on the origin of the *Confessio Augustana* by Wilhelm Maurer). Clearly, the Lutheran reformers in 1530, conservative toward past tradition and structures as they were, would have been willing, indeed preferred continuing, to have bishops, but bishops who permitted, if not encouraged, the preaching of the gospel as the Reformation understood it. So it was that the Augsburg Confession, in its second section on "abuses" and "matters in dispute," dealt with the power of bishops in Article 28, as well as in the first part on the chief articles of faith—about which, it was hoped, there was no dispute—concerning "the office of the ministry" in Article 5 and "order in the church" in Article 14.

The Maurer approach argues one should begin with Article 28, because it "was among the first to be drafted, and is much the largest in the entire Confession" (Dulles and Lindbeck, p. 147). This means that the underlying assumption about ministry in 1530 is, as the Apology was to put it, a "deep desire to maintain the . . . various ranks of the ecclesiastical hierarchy" (Apol. 14, 1-2, Tappert ed. p. 214). It also leads to the claim that such a willingness to retain episcopacy shapes what is said in the "undisputed" articles, 5 and 14, on ministry. Upon examination, Article 5 turns out to be really about "the gospel and the sacraments" through which God gives the Spirit and works faith (that is the *id est* provided for the statement "God instituted the office of the ministry"; the titles of Article 5, "Von Predigtamt" and "De ministerio ecclesiastico," are somewhat later). And hence, as reported in my study for the LCA (note 15, above), the claim that in the brief Article 14 the words *rite vocatus* ("nobody should [Piepkorn: 'must'] teach publicly in the church or administer the sacraments unless he is *regularly called*") meant "ordained," and that by a bishop, in the 1530 context.

The approach here indicated (for details, see Maurer) deserves—and has received—discussion by experts in the Confessions. It is fact that the Torgau Articles of late March 1530 provided the basis for what became the "abuses" part of the Confession read at Augsburg in June 25 of that year, and they deal with much of what became Articles 22-28 in the *Confessio Augustana,* including the sovereignty of bishops. It is, of course, also true that what became prior articles in the CA in the irenic section, had appeared in documents even earlier; i.e., number 7 in the Schwabach Articles of summer 1529: "to obtain this faith, or to bestow it upon us men God has instituted the ministry, or the oral word, viz., the gospel . . . " (cf. CA 5). The contention is, from source criticism and in terms of document's historical development, one should "begin with CA 28 in the study of the CA as a whole" (Dulles and Lindbeck, p. 147). It becomes the interpretative key on ministry.

Further questions arise, however. What was Melanchthon's intent as he drafted the CA? Was it to mute the abuses section with an irenic beginning, emphasizing agreements, as over the ministry, before getting to abuses in the episcopal office? Did he have a "doctrine of the ministry" in mind or was the aim to say quite little, focusing on the hope for a reformed episcopacy in Article 28? (It is sometimes contended that the CA offers no doctrine of the ministry, but that Lutherans have subsequently made it into one.) Is the "deep desire to maintain the church polity and . . . hierarchy," already referred to, compromised—fatally, from a traditionalist point of view—by the phrase Melanchthon goes on with: "although they were created by human authority" (Apol. 14.1; cf. the distinction in CA 28, 21, and 29 between divine right and human right)? Or does this show that episcopacy was in mind in the phrase "rightly called" in CA 14?

Above all, there is the hermeneutical problem. The approach we are examining assumes the CA as the norm, the CA text as "hermeneutically primary," without use of what Luther or Melanchthon said on ministry elsewhere and without attention to later developments after 1530. So Dulles and Lindbeck, pp. 157-59. This is a kind of "canonical criticism" that focuses on the finished doctrine "as is," not its contemporary context or subsequent trajectory. But this stress on meaning for "the original audience" (p. 159, the Diet at Augsburg? the Catholic opponents? the "Lutheran" adherents?) is modified in one significant way: the historical development of the CA, from its sources and in its sequential drafting process, is admitted to the inquiry and indeed becomes the key step in deciding to begin with CA 28.

In this proposal it is as if we canonized the finished document as it stands but allow what has priority in its historical genesis to call the shots. Thus CA 28 is said to tower over Articles 5 and 14 (and 4 on justification, or 3 on Christology, or a constellation of articles like 3-5 on the Holy Spirit or 7-14 plus 16 on the right-hand and left-hand reign of God; all have been proposed as alternatives for finding a "center" to the Augsburg Confession). Lutherans thus have a question before them of how they read their chief symbolic book.

The Dulles and Lindbeck article (pp. 166-67) concludes with a summary on "the CA's teaching on ministry" drawn up by Harding Meyer for a volume on the Augsburg Confession and the Roman Confutation that was written against it in 1530; it is worth citing this list in full [translation altered in point 4]:

1. There is a single ministerial office instituted by God and therefore *de iure divino* and, in the full sense, essentially necessary to the church (cf. CA 5).
2. A series of functions belong *de iure divino,* to this office, some of which (especially the proclamation of the gospel and administration of the sacraments) are exercised by the pastor or priest (i.e., the leader of the individual congregation), while others—often designated in our day by the concept of episcope—can be effectively carried out only by officeholders at a higher level. These latter exercise church and, more especially, teaching discipline, and in cooperation with the congregations call and ordain new pastors or priests.
3. The obvious ways to exercise the functions of episcope is by means of the institutional structure which has in fact developed for this purpose, *viz.,* the historical succession of bishops in office. This structure should be maintained when possible for the sake of the preservation of the unity of the church. Yet when, for the sake of the gospel, it cannot be maintained, the church's being is not thereby lost.

   The CA is open to the following further interpretation suggested, after centuries of development, in view of the variety of contemporary church situations:
4. Although the differentiation of the ministry into presbyterial and episcopal offices [occurs] in an historical structure arising from "human authority" (according to Apol. 14, 2), yet the guidance of God's Spirit can be seen in its development. Thus the historic episcopate is, on the one hand, a human order, but it is also at the same time more than that. This position corresponds to the more flexible understanding of *ius divinum* sketched above [p. 165, no neat distinction can be drawn from *ius humanum*].
5. Even if the decision of the Reformers to deny obedience to the bishops of their time for the sake of the gospel was unavoidable, damage was yet done to the ecclesial reality of the church by this breach in its continuity and structural unity.

6. Although we [as Lutherans] affirm that this breach did not deprive the churches [i.e., the Reformation communities of their being as church] (cf. no. 3. supra), yet the resultant ecclesial deficiency (a deficiency in the church's unity) constitutes for both sides an abiding challenge to seriously consider the importance of the historic episcopate for the unity of our churches.

(From "Das Bischofsamt nach CA 28," in *Confessio Augustana und Confutatio,* ed. Erwin Iserloh and Barbara Hallensleben, Religionsgeschichtliche Studien und Texte 118 [Münster: Aschendorff, 1980], pp. 489-98.) Lutherans will want to decide whether they agree, or that too much has been conceded. So with Catholics.

The most significant treatments of episcopacy by Lutherans in the dialogues has probably been in the discussions with Roman Catholics and with Anglicans.

From the international Roman Catholic/Lutheran Joint Commission, the volume on *The Ministry in the Church* (German 1981; English 1982) was drawn up "with special reference to the episcopate" (§2). Episcopal polity is treated in §§41-73, including apostolic succession and the service for universal unity of the church performed for Roman Catholics by the pope. We may note, in the interpretation of the Lutheran ministry, a distinction offered between "local congregational ministries and superordinated regional ministries." (An earlier statement, *Ways to Community* [1980], §23, spoke of "supracongregational ministries.") While "the Lutheran office of pastor . . . has really taken over the spiritual functions of the bishop's office," the function of oversight (*episcopē*) is carried out through the "superordinated" (i.e., bishop, church president, superintendent) (§§43-45). "Bishop" and pastor are thus distinguished as to the geographical area of each one's ministry (§47). As to teaching authority, which Catholics assign especially to the bishops, Lutherans see the decisive role in interpreting and developing church doctrine to be "played by teachers of theology together with non-ordained church members and ordained ministers" (§55). "The holders of the episcopal office" are especially to watch over the purity of the gospel as preached and taught (§53).

A still later document from the Joint Commission, *Facing Unity: Models, Forms and Phases of Catholic–Lutheran Church Fellowship* (preface dated 3 March 1984; English, Geneva: LWF, 1985), proposes ways a "jointly exercised ministry of fellowship" could be developed, including *episcopē* (§§117-45). Primarily there would evolve, for example, a working relationship developed between those who exercise *episcopē* in the two churches in a given region; then a mutual act of recognition; eventually a "single *episcopē* in collegial form," as an interim step to the patristic idea of one bishop in a given place; then the gradual establishment of a common ordained ministry. This is, in a sense, a solution from the top down, frankly recognizing the cruciality of episcopacy to Roman Catholics and the unlikelihood of solving "the ministry question" without prime attention to the leadership function within the ordained ministry. Pipe dream or realistic proposal in what is unexplored terrain?

The several rounds of Anglican-Lutheran dialogue, in the United States and internationally, could not avoid the topic of bishops. It has traditionally been a dividing line, especially since the Lambeth Conference in 1888 insisted on the historic episcopate as one of the four essentials for a reunited church, along with Scripture, creeds, and the two sacraments. The U.S. Lutheran–Episcopal dialogue, round I (1969–1972), in tackling apostolicity, agreed that in any "one church" in the future there must be *episcopē,* and that its "functional reality . . . is in flux in both our communions" (*Lutheran–Episcopal Dialogue: A Progress Report* [Cincinnati: Forward Movement Publications, 1973], p. 22). LED II issued a report, the longest section of which was on apostolicity, with considerable agreement on succession in mission, Scriptures, creeds, sacraments, and Ordained Ministry. It then offers this nuanced statement: "Lutherans see *episcopē* exercised in the ministry of parish pastors as well as in bishops' supervision of local congregations, while Episcopalians see the *episcopē* as shared by bishops with their clergy." (*The Report of the Lutheran-Episcopal Dialogue, Second Series 1976-1980* [Cincinnati: Forward Movement Publications, 1981], p. 40.)

The *Anglican-Lutheran International Conversations* (London: SPCK, 1973) reported different ways the two communions have seen episcopacy preserved and that both "are open to new ways in which episcope may find expressions appropriate to the needs . . ." (§§79-82). The regional dialogue in Europe, 1979-1982, terming LED II "so far the most important Anglican–Lutheran dialogue on a national level" (p. 2), chipped away at "a difference between us" (in spite of much agreement) that, "while Anglicans cannot envisage any form of organic church unity without the historic episcopate, Lutheran churches are not able to attribute . . . the same significance for organic church union" to it. Nonetheless, it was felt that "there exists sufficient agreement between our Communions for the mutual recognition of Anglican and Lutheran ministries" (*Anglican–Lutheran Dialogue: The Report of the Anglican–Lutheran European Regional Commission* [London: SPCK, 1983], §§40-43). The prototype agreement came in the United States in 1982 when the Episcopal Church in the United States, the ALC, AELC, and LCA agreed officially to Interim Sharing of the Eucharist, although "historic episcopate" and "ordering of ministry" must be resolved before "full communion" can be established.

More recently the international Lutheran–Methodist dialogue has been able to agree that their churches "regard oversight (episcopē) as fundamental in the life of the church." Exercised "in a variety of ways" but mostly among

Lutherans and Methodists by bishops, it is "not . . . an essential mark of the church" but rather involves "a minister set aside for superintending pastoral functions" (Lutheran–Methodist Joint Commission, *The Church: Community of Grace* [Geneva: LWF: and Lake Junaluska, N.C.: Methodist World Council, 1984], §39). The U.S. Lutheran–Methodist dialogue reached similar agreement at a 1985 session that bishops are beneficial to the church but not essential. Methodist bishops were perceived as having more power than Lutheran counterparts, e.g., with their own life tenure and in appointing pastors to congregations, but within a system described as "fiercely democratic."

A final piece of evidence for Lutherans to mull over is a Statement by the Consultation on Episcopé, sponsored by the LWF Department of Studies and published in its Reports and Texts series, *Lutheran Understanding of the Episcopal Office* (Geneva, 1983). Meant to build on the 1970 volume, *Episcopacy in the Lutheran Church?* mentioned in my paper, it is of a piece in a trilogy with the booklets already referred to, *The Lutheran Understanding of Ministry* and *Women in the Ministries of the Church* (also 1983). Each repeats the same definitions of "ministry" (of all), "ordained ministry," and here "episcopal ministry and episcopal office"—the latter "denote the task of pastoral leadership and spiritual supervision. Persons exercising this task in Lutheran churches are called either bishops or by some other title" (p. 3). This might suggest a threefold ministry of laity, the ordained, and bishops, but the report clearly affirms the ordained ministry as one, whether local pastor or episcopal leader (§6).

This consultation, in which there participated from Canada the ELCC President S. T. Jacobson and from the United States Dr. David Preus (ALC Presiding Bishop) and Bishop Wilson Touhsaent, Northeastern Pennsylvania Synod, LCA, reflected the dialogues in seeing Lutheran churches "in unbroken succession of the ministry of the gospel" yet "open to the historic succession of bishops" (§§9, 11). For a converging picture of the bishop's office they cite *BEM* §3/29 (see Chap. 5, below) and the international Lutheran–Catholic statement, *The Ministry of the Church*, §44, about "superordinated regional ministries," quoted above. Further reflection on "episcopal ministry in individual Lutheran churches" is encouraged.

A United States Lutheran Council DTS study on "The Historic Episcopate," completed in 1984, offers a clear Lutheran overview on that topic and definitions of that term and of *ius divinum* ("divine law," according to God's word, by Christ's institution). Biblically, bishops in historical succession are not mandated, and hence that institution is not necessary. But *episcopē* there must be. "American Lutheranism is free to create under the guidance of the Spirit forms of leadership that embody *episcopē* and hold ecumenical promise."

In light of these subsequent discussions and events, the further issues from the formal adoption by the LCA of the title bishop in 1980 are how a new Lutheran church would move on the matter; an inner-Lutheran question of how to interpret one's own confessions, above all, the CA; what to respond to the ecumenical solution proposed by *BEM,* of bishops in threefold ministry; and living out the constitutional change to *bishop* in the last seven years of the LCA (and the de facto shift to the term in the ALC).

Some of these questions will be taken up in Chapter 5. I have the impression that within the LCA the use of *bishop* did bring about quite often a more pastoral tone within the necessary structures. Externally, it brought more ready recognition of the person as an ecclesiastical leader, without having to explain, "President of what?"

4

"Authority" in Ministry: The "Teaching Office" according to the New Testament

No ministry can function very long without the question of authority being raised. By what right does it forgive sins, make statements about God or in God's name, admonish or discipline, or even help others on behalf of its Lord, Jesus Christ? Such questions pertain to average Christians as well as to ordained clergy carrying out their tasks or making assertions on Christ's behalf. Jesus too was asked "by what authority" he spoke and acted; "Who gave you this authority to do these things?" (Mark 11:28).

In particular, the authority to teach, to formulate and promulgate Christian doctrine, has been a concern both practically and on the theoretical level ecumenically. Does the "office of teaching" belong to all the people of God or to the clergy or to just the bishops? In Roman Catholicism the teaching office (Latin, *magisterium;* German, *Lehramt*) has come to be associated above all with the bishop of Rome, the pope, and in 1870 the dogma of papal infallibility was formally defined by the First Vatican Council.

The Lutheran–Roman Catholic dialogue in the United States tackled such problems in two stages, dealing with "papal primacy" in a statement published in 1974 (see note 46, below) and then with "teaching authority and infallibility" over a six-year period. As part of this latter study, the Rev. Joseph A. Fitzmyer, of the Catholic University of America, was asked to prepare a paper in 1974 on "The Office of Teaching in the Christian Church According to the New Testament." The counterpart Lutheran paper, reprinted below, was entitled "Teaching Office in the New Testament? A Response to Professor Fitzmyer's Paper." Both appeared in volume 6 of Lutherans and Catholics in Dialogue, *Teaching Authority and Infallibility in the Church* (Minneapolis: Augsburg, 1980), pp. 186-212, 213-31, respectively, with notes on pp. 328-35 and 336-42. Interested readers ought by all means to read Father Fitzmyer's basic analysis there, but the fact that the response summarizes each section briefly before commenting on it allows one to follow the discussion within the pages that follow.

At issue, first, are matters of methodology. On these there was little dispute in the two papers for the dialogue. The joint findings, however, often differ from later, traditional views in what they report concerning the variety within the New Testament. Second, there is the question of authority. Here "gospel" or "kerygma" emerges as the matrix out of which teaching authority derives. Third, there is considerable agreement on the Spirit-filled Christian community as locus for authority of teachers and teaching. Fourth, teaching and preaching the gospel seem to be intertwined.

Any reply to Professor Fitzmyer's excellent survey on teaching and teachers in the New Testament not only must deal with the mass of data and the conclusions which he has set forth but also must indicate possible application of the scriptural material to the problem of teaching office in the church and infallibility. This response hopes in addition to note some alternative methods of approach.

After a few initial observations, I shall generally follow his order of presentation, *(a)* highlighting briefly what I understand him to be saying and *(b)* indicating points under dispute in New Testament studies and theological dialogue. (This list will be selective, for obviously in a presentation dealing with so many passages, where opinions vary, on any issue divergent scholarly opinions can be cited, most of which are irrelevant for our purposes.) Finally, suggestions about applications and future concerns will be offered. At the outset I record my gratitude for his encyclopedic study, with its clarity, honesty, and thoroughness.

I. Initial Observations

1. There is comparatively little overlap between the passages treated in the essay on "The Office of Teaching" and those listed for the dialogue in an unpublished paper by Father Jerome Quinn on traditional "Scriptural Loci on Infallibility." Among the verses noted for both topics were Matt. 28:18-20; John 14:26; Acts 2:42-46; Eph. 4:11-15; and 1 Tim. 3:13-15, but each would have to be examined to see if and how the topics really connect. Does this not mean that *infallibility* and *teaching office* are separate terms, each with its own history, occasionally intertwined, or at least that their concatenation is a postbiblical development?

2. Professor Fitzmyer's methodology stresses the word-study approach and tradition history as an avenue to our topic.

a. Application of the tradition-history method leads to treatment of our sources in the New Testament in roughly the presumed chronological order of the documents: genuine letters by Paul, doubtful Pauline epistles, the Synoptic Gospels, Acts, deutero-Pauline letters, James, and the Johannine literature, with due attention in the Gospels to the *Sitz im Leben Jesu* (situation in the life of Jesus) and *Sitz im Leben der Kirche* (situation in the life of the church).

One may question whether even this careful sequence, akin to that followed in *Peter in the New Testament* (cited below, n. 46), allows full attention to such stages as pre-Pauline Christianity (Jewish Palestinian, Jewish Hellenistic, and Greek Hellenistic) and, in the Gospels, *Sitz im Gemeindeleben* (situation within community life) distinguished from *Sitz im Leben des Redakteurs* (situation in the life of the editor). Hence it may be helpful to ask, even more than has been done at times, about Paul's connection with those who were "in Christ" before him (especially when he is called "the first Christian theologian"), and about the distinction of redactoral verses in the Gospels from community tradition and genuine "Jesus material."

b. In the essay, hope is expressed at the outset for a possible "trajectory" of the teaching office *(Lehramt)* and, more tentatively, of infallibility. More modestly, the goal is to show a New Testament concern for "authoritative teaching, a teaching function, and even traces of a Ministry of authoritative teaching."

The findings, however, are able to sustain as conclusions only that: (1) the teaching function "played an important role in the growth" of the early church (*not* a steady growth of the teaching office); (2) teachers in the Christian community varied in their situations; and (3) their function was "nothing more than a development or extension" of preaching the gospel, and "the truth of the gospel" served as the norm. Even so, (4) there are "cautions" in the New Testament about teachers and teachings, and (5) in the Johannine literature it seems the whole community, under the Spirit, rather than any group of teachers, is charged with guiding people "into a more profound understanding of what the kerygmatic message was." Hence it must be allowed that whatever infallibility means as a modern term for "a quality of Christian teaching," the term is not biblical, "nor is the concept with all its specifications and conditions" to be found in the New Testament; Christians "only adverted" to *infallible* as a predicate for their teaching "after many centuries."

The gap between expectations (remembering that traditional views have often claimed far more to be lodged in the New Testament) and actual findings (even assuming all the above conclusions) is, of course, created by our assigned topic, "The Office of Teaching" set in the context of "Teaching Authority and Infallibility in the Church." For the topic in that context is looking in the New Testament for what are *later* concepts. That *infallibility* is not a New Testament term has already been noted. *Lehramt* may also be a cause for difficulties as a term. The German need mean no more than "office of teacher," but it can also carry overtones, which it has developed in Roman Catholic history, of a strongly dogmatized institutionalizing of the original task of witness by Christians into a *magisterium* of the Church, hierachically conceived.

Perhaps a further difficulty lies in the term *trajectory*. Its application in biblical studies stems from the work of Koester and James Robinson.[1] They sought to show that the ancient, biblical world was not simply a matter of "fixed points" with static "backgrounds," but rather movement and development, with dozens of trajectories, like rockets lighting up the sky. At the least, in a topic such as ours, we must look for several possible trajectories, often with ups and downs, not merely evolutional ascent. But the very term suggests a hand which launches the trajectory and controls it—theologically put, God's hand! That begs the question of whether historical developments, often quite ambiguous, were by divine direction (*iure divino*, "by divine law") or from the vicissitudes of history (*iure humano*, "by human law"). A more neutral term, like "lines of development" is to be preferred. (*Entwicklungslinie* is employed in the German translation of Koester and Robinson.)[2]

c. The word-study method is assiduously followed throughout the essay, involving terms for teaching (*didaskō, didachē, didaskalia*) and for preaching (especially *kēryssein* and *euangelizesthai*); hence the frequent use of articles from the Kittel *Theological Dictionary of the New Testament*, supplemented by other bibliography and the author's own astute observations.

In pursuit of this method it can be asked whether related and seemingly important terms like *katēcheō/katēchēsis, paradosis*, and even *paideuō* ought not to be included and be further pursued in order to get at the early Christian view of what was taught in the churches and how it was taught.[3]

A bigger question, quite apart from James Barr's overall strictures about the word-study method,[4] is whether this procedure takes us very far. Does it not leave us with many bits and pieces, without grasping the historical development? The word-study approach, by its very nature, may cause us to concentrate on individual terms, of a certain type at that, twigs and trees at the expense of the forest.

d. The role of certain backgrounds or other trajectories might also be noted at this point. One has to do with Old Testament-Jewish antecedents. Granted, the title of the paper is "The Office of Teaching in the Christian Church according to the *New* Testament," but early Christianity derived many of its offices from the Old Testament and Judaism. Granted, too, such backgrounds are brought in at pertinent points. Thus (on p. 193 of Fitzmyer's essay) K. H. Rengstorf's opinion is set forth that *didaskein* has a Jewish content of "teaching Torah" and Paul worked in a Hellenistic context, so that the term *didaskein* had greatest use in the world of Jesus and the earliest church rather than in Gentile Christianity.[5] Note 41 does point out the Palestinian-Jewish background of Jesus' teaching (Hebrew *limmēd*).[6] One cannot do everything at once, and any presentation must adopt its own order and limits, but there is need to keep in mind these Jewish and Old Testament roots, both as a positive influence and as something Christianity reacts against, in developing its own teaching offices.[7]

A similar example concerns the Spirit and the "spiritual" (*pneumatika*) or "grace" gifts (*charismata*) granted from God. Father Fitzmyer's presentation must several times refer to this setting for New Testament discussions about *didaskaloi* (1 Cor. 12:28; Eph. 4:11; Luke 12:12; John 14:26). Indeed, we are again and again forced to say, as in John, that the gift of the Spirit to all the members of the Christian community is what makes teaching-witness by believers possible. Mutatis mutandis, the same thing could be said of the church as depicted in Acts, and the Pauline community in Corinth.[8] It would be well to bear in mind the New Testament communities' claim about having received the Spirit as background to any authority posited for their teachers and teaching. Indeed, the *Lehramt* and teaching-trajectories, if there be such, must intersect often with the trajectory of the Spirit, or even commence with it.

3. The matter of difference between preaching and teaching (*kērygma and didachē*) frequently appears in the essay. To be sure, the topic is first introduced as a question, and it is asked whether they are adequately distinct. But the New Testament data are said to provide "distinct terms" for two "distinct functions" (p. 187), though then it is allowed that "it is difficult to single out . . . the crucial difference" and "the nuances" in each case. Nonetheless, this does seem an operating distinction in the paper.

The New Testament evidence at times is disquieting, however. In Acts, "teaching and preaching/proclaiming are not infrequently juxtaposed, so that one wonders about the distinction between them" (p. 203); Luke thinks about them "in such a way that it is not easy to distinguish between them" (p. 204). In Colossians(–Ephesians) "the lack of a clear distinction between teaching and preaching is found"; instead, possibly "an extension of the function of proclaiming to teaching" (p. 195). Hence the conclusion on teaching that "at times it was difficult to say whether it was regarded as a function distinct from the function of preaching the gospel" and that "undoubtedly . . . the teaching function was nothing more than a development or extension of the latter" (p. 211).

Such frequent reservations raise questions about the whole *kērygma*/*didachē* distinction so long and widely accepted in scholarship. The differentiation is one we owe especially to the writings of C. H. Dodd.[9] These give the impression of *kērygma* as the apostolic message about what God has done to deliver us, preached to the world, and of *didachē* as apostolic teaching or ethical instruction, directed within the believing community. (Such an understanding carries with it many implications about what preaching is and for worship; it is also related to, but not to be confused with, the debate over "indicative" and "imperative.")[10] Yet Dodd himself did not always speak in such limiting terms and at times insisted that *didachē* was more than ethical instruction, embracing also apologetic and the exposition of theological doctrines;[11] it is all that happens after the *kērygma* is announced.

There have been many voices dissenting from Dodd's analysis. What if *kērygma* were not so propositional and unified as Dodd made the apostolic preaching? Even on Dodd's own showing, one ought to speak in the plural of (Pauline and Jerusalem) *kērygmata*.[12] In the opinion of some, the starting point was really a series of confessional formulae and creedal slogan;[13] in that case both preaching and teaching would be the drawing out of the implications from such a credo in a given situation.[14] Another type of conceptual analysis was offered by H. G. Wood[15] against the view of Dodd (and also in Bultmann)[16] that "Apostolic Preaching" and "Apostolic Teaching" were "separate entities"; according to Wood, "Kerygma and Didachē were distilled out of a tradition that included both" and thus "Didachē and Kerygma together make up Euangelion."

More impressive as hard evidence is the kind of analysis done by Robert H. Mounce[17] and others, arguing that Dodd "drew too sharp a picture between *kerygma* and *didachē*," for the New Testament usage is not so clear. The vagaries of the data are apparent enough. In Matthew 4:23 the evangelist says: Jesus went about all Galilee,

teaching (didaskōn) in their synagogues
and *preaching (kēryssōn)* the gospel of the kingdom
and *healing* every disease and every infirmity among the people.

The Marcan parallel on which Matthew draws has simply: And he went throughout all Galilee,

preaching in their synagogues
and *casting out* demons (1:39).

(Luke 4:44 keeps only: "he was *preaching* in the synagogues of Judea.") Presumably Matthew has made the editorial changes quite intentionally, for he repeats virtually the same wording in 9:35, the two summary statements providing a frame for Chapters 5–9. "Teaching" in 4:23 and 9:35 is meant to refer to the type of material in Chapters 5–7, the Sermon on the Mount ("And he opened his mouth and taught them . . .," 5:1). "Healing" is described in the miracle stories in Chapters 8–9. "Preaching the gospel of the kingdom" has been tersely described in 4:17 (derived from Mark 1:15, but also on the lips of John the Baptist in 3:2). What we seem to have here is a

distinction between *kērygma* and *didachē* (or is it between teaching and healing?—cf. Acts 1:1, "all that Jesus began to *do* and *teach*"), but it is plainly
Matthean theology, not found in Mark or at this point in Luke. It deserves
to be followed up in the context of Matthew's thought, where teaching seems
"the highest apostolic function" [18] (cf. 28:19). But did Matthew's predecessors
make any such distinction?

Mark 1 is instructive here. Verses 14-15 portray Jesus *preaching* a "little
kerygma." Then in v. 21 he enters into a synagogue and teaches, but what
he taught we are not told. In vv. 23-26 he casts out an unclean spirit. The
people exclaim: "What is this? A new teaching! With authority he commands
even the unclean spirits . . . ," or (NAB) "What does this mean? A completely
new teaching in a spirit of authority! . . . ." Is the *didachē* here some unreported
sayings, or the miracle, or his *kērygma?* For this passage Rengstorf's judgment
applies: "When the Synoptists speak of the *didachē* of Jesus, . . . they do
not mean a particular dogmatics or ethics, but His whole *didaskein,* His
proclamation of the will of God as regards both form and content," [19] and
apparently his doing of it too, including miraculous deeds.

Akin to such Synoptic passages is Acts 13:12, where the proconsul Sergius
Paulus believed when he saw how Bar-Jesus was miraculously struck blind
at Paul's rebuke, "for he was astonished at the teaching *(didachē)* of the
Lord."

More examples might be explored, but my points are (1) the distinction
between *kērygma* and *didachē* is not so stark in many New Testament writers
as Dodd assumed; (2) *kērygma* and *didachē* blend and overlap, probably in
early sources as well as late ones, and indeed it may be only a few theological
minds (e.g., Matthew) who distinguish them, and then not in Dodd's way (in
Matthew *didaskein* seems to be the dominant term, really including "to
preach"); (3) in any analysis, the role of miracles and mighty works must be
considered; (4) the real question in preaching-teaching-healing is that of the
authority *(exousia)* involved; note especially (5) the need for distinguishing
redaction from tradition (e.g., in the Synoptics) and (6) the need for attention
to additional terms (e.g., *katēcheō* in Gal. 6:6, what is "the word" which
"he who teaches" sets forth?).

My own impression is that *kērygma* and *didachē* are more holistically
conceived in the New Testament than our modern dichotomies allow. Elsewhere I have argued that the gospel (in the sense of good news) includes both
our *"kērygma"* and *"didachē"*;[20] the latter involves, among other things,
reiteration of the basic saving message and drawing out of its implications—
what D. M. Stanley called "induction into the *sensus plenior* of the *kērygma.*" [21] I understand *didachē* (for Paul especially) as including (1) instructional
material from Jesus[22] and (2) catechetical materials[23] developed in the be-

lieving community from a variety of sources, presumably, in the opinion of the community, under the aegis of the Spirit.

Such an understanding of *kērygma* and *didachē* as proclamation about what God has done in Jesus and how in turn believers respond (the material being variable in content but remarkably fixed in certain persistent formulas) has implications for the way we understand preaching/teaching. Theologically it means that any teaching office works from the gospel as its norm. For topics on which the church needs to speak, such as modern problems in social ethics, it means that, while there may be data and influences from the contemporary sciences and from reason, nature, church traditions, and past practices, the gospel stands as norm over all of these. The church's imperatives derive from this central *kērygma*.[24]

II. Exegetical Analysis

A. The Pauline "Trajectory"

Summary of Professor Fitzmyer's paper

I. *The genuine Pauline letters:* Paul does not often describe himself as teacher (but cf. 1 Cor. 4:17), because he was not taught the gospel which serves as the norm (Gal. 1:12) and which is indeed the truth (Gal. 2:5,14). But he knows of teachers in early Christianity (mentioned in two lists of charismata, 1 Cor. 12:28; Rom. 12:7) and he knows of official teaching (Rom. 6:17) and doctrine (16:17). *Didaskein* is rare as a term in his Hellenistic churches, since it implies a Jewish concept ("to teach Torah").

II. *The doubtfully Pauline letters* lay greater emphasis on the subject. "The traditions you were taught by us" (2 Thess. 2:15) as a phrase suggests either gospel-tradition details which had become the object of teaching or a broader post-Pauline sense. Colossians blurs distinctions by relating teaching to admonition, wisdom, and the receipt of kerygmatic tradition. In Ephesians teachers are fourth in a list of functions but still "charismatic"; teaching relates also to conduct.

V. In the *deutero-Pauline letters* "official teaching" emerges, related to office *(episkopoi-presbyteroi),* the holders of which are obliged, in succession from the apostle, to teach sound doctrine (*kērygma,* piety, etc.).

1. For analysis we may take these three sections together as the Pauline course of development. Regardless of where we draw the line between what is "authentically by Paul himself" and "the work of his school," we have a continuity which shows definite development and where Paul is on the way to becoming what he is in patristic tradition, "the divine apostle."[25]

2. The pre-Pauline picture does not emerge as clearly as it could. Obviously Paul knew of the idea of oral tradition *(paradosis),* both in the Jewish sense

of "the traditions of my fathers" (Gal. 1:14) and with reference to Christian teachings (1 Cor. 11:2; 2 Thess. 2:15; 3:6). He also reflected the rabbinic pattern of transmitting oral tradition (1 Cor. 15:3; 11:23).

Precisely what makes the difference in Paul is not the method of passing on the materials, but (1) the content and (2) the freedom with which Paul handled what he has received; "for Paul tradition is not sacrosanct";[26] Christ, the Spirit, and the gospel dominate. His fidelity (to Christ and the gospel) and the freedom with which he handled *paradosis* deserve further exploration. Particularly helpful insights may come from exploring his treatment of authoritative citations from the Hebrew Scriptures and of the sayings of Jesus.

3. In tracing the rise of Christian teachers in the communities Paul knew, if evidence is difficult to come by as to whether *didaskaloi* arose out of a Jewish background (and first appeared in Jewish Christianity) or out of Hellenistic Judaism,[27] a more sound starting point is with the earliest Christian reference to a teacher engaged in oral instruction of "the word," Gal. 6:6 *(ho katēchōn ton logon)* (cf. 1 Cor. 14:19; Acts 18:25; perhaps Luke 1:4; and note 3 above).

The list in 1 Cor. 12:28 may be dated a bit earlier than that in Romans 12. Conzelmann sums up well the issues and opinions on the Corinthians passage, "First apostles, second prophets, third teachers" (v. 28) refers to three charismatic offices for the church as a whole, traveling from local community to local community (Harnack). Paul did not distinguish charismatic and other offices (Kümmel); all community functions are charismatic. And (Greeven) the prophets and teachers did not travel, they were tied to the local congregation (cf. 1 Cor. 14); a similar view is held by Barrett and Wegenast.[28] Does that mean that apostles were the itinerant regional figures, and teachers the fixed local ones? That teachers are third also in the Romans list (12:6-7) is less impressive when we note that the first two are not "apostles, prophets" but functions: "prophecy" and "service" *(diakonia)*. That, incidentally, is one reason why the footnote in *Eucharist and Ministry*[29] puts teachers in the "special Ministry of the church" (1 Corinthians 12) but hedges on "healing and teaching" (which could go either way), while putting "acts of mercy, aid, and helping" (cf. Rom. 12:7-8) under "the ministry of the people of God."

If one has to guess what teaching by such teachers in these brief references encompassed, it presumably concerned the setting forth of the Christian message (in an ever deepening way), with all its implications (especially for life and conduct), drawing in the Hebrew Scriptures, thus passing on and applying the gospel tradition.

4. Prophets occur ahead of teachers in the Pauline lists at 1 Cor. 12:28; Rom. 12:6-7; cf. Eph. 4:11, and are mentioned in churches like Corinth as exhorting, comforting, edifying, and communicating knowledge and mysteries (1 Cor. 14:3, 24-25, 31; 13:2). Does a teaching function not occur when

such Christian prophets deliver a "sentence of holy law" (such as 1 Cor. 3:17; 14:38; 15:51-52; 16:22; Gal. 5:21; 1 Thess. 3:4 have been analyzed to be)? The proposal of Ernst Käsemann, though it has not gone unchallenged,[30] holds that in small (Galilean) Palestinian communities charismatic figures spoke for God or the risen Christ, and statements from them or later prophets appear in Paul's letters and the Synoptic tradition. Such material would be teaching of highest authority, pointing to divine judgment, from a very charismatic teaching office.

5. With regard to 1 Cor. 4:17 (which turned out to be the "one occasion" where Paul did "describe himself as having taught"), the meaning of "my ways in Christ" can be defined more clearly than as "something broader than the gospel, though based on it" or as "something more than merely faith in the preached gospel" or "imitation" (of what?). The reference is not to lifestyle or idiosyncrasies of Paul himself, but to his catechetical teachings (and thus to his gospel). They are just "as I teach them everywhere in every church" (no need to delete this ecumenical reference, as J. Weiss proposed, for, as Conzelmann notes, such references also appear at 7:17; 14:33; 1:2; 11:16). Possible background may be "the ways of life" in which one walks according to the Old Testament (Pss. 25:4; 18:21; *derek; halakah;* cf. "the Two Ways" in Didache 1–6). It is catechetical material, if not a primitive catechism, that is meant. Old Testament background for imitation of the Christ as a Christian "way" has been argued by E. J. Tinsley.[31] The dissertation by Donald Manly Williams, "The Imitation of Christ in Paul with Special Reference to Paul as Teacher" (1967), referred to in note 14 of Professor Fitzmyer's essay, connects the phrase with Paul's personal example as well as his *paradosis* and argues that his teaching on love in 1 Corinthians 13—termed a "way" or *hodos* in 12:31—is one of his *hodoi.*

6. Romans 6:17*b* is likely a later gloss, interrupting an antithetical sentence in Paul's letter. Paul wrote, Thanks be to God, that

you were once slaves of Sin . . .
and, having been set free from Sin, have become slaves of righteousness.

Between the contrast of "slaves of sin" and "slaves of righteousness" someone inserted the comment, "have become obedient from the heart to the standard of teaching [*typon didachēs*] to which you were committed." As an insertion it makes the obedience *prior to* the liberation from sin and captivity to God's righteousness. Its content is singular. Normally tradition is handed on to believers; here believers are handed over to a *typos didachēs.* The whole is uncharacteristic of Paul's emphasis on freedom. Whether by Paul or a later hand, it refers, I agree, to the catechetical tradition.[32] There are pre-Pauline formulas of the type envisioned in Romans at 1:3-4; 3:24-26; 14:8; and elsewhere.

7. If Rom. 6:17*b* is thus bracketed out or is citing a phrase from catechetical paraenesis, if 1 Cor. 4:17 is taken to refer to catechetical teaching, and if Gal. 6:6 *(katēcheō)* and uses of *paradidōmi* are given their due, then attention to how Paul handled tradition in shaping teaching becomes even more imperative. (The standard study is by Wegenast, whose views I am frequently citing; see especially note 26.)

8. There is growing emphasis in the Pauline corpus, chiefly beyond the uncontested letters and above all in the Pastorals, on (right) "doctrine" *(didaskalia)* and the "deposit" of faith "which has been entrusted" *(parathēkē,* 1 Tim. 6:20; 2 Tim. 1:12, 14). The Pastorals no longer feel the pejorative sense common in the Septuagint and Gospels of *didaskalia* as "human doctrines." "No tension is felt between the gospel, constantly preached afresh, and doctrine to be learnt, kept pure and defended against heresies."[33]

B. Jesus and the Synoptics

Summary of Essay

III. Though use of the sources is complicated by the two *Sitze im Leben* (situations or settings in Jesus' lifetime and in that of the early church) Jesus can be seen historically in his Palestinian setting as a teacher (rabbi?), but as more than an expositor of Torah. Redactionally, *Luke* emphasizes teaching activity on the part of Jesus (to ground securely what his church was doing). *Matthew* rejects *rabbi* or *master* as a title within the community (23:8-10), for Christological reasons, and roots teaching (of what?) in a commission from Jesus himself (28:18-20).

1. Method: It has already been suggested that we may need to pay more attention to the oral period and sources like Q in order to develop any trajectory here; we may also need to pay more attention to Mark. Redaction might be more consistently distinguished from tradition. Thus for getting at each gospel's picture of Jesus there would be fuller evidence than just the word-study approach affords.

2. As to the historical Jesus, clearly he was a teacher. Whether the term *rabbi* was used in his lifetime depends on when it became a *terminus technicus* in Judaism, and whether we insist on its being a technical term when applied to Jesus. I assume he was "rabbi" in that he taught and had pupils (disciples), but not in the (later) sense of having studied formally and been ordained. What distinguished him was his authority, in which the miracles played a part, as well as his radicalizing of the message about God's reign and will. The picture of him as teacher has doubtless been enhanced by later efforts, in the light of Christology, to gather his teachings and depict him as *the* teacher (of wisdom). The recent attempt by Etienne Trocmé[34] to show Jesus as he might have been looked upon by various groups in his day, on the basis of

different forms of oral materials, might be noted: Jesus appears, e.g., to us as seen

| by disciples | in dominical sayings and apophthegms, | as a { prophet and teacher |
| by middle- and lower-class non-Christians | in parables | as a   moralist. |

3. How do we deal with a possibly nonchristological portrait of Jesus in the Q source? Here he seems to appear as one whose authority as teacher (which was considerable) lay in the fact that he was to be the coming judge.[35]

4. Mark: The faultiness in distinguishing too sharply between *kērygma* and *didachē* has been noted. What Jesus preached (Mark 1:14-15) was the coming kingdom in its imminence and the necessary human response; what he taught (*didaskein*, 4:2, and the following chapter of parables) was the coming kingdom in its imminence and the necessary human response. Teaching for Mark apparently encompasses miracles (1:27), controversy with opponents (12:35-40), Old Testament interpretation (12:35-36), and "the way of God" (an Old Testament phrase? 12:14). Indeed, *didaskein* seems a sort of general, redactional term in Mark to describe Jesus and his message.[36] In the Gospels generally the teacher becomes the teaching, and the content of Mark's message is Jesus himself (8:35; 10:29).[37]

5. Luke: The evidence for "the Lucan emphasis on teaching" noted by Father Fitzmyer (pp. 199-200) becomes ambiguous when we are told that references to Jesus as teacher are "almost as great" in (shorter) Mark as in Luke. Use of infancy material and parallels with John the Baptist seem an indirect way to get at the topic. Jerome Murphy-O'Connor concludes rather that "Luke appears to have felt the inadequacy of 'Teacher' as a Christological title"; Glombitza holds that "in the Third Gospel Jesus is a 'teacher' only as far as strangers are concerned (e.g. 10.25 and 22.11)"; " 'Teacher' is a title based on superficial observation, and it is never employed by the disciples. . . ."[38] If we wish to see Jesus teaching in Luke, Chapters 20–21 (in the Temple!) and 4:14-27 (use of Old Testament) afford examples.

6. In Matthew, 28:16-20 is to be regarded as the best interpretative starting point for the gospel (cf. W. Trilling, Peter Ellis). The content of the teaching there ("all that I have commanded you") must have some connection with the five great discourses in Matthew; these are Jesus' *didachē* and commandment (cf. Deut. 5:30-31). The commission comes from the risen Christ; the content of the teaching comes from the earthly Lord (in Matthew, the

disciples call Jesus "*kyrie*"; "though Matthew frequently uses the title *di-daskalos* or, alternatively, *rabbi,* he never uses it as a mode of address in the mouth of the disciples, with one exception—Judas Iscariot," in 26:49 and 26:25![39]

Matthew 23:8-10 contains many enigmas (well-posed as questions in Father Fitzmyer's essay). In Jewish use, or if spoken by Jesus himself, "teacher" in v. 8 would have referred "clearly to the Father" (see p. 200); but in the redacted form one cannot be sure if it does; it is more likely christological. The *Kyrios* Jesus is the one *didaskalos,* who sends forth followers to teach what he has commanded. Matthew's church may well have eschewed "teachers/rabbis" in the Jewish sense, out of reaction to "the synagogue down the street."[40] Jesus is *the* Teacher; there are no others.

However, the Matthean community may well have had a "school of scribes" (13:52) as well as "prophets and wise men" (23:34) who immersed themselves in Scripture in light of the gospel and brought out "what is new and what is old." Is that teaching? One need not be concerned if structures here differed from the charismatic teachers in Corinth 30 years before. The lines of development need not be the same, and besides the Matthean community probably had its troubles with, and reasons to avoid, such Hellenistic wonder-working charismatics.[41]

Last of all, is there in Matthew "the prohibition of a teaching office" in 23:8-10? Professor Fitzmyer (p. 200) wrestles with this possibility. Wegenast offers the following opinion apposite to the concerns of this dialogue:

> . . . for Matt., Jesus is the teacher of the *church* who supersedes the Sinaitic revelation and its rabbinic interpretations ("it was said to men of old") in order to lay a new foundation ("but I say to you"). After the death of Jesus, Peter guarantees this foundation (Matt. 16:18), holding the office of the keys . . . which to the Jews meant the office of a teacher [*das Lehramt*]. The foundation guaranteed by him is no new law but the fulfillment of the old, now freed from rabbinic distortions. Only now does the original intention of the law become clear (Matt. 19:8: "from the beginning"). These two verses (Matt. 16:18; 19:8) throw light on Matt. 5:19: he who lives without the Torah is without righteousness. The follower of Jesus is called not to lawlessness but to a superior righteousness, the foundation of which is the law and Christ's interpretation of it. This is why, after his resurrection, this interpretation must be passed on through teaching (Matt. 28:20).[42]

Wegenast's analysis points to Jesus as *the* Teacher. The disciples were not above their Teacher (10:24-25). Peter (in the particular role noted above) and presumably all the disciples taught what he, the earthly Risen One, had taught—messianic Torah, in Jesus' interpretation. But they were not themselves teachers—not even Peter. Indeed, the eleven on the mountain remained "men of little faith" who both worshiped and doubted (28:17).[43]

It is agreed that the commission to the eleven relates to Christ's promise and presence; their preaching/teaching was to announce the kerygma and all that Jesus commanded, perhaps even to be a "reformulation of the essential kerygma to meet new problems" (p. 202). But is there a *Gegenüber* (over-againstness) in Matthew which implies an office of teacher in the church "overagainst the community of believers" (p. 201). The Malta Report (par. 50) admittedly referred *Gegenüber* to the gospel proclamation, not to an office of teaching (the report used the phrase "office of the ministry"). Again, the exact sense of *Lehramt* may be a cause of confusion. We must be careful (in light of the way Matthew uses *didaskein* terms and of his whole view of the church)[44] not to read in an office of teaching in opposition to church members, without further evidence, on the grounds that it is implied by 28:16-20.

C. Acts

Summary of paper

IV. Acts amplifies the picture in Luke's Gospel. The book knows of teachers in the local community (13:10) and stresses the apostles and others, teaching/preaching, on Jesus' commission, with some concern for correct doctrine.

In this helpful sketch, with which I am in general agreement, the evidence seems again to point to teaching as reiteration of *kērygma (logos)*, as scriptural development, and as ethical implications of the *kērygma*. It is not concerned, as in Matthew, with exposition of Torah in the sense of laws. What is blurred is not Luke's concept but modern distinctions. What is taught seems more important than who teaches it, even given Luke's emphasis on "the Twelve" (or thirteen).

D. James

Summary of paper

VI. James 3:1 shows the author to be a teacher, without official position, but with the awareness, under God's judgment, that teachers may err.

Perhaps this passage should be related to the "teacher of wisdom" tradition. The role of teacher is viewed here as not unimportant in the church, but with modesty, subject to "sins of the tongue" (3:2-12).

E. Johannine Literature

Summary of paper

VII. The Fourth Gospel contains most of the references here, references chiefly to Jesus as the teacher whose source of authority is in the Father and whose teachings will be explicated by the Paraclete. Believers are "taught by God" (6:45), have a *chrisma,* the Spirit (1 John 2:27), and must teach as part of their witnessing (9:34). In the Gospel of John there is no church structure, yet there is an emphasis on unity (from gospel doctrine?).

This Johannine picture is extremely important for grasping New Testament pluralism. It is a different world from that of Paul or the Synoptics. Jesus is the "apostle"; disciples abide in him. Is witness really directed outward to the world, except in controversy with "the Jews" (the world), or only inward, to development of the community? Clearly, the content of the teaching is Jesus himself, as Revealer.

Those Christians who have the anointing need no further teaching (1 John 2:27; cf. 3:24), and have all knowledge, knowing the truth already (2:21). Is a *Lehramt* conceivable here, or only a proclamation (1:3) to remind hearers of what they already are, of implications of their confession (1:1-2; 4:2, for example), and of the need to keep doing the truth? Note also 2 John 9-10, about "abiding in the doctrine of Christ (*didachē tou Christou*)," which is in content "nothing else than the message of Jesus in John 7,"[45] i.e., about himself, coming from the Father (John 7:16-36).

III. Concluding Comments and Further Concerns

1. The essay lays a good groundwork for a difficult subject.

2. It is agreed that the teaching function did exist in early Christianity and grew stronger, if not always clearer (but not in an ever-steady, ascending trajectory). It does become connected, at times, with *episkopoi/presbyteroi* in the Pastoral Letters, but here the gospel of Paul the apostle dominated those who did the subsequent "traditioning" and teaching. Romans 6:17 well expresses this situation: they "were handed over to the *typos didachēs*." And the "traditions" involved here, whether written or oral (cf. 2 Thess. 2:15), seem to have been already openly known and accepted by the community of faith.

3. The cautions expressed by Father Fitzmyer (on p. 212) are well taken: there is only one Teacher, Jesus Christ, according to Matthew; a certain modesty about teachers and their fallibility is noted by James; the community as a whole, rather than any group within it, serves as Spirit-guided teacher, according to the Johannine literature.

4. There are grounds to question any sharp dichotomy between preaching and teaching. The gospel, consisting of both didactic *kērygma* and kerygmatic *didachē,* seems a better way of conceptualizing what is involved in "the Word of God."

5. It seems necessary to trace *several* lines of development: at the least the Pauline line of development, the Synoptic (with bifurcating lines for each Gospel), and the Johannine. Should others be added to those (e.g., "Jesus as Teacher," "the Spirit as Teacher," and "the wisdom trajectory")?

6. An overall impression, as so often with the New Testament, is one of the tremendous variety within the early church—a variety which must, within

certain limits, have been "pleasing to God," orthodox, evangelical, and catholic. Apparently all these teaching models in the New Testament "seemed good to the Holy Spirit and to us" (the early Christian church).

7. One is struck, from the evidence presented in Professor Fitzmyer's essay, with the centrality of the kerygma or gospel in explaining New Testament teaching. The latter overlaps with or derives from the former again and again. The key New Testament phrase is "the truth of the gospel" (Gal. 2:5,14). The gospel is the truth which serves as the norm for all teaching and conduct, even of apostles in Antioch and Galatia, and of all teachers and teaching ever since.[46]

SUPPLEMENTARY COMMENTS

This paper, together with that of Father Fitzmyer, aided in producing the Common Statement about "Teaching Authority and Infallibility in the Church" on which the Lutheran and Catholic theologians in the U.S. dialogue were able to agree in 1978.[47] That statement treated the question of infallibility, both as later asserted in Roman Catholicism with regard to the pope under certain conditions defined in 1870 (see §§21-22, 30-33 in the Common Statement, and in the Roman Catholic Reflections especially §§12-20) and by Protestants at times with regard to the Bible (see §16 in the Lutheran Reflections), within the framework of "a fresh look at doctrinal authority."

This "fresh look" drew especially on "modern historical studies in Scripture" (Common Statement, §4). It was argued that "God . . . is the source and ground of authority for the Church of Christ" and that "the gospel . . . is an expression of this authority" (§5). In light of Jesus the Christ as our authority, "himself the gospel," a gospel in which "the risen Lord's authority and power in the Christian community are expressed" (§§6-8), it was agreed that "this gospel

(a) was proclaimed by witnesses—apostles and other—in the early Church [§§9-10];

(b) was recorded in the New Testament Scriptures, which have 'a normative role for the entire later tradition of the Church' [§11];

(c) has been made living in the hearts of believers by the Holy Spirit [§12];

(d) has been reflected in the 'rule of faith' (*regula fidei*) and in the forms and exercise of church leadership [§13];

(e) has been served by Ministers [§§14-16]" (§5).

While subsequent history, doctrine, and cultural contexts have given this ordained Ministry varied shapes, so that Catholics and Lutherans "have sought to assure . . . transmission of the gospel along different lines" (§29), there is agreement on "the primacy of the gospel" (§43) and "the privileged authority of Scripture" (§45), as well as on recognition that "all members of the people of God share in principle the responsibility for teaching and formulating doctrine" (§47) and appreciation that the Spirit works through Scripture, tradition, and teaching authority (§50). Thus the gospel grounds ministerial authority.

This position received further affirmation in the 1981 document from the international Roman Catholic–Lutheran dialogue in a report by its Joint Commission entitled *The Ministry in the Church*.[48] It spoke of "the christologically based authority (*exousia*) of the ministry" that "must be exercised in the Holy Spirit" (§22), involving "the participation of the whole community" (§24). "Both churches know that their norm is the gospel" for teaching ministry and teaching authority (§57). There is also a mutual emphasis on ordination, which is "primarily the act of the exalted Lord who moves, strengthens and blesses the ordained person through the Holy Spirit" (§34).

Then in 1983 a similar assertion was articulated in "The Lutheran Understanding of Ministry,"[49] a Lutheran World Federation study, which spells out a view of ministerial authority in some detail. It speaks first of Christians as "a people to whom God has given the gifts of the Holy Spirit (*charismata*) to empower their common life and their mission in the world." Because they are "empowered by the same Spirit Jesus received at his baptism, the baptized people of God are sent to carry out Christ's ministry" (§3). This includes a ministry of worship (*leiturgia*), of witness (*martyria*), and of service to others (*diakonia*) (§§5-10; cf. *The Ministry in the Church*, §13).

Within the wholeness of this one ministry of the people of God, the ordained ministry "exists to serve the Christian community" (§18). It is "divinely instituted as the necessary instrument in the service of Word and Sacrament" (Augsburg Confession, Article 5) (§19). "The authority of the ordained ministry is rooted in Christ who received it from the Father," but, since Jesus came to serve, "ordination inaugurates an authority not of status but of service," a service that "centers in Word and Sacrament" (§20). The ordained, who "stand both within the congregation and over against it" are thus part of "the one ministry of the Church" but also "bear the authority of God's word—but only insofar as their proclamation is faithful to the Gospel" (§21). Their authority is thus "Gospel-authority" (§24).

It may be remarked that in the LWF statement this gospel matrix for ministry is more overtly asserted in the case of the ordained. For the nonordained ministers it is their baptism (also "gospel"!) that provides the context (§2); in some cases a "commissioning" is also involved (§45). To the clergy "ordination gives authority publicly to preach the Gospel and administer the sacraments" (§47); it is "a calling, blessing and sending for a God-given ministry in the midst of and for the people of God" (§52). On the other hand, "the ministries of most Christians are carried out primarily outside the life and activity of the institutional Church. Thus they constitute the frontline of the Church's ministry to the world" (§15).

The LWF study lifts up the ministry of the laity in a way Lutheran–Catholic dialogue statements do not have occasion to do. It shares with them a view that ministry and its authority for teaching and other functions arise out of the gospel.

But this convergence between Lutherans and Roman Catholics on the point that "the Ministry of Word and sacrament" serves the gospel and is a means "by which Christ preserves the Church in the truth of the gospel" (1978 Common Statement. §41, 6) does not mean full agreement on the Ministry has been achieved between these two confessional traditions. For Catholics stress in addition "the authority of the Church's institutions, particularly of the structures of the Ministry of bishops and priests under the primacy of the bishop of Rome" (§40). While the U. S. discussions between Lutherans and Roman Catholics had in 1974 been able to report a significant and widely heralded agreement on "papal primacy,"[50] the dialogue's earlier volume in 1970 on *Eucharist and Ministry* has not always been regarded, especially in some Catholic responses, as having made a satisfying case for Rome's granting recognition to the validity of the ordained Ministry among Lutherans. See the 1984 critique by the "Committee on Doctrine of the National Council [Conference] of Catholic Bishops," together with "Observations" on this critique by the present Roman Catholic members of the dialogue (1986), and the evaluation by the "Bishops' Committee for Ecumenical and Interreligious Affairs" (1986), all reprinted in *LQ,* New Series 1 (1987): 125-69, especially pp. 128-30, 144-47, and 167-68.

Thus recognition of the authority and validity of the ministers—and hence ministry—of other churches remains a disputed matter on the ecumenical agenda. "'By what authority' do they act? Do we recognize it?" most churches ask of the others' ministrations.

Broadly speaking, there are some half-dozen ways in which the authority of a ministry can be "validated." Often, elements from several of these methods may appear in a church's understanding of what constitutes an acceptable ministry. But by and large each denominational tradition emphasizes one particular approach to authority for ministry. (With the analysis that follows, compare also above, in Chapter 2, Part B, section II on "ecclesial recognition.")

One obvious approach is to stress *the Spirit*. God's Spirit calls persons into tasks of ministerial leadership, endows them for the work, and grants manifestations of pneumatic power and presence as proof that the person is chosen by God. The modern Pentecostal movement reflects such an understanding; "signs and wonders," as in the book of Acts, are said to testify that God is blessing a ministry.

Closely related, but a second method, involves *charismata,* the raising up of charismatically endowed leaders. Here gifts of God's grace make it apparent that this person or that is equipped to lead. These charismata might be natural talents raised to new heights for the situation or unexpected gifts suddenly given. The charismatic leader can appear even in groups that do not stress the Holy Spirit.

We find examples of these two, often related types of leadership in ministry early in Israel's history in the judges whom God raised up, in certain prophets, and in the young church of the New Testament. But Israel's kings could also claim, at least in the portrait of the ideal Davidic ruler, to be blessed with gifts like wisdom, understanding, counsel, and fear of the Lord from the Spirit of God (e.g., Isa. 11:1-2). And Paul, in writing the Corinthians, assumed that every Christian possessed the Spirit (1 Cor. 12:13) and therefore certain gifts from the Spirit (12:11), such as wisdom, knowledge, faith, the gift of healing, miracle-working, or tongues (12:4-10). These he called "spiritual gifts" or the individuals "spiritual persons" (12:1), possessing charismata (12:4). As part of God's endowing of the congregation with such gifted persons, Paul lists types of people and functions: "first apostles, second prophets, third teachers, then workers of miracles, healers, helpers, administrators, speakers in various kinds of tongues" (12:28) and the still better way of self-giving love in life (12:31—14:1).

Among the difficulties with verifying a ministry from the presence of the Spirit and such charismatic gifts is the problem of discerning what are often subjective qualities and the competing rivalries of those claiming such endowments. Paul in Corinth had to urge the tests of whether gifted leaders built up the community (8:1) and conformed to "Christ crucified" (1:17, 23) as the gospel. There is also the fact that, at least for the Pauline and Johannine churches, all Christians have the Spirit (the Paraclete) and some spiritual gift or gifts (or charism); cf. John 14:15-17, 25-26; 15:26-27; 16:13-15; 1 John 2:20, 27; 4:13, for some of the Johannine evidence. Human discernment finds it hard to evaluate claims of endorsement by the Spirit perpendicularly from above. Furthermore, almost every Christian tradition prays for the Spirit to assist its (ordained) ministers and indeed endow them with appropriate gifts of grace. Thus in countless liturgies it is prayed, "Pour out, O God, upon these thy servants and all called to the Ministry of the Word and the Sacraments thy Holy Spirit and the gifts of thy Spirit . . ." (examples in *The Ministry of the Church,* pp. 38-41, 43, 57-60).

Other approaches to validating an authentic ministry think horizontally, of *conformity and continuity with past tradition,* rather than of a "tap on the shoulder" or a new endowment from above. A third method for assuring that the teaching, pastoral leadership is proper looks to its agreement with venerable *predecessors.* The new leaders are expected to be a contemporary extension of the views of ancient teaching and practice. Often, an oral tradition is involved on which and within which the current leaders take their stand. Emerging Judaism in New Testament times exemplified this approach in rabbis who "sat on Moses' seat" (Matt. 23:2) and taught as voices for the current day, applying the oral traditions to new needs. Early Christianity too had its oral traditions (*paradoseis*) to be maintained (1 Cor. 11:2; 2 Thess. 2:15; 3:6) and its teachers of oral catechesis (Gal. 6:6).

While there is a sense in which every denomination measures authentic leadership by unwritten traditions or may have a lore that is passed on apart from books, perhaps as part of "spiritual development" or piety, it is far more common, especially as the decades and centuries go on, to seek to link the valid teacher, preacher, priest, or other leader with a *written standard or norm*. The "traditions of the fathers" or "of the elders" in Judaism (cf. Gal. 1:14; Mark 7:3, 5) rested in fact on written documents, the Scriptures. Increasingly Christianity made appeal to apostolic writings, eventually to the canon. Conformity to Scripture has long been a factor in assessing the propriety of a ministry. Protestantism in general and Conservative Evangelicalism in particular evaluate the authenticity of a minister by his (or her) congruity with Scripture as the group understands it.

Agreement with "the Book" or with an even broader heritage found in other writings and oral traditions is thus a further way of validating ministry. Note that this criterion can apply to all Christians and to clergy as well. The difference between clergy and laity in this approach would be the degree of rigor with which the person is expected to conform to the norm. Of the ordained a higher standard is demanded.

A fifth way of deciding when a ministry is valid is the *institutional* test. Does the person stem from and conform with the right structures? The church is here the basis for ministerial validity. In some approaches it is the local congregation that provides the source and standard. The group of people making up the local church designates one of its own to minister in its name. The congregation may then also be able, just as readily, to remove that person from the ministry. So in Congregationalism, some storefront churches, or the "transfer theory" in parts of Lutheranism (see above, Chapter 1, §59). Of course the institution involved may also be a national church or even an international structure. This approach permits the group, large or small, to make clear rules and keep rolls on who is "in" and who is not in its ministry.

A sixth way to validate ministry involves a *hierarchical* approach. Within the institution there is found a structure of church governance. Its upper level(s), usually the bishops, ordain and thus determine who is a minister/priest; they also discipline and may remove persons from the ordained ministry. So Roman Catholicism, Eastern Orthodoxy, Anglicanism, and other groups. Here the ministries of clergy and laity are sharply separated.

Perhaps a seventh approach involves *age, wisdom, and experience.* The concept of "elders" played a role in the Jewish synagogue, and early Christianity at times recognized "those who are older" in contrast to "those who are younger" (1 Tim. 5: 1-2; 1 Peter 5:5). Eventually Christian elders (Greek, *presbyteroi*) became a clear and distinct type of minister, the presbyters (1 Peter 5:1; James 5:14; Titus 1:5; 1 Tim 5:17-19; 2 John 1; 3 John 1). Subsequently the presbyters became "clergy," not necessarily older persons, and the idea of age and wisdom attached itself often to the bishop as leader within the hierarchical structure.

Although certain of these approaches have been identified above with specific denominational or confessional groups, the fact is that several aspects are often combined in determining for a church who its "valid ministers" are. While Lutherans, e.g., may derive ministerial authority from the gospel, that does not exclude prayer for the Spirit and for spiritual gifts for ordinands or the demand for conformity with biblical and other traditional (confessional) teachings, and even at times hierarchical tendencies. The fact that Roman Catholic clergy stand in a hierarchical structure of bishops and pope does not mean other factors listed above are not also part of the picture in validating office in the Church of Rome.

Perhaps reflection on which aspects of certifying ministry a church most cherishes could help in attaining clarity and even future convergences with other churches on the question of the ministry/Ministry and its authority. But different denominations do emphasize different approaches. That "authority question" in ministry is part of the tangle that the ecumenical movement has had to address.

5

Current Crisis Questions about Ministries

The 1980s have brought to all churches a proposal directly confronting their customary way of looking at the ministry. It comes in the statement completed at the Faith and Order Commission's meeting in Lima, Peru, in 1982, *Baptism, Eucharist and Ministry.*[1] It asks all churches, whether in the World Council of Churches or not, to what extent each can recognize "the faith of the Church through the ages" in this document, and what consequences, guidance, and suggestions for further work each can draw. In *BEM*, Part III, on "Ministry" (hereafter cited as 3/ and the paragraph number, or just by number where the section is obvious), statements are made concerning laity as "the whole people of God" and in even more detail about the ordained ministry. There are quite specific proposals on "threefold ministry," including bishops, though nothing specific on women and their ordination. What is presented may or may not bring about a crisis in a denomination, but the potential is there for a considerable shake-up in how things have traditionally been viewed in almost all churches, catholic or/and evangelical.

Lutherans thus are not alone in having to deal with the ideas of *BEM*. Nor are they alone in having brought together several churches into one in the 1980s. Presbyterians in the United States, for example, did too. But Lutherans probably had to deal with more variety in their tradition on the issue of the ministry than many other groups do; polity is not a Lutheran hallmark as it is with Presbyterians. Three Lutheran bodies between 1982 and 1986 dealt with the question of structure for a new church of more than five million members and did this in considerable proximity to *BEM*—in terms of time, people, and ideas—and to influences from the ecumenical dialogues. And by doing all this in a commission of 70 elected members, chosen from the outset with categories for women, laity, and minorities, and with task forces usually reflecting the same egalitarian principles, Lutherans tried to work through problem areas like the ministry with a cast of decision-makers that was scarcely a bishops' committee, professional theologians' assembly, clergy caucus, or "old boys' network." It may have been the largest body, most deliberately balanced or weighted (in some categories), for planning a church to date in history. An account of its examination of and crises over the ministry (and there were other topics of debate, like ecumenism, the property of the local congregation, and the pension system) may be read by others as a case study, but for those entering the Evangelical Lutheran Church in America (ELCA), legally to be begun January 1, 1988, this shared history is background for further, future discussion. For the ELCA is pledged to complete a fuller study on the ministry by 1994 at the latest. The tugs of persons and principles in various directions that will ensue may be more clearly understood in light of the 1982–1986 discussions within the Commission for a New Lutheran Church (CNLC).

These two foci in this chapter, *BEM* and CNLC, come together in that the forthcoming ELCA study on ministry mandates consideration of ideas in *BEM* like the "threefold ministerial office of bishop, pastor, and deacon." As explained in the Introduction, I do not regard the treatment below as definitive, but perhaps sufficient to share some history and some themes discussed about ministry. I write as an interested follower of *BEM*'s progress, not a participant in its process or even one who served on committees that drafted Lutheran responses. With regard to the CNLC, I was involved as one of the 70 but never served on any of its many committees that tackled the ministry. Forewarned, readers may wish to see Part B of this chapter as a personal interpretation, and some opinions as just that—private (and possibly minority) views. In all instances these lines are written about past events of recent years but with an eye to the Lutheran and ecumenical future.

A. THE ECUMENICAL IMPACT OF THE FAITH AND ORDER STATEMENT ON *BAPTISM, EUCHARIST AND MINISTRY* (1982)

The Lima text of 1982 has a history that goes back even before the Lausanne Conference of Faith and Order in 1927, beginning with the pioneer days of ecumenism and the hopes and priorities of leaders like William Temple ("reunion" ahead even of "women's rights"), alluded to in the Supplementary Comments to Chapter 2. Indeed, already at a 1916 planning meeting in Garden City, Long Island, that led to this movement which emphasizes the content of the Christian faith (Scripture, creed, and sacraments, e.g.) and the ordering or constitution of the church (especially involving the ministry and, for some, the "historic episcopacy"), the theme of the ordained leadership was present.[2] This stemmed in part from Anglican insistence on such a role for bishops in the Lambeth Quadrilateral's listing of essentials for reunion in 1888. Thus at Lausanne one section was devoted to discussing "The Ministry of the Church."

Each of the three parts making up the total *BEM* statement has had a history of its own. The development of what Lima finally said on baptism, though in draft form by 1970, underwent radical recasting, especially after intense discussion with Baptists at Louisville in 1978. The eucharist section evolved between 1967 and 1982. While a first version of a statement on Ministry was ready in 1972, it expanded into a longer version printed following the Faith and Order meeting at Accra, Ghana, in 1974,[3] but was then shortened over the next eight years. The milestones on the way to Lima's statement on the ministry were sessions in Louvain (1971), Marseilles (1972), the commission meetings at Accra and then Bangalore, India (1978), and special consultations on episcopacy (Geneva, 1979), for the Eastern Orthodox (Chémbesy, Switzerland, 1979), and in the same year on women at Klingenthal, France (noted in the Supplementary Comments to Chapter 2, above). The long process has been likened to a stream, the tributaries of which feed a growing river in which the ecumenical bark of the church sails onward, a process I have charted elsewhere.[4]

Overall, *BEM* can be described, I think realistically and I hope not harshly, as a series of combinations or even "both/and compromises" on big issues that have long divided major Christian traditions. With regard to baptism, *BEM* asked whether mutual recognition cannot be given for both infant baptism and believers' baptism (1/11-12). Among controverted areas regarding the eucharist, attempts are made to speak on "the mystery of the real and unique presence of Christ" there in a way that satisfies many understandings and to raise the issue of "the inclusion of baptized children as communicants at the Lord's Supper" (2/19, Commentary), thus bridging Eastern Orthodox infant communion with Western Christian custom. The Ministry section seeks to present the threefold ministry as a traditional but post–New Testament pattern (3/19-25) that all could accept "in the order of life of a reunited Church" but not as divinely given (3/26, Commentary). Can such a concatenation of possibilities prove acceptable? Can one conjure with a situation where there might be infant communion *and* believers' baptism, or the (historic) episcopate *together with* the recognition that "the reality and function of the episcopal ministry have been preserved" in some churches often "without the title 'bishop'" and that the office has not always been "a guarantee, of the continuity and unity of the Church" (3/37, 38)?

Such a description of *BEM*'s proposals, of course, only highlights some of its most striking and controversial ideas. We miss thereby the solid work done on so many other aspects of each topic, showing how to state agreements and present convergences. It is the commonalities among the churches—or ways to see each paragraph of the document as amenable to one's particular denominational features of identity—that should first engage attention, and only then the controverted areas where suggestions may or may not prove acceptable to a church.

It should also be repeated that *BEM* focuses on these three disputed areas, taking up the two sacraments and the ministry within which they function, in light of broader agreements about Scripture and the Christian faith and with a vision of the possible future expression of that faith together in a fresh way. The matrix for *BEM* should be seen in the Montreal statement of Faith and Order in 1963 about Scripture.[5] All these studies can be accommodated under a long-range project, "the Common Expression of the Apostolic Faith," perhaps to be completed by the year 2000.[6]

BEM *on Ministry*

Faced at the outset by the apparently dismaying variety, contrasting views, and even mutual rejections of each other's ministries that one encounters when comparing what each church holds on the topic, Faith and Order plugged away over the years at finding what agreements there are. If originally the Anglican presence posed the demand for episcopacy, the entry of the Roman Catholic church into ecumenism, following Vatican II, reinforced such emphasis and, along with frequently increased Eastern Orthodox involvement, made Faith and Order into far more than a drive towards Protestant reunion. The *BEM* draft on ministry in 1972 operated with heavy use of quotations from previous ecumenical documents. These came especially from the Montreal and Louvain meetings. The 1974 document at Accra reflected much more the creative ferment of the 60s. The final text from Lima—on which there was unanimous agreement of the delegates to transmit it to the churches, not because all agreed with every item, but because it had been perfected as much as possible—this 1982 version is leaner, more realistic about what is possible, and offers a certain balance of past praxis and new possibilities.

Yet Lima ducks some divisive issues, topics that were perhaps not resolvable. For example, *papal ministry*. The place of the pope is not touched on in connection with bishops in the church. Yet, without agreement here there could be no Roman Catholic assent to the section on ministry. The proposals on *mutual recognition of ministries* that had been framed at Accra (§§88-106) have been drastically curtailed. They amount to just two questions, both about "episcopal succession": *(a)* Can churches that have preserved it recognize "both the apostolic content of the ordained ministry" and "a ministry of *episcopé*" in those that have not? *(b)* Can churches without this succession grasp "the continuity with the Church of the apostles" expressed through "the successive laying on of hands by bishops" and feel a need to recover this sign? (§53). The question of *intercommunion*, which frequently relates to views on the "validity" of each other's ministries, appears in *BEM* in the eucharist section (2/33). There it has become more muted. Whereas Accra dared to speak of "the problem of intercommunion" moving "toward its solution" as the churches "move toward the fullness which is in Christ" (§36), Lima refers only to how "increased mutual understanding . . . *may* allow *some* churches to attain a greater measure of eucharistic communion" (italics added).

Perhaps the most noticeable place in the Lima text where discretion overrules boldness, concerns *the ordination of women.* The Accra draft (§§64-69) plunged right into that problem by stating, in its section on ordination, "The Church is entitled to the style of ministry which can be provided by women as well as that . . . by men." While "the force of 19 centuries against the ordination of women" was noted, the position of "those who advocate" the step "out of their understanding of the meaning of the Gospel and ordination" seems to be more emphasized. That passages like Gen. 1:27 and Gal. 3:28 are being read "with a sensitivity arising out of new circumstances and new needs" is affirmed (§66). The social, cultural sicknesses are named: "the predominance of male imagery" (§67), "the feeling of some men that their security and authority are challenged" (§68), and even the sheer fact that "for some churches these problems are not yet alive" (§69). Opinion is growing, it was said, that "doctrinal considerations either favour the ordination of women or are neutral," so "the possibility is open that a future ecumenical council might deal with the question"—favorably, one presumes (§69). So the Accra *Agreed Statements.*

The Lima document, eight years later, places its much briefer reference to women in an entirely different context, not under "V. Ordination," but at the end of "II. The Church and the Ordained Ministry." There, after reference to the ordained within the whole people of God, the authority of the ordained and their particular priesthood, a paragraph follows that is headed "The Ministry of Men and Women in the Church." Note that the subject is not "ordained ministers" but "the Church":

> 18. . . . The Church is called to convey to the world the image of a new humanity. There is in Christ no male or female (Gal. 3:28). Both women and men must discover together their contributions to the service of Christ in the Church. The Church must discover the ministry which can be provided by women as well as that which can be provided by men. . . .

Note that it is not stated that this ministry is the same in each case. The rest of §18, as well as the Commentary on it, descriptively present what churches hold that ordain women "because of their understanding of the Gospel and of the ministry" and what those who hold to the 19 centuries of tradition believe. There is no hint of a trend, let alone of an ecumenical council taking up the "women's question."

We ought not to be surprised on this score that, amid the pressures in getting out a consensus statement on which major churches might agree, the consultation with the Orthodox likely weighed heavier than that on women, or that the Vatican statement of 1976 against women being ordained counted for

more than the slowly rising number of women ministers in Protestant, Lutheran, and Anglican churches. In short, the tradition of the centuries was
more impressive than the mixed attitude in even the churches newly allowing
women into their ministries. A statement like Lima almost had to deal thus
with the issue of women priests/pastors/presbyters in order to get a statement
out, referring the discussion back to the churches because answers are so
divided. Compare also §54, where it is hoped that differences on women's
ordination will not hinder mutual recognition of ministries.

What then does *BEM* contain on Ministry? We stress here four themes, one
with subpoints, out of its general outline, which runs like this:

    I. The Calling of the Whole People of God (§§1-6) (see below)
    II. The Church and the Ordained Ministry (§§7-18) (noted, in part,
       above)
    III. The Forms of the Ordained Ministry (§§19-33) (see below)
    IV. Succession in the Apostolic Tradition (§§34-38) (see below)
    V. Ordination (§§39-50) (see below)
    VI. Towards the Mutual Recognition of the Ordained Ministries (§§51-
       55) (see above).

Out of the eight subissues that might appear in ecumenical dialogue on
ministry,[7] the Lima text, we have seen, (1) passes over papal ministry; (2)
mentions the ordination of women descriptively as a problem, and has little
(compared with earlier drafts) on (3) mutual recognition of ministries and (4)
intercommunion. It does its fullest work on four other topics. What might
seem the key issue, ordained ministry, appears at times to take a back seat
to *episcopē* and bishops. That impression might, however, be misleading if
we note the main headings in *BEM* (above) and observe that the "Ordination"
section deals with the act of entering the ministry, with only one sentence in
§39 about "different intentions" in the liturgies "according to the specific
tasks of bishops, presbyters, and deacons." But as already noted, "mutual
recognition" seems to hang on solving not just "ordained ministry" but "episcopal succession."

Of the four subissues on ministry that *BEM* treats substantively, we may
begin with (A) *the whole people of God,* as the Ministry section itself does.
(The term *laity* is not used, unless the Greek *laos* is sensed behind "people."
Instead "the Church," "all members of the Church," "members of Christ's
body," and "the community" are the subjects of sentences in this section.)
The section is Trinitarian ("God calls," Jesus died and rose, "the Holy Spirit
unites"), but very christocentric ("the life of the Church is based on Christ's
victory") and pneumatic ("the Holy Spirit bestows on the community diverse
. . . gifts"). More may be said about the Church than what members do, but
they are "called to confess their faith and . . . hope," to "identify with . . .

people," and "struggle with the oppressed," in relevant witness and service (§4).

It is over "how the life of the Church is to be ordered" that Christians differ, particularly "the place and forms of the ordained ministry" (§6). While a "charism" or gifts of the Holy Spirit may be bestowed on any Christian for "the building up of the community and the fulfillment of its calling" and there is thus a "ministry in its broadest sense" as service, "ordained ministry refers to persons who have received a charism and whom the church appoints for service by . . . ordination" (§7). "The chief responsibility of the ordained ministry is to assemble and build up the body of Christ by proclaiming and teaching the Word of God, . . . the sacraments, and by guiding . . ." (13).

How, then, do lay and ordained members relate? Interrelatedly. They need each other. Then, it seems to me, *BEM* takes a step that reflects the notion of the priest as acting "in the person of Christ" (*in persona Christi*), as "another Christ" (*alter Christus*). This has long been a watershed area of Catholic exaggerations and Protestant fears about damage to the sole mediatorship of Christ.[8] When *BEM* says the presence of ordained ministers "reminds the community of the divine initiative, and of the dependence of the Church on Jesus Christ" (3/12), that is to be read along with the statements that "it is especially in the eucharistic celebration that the ordained minister is the visible focus of the deep and all-embracing communion between Christ and the members of his body" (3/14) and the earlier statement, "The minister of the eucharist is the ambassador who represents the divine initiative and expresses the connection of the local community with other local communities of the universal Church" (2/29).

Both the ALC and LCA responses were to criticize the concepts here as "problematic."[9] Perhaps that also applies where *BEM* says the authority of the ordained is "rooted in Jesus Christ" through ordination (§15; one misses the note, found in Lutheran statements, of "gospel authority," where there is authority but only insofar as the minister's proclamation is faithful to the gospel, as in the LWF 1983 statement on Ministry, §21, cited previously). From a Lutheran standpoint the theme of priesthood is applied to clergy in a strained way. Section 17 begins by asserting that "the Church as a whole can be described as a priesthood." All Christians, the ordained included, thus "are related . . . both to the priesthood of Christ, and to the priesthood of the Church." Then a sentence follows to justify use of "the word *priest* to denote certain ordained ministers" in some traditions (§7): ordained ministers "may appropriately be called priests because they fulfill a particular priestly service by strengthening and building up the royal and prophetic priesthood of the faithful through word and sacrament, . . . prayers of intercession, and . . . pastoral guidance . . ." (§17). Is this "priesthood" in a broad and then in a narrow sense (as "ministry" was thus used)? Or is it the issue of mediatorship, the role of the clergy with (or against) the role of the One Mediator, Jesus Christ? (The ALC response to *BEM* saw raised an "issue of mediatorship which contradicts the universal priesthood of believers.")

We began point (A) by inquiring after what the Lima document says on the whole people of God, and soon found the text to be talking far more about the ordained ministry. Hence the judgment from the ALC: "the roles of the laity appear to be neglected." The test area of how the ordained and the rest of the whole people of God are related seems clergy-oriented, even if it is allowed that "the ordained ministry has no existence apart from the community" (§12). The LCA response felt too that *BEM* "does not stress adequately the active role of the universal priesthood in the proclamation of the Gospel."

Overall, the Faith and Order statement is so interested in the traditionally divisive question of the ordained ministry that it fails to do much justice to the ministering of church members, in spite of the titles to parts I and II of its outline.

(B) *The Ordained Ministry and Its Threefold Form:* Here we move into what is, in many ways, the heart of the Lima document. Section III also represents much new material, at least by comparison with the 1974 Accra text. The *Agreed Statement* at Accra, in its section on "diversity of ministry," had spoken of "the threefold ministry of bishop, presbyter-priest and deacon" and allowed even that this structure "predominates," but quickly added that "it would be wrong to exclude other patterns of ministry which are found among the churches" (§25). Accra spoke of difficulty in imaging "any structure of ministry which did not incorporate *episcope*" (oversight) and *"presbyteral* function understood as the proclamation of the Gospel and the administration of the sacraments," with both "episcopal and presbyteral functions . . . sharing in the *diakonia,* that is . . . service. . . ." Possible renewal of "the office of deacon and deaconess" was mentioned. *BEM* seems to stress far more "Bishops, Presbyters, and Deacons"—that is indeed the first subhead in section III. But one must observe exactly what is said in *BEM.*

"The Ordained Ministry" is traced by *BEM* (§§8-11) from the time of Jesus. He chose disciples. "The Twelve and other apostles" show that "there were differentiated roles in the community" from the very beginning. "After the resurrection . . . the apostles prefigure both the Church as a whole and the persons within it who are entrusted with the specific authority and responsibility." Apostles, as unique "witnesses to the resurrection," differ from "the ordained ministers whose ministry is founded on theirs." But Christ does continue through the Spirit to "call persons into the ordained ministry."

One must give heed to a careful distinction then made by *BEM,* based on much modern, critical scholarship: "The New Testament does not describe a single pattern of ministry which might serve as a blueprint or continuing norm for all future ministry in the Church." Rather, there was "a variety of forms." Only later, "during the second and third centuries, a threefold pattern of bishop, presbyter and deacon became established. . . . " But "in succeeding centuries" this threefold structure underwent "considerable changes" (§19). Sections 20-21 trace out some of the shifts with regard to *episcopē* by bishops and the resulting changes for presbyters and deacons. One could amplify by saying that by the Middle Ages, in the West, the threefold ministry became a sort of "2.1 structure," as the diaconate became a momentary stepping stone to the priesthood, or, with the pope, a fourfold structure evolved.

Then comes the other half of *BEM*'s presentation. Even though the threefold ministry is thus post–New Testament and for many Protestants, including Lutherans but not necessarily Anglicans, not divinely mandated, "nevertheless the threefold ministry of bishop, presbyter and deacon may serve today as an expression of the unity we seek" (§22). The pattern admittedly stands in need of reform (§24), but does it not have a "powerful claim" on all to be accepted by them—but with the proviso "useful for unity" but not by "divine command" (§25)?

After emphasizing that ordained ministry must be exercised by persons sharing together in the common task, rooted in the community—the personal, collegial, and communal aspects of an ordained ministry that "needs to be constitutionally or canonically ordered" (§§26-27)—*BEM* offers "in a tentative way" functional descriptions of each ministry.

(1) *Bishops* preach, preside at the sacraments, and administer discipline, with "pastoral oversight of the [geographical] area to which they are called" and "leadership in the Church's mission" there. They serve "apostolicity and unity" by relating a geographical region "to the wider Church" and "the universal Church to their community." Then an important sentence on interrelatedness: "They, *in communion with the presbyters and deacons and the whole community,* are responsible for the orderly transfer of ministerial authority in the Church" (§29). (The italics are added; how many varieties of shared responsibilities can this cover?)

(2) "*Presbyters* serve as pastoral ministers of Word and sacraments in a local eucharistic community." They preach, teach, exercise pastoral care, discipline there, and prepare members "for Christian life and ministry" (§30).

(3) "*Deacons* represent to the Church its calling as servant in the world. By struggling in Christ's name with the myriad needs of societies and persons, deacons exemplify the interdependence of worship and service. . . ." Then far more is said about service in the church—in worship, teaching, administration, and governance—than about exercising love in the community (the neighborhood? or the church community?). Only the "deacons" paragraph

(§31) receives a commentary. Here we learn that, while there is "a strong tendency in many churches to restore the diaconate," there is also "considerable uncertainty" about need, rationale, status, and function for it. The hope is voiced that "there may be united in this office ministries now existing in a variety of forms" and under several names, and that "differences in ordering" here should not hinder "mutual recognition of the ordained ministries."

Such are the *BEM* proposals on ordained ministry, given the variety of charisms and impulses that may call for responding to all sorts of needs, temporary or permanent, through recognizing the Spirit's gifts; this happens, e.g., in religious orders or special ministries. Ministry, one might say, needs to be both fixed and fluid.

The responses of U.S. Lutherans to this key section of *BEM* commend the paragraph (§13) on the responsibility of the ordained ministry to proclaim Word and sacraments and guide worship, mission, and caring ministry (ALC, D.2). Likewise on the way *BEM* "grounds the ordained ministry in the Gospel" (so LCA, p. 7, point 4.b; but does it? cf. 3/15 where the line seems to be "Christ-ordination-authority of the ordained") or its authority "as being derived from the authority of Christ" (ALC, D.2). But on the "threefold pattern" the LCA response commented, "There is no Lutheran consensus," and the ALC took exception to the judgment in *BEM* (§22) that such a ministerial structure "may serve today as an expression of the unity we seek" by noting "disunity among churches that employ the threefold ordering of ministry" (D.4). The LCA also criticized a lack of focus on "the pastoral sense of the ordained ministry" (4.c).

One may see in *BEM* a trial balloon. To what extent could a great number of churches agree on a reformed version of threefold ministry, a structure that is of human origin, not divine mandate? It is questionable whether some of the churches which stress such a ministry could allow that it is merely "by human right." And in a reunion where some hold it to be divinely given and others find it ecumenically expedient, it is far from certain that in time a "divinizing" aspect would not rub off onto the structure. But Lutherans confessionally are not closed-minded to the ordained ministry of episcopal-presbyters. The thicket of problems about "the deacon" (and deaconess) is another matter. For the great variety of views expressed at the Ecumenical Consultation on the Diaconate held February 25-27, 1987, at Douglaston, New York, see *JES* 24 (1987): 188-89.

(C) *Succession* has long been a stumbling block in discussions about church and ministry, especially when tied to the historic episcopate and views that a ministry is valid only when the person is ordained by a bishop (or bishops) who in turn was inducted into office by bishops going back, in pedigree, to the original apostles—Roman Catholic thought would add, bishops in com-

munion with the bishop of Rome, the pope. *BEM* makes an immense contribution here, as a result of modern historical and theological scholarship,
perhaps even "solving" this problem. Its Section IV is even in some ways
an improvement here, in my judgment, over the Accra *Agreed Statement.*

In the 1974 version "Apostolic Succession" was quite prominent as Part
II of the Accra text. In the Lima document the heading is, better put, "Succession *in the Apostolic Tradition"* (italics mine), and this unit (§§34-38)
appears as Part IV, *after* the discussion of ordained ministry outlined above.
The *BEM* presentation first mentions the apostles' proclamation and how
"apostolic tradition" means "continuity" in "witness to the apostolic faith,"
"proclamation [but not just reiteration] and fresh interpretation of the gospel,"
the two sacraments, "transmission of ministerial responsibilities," and "communion in prayer, love, joy and suffering" as well as service and sharing
(§34). Then it is stated that "the primary manifestation of apostolic succession
is to be found in the apostolic tradition *of the Church as a whole"* (italics
added), especially via the ordained ministry which preserves and actualizes
the apostolic faith (§35). Only then is "the succession of *bishops"* mentioned
as *"one* of the ways . . . in which the apostolic tradition of the Church was
expressed" (§36; again, italics added for emphasis), indeed at times even
without the title *bishop* (§37). Episcopal succession can be "a sign, though
not a guarantee" (§38).

This striking approach somewhat stands on its head the notion that "historical episcopate" is *the* "pipeline" that guarantees ministerial validity and
even the gospel. (It is striking enough that §38 warns that the considerations
noted "do not diminish the importance of the episcopal ministry," §38). As
an approach, the section owes a great deal to the persuasive analysis of
apostolic succession by Edmund Schlink, a Lutheran systematician at Hei-
delberg University.[10] This way of viewing apostolicity has repeatedly been
asserted in the bilateral dialogues, notably Lutheran–Roman Catholic.[11] Much
of the content was already in the Accra statement in 1974 (§§27-37), even a
sentence reflecting the U.S. Lutheran–Catholic dialogue and historical research concerning "cases in the history of the Western Church in which priests,
not bishops, have with papal dispensation ordained other priests to serve at
the altar" (§32). Both the ALC and LCA responses applaud what *BEM* has
said on apostolicity.

(D) *Ordination* is a theme in the Lima text about which U.S. Lutherans in
their official responses to *BEM* found nothing to criticize. The treatment in
§§39-50 moves from origins in the invoking of the Spirit and laying on of
hands for certain members of the New Testament church to the developed
practices at the (liturgical) act of ordination and the varied conditions for being
ordained. The term is said to denote "an action by God and the community

by which the ordained are strengthened by the Spirit for their task and are upheld by the acknowledgment and prayers of the congregation" (§40).

All this is not to say there may not be aspects of ordination worth further discussion. The careful linguistic analysis in Accra §41, where the cultural difference is stressed between the Greek verb *cheirotonein*—translated as "ordain" by the King James Version in Acts 14:23 but meaning no more than to "appoint" (so RSV)—and the Latin *ordinare* with its legal connotations, has been relegated to the Commentary in *BEM* (§40). We have already called attention to the fact that once in §39 *BEM* introduces the idea of different intentions at ordination, i.e., not necessarily to a single office but to "tasks of bishops, presbyters, and deacons" (§39).

Reactions to Faith and Order Paper No. 111

All churches were asked to respond to *BEM* by 1984, a deadline later. extended till the end of 1985. Consideration of the document was worldwide. The volume became an unexpected "best seller," with over 300,000 copies printed in 30 languages. By early 1986 more than 100 official responses were received by the Faith and Order Commission, representing "a treasure of ecumenical thinking," according to Dr. Günther Gassmann, Director of its Secretariat, a German theologian formerly on the LWF staff. The U.S. Lutheran churches responded, each according to its own processes, and some of their thinking has already been noted above.[12] The LCA began soliciting reactions in 1983 and through a drafting committee under its Director for Ecumenical Relations, Dr. William G. Rusch, presented a text to the LCA's highest authority, the biennial convention. This text was slightly revised by the Toronto convention in July 1984. The ALC, in response to a request at its 1984 convention, had its Standing Committee on Inter-Church Relations draw up a briefer paper, which was adopted by the ALC's Church Council in June of 1985. (I leave out of the picture, in order to compare these two responses, the reactions in the AELC and other Lutheran replies.)

It has been said that the ALC wrote "one of the stronger critiques of *BEM*, saying that the document obscures Martin Luther's teaching of justification by grace through faith in Jesus Christ" (LCUSA news release 86-02). Perhaps. At least it is a popular impression that LCA was more positive. Because of such statements I have begun above with examples of a certain ALC-LCA commonality on specific points. What the ALC statement said on justification (A.4) is that *BEM* "reflects a conceptual framework that is dominated by Catholic understanding and appears to slight evangelical understandings. The centrality of justification by grace through faith is thereby obscured." Actually, the LCA response makes a similar point when it asks consideration of "four motifs . . . especially in light of the Lutheran understanding of the Gospel as justification by grace through faith which they regard as their witness to the Church catholic" (p. 6). The LCA states its ecumenical stance thus:

> In a Church Catholic, Lutherans want to say the Gospel.
> In a Church Evangelical they want to say a word catholic.
> It is in making both of these affirmations together that Lutherans are ecumenical (p. 8).

It specifically asks "whether there is some imbalance which slights the evangelical" in *BEM* (p. 5).

The four LCA motifs I find paralleled in the ALC response too. It is contended that *BEM* needs further consideration with regard to these elements:

1. *A stronger articulation of the Word and what this means for an understanding of baptism, eucharist, and ministry.* (ALC, p. 3: "The text fails to articulate an emphasis on the centrality of the Word and proclamation.")
2. *A clearer expression of the dynamic of sin and grace and what this means* for the three themes. (ALC, p. 3: It "does not articulate . . . the dynamic of sin and grace. . . .")
3. *The priority of a certain period of history as normative for the faith*, i.e., the 2nd or 3rd century at the expense of the 16th or, above all, of the first or New Testament century. (ALC, p. 4: "The text appears to regard certain periods of history as normative. . . .")
4. *A wider perspective on ministry.* (ALC, p. 6, "The roles of the laity appear neglected.")

It would appear the ALC deliberately echoes the earlier LCA critique here.

Both responses also note the attempt of *BEM* to create new theological language (that turns out to be "frequently ambiguous," according to the ALC, and "both a contribution and a problem," LCA), and each scores *BEM* on its minimal reference to the ordination of women. (At the LCA convention this section was beefed up by floor request and now states, "Our commitment to the ordination of women is an integral part of our obedience to the Gospel," p. 7, d.)

Where do the responses then differ? Not unexpectedly, the LCA welcomes "the ethical imperatives for justice in connection with the Eucharist" (p. 8), while the ALC paper feels the text is not "mission-oriented" (p. 4). The ALC affirmed the emphasis "on the corporate nature of Christian faith and life" as "a theological truth that many in our American churches need to hear . . ." (p. 3). That is worth saying against American and pietist individualism. I do not find the same affirmation in the LCA statement.

Whence the impression that the ALC response is more negative? Not so much on Ministry as, I suggest, on the eucharist, a topic on which the LCA response touches but little (cf. p. 4, where it talks about "a renewed appreciation of the sacraments as a means of grace" having occurred quite apart from *BEM*, and a section on p. 8 that includes the request for attention to "the rationale for frequency of communion, along with other forms of being nourished by the Word"—that is *not* paralleled in the ALC's longer "Observations on the Eucharist"). Finally, there is a matter of general tone and the fact that the LCA response gives a much more positive setting for its answer by reviewing its ecumenical posture and the congruence of that with what *BEM* seeks. By limiting its praise to a single paragraph or two (p. 3, points 1 and 3, about the theological character and seriousness of *BEM*), the ALC paper invites attention to its repeated use of words like "concern" and "reservations" or "we take exception."

This *BEM* document and emerging reactions to it were on the consciousness of at least some of the members of the Commission for a New Lutheran Church as it did its work. *BEM*'s ideas remain before U.S. Lutherans (and all others) as they study and work with ministry in the years to come.

B. TOWARD THE EVANGELICAL LUTHERAN CHURCH IN AMERICA (1988)

Most Lutheran bodies in the United States, except the Lutheran Church–Missouri Synod, have gone through one or several mergers, bringing together waves of ethnic immigrants who arrived at varying times. Recent major consolidations occurred in the early 60s when the ALC was formed in 1960 from Norwegian, German, Danish, and other groups, and the LCA in 1962 from German, Swedish, Finnish, Danish, and other groups, some of them "Americanized" for several centuries. While the understandings of ministry in these groups exhibited some variety from the backgrounds in Europe (see Chap. 1, above, §§38-48), there was shared a common emphasis on what the Scriptures teach, the 16th-century confessional heritage, and the experience, for a greater or lesser period, of the religious pluralism and freedom of the new world. Generally the ministry was not a doctrine that proved divisive at merger time, but there was frequently earnest debate about things as important as the priesthood of all the baptized and the office of Word and sacraments.

Most Lutheran churches in America, except Missouri, had also worked together in an international expression of Lutheranism, after World War II by membership in the Lutheran World Federation. The U.S.A. National Committee of the L.W.F. sponsored, with Roman Catholic authorities, the U.S. Lutheran–Catholic dialogue, with the LCMS providing representatives too. In 1966 the Lutheran Council in the U.S.A. was formed by most Lutheran bodies in the country, the Missouri Synod included. All of these organizations provided occasions to discuss topics like ministry, and references to papers generated by each of them have dotted the pages of this book in almost every chapter.

By the mid-70s it was clear that the Consultation on Lutheran Unity, where there had once been hopes of bringing ALC, LCA, and LCMS together, was going nowhere—in part because of the ordination of women by the first two groups. But in 1975 an ALC/LCA Committee on Church Cooperation began work and invited also the Association of Evangelical Lutheran Churches to participate. This group had been formed in 1976 by an exodus of more than 100,000 persons from the Missouri Synod. In 1978 the AELC issued "A Call to Lutheran Unity," and the 2,967,000-member LCA and the ALC with 2,389,000 members set up with the AELC "The Committee on Lutheran Unity." This CLU in turn produced proposals that led the three churches to commit themselves enthusiastically, at their conventions in the summer of 1982, to form one church and to elect, by categories such as "clergy and laity, male and female persons, racial and ethnic groups, age groups," etc., 31 persons each from ALC and LCA and 8 from the AELC to a commission to draw up specific plans.

The Work of the Commission for a New Lutheran Church

It is a tribute to the high commitment of the churches that the Commission for a New Lutheran Church could meet less than a month after the church conventions, in September 1982, with virtually perfect attendance. This initial CNLC session already had before it a series of study papers assigned by the CLU; none of these was directly on "the ministry," but several touched on ministry issues. In what follows, we shall focus solely on "the ministry debate," as it came to be called, leaving the fuller history of the CNLC to be told by others in the future.

The initial CNLC meeting at Madison, Wisconsin, made the important decision to appoint Task Forces on Theology and on Society. Such working groups were to produce studies for the CNLC throughout its life, but it must be remembered that these task force reports had no authority (other than their intrinsic wisdom) until the Commission voted something from their pages. Also, at this early stage, these first two task forces were perhaps less balanced on counts of gender, lay status, and for minorities than subsequent task forces were to be. There was probably also a higher number of Commission members on the Task Force on Theology (I was not one of them) than became the rule thereafter. This could be defended at the outset by the fact that familiarity with the Commission's work helped expedite the process. The aim was to do theology with proper attention to the societal context in the United States, then and in years to come.

Before describing what the Task Force on Theology did (and its work was to be foundational though not canonical for much of the future considerations by the CNLC), it is advisable to sketch the picture—whether true or a caricature—which many, including the 70, brought to the task. For we inherited a great deal of past history, from Luther to *BEM*, on the ministry, plus all the ferment of the 60s, anguish in Lutheranism of the 70s, and brave hopes for the 80s. It was conceded that we would likely be able to come to ready agreement about a "doctrinal article" for the new constitution, with the issue of "inerrancy of Scripture" the only one possibly to cause discussion, as some voices would demand an emphasis on biblical errorlessness. Ecclesiology might be harder, especially on practical questions of how a church with 5.5 million members should be structured.

As for images, the LCA was often regarded as a somewhat clerical body, though not without strong trends toward lay ministries. Its synods were more organizationally significant, and so its synod presidents ("bishops" after 1980) played a role that ALC districts and their "bishops" often did not. The ALC was viewed as far more "congregationally" oriented in its polity, though not, of course, without a sense of the national church and its offices. There was often in the ALC a less strong emphasis on the ordained ministry; parish pastors, for example, were not automatically voting delegates at district meetings, as they were in the LCA, and seminary faculty and other clergy outside parishes were less involved in the church's parliamentary life. Yet for all the "congregationalism" attributed to the ALC, it must be remembered that this was also the body with the heirs of Loehe (through the Iowa Synod) and of Grabau (and the Buffalo Synod) who held a "high" view of the pastoral office (see above, Chap. 1, §§58 and 54).

The AELC brought into the scene an inheritance from—and sometimes a sharp reaction to—its Missouri Synod background. The LCMS was quintessentially oriented to the local congregation through the theory of "transfer" of authority from the lay priesthood to their "designated clergy" (see above on the *Übertragungslehre,* Chap. 1, §§44 and 59). Yet this had evoked, as a counterbalance, a strong emphasis (sometimes overdone) on the authority of the pastor's office. One may compare some of the articles by Professor Arthur Carl Piepkorn, cited in connection with the Catholic dialogue (above, in Chap. 1, Supplementary Comments), for a high view on "Sacred Ministry." The AELC as a whole has probably brought more of the clerical than the congregational position into its life, though its very name suggests an association of congregations/churches. We have already seen how AELC from its beginnings reversed Missouri views by ordaining women. It also resolved for itself the long LCMS debate over the status of Christian day-school teachers by deciding to include "teachers or directors of Christian education in congregations, in Christian day schools at the primary level, in church-related colleges, and in seminaries" within the office of the ministry.

Inasmuch as such teachers in parochial schools were to become an important issue in later CNLC discussions, it is worth quoting here from a presentation by Dr. John H. Tietjen on "Ministry in the AELC," requested by the Commission, at its Los Angeles meeting, October 30, 1984. (The quotation in the previous paragraph is also from that paper.) In brief, the office of the ministry is seen as having several forms: the pastoral ministry; teaching ministry, as outlined above; and diaconal ministry. "Ordination is the term used to set apart people for pastoral ministry. Commissioning or consecration are terms used to set apart people for teaching and diaconal ministry." More of this later, when we get to the period of most intense confusion in 1984 over what the CNLC should do. But the question of status for teachers, inherited from the Missouri Synod problematic, was known to many when the Commission began work.

Finally, regarding "bishops," it was clear from the day the Commission first met that all three churches used the term, though somewhat differently. The LCA has it constitutionally for synod presidents and the President of the church. The ALC had even longer used it informally for district presidents but preferred the title "Presiding Bishop" for the President of the church. The AELC had a national and regional bishops, and more locally, in some regions geographically large, "auxiliary" bishops as well. How would the term be used in a new Lutheran church? The CNLC set to work with such questions in mind, along with its inherited Lutheran history and the currents in an ecumenical stream of which *BEM* was a part. It listed in its *Progress Report #1*—a device for reporting regularly and promptly to the churches— in early 1983, among the basic issues to be faced: relation of "the Office of the Ministry" to "the ministry of all believers"; character and responsibility of the ordained ministry; "oversight"; status of ministries like those of parish school teachers; and teaching authority in the church.

Beginnings, with the Task Force on Theology

"The Report of the Task Force on Theology" to the CNLC[13] was the work of a blue ribbon group of 21, three of them members of the Commission (Fred W. Meuser, who served as chair; Gerhard O. Forde, and John Tietjen). Eleven were seminary faculty, then or previously. Only five were women. Less than one-third were lay people, and one of these taught theology and another was studying in seminary. Expertise, in theological disciplines, was thus a prime consideration. This group met four times between November 1982 and June 1983, when its 10-page report was completed. One of its sessions was jointly with the Task Force on Society. A quarter of its report deals with "Confession of Faith" and the rest with "The Church." Out of the first part the Commission made its own the view of the report that no new confession of faith was needed (though there must be constant confessing of its faith), and from what the report presented, the CNLC affirmed summary emphases on the Word of God and Scripture. Here was a lasting contribution toward the chapter in the ELCA Constitution on Confession of Faith.

What the Task Force on Theology said on the Ministry, however, served to set in motion three years of intense discussion. The document began with the church, in Part II of its report, as "a people called and sent by the triune God" and affirmed that "the means God uses to create this community is the Gospel given to us through the ministry of word and sacrament" and that "the salvation in Christ which comes through the means of grace is received in faith, active in love, looking forward in hope." The purpose of the church is mission, which is the task of "the general ministry of the church," all believers (the term "priesthood" is used just once). Mission takes place by proclamation of the gospel in words (*kerygma* and confession), deeds (*diakonia*), and "by the very being of the church (*koinonia*)," i.e., as "one, holy, catholic, and apostolic." The "three main forms of the ministry of all believers" (§§48-51) are traditional evangelism (witnessing outside the church); tasks within the parish or larger church, including worship leadership; and "exercising secular vocations for the good of society and for the care of the earth." It is specifically warned, "The new church should guard against any tendency to equate the ministry of all believers with traditional church work" (§52).

"Within the people of God and for the sake of the Christian ministry entrusted to all believers, God has instituted a specific ministry," the task force report begins its next section. It rejects notions that this ministry exists merely for the sake of good order, for it is "given by God to the church" (§55). In addition to the Augsburg Confession, Articles 5 and 14, the report grounds "a twofold institution of the ministry," as general and specific, in Easter commissioning scenes like Matt. 28:16-20 and Luke 24:44-48. In the former, "the 11 disciples function not only as the first Easter community but also as the specially elected messengers who are mandated to teach with authority" (§56). (The idea can be paralleled in *BEM* 3/10: "the apostles prefigure both the Church as a whole and the persons within it who are entrusted with the specific authority and responsibility.") But I confess to having been always of two minds whether this is a brilliant insight, equalizing the origins of both types of ministry, or an arbitrary statement to solve the "transference theory" debate. I am tempted to think, not that there were six "clergy" and five "laity" on the mountain with Jesus; or that the eleven were future bishops and priests but those who "doubted" were lay folk who had slipped up on the mountaintop unannounced (an old sacerdotal explanation); but rather that all eleven both believed and doubted, as "little faiths"; our concept of "clergy and laity" may not be germane to Matthean thought. (The Lucan passage is different, for the eleven and "other disciples" are mentioned in 24:33, and Luke has a clear doctrine of apostleship.) But such exegetical matters one never had time to discuss in CNLC sessions.

The Specific Ministry, the report goes on, has (1) the pastoral ministry as its "chief form" and (2) "other forms of Specific Ministry." Under the first category, functions of pastors are spelled out (§§59-66) but specialization is noted too, as in "military and institutional chaplaincies, seminary and college professorships," etc. (§67). Bishops, having jurisdictional oversight in a region, belong in this category of pastoral ministry. Their functions are also listed, as are questions like their tenure and teaching authority (§§68-78).

For "other forms of specific ministries" the report invokes Ephesians 4, 1 Corinthians 12, and the Pastoral Epistles in a quite general way, and then becomes descriptive: "Two such other forms of ministry present in our churches are the diaconate and the parish school teacher" (§80). "The church in its freedom has established still other forms of ministry," like catechist and cantor; criteria are suggested (§81). Ordination had been briefly discussed in connection with "the pastoral ministry" (§66), and while "it would be possible to use the same term" for these other ministries, the preference is to use currently employed terms like "commissioning" or "consecrating" (§82).

There is attached at this point the single but lengthy footnote to the entire report. It lists one member's summary of other points of view that surfaced within the task force. Striking is the opening paragraph with its claim that Lutherans have generally agreed "there can be a variety of forms in which the ministerial office is present. In the past they had also agreed there can be only *one* office of ministry, 'the specific ministry, instituted by God.'" (Does that mean the task force no longer agreed?) Since the report might seem to make "other forms" into "lower forms," the options were these:

(1) What the report itself said;

(2) Ordain parochial school teachers, deacons, etc. But that might "establish a lower form of clergy" and make ordination "purely functional."

(3) Ordain them into "the one ministerial office," specific ministry, lifelong.

(4) Connect deacons and parochial school teachers with "the ministry of all believers," though they are full-time church workers. This, the note goes on, does not downgrade their status unless you have succumbed to clericalism and regard "laity as the folks who provide bread and butter for the lower or higher clergy."

On this foundation the CNLC attempted to build, with regard to the ministry. It would, late in the CNLC process, be urged that the new church had no "ecclesiology." To the extent indicated, the task force provided a progression of "Church—Mission and General Ministry" before taking up ordained ministry, which it called "Specific Ministry." While the Task Force on Theology was doing its work, the Commission held its second meeting, in Chicago, February 7-11, 1983, and received a progress report. Potentially more important was a coincident series of lectures and discussions on "issues facing American Lutheranism" set up at the Lutheran School of Theology at Chicago, on overlapping dates. Even with the best of intentions, traipsing through the snow from meeting site to the campus, commissioners, even those who wanted to, could take in only a portion of the LSTC sessions. The CNLC had its own schedule and was determined to do its own work. Later a volume of essays from the seminary symposium was given to each commissioner,[14] as another resource. But the task force report was the platform for much of the future discussion over Word-and-sacrament and other ministries.

The third meeting of the CNLC, in Columbus, Ohio, September 24-28, 1983 began discussion of the task force reports on theology and on society, attempting to coordinate them at points, and being forced to admit that the assignments given were "limited in scope." More input would be needed at points, and so "a research paper on the nature and function of the office of bishop" was requested, either fresh or an existing study, with reactions from scholars "of varying viewpoints." Determination was also made not to adopt the first two task force reports but receive them as "working documents." A summary of what had been said on ministry by the task force appeared in *Progress Report #2* for all constituencies to ponder. Among those who discussed it were the ALC/AELC/LCA bishops, meeting in a conference in October 1983. They asked for greater clarity about "specific ministry" and the office of bishop, among other things.

The Debate Grows More Intense, 1984

Help on the title *bishop* came in a paper by Dr. Joseph A. Burgess, Executive Director of LCUSA/DTS, where a study was under way on the office of bishop and the historic episcopate (see above, Chap. 3, Supplementary Comments). "What Is a Bishop?" as the paper was called, received responses from five commissioners and plenary discussion at the fourth CNLC meeting, in Minneapolis, February 18-22, 1984. LWF statements on the ministry were also distributed. An ad hoc committee consisting of three CNLC members—Fred Meuser, the chair of the Task Force on Theology; Janet Baumgartener Schwanke, AELC, involved in Christian day schools; and William Diehl of the LCA, active in promoting lay ministry in the world, brought recommendations to change "general" to "universal" ministry, provide recognition for "'specific ministry' beyond the church," and employ but two rites to set aside persons, namely, "ordination" for the pastoral ministry and "commissioning" for all other types. Small groups and CNLC debate allowed *Progress Report #3* in the spring of 1984 to present "A Perspective for Ministry":

> (A) the new church will "affirm persons who seek to carry out their baptismal vocation in the public realm or . . . the church and implement this through an appropriate rite";
> (B) "two forms of specific (or public) ministry: ordained . . . and commissioned";
> (C) an office of oversight, using
> (D) *bishop* as the title.

Because 1984 was a convention year, when each church met in national assembly in the summer or fall, the CNLC met an extra time, June 14-16, at Valley Forge, near Philadelphia. This fifth meeting spent a considerable amount of time reviewing responses from synodical district meetings in the spring (e.g., 77% agreement on the title *bishop*) and reevaluating the form in which *Progress Report #3* should go to the national conventions. Two more ad hoc committees tried their hand at brief statements on "Ministry" and "Bishop." The net result was that the commission adopted a resolution with regard to its report on ministry: items A and B, above, stand unamended, but issues will be further studied. (The vote at synod and district meetings found only 56% agreeing with B in principle, and a relatively high percent "not ready to express myself.") More important: "that further study of ministry be undertaken," tabulating "statements of doctrinal consensus and variant theological viewpoints." The matter thus grew more complex.

By the time the Los Angeles meeting of the CNLC rolled around, October 29–November 2, 1984, more data were accumulating. A "Design Task Force on Specific Ministry" made its report. It called for "one ministry" of the whole people of God, within which are "two public ministries":

The Public Ministries of the Church
should be

Office of Word and Sacrament		Office of Word and Service
	for which people are set apart through	
ordination		commissioning
	for	
pastoral work (parish pastor, etc.)		diaconal work (day-school teacher, etc.)

It was for this meeting also that each church body bishop had been asked to select a theologian from the Commission to speak on that body's doctrinal position concerning ministry and current theological viewpoints on it. (Another person spoke on practical considerations, like rostering for each church.)

Dr. Gerhard Forde spoke for the ALC, citing from its *United Testimony on Faith and Life* (1952), in light of the Augsburg Confession. Later theses in

Guidelines for the Calling and Sending of Clergy, adopted by the ALC convention in 1976, he thought, tended more toward the transference theory, which he further felt the Task Force on Theology had sought to avoid by having the institution of the general and of the specific ministry take place "simultaneously" (the famous §56, Matthew 28, mentioned above). The ALC also has "Commissioned Church Staff Ministries" but is "somewhat more restrictive than the Task Force Report" on ordination for such lay church workers. He saw the current concerns to "avoid the erosion of pastoral identity" and "to involve all people and avoid domination by the clergy" to be at odds with each other.

Dr. H. George Anderson, of the LCA, understood the assignment to be to review CNLC discussion and the differences involved. This his brief paper did, listing four options: (1) Resist singling out certain occupations as requiring liturgical recognition beyond baptism, except for ordination to pastoral ministry. (2) Interpret such ordination broadly, to include teachers of religion. (3) Have a variety of offices in addition to the ordained ministry. Here it was added that the LCA has never grouped these offices such as deaconess or missionary into a single "commissioned" category. (4) The threefold ministry, with "commissioned ministry as a step toward it." LCA practices were then further indicated by Bishop James R. Crumley Jr. A revised report by Dr. Anderson on the LCA position appeared with the Agenda for the February 1985 meeting of the Commission (Exhibit M, pp. 3-5). Pointedly he there wrote that "the LCA has not argued for a 'two-fold divine institution of . . . the general ministry and the specific ministry . . . simultaneously'" (Matthew 28 again) and noted that according to the LCA's 1980 "A Study of Ministry" it is "only the office of Word and Sacraments" that "can claim divine institution. Further, the description of the possible functions of bishops in the Task Force Report goes beyond present LCA descriptions of the office." As for "specific ministries" like cantor or college religion teacher, "the LCA would be more likely to include" such activities "as specialized forms of *lay* ministry," thus coming closest to the fourth option in the footnote to the Task Force on Theology report, recounted above. But these comments came only after the Los Angeles meeting.

What Dr. John Tietjen said on the AELC position has already been in part cited. He underscored New Testament variety and that "the AELC affirms that there is no divinely instituted form or forms of the office of the ministry." Hence, after referring to its three forms of the office of the ministry, he said "the AELC would have doctrinal problems" if a decision were made "not to recognize other forms of the office of the ministry besides pastoral ministry . . . if . . . based on the assumption that pastoral ministry is the only divinely-instituted form. . . ." Further presentation by Elwyn Ewald, of the AELC, showed there to be a distinction within the ranks of teachers and directors of

Christian education: those who meet criteria in theological studies are "called" and have "minister of religion" status with the Internal Revenue Service; those who do not are "contracted" and do not have such status.

These presentations and ensuing discussion were to be welcomed, even if the result was another committee from within the Commission, this time of seven persons. The upshot of complicated amendments and voting was a simple statement in *Progress Report #4* (fall 1984):

> Initially the new Lutheran church shall recognize four public ministries that exist in various of the three uniting churches:
> 1. Ordained pastors, including bishops;
> 2. Commissioned day school teachers;
> 3. Consecrated deaconesses/deacons, and
> 4. Certified and commissioned lay professionals.

This recognition, it was added, acknowledges differences but, an amendment stated (seeking to save embarrassment with regard to what Lutherans had said, e.g., in the Catholic dialogue), "does not establish a position in the ongoing ecumenical debate on ministry." Further study was encouraged in the new church. Small wonder a press release headline opined, "Lutherans Decide Ambiguity Best Route on Thorny Issues."

1985, Year of Decision

When the CNLC held its seventh of ten meetings, at Atlanta, February 16-20, 1985, it had received a number of reactions expressing dissatisfaction with its last report on ministry. Although the Report on Findings could state that "a strong majority agrees," especially in the AELC, it had to note that bishops who responded were "considerably less favorable" and that among those who added comments "critics (totalling 40%) feared primarily an undercutting of the ministry of the laity and argued for recognizing only the ordained clergy, not other 'public ministries.' " The action on the issue began on February 17 with an ad hoc committee of commissioners, William Lazareth, Lloyd Svendsbye (ALC), and John Tietjen, recommending that the CNLC authorize this group of three "to draft a position on ministry" for the September 1985 meeting of the commission, meanwhile reporting to the churches that further study was under way. After some discussion, any vote was deferred until a two-hour session on the issue February 19.

That discussion on Tuesday, perhaps the longest and most confusing procedurally on the topic in the CNLC's history, can best be understood if three proposals are noted, along with the outcome. Perhaps the simplest, in essence referring the matter to the churches for further comment, was read by William Diehl, for himself and Robert Brorby (LCA), serving notice it would be moved, in case the proposal by Bishop Herbert Chilstrom (Minnesota, LCA), which will be described below, were defeated. The Brorby-Diehl motion first affirmed for *Progress Report #5* something of what *Report #3* had said about laity:

> all the people of God, by virtue of their baptism, are called to ministry in the world and in the church.

It then went on to list four alternatives which the church bodies should consider; these were intended to pick up some of the categories in the Task Force on Theology (TFT) report and previous ideas floated or approved for a progress report in the Commission:

Alternative 1—one office of pastoral ministry; "all other forms . . . are laity" (cf. TFT footnote, option 4, and H. George Anderson's remarks for the LCA, noted above under the Los Angeles meeting);

Alternative 2—"affirm forms of ministry present in the three church bodies" (TFT provided for this, and *Progress Report #4* envisioned the new church beginning thus);

Alternative 3—"the threefold pattern of ministry," with "the diaconal office . . . as an umbrella for . . . day school teachers, deacons, deaconesses, administrators, youth workers, parish workers" (*BEM,* with almost all church workers made deacons; attractive to the AELC);

Alternative 4—no decision now, "accepting present forms of ministry," with "resolution in the new church" (cf. *Report #4*).

As can be seen, this proposal stressed lay ministry and not deciding at Atlanta. It was against having the ad hoc committee of three report at the next meeting. It did not enter into our voting on the two proposals formally before the house (see below). (The CNLC operated with a procedure whereby two motions, or more, could be before the house for perfecting with amendments, simultaneously. The 70 sometimes felt that a host of propositions was parliamentarily encamped against them.)

The first proposal actually moved was a threepart one by Bishop Chilstrom. Part A repeated what *Progress Report #3* had said about recognizing and affirming ("through the appropriate rite," as in the *Occasional Services Book*) "persons who seek to carry out their baptismal vocation" in the public realm or in the church. Part B provided that the new church "will *ordain* persons . . . for the ministry of Word and Sacrament"; included within this "ordained" category will be bishops. It will also, Part C, "*commission* persons . . . for the *ministry of diaconal service,*" initially of five sorts: deaconess, deacon, day-school teacher, lay professional, and lay missionary. To the typed form as distributed, Dr. Chilstrom added Part D, that the new church should be encouraged "to engage in further study," a point that had been made in *Report #4* also. This motion obviously emphasized laypersons, the ordained ministry, and reflected ALC and LCA practice on commissionings; it, of course, angered AELC representatives, as did the other proposal even more which was made 15 minutes later.

Dr. Robert J. Marshall, a former President of the LCA and now a seminary professor, moved that the CNLC recommend that the new church:

1. Affirm the ministry of all the baptized people of God;
2. Receive all in any specially recognized status of ministry in the uniting church- es and retain them in that status on the role [sic] of ministers with the privileges and responsibilities they have had [this was a "grandfather"—or "grand- mothering"—clause];
3. Add to the role of ministers only those who are ordained;
4. Ordain only those who are called to the office of the ministry of Word and Sacraments;
5. Maintain a roster of lay workers who have been on such rosters in the uniting churches and develop these rosters according to such categories, standards and expectations as the new church shall decide.

This motion was even more negative on the AELC idea of ministry, though it removed no one from any present status; it simply precluded future ordi- nations (or commissionings) to such positions.

The CNLC thus had before it two motions (and notice of a third), all by LCA commissioners. All three stressed the ministry of the baptized, and the two from Drs. Chilstrom and Marshall the ordained ministry. They differed over the future for diaconal ministries, the Marshall motion closing the door on any place in the office of ministry for day-school teachers and others. The new church was left with more work ahead by the Chilstrom motion than by the Marshall proposal.

One need not here rehearse details of the spirited debate, the use of "a Quasi-Committee of the Whole" during coffee break(!), all the amendments proposed (passed or defeated) to the Chilstrom motion, and the final series of actual votes about 4:55 P.M. that led to a resolution that was passed by the CNLC for *Progress Report #5*. There were many pressures. The "ministry issue" was called "the most important question" that the commission faced (Bishop Crumley). There was a certain loyalty to what the ad hoc committee had proposed. It was urged the next progress report must say something more on ministry than had the previous one "or else we're on the brink of losing credibility." The Chilstrom and Marshall proposals were both hailed as modest for *not* trying to write a new theology of Lutheran ministry. Bishop Preus, referring to all the data, including that from the dialogues, saw no call for a major change of course, indicating a preference for the Marshall motion. Speaking for the AELC, Elwyn Ewald argued for the ad hoc committee; the

Chilstrom plan is better than the Marshall motion, which represents a "judgment" against the AELC and implied the AELC was a failure which "we will accept . . . but we'll straighten it out as time goes by." Appealing to the Task Force on Theology report, it was argued that Word-and-sacrament ministry could take many forms; we could ordain (not just commission) deacons; "I want their numbers to grow." John Tietjen argued for the AELC that "when we had the opportunity, we were able to convince people in the TFT or the Design Task Force on Specific Ministry."

A "no win situation" for the three churches is how Elizabeth Bettenhausen LCA) described things. Deep theological division exists; the CNLC needs to moderate any pain that may result from a decision, but, she stated, "to use a grandparenting clause is not to admit that what had happened in the past is a failure." There was no disagreement, Tietjen summed up, on the whole people of God or the office of Word and sacrament. "The disagreement is whether there are other forms of ministry." William Lazareth spoke of the need for a variety of "serving ministers" to supplement the ordained, but did not regard the wording (in Chilstrom, Point A) to be an extension of the AELC position. To a further question, Lazareth went on, "When Lutherans deal with ministry, the means of grace are essential, whereas church structure is only beneficial. There are many critical needs to be met in our society. Therefore, in the church it is both professionally possible and pastorally advisable to structure various forms of service ministries among God's people that can complement and reinforce the ordained office of word and sacrament for human salvation." (ALC news release 85-27; LCA 85-11; my own notes; the CNLC minutes, pp. 359-62 and 394-98, report only motions and votes.)

On February 19 the AELC dodged a bullet—or, properly stated, two. To make a long story short, the vote to substitute an amended version of the Chilstrom motion for the original proposal (reported by Lazareth for the ad hoc committee) lost. The recommendation that Lazareth, Svendsbye, and Tietjen draft a position for the September meeting was voted. So it looked as if three theologians would settle the matter thus. But, reflecting CNLC style, the motion was amended to have the chair appoint "four more persons from CNLC" to this latest ad hoc committee, "including a lay person, a parish pastor, a bishop and a lay person employed by the church," at least two of these to be women.

So ended the battle at Atlanta. *Progress Report #5* that spring repeated what *Report #4* had said and then listed issues that require "further serious attention." It stated the opinion "that it is possible to produce a position on ministry . . . that will be acceptable to CNLC and the uniting churches." One detail that never was clear is how many persons were affected in the AELC in its push for a place in the office of the ministry for day-school teachers and others. The figure commonly cited was "more than 250 teachers, ministers of religion, Christian education directors, and approximately 50 deacons and deaconesses, many of whom have been commissioned as ministers and share some of the same privileges as ordained ministers." Occasionally ALC/LCA directors of education in parishes and nursery school teachers were tossed in, to yield a figure of 1600-2000. As a member of the CNLC, I received letters from parish secretaries wanting to be included in the ranks, and one woman in a synodical program of diaconal service in local churches described "us deacons as like cockroaches," primeval and ubiquitous. But I never saw firm figures as to how many of the AELC persons involved were "commissioned" and how many "contracted," a distinction that the AELC had found necessary to set up (see above in Elwyn Ewald's report at the Los Angeles meeting).

One event that occurred on the way to the September CNLC meeting was a joint session of bishops from all three merging bodies in Minneapolis, March 4-8, 1985. While a snowstorm spoiled hopes for fuller discussion together of the now emerging plans for a new church—the CNLC accomplished many things besides talk about the ministry—the 50 or so ALC, AELC, and LCA leaders did vote a recommendation with five parts:

A. To affirm the ministry of all the baptized people of God, though clarification is needed on the term *ministry.*

B. "The office of Word and Sacrament is the only constitutive and necessary office in the church," though its "uniqueness" must be "defined within the context of the ministry of all the baptized. . . ."

C. "In addition . . . there should be forms of lay ministries recognized and certified by the church," with "appropriate rites" to set apart such persons.

D. The new church's position on ministry "should not be determined in isolation from the larger ecumenical community."

E. The issue in (B) and (C) above should be resolved before formation of the new church.

The vote was 47 yes on this statement, 0 no, and 1 abstention, but not without "pain to the representatives of the AELC" (ALC news release 85-38).

The ad hoc committee that was to make the final proposal on the ministry was expanded by appointment of ALC Bishop L. David Brown (Iowa); Mrs. Gwen Boeke, Cresco, Iowa; the Rev. LaVern Grosc (LCA), Lincoln, Neb.; and Ms. Laura Klick, Des Moines, an LCA professional leader. (I know the resolution said "persons from CNLC," but this was the decision.) Dr. Lloyd Svendsbye had declined to serve and was replaced by Prof. Gerhard Forde for the ALC. The seven met July 22-24, and their proposal came through the CNLC Planning Committee to the eighth meeting of the commission.

Overland Park, Kansas, was the scene of the meeting where the CNLC finally reached agreement on a motion about ministry on Tuesday, September 24. This date I described in my notes as "probably the best day in the CNLC's history" in terms of getting things done, for a great deal was put in place as to the constitution's statements of faith and purpose and with regard to "narrative design" for the new church. As for the ministry, the final ad hoc committee moved, in an action that the CNLC made its own:

  A. That the new church strongly affirm the ministry of all the baptized people of God.
  B. That for the initial period of 1988–1994, CNLC recommend that the new Lutheran church:
      1. receive all in any specially recognized status of ministry in the uniting churches and retain them in that status on the church's roster with all the privileges and responsibilities they had had;
      2. add to the roll of those who serve in the office of Word and sacrament only those who are ordained as pastors;
      3. maintain a roster of lay workers who have been on such rosters in the uniting churches and develop those rosters according to such categories, standards, and expectations as the new church may decide.
  C. That CNLC recommend that during the same initial six-year period of 1988–1994, the new church engage in an intensive churchwide study of the nature of ministry resulting in decisions regarding appropriate forms that will enable the church to fulfill its mission; and
      That special attention be given to:
      1. the possibility of articulating a Lutheran understanding and adaptation of the threefold ministerial office of bishop, pastor, and deacon and its ecumenical implications;
      2. the appropriate forms of lay ministries to be officially recognized and certified by the church including criteria for certification such as Christian faith, preparation and education, vocational commitment and accountability.

These recommendations were preceded by 10 pages of edited material from the Task Force on Theology's original 1983 report, on the church, the mission and ministry of the baptized, and the ministry of those officially set apart. "There is no divinely instituted form or forms of the office of Word and sacrament," it was argued. Descriptively, the ALC and LCA have limited the office, the AELC has recognized two other forms. How the new church should exercise its freedom was spelled out in the three recommendations. The chair of the ad hoc committee, Dr. Lazareth, described them as not doctrinal compromises but mutual concession. "Our doctrinal position is that this is not a doctrinal issue."

Discussion was brief, consisting chiefly of questions. A note was added after an asterisk on "privileges" in B. 1, explaining, "Any privileges of representation in synodical assemblies shall be governed by decisions on governance of synods." It did not sit well later with clergy, especially in the LCA, when for synod meetings some lay professionals were given a vote but retired pastors were not. Interests of the laity, stressed in a letter from William Diehl in August 1985, were noted. The ad hoc committee's report submitted its pages before the recommendation (adapted from the TFT report) "for adoption in principle and for use as background." The official action was to "receive the Report." *Progress Report #6* presented the three commission recommendations as the totality of its report on ministry.

What had happened? Solomonic wisdom? Behind-the-scenes agreements? A feeling this was the best that could be done in a no-win situation? A willingness to grandparent and in no way be vindictive? All of the above? It is worth noting that the measure as voted includes wording from the Marshall proposal at the previous meeting in point A virtually verbatim, B. 1 and 3 likewise, and B. 2 as a rephrase of Marshall items 3 and 4, right down to the phrase "only those who are ordained" (as pastors). What is new is the six-year study, with its reference, reminiscent of *BEM,* to "threefold ministerial office" (note the singular) and attention to "forms of *lay* ministries" (italics added). To some the final report seemed a triumph for what the original Task Force on Theology had said, but Dr. Fred Meuser, chair of that task force, hoped that this action would not let questions fade away that had been raised, for seemingly the TFT's outlook was more "liberal," progressive, loose—call it what you will—on those "other forms of specific ministry."

Subsequent Skirmishes and Changes

In 1986 at its February meeting in Minneapolis the CNLC began to put these agreements on ministry into constitutional language. There appeared in *Progress Report #7,* as Chapter 9 of the ELCA Constitution, a little more than two pages on "Ordained Ministers, Consecrated Deacons and Deaconesses, Commissioned Teachers, and Certified and Commissioned Lay Professionals." That covers all the recognized statuses in the uniting churches! But the work was not finished yet.

The LCA bishops at their March 31–April 2 meeting in New York surfaced five issues where they felt substantial change was needed in the CNLC documents. These were the nature of the church (how congregations relate to the wider church); ecumenism; quotas in representation and staffing; the pension plan; and, of course, the ministry. These issues ultimately came to the Commission with broad support from sense motions at LCA synod meetings. All were matters on which a church had a right to speak, though some felt these interventions came late in the game. The LCA had not previously implied there were "nonnegotiables," though in effect each of the other bodies invoked such a position at one time or another. Now that the whole picture was relatively clear, the LCA spoke. I confess to mixed feelings on the five matters, which were worked out for presentation in terms of revisions of the constitution and bylaws.

To illustrate, one result was to insert into the ELCA Constitution at the June meeting of the commission a new chapter on the "Nature of the Church."

While this came out of the LCA Constitution, it supplied a gap in ecclesiology that existed in previous drafts.

Less happy may be one of the changes made in the interests of ecumenism. The LCA had inherited a stance from one of its predecessor bodies, the ULCA, that no new doctrinal agreements are necessary for Lutheran unity. The United Lutheran Church in America had put it thus: the ULCA "acknowledges all churches that" hold "the Unaltered Augsburg Confession to be entitled to the name of Evangelical Lutheran" (Constitution, II. 3). The LCA in 1962 had escalated this to say in its Constitution (II. 5), "This church . . . acknowledges as one with it in faith and doctrine all churches that likewise accept" the Augsburg Confession and Luther's Small Catechism. The ELCA, up till its very last meeting, used such language in its Statement of Purpose (Chap. 3. k) about relating to "Lutheran and other Christian churches for the sake of mission and the oneness of Christ's church." The LCA bishops now insisted that this be in the ELCA constitutional Chapter 2 on "Confession of Faith," thereby "acknowledging as one with it in faith and doctrine all churches that likewise accept the teachings of the Unaltered Augsburg Confession." Is that a very ecumenical standard, so that doctrinal unity would follow automatically if the Reformed Church in America added the CA to its list of authoritative statements or Roman Catholics made it exhibit #3358 in the *Enchiridion Symbolorum?* Or is it to be pressed to show they must actually live by all teachings in the Augsburg Confession? (The matter was perhaps solved with regard to ministry for the final year or so of the LCA's life by an action at its 1986 convention that "synods may receive . . . ordained ministers from churches which believe, teach, and confess the Apostles', the Nicene, and the Athanasian creeds." Presumably this "validates" ministries without a word about the Augsburg Confession!)

The LCA bishops clearly wanted a stronger affirmation of the ordained ministry, preferring to speak of ministry as "either ordained or lay." "The ministry of the church is given to the whole people of God by Jesus Christ" (compare and contrast CA 5); "within this ministry there is only one office" of essential ministry, that ordained, of Word and Sacrament; but "the church may authorize . . . other ministries for . . . its mission." From the LCA came therefore the proposal of three chapters in the constitution on (9) the ministry of the whole people of God, (10) Ordained Ministers, and (11) deacon(esses), teachers, and lay professionals, instead of the omnibus chapter in *Progress Report #7*.

As if this wasn't enough to make lively the final meeting of the CNLC, in Seattle, June 23-25, 1986, a new draft was proposed that, under "Ministry" in Chapter 10 of the Constitution, would closely parallel "Ordained Ministry" with a newly created category of "Associates in Ministry." Here AELC commissioned teachers, deacons, and deaconesses could be joined by LCA and

ALC lay professionals and others. As one LCA bishop wrote me, before the meeting, the provisions for the Associates in Ministry are "patterned too closely to the office of ordained ministry," and that prejudges the future ELCA study.

The final *Report and Recommendations* of the CNLC, completed June 25, put all these concerns together in a constitutional chapter (now 10) on "Ministry" with three subheads: of the Baptized People of God, Ordained, and Associates in Ministry. The primary motion voted in September 1985 appears as a continuing resolution. Further, necessary provisions are spelled out in the constitution and bylaws. Terms like "call" do not appear in connection with the Associates in Ministry, but rather "letter of appointment." The roster here will include those in existing categories of the three churches who *choose* to be certified by December 31, 1987 and those so certified in the new church.

The complexity of convention action in August 1986, by the ALC in Minneapolis, the AELC in Chicago, and the LCA in Milwaukee on the CNLC report can mercifully go without description here. Changes were difficult, with concurrence necessary, the two larger churches having in effect each a veto power. The major addition was a new paragraph 10.21 on Ordained Ministry:

> Within the people of God and for the sake of the Gospel ministry entrusted to all believers, God has instituted the office of the ministry of Word and Sacrament. To carry out this ministry, this church calls and ordains qualified persons.

It was ALC-proposed and then approved by the LCA (whose convention had passed a similar wording for insertion earlier, which the ALC declined to act upon). The AELC declined to approve section 10.21, but, by the rules, it stood. The continuing resolution from the September 1985 CNLC meeting went through unchanged except for adding that the future study should also give attention to synod relationship and discipline for lay ministries. The ELCA was thus launched with ministry of the universal priesthood, the ordained, and associates in ministry.

Assessing CNLC on Ministry

This far the CNLC was able to go, leaving a major study ahead, with many possible decisions, for the Evangelical Lutheran Church in America to complete by 1994. Why didn't the Commission of Seventy get further on the topic of "ministry"?

The *ferment of the times* within the churches was one factor. Any group working in the period of the CNLC, from 1982 to 1986, would, of necessity, inherit a multitude of currents from recent decades. Probably no church, with the possible exception of the Eastern Orthodox, could be unaffected in the

1980s by such pressures to test old views and to consider changes. This applies even for those with a traditional "threefold ministry." Roman Catholics, for example, had dealt partially with the papal office of ministry in 1870 and especially with bishops, among other aspects of the ministry, at the Second Vatican Council, but in the '80s Rome was still working out the relationship of the pope with the newly developing role of bishops, and was seeking as well to revive a permanent diaconate and to identify contemporary under-standings of priesthood that would attract sufficient male candidates. Mean-while, debates and skirmishes were going on over women in ministry and development of the lay apostolate. Anglicans were at this time in some branch-es of their communion welcoming women into priesthood (and elsewhere standing against it), but the question of women in the higher office of bishop touched off further debate, and exactly what deacons are and the expanding role of laity occupied the energies of other Anglicans. So with most denom-inations. There were lively experiments or proposals over new forms of min-istry.

Even in communions where issues about ministry were relatively quiet, *the BEM statement* had put old and new questions before the leadership and decision-making process of these and of all churches. Churches were asked to please indicate:

- the extent to which your church can recognize in this text the faith of the Church through the ages;
- the consequences your church can draw . . . for its relations and dialogues with other churches . . .;
- the guidance your church can take . . . for its . . . life and witness;
- the suggestions your church can make for the ongoing work of Faith and Order as it relates . . . to its long-range research project "Towards the Common Expression of the Apostolic Faith Today."

As if internal ferment and ecumenical challenges were not enough, there were also *shifts* going on *in society*. Secularization and urban complexity; ethnic diversity and changes of population in the heartland of many denom-inations; the advance of government into institutions like schools and hospitals and into the care of orphans, children from broken homes, and the aged; plus the multiplication of new borderlands in society and technology like single parenting, streetpeople, the desperately poor, or biomedical ethics—all these gave Christians new and bewildering areas in which to minister.

But the CNLC's task on ministry was also conditioned by many specifically Lutheran factors. One was a *pluralistic heritage*. German *Landeskirchen* in Bavaria, Württemberg, the Rhineland, and the north were by no means exactly the same. Each Scandinavian church brought different accents, not only in language but also in ecclesiology and ministry. The waves of immigrants even from the same area in Europe might differ from 1750 to 1850 to 1920. America was a vast country, and the religion of the frontier differed from religious life in an eastern city like Philadelphia or Baltimore. Lutheran settlers could take on very different colorations when influenced by (or in reaction to) the Baptist south, Puritan-Congregationalist (and later Roman Catholic) New England, or Calvinist or Catholic neighbors in the midwest.

Moreover, Lutherans, by confessional heritage, were a group for whom *church polity was not of the essence;* a supposedly divinely given form of church governance was not what held them together. As regards ministry, they mostly all emphasized that there should be an ordained clergy, with one office of the ministry; a succession into that office that was done "decently and in order" by ordination; a royal priesthood of all baptized believers, so that laypeople felt a vocation as Christians in their general work; and for all else, a certain freedom and flexibility, to meet new situations.

It must also be acknowledged that *the nature of the CNLC* itself contributed to the difficulty of solving, definitively, the problem of the ministry. Seventy is a large number of people, falling somewhere between a convention where *Robert's Rules of Order* are demanded and an informal gathering that can proceed by consensus. The Commission included people accustomed to following parliamentary procedures with great adroitness and people who remembered fondly the style of the 60s with small group discussion and arriving at "a sense of the meeting." It took people so diverse two or three meetings to get to know (and trust) each other. For a while it seemed that people had to caucus before agreeing on an agenda, but meanwhile time went by on a tight schedule, and key decisions were made, as on the Task Force on Theology and its report, before the 70 had jelled into a cohesive body. Had the Lutheran doctrine of the ministry already been gerrymandered in the TFT report so as to accommodate the political reality of AELC concerns about the teachers it had unilaterally made part of the office of the ministry?

It is only honest to report that the commission was probably as *divided into a variety of opinions on ministry* as the three churches were as a whole. We probably had some inclinations toward "high" clerical views and perhaps more "populist" thinking on lay and congregational leadership, though there were seldom expressed extreme views in either direction. Here and there, it seems, doubt existed whether we needed clergy, others felt we needed to expand the clergy ranks to include day-school teachers and others in all sorts of diaconal functions. And there must have been many bewildered by the whole plethora of opinions, who simply longed to continue doing things as they had been. Why not? "If it ain't broke, don't fix it." And others who brought hopes of reform under the banners of ecumenism or lay ministry, or feminist concerns.

At least passing note must be taken of "the Pittsburgh situation." Here the Denominational Ministry Strategy group, partly begun with LCA funding as an activist effort to aid those thrown out of work as steel plants closed, escalated into confrontation, acts of protest, and some violence, especially in several LCA congregations. We shall not try to recount the whole story, with its rights and wrongs, but two pastors of the Western Pennsylvania–West Virginia Synod were, following disciplining procedures, deposed from the LCA clergy roll. The unfolding events provided a backdrop—and sometimes were directly invoked or the pastors involved appeared at CNLC meetings (and took over the platform of the 1986 LCA convention)—during deliberations. This history and some fishing in the troubled waters of Pittsburgh by a commission member or two impacted more on CNLC decision making about clergy discipline and congregational ownership of property, in my judgment, than on general discussion about ministry. Certainly, a very high view of the ordained pastor's office (at least his own) was reflected, however, in the letter from the Rev. John Tietjen dated 3 September 1986 (he had earlier sought to work with the pastors involved): he excommunicated them not simply from a denomination's clergy roll but from the kingdom of heaven. Wrote Dr. Tietjen:

> In the name of the Triune God and by the authority invested in me by the Lord Jesus Christ I exercise the office of the keys to declare that you are outside the kingdom of heaven and not a member of the body of Christ.[15]

That, of course, is more than the Matthean church did, whence we get the idea of "the keys" (16:19), for the Gospel of Matthew leaves the sorting of wheat and chaff between God's kingdom and Satan's to the final judgment at the parousia (13:30,40-43; 22:11-13).

Perhaps the miracle is that the CNLC eventually arrived at constitutional provisions that passed the test in all three churches along with a plan for future study in the united church.

The Study Ahead

The ELCA has many options that could result from the study following its 1988 inception. At the one extreme, reflecting the Grabau and Loehe strand of tradition, could be the "threefold pattern of bishop, presbyter, and deacon," in accord with *BEM* and reflecting "catholic" styles of church governance. A less extreme version is the *BEM* proposal itself, where the threefold ministry is regarded as a second or third century A.D. development, postbiblical, and therefore not of "divine law" in the Lutheran understanding. It would be something to be accepted voluntarily for the sake of unity. Against such views is the consistent Lutheran commitment to a single office of the ministry and the fact that one church's *iure divino* readily rubs off on structures that Lutherans find to be of human origin. The ELCA study calls for attention to "articulating a *Lutheran* understanding and *adaptation*" of this threefold ministerial office. What might the "ecumenical implication" of such a construction be?

At the other end of the spectrum would be a purely congregational concept of ministry, rooted in the universal priesthood of believers. In this ecclesiastical version of Rousseau's social contract, a local group transfers its ministerial rights to some "designated minister." Such "transference theories," however, found little open support in discussions that led to the ELCA. A less extreme version, however, might take seriously where *BEM* itself begins, with the whole people of God. The Faith and Order statement talks primarily of their "witness" or "service" ("*ministry* in its broadest sense," §7b). However, the Lutheran tradition and ELCA Constitution affirm more vigorously the universal priesthood. "It is within *this context of ministry* that this church calls or appoints some . . . for specific ministries" (10.11, italics added). What might be the shape and implications of a Lutheran church that really showed commitment to "all its members for their ministries in the world and in this church"?

Between the lay "people of God" and the ordained ministry, the ELCA study faces its challenge with those tentatively placed together as "Associates in Ministry." The AELC "commissioned teachers" have been the spearhead for expanding the office of the ministry, along with AELC deacons and deaconesses, so as to include teaching and diaconal ministry with the pastoral. ALC "commissioned church staff" have enjoyed no such status, nor have LCA (and ALC) deaconesses ("sisters") sought it. "Lay professional" leaders in the LCA have not been grouped with "the clergy" either. But this is not to say there have not been "professional" emphases and desire for "ministerial" status among persons in most of these groups. The deacon picture is the most clouded, since the term covers a great variety of congregational and local programs, with differing synod structures in Upper New York, Center City Lutheran Parish of Philadelphia, and in Baltimore churches, just in the LCA. When someone says, "I'm a deacon," I've learned to respond, "Just what does that mean?"

Among the options for the new church study are to see such persons within the context of the universal priesthood, or to set them within "the office of ministry of Word and sacrament," or to create a third category. Some would solve it with a magic wand they see in *BEM,* by making such people "deacons," the third office of the ministry, or in a Lutheran version a corner of the "one office" of ministry. But can the presbyterate-episcopate be stretched that far? Would Christian day-school teachers really be akin to deacons in the Eastern Orthodox or Roman Catholic understanding of the diaconate? (The move would ring truer were Catholic male parochial school teachers regarded as permanent deacons by virtue of their teaching office.) To speak of such status for those who teach math or English in a parochial school often drives those interested in lay ministry in the world to propose, "Why not then give dedicated Christians who teach in *public* school the same office?" Where to draw the line?

A consultation on the diaconate in February 1987, sponsored by LCUSA, COCU, the Roman Catholic Bishops' Committee on the Permanent Diaconate, and the Commission on Faith and Order of the National Council of Churches showed how varied the situation is. *Diakonia* there must be, indeed, "institutionalized" in some ways, but is an office of deacon necessary to accomplish it (LCUSA press release 87-08)? Cf. *JES* 24 (1987): 188-89.

One real danger, some charge, is that in structuring ministries the church will concentrate on internal service inside the walls of a church building— cantors, musicians, assistants at worship, teachers, etc., to the detriment of building up witness in the world. "Ministry in Daily Life" was the name chosen in late 1986 for a network of groups interested in equipping and supporting ELCA laity for their ministries in world and church (ALC's "Discipleship in Society," "Kogodus," and LCA's Laos in Ministry). I find it hard to believe that the cutting edge in ministering for a church approaching the year 2000 in the United States lies in refining ranks and status for internal activities—not to get into the whole question of whether parochial schools are desirable, to begin with—rather than in pushing the witness of believers in the world as ministry.

Priesthood and Ministry

Some years ago, for the Anglican–Roman Catholic dialogue, the Dominican, J. M. R. Tillard, of Ottawa, wrote a paper with the intriguing title, "What Priesthood Has the Ministry?"[16] It deals with Catholic views of ministry, Roman and Anglican, and, in making some interesting points for that dialogue, raises questions for us.

Tillard, a member of the Faith and Order Commission, was struck by the fact that in Roman Catholic tradition, bishops alone possess "the highest dignity of priesthood"; presbyters or priests have a "second level" of ministry, "dependent on the bishops in the exercise of their power" (deacons, "upon whom hands are imposed 'not unto priesthood, but unto a ministry of service,'" are at a lower level, *Lumen Gentium* §§28, 29). A somewhat similar view of "sacerdotalness" for bishops and priests Tillard saw in Anglican tradition, with the implication that " 'sacerdotal function' immediately suggests . . . a sacrificial act," i.e., traditionally the priest offering the eucharistic sacrifice. This he contrasted with the Reformation position, as in the *Second*

Helvetic Confession of 1556: "The priesthood and the ministry are very different from one another. For the priesthood . . . is common to all Christians; not so the ministry." In such a taxonomy, Lutherans with their priesthood of all the baptized and an ordained ministry, fit in the Reformation category. That accounts for why we have not often heard the Latin term *sacerdos*, "priest," in our discussion of Lutheranism.

Tillard's detailed investigation of the New Testament concludes that sacerdotal vocabulary is *not* used there to describe the ministry, even in Hebrews. In 1 Peter, Christ is not priest but victim (2:21-25; 4:1); the "holy priesthood" (2:5) involves daily life and conduct of the Christian believers. Here the two types of priesthood are, he says, the "existential" (as at Exod. 19:6) and the Levitical, but the former—not the latter—is what interests 1 Peter. When then did "Levitical" views of Christian priesthood come into the church? Not in the New Testament, even in connection with the eucharist, Tillard finds, for "nowhere does Scripture tell us . . . who presides," and at Passover it would have been "the father of the family or the chief of the little fraternity" that assembled for the occasion. Only in Tertullian and Hippolytus (late second, third century) do we find Christian ministers described by the Latin *sacerdos;* priesthood is now separated from the lay state, at a time when the eucharist was being taken more and more as a sacrifice the clergy "offered."

Tillard's intricate argument contrasts the position (Catholic, Anglican) that combines Scripture and tradition from later centuries over against the Reformation determination "to say nothing that is not in Scripture." He sees the former as identifying "minister" with "priest" who has "his role in the offering of sacrifice." The Reformation (Reformed) view, he charges, could on its part "confuse the two levels of priesthood" and interiorize "ministerial priesthood" in a holy life.

"What Priesthood Has the Ministry?" we may ask, in somewhat different ways. Ecumenically today the differences really are over ordained ministry. Whose clergy are valid? Less and less do battles rage over baptism. More and more churches tend to accept each other's baptized laity as part of the universal priesthood. The issue in these terms is, Which priesthood has the "right" ordained ministry? Is it possible, we may ask, that a fruitful starting point for ecumenical discussion might be with the universal priesthood, in the context of which all special or ordained ministry exists?

But the question can also be asked of the two types or levels (in some traditions) of priesthood. Which has the ministry, the priesthood of all the baptized or the priests in the sense of the presbyters, the ordained? Here the answer is, from our examination of the Lutheran tradition, both. Every believer, each member of the universal priesthood has a ministry; so does every ordained (or commissioned) minister, no matter how we structure the Ministry within the ministry.

Which priesthood has the ministry in terms of "the Levitical" and the "existential"? Here the New Testament answer was already that "royal priesthood," the whole people of God, in 1 Peter 2:9 had the *diakonia* of declaring the wonderful deeds of God who had called them from darkness to light. Yet with regard to priesthoods that have adopted Levitical self-understandings (as when the Council of Trent spoke of clergy as first and foremost "sacrificing priests"), Lutherans in dialogue have been willing to affirm of Roman Catholic priests that they "are engaged in a valid Ministry of the Gospel." So the answer is, both are.

To ask, "What Priesthood Has the Ministry?" is, taken along these lines, to stand some of our conventional questions on their head. Can one, without succumbing to a theory of congregational transference, take seriously the context of the whole people of God?

If Luther had a flair (and sound theological reasons) for doing "Christology from below"—beginning with Christ in his humanity and not with heaven's eternal decrees—perhaps there is room, and now the opportunity, to do ecclesiology and ministry "from below," with the whole people of God.

For sure, the ministering is there to be done, in God's world, in Jesus' name. The tragedy for a new Lutheran church, as well as for all Christians, would be to spend our energies defining rather than doing, for the God whose service is freedom.

Notes

Introduction

1. *The Diaconia of the Church in a New Age,* a colloquium to celebrate 20 years of partnership between Valparaiso University and the Lutheran Deaconess Association in the education of deaconesses for The Lutheran Church–Missouri Synod, May 1-3, 1964; pp. 1-27.

2. *The Ordination of Women: A Report Distributed by Authorization of the Church Body Presidents as a Contribution to Further Study, Based on Materials Produced through the Division of Theological Studies of the Lutheran Council in the U.S.A.,* condensed by Raymond Tiemeyer (Minneapolis: Augsburg, 1970).

3. For fuller discussion on the Scripture issue, see *Studies in Lutheran Hermeneutics,* ed. J. Reumann in collaboration with Samuel H. Nafzger and Harold H. Ditmanson (Philadelphia: Fortress, 1979). The use of historical-critical methods remains at issue. My essay, "The Augsburg Confession in Light of Biblical Interpretation," on a theme assigned for a consultation of the Strasbourg Institute for Ecumenical Research, had as its task to explore, for the 450th anniversary of the *Confessio Augustana* in 1980, what has changed in biblical studies since 1530 in the areas of justification and Christology (printed in *Confessio Augustana 1530–1980: Commemoration and Self-Examination,* ed. Vilmos Vajta [LWF Report, 9; Geneva: Lutheran World Federation, 1980], pp. 3-34). It was cited specifically in a resolution (3-20) voted at the 1981 convention of the Lutheran Church–Missouri Synod, asking the Lutheran Council's Division of Theological Studies to place the Reumann essay on its agenda for discussion "as a matter of urgency." The official "Response to John Reumann's 'The Augsburg Confession in the [sic] Light of Biblical Interpretation,'" by Horace D. Hummel, printed in *Concordia Journal* 9 (1983): 171-79, declined a "point by point engagement" in order to concentrate on "basic presuppositions" on the Bible. The subsequent LCUSA study resulted in a DTS statement, transmitted by the Council's November meeting in 1986, on the use of historical criticism in studying the Bible, subsequently published as *Statement on Historical Criticism* (New York: LCUSA/DTS, 1987).

4. *Peter in the New Testament: A Collaborative Assessment by Protestant and Roman Catholic Scholars,* ed. Raymond E. Brown, Karl P. Donfried, and John Reumann (Minneapolis: Augsburg, and New York: Paulist, 1973).

5. *Mary in the New Testament: A Collaborative Assessment by Protestant and Roman Catholic Scholars,* ed. Raymond E. Brown, Karl P. Donfried, Joseph A. Fitzmyer, and John Reumann (Philadelphia: Fortress, and New York: Paulist, 1978).

6. *The Supper of the Lord: The New Testament, Ecumenical Dialogues, and Faith and Order on Eucharist* (Philadelphia: Fortress, 1985), pp. 137-77.

7. *Report and Recommendations of the Commission for a New Lutheran Church to The American Lutheran Church, The Association of Evangelical Lutheran Churches, Lutheran Church in America, as Amended and Adopted by the Thirteenth General Convention of The ALC, the Sixth Delegate Assembly of the AELC, the Thirteenth Biennial Convention of the LCA, August 29, 1986,* p. 42, item 10.11. A 87, b. 2.

1. The Ministries of the Ordained and of the Laity in Lutheranism

1. Cf. G. Wendt, "Klerus und Laien," in *Die Religion in Geschichte und Gegenwart,* 3rd ed. (=*RGG³*), edited by Kurt Galling and others, 7 vols. (Tübingen: J. C. B. Mohr [Paul Siebeck], 1957-1965), 3:1663; William H. Lazareth, "Priest and Priesthood," in *The Encyclopedia of the Lutheran Church (=Enc. Luth. Ch.*), edited by Julius Bodensieck, 3 vols. (Philadelphia: Fortress, 1965), 1964–1966; e.g., *Evangelisches Laien–ABC,* edited by W. Natzschka (Hamburg: Furche-Verlag, 1952), s.v. "Laie," p. 121: "Der wesentliche Unterschied zwischen L[aien] und Priester ist in der kath. Kirche ein Glaubenssatz und beruht auf dem Sakrament der Priesterweihe. . . . Der Ausdruck L. hat sich auch in der ev. Kirche erhalten und bezeichnet ein nicht theologisch gebildetes und nicht mit dem Pfarramt betrautes Gemeindeglied. Zwischen dem L. und dem Pfarrer besteht zwar kein grundsätzlicher Unterschied wie in der kath. Kirche, aber ein sachlicher, der in der bes. Aufgabe des geistlichen Amtes begründet ist. . . ."

2. Edgar M. Carlson, "The Doctrine of the Ministry in the Confessions," in *The Lutheran Quarterly (=LQ)* 15 (1963): 118-19.

3. E. g., "Symposium on Ordination," in *Dialog* 8 (1969), p. 172 (a seminary student): "It is possible that part of the problem is because the Reformation Church itself is that kind of provisional emergency structure which never really intended to perpetuate itself indefinitely, and therefore we have more or less found ourselves stuck with emergency orders and emergency offices which are not very well defined."

4. G. Wendt, loc. cit.

5. Werner Elert, *The Structure of Lutheranism,* vol. 1, trans. W. A. Hansen (St. Louis: Concordia, 1962), p. 344.

6. Carlson, op. cit., p. 120.

7. WA 6, 564, 11-12 ("The Babylonian Captivity of the Church," 1520) = *Works of Martin Luther* (Philadelphia: A. J. Holman, hereafter cited as PE, "Philadelphia Edition"), vol. 2, p. 279; = Luther's Works, American Edition, (hereafter cited as LW-AE), vol. 36, *Word and Sacrament,* ed. A. R. Wentz, p. 113.

8. WA 31, 1, p. 211, 17-19 ("Exposition of Ps. 82," 1530); = PE 4, 314; = LW-AE, 13, 65.

9. WA 30, 3, p. 525, 24 ("Von den Schleichern und Winkelpredigern," 1532); = LW-AE 40, 392. Cf. also lines 20f. (= LW-AE, 40, 391), Paul "makes an even clearer distinction when he speaks of the congregation as the laity" at 1 Cor. 14:16f.

10. Brian Gerrish, "Luther on Priesthood and Ministry," *Church History* 34 (1965): 416, 409. Something of the same tension is seen in the articles by Klaus Tuchel, "Luthers Auffassung vom geistlichen Amt," *Luther-Jahrbuch* vol. 25 (Berlin: Lutherisches Verlaghaus, 1958), pp. 61-98, and Regin Prenter, "Die göttliche

Einsetzung des Predigtamtes und das allgemeine Priestertum bei Luther," *Theologische Literaturzeitung* 86 (1961): 322-332. Tuchel holds that Luther sees the ministerial office as instituted in Christ and created for the sake of order, but no real "doctrine of the ministry" emerges. Prenter finds only one origin, namely, in "salvation history" (*Heilsgeschichte*), through Christ himself. Tuchel seeks to write as an objective historian; Prenter operates more as a systematician.

11. Lowell Green, "Change in Luther's Doctrine of the Ministry," *LQ* 18 (1966): 174, 178-79.

12. So Robert H. Fischer, "Another Look at Luther's Doctrine of the Ministry," *LQ* 18 (1966): 260-271. "Green is wrong in thinking that Luther's solution was to switch from a 'transferal theory' of the ministry to a divine institution theory" (p. 267).

13. Hans Storck, *Das allgemeine Priestertum bei Luther,* Theologische Existenz Heute, N.F. 37 (Munich: Chr. Kaiser, 1953), p. 53, sees three functions designated in Luther by this phrase which stems from Exodus 19:6 (1 Peter 2:5, 9; cf. Rev. 1:6; 5:10; 20:6): "the unmediated and unbroken relationship in which the Christian stands to his God"; "the sacrifice which the Christian in all offices, presents for his neighbor"; "the power of the Christian to fulfill every spiritual office and its activity, which serves the further transmission of God's love." Universal priesthood does not mean the same thing as the office of the word; the two supplement each other. Wilhelm Brunotte, *Das geistliche Amt bei Luther* (Berlin: Lutherisches Verlagshaus, 1959), pp. 142, 200, emphasizes four features in Luther's concept: the equal spiritual authority and dignity of every Christian; the Christian's unhindered access to God and his word; the priestly office of offering oneself to God; and the task of proclamation given the Christian in his specific, given area.

14. So Fischer, op. cit., p. 268, against Gerrish, who accepts a "delegation theory" as Luther's intention.

15. Fischer, ibid., p. 269. The "proof" passage Gerrish cites is WA 50, 632-33 ("On the Councils and the Church," 1539) = PE 5, 275-76 = LW-AE 41, 154.

16. Fischer, loc. cit. The only passages cited directly in Luther on the institution of the church's public ministry are Matt. 28:19-20 (the Great Commission from the risen Lord Christ) and 1 Cor. 14:40 ("all things should be done decently and in order"), though indirect institution is seen in Titus 1:5-6, Eph. 4:8,11, and in use of general terms like "servants of Christ" in the epistles (Brunotte, op. cit., pp. 127-129). It is characteristic of Luther and Lutheranism that an office of the ministry is insisted upon, as instituted by God through Christ; this ministry is accepted as biblical, but no attempt is made to ground it very specifically in biblical texts, certainly not in the historical Jesus.

17. Fischer, op. cit., p. 270.

18. On Melanchthon, cf. Green, op. cit., p. 180, n. 19; Elert, op. cit., p. 353; and Helmut Lieberg, *Amt und Ordination bei Luther und Melanchthon* (Göttingen: Vandenhoeck und Ruprecht, 1962), pp. 245ff. Lieberg (p. 384) concludes that the major difference between Luther and Melanchthon on this point is that, in the latter, derivation of the ministerial office from the universal priesthood is lacking, but Luther's emphasis on the divine institution of the office means there is no contradiction.

19. Cf. the General Index in *The Book of Concord: The Confessions of the Evangelical Lutheran Church,* edited by Theodore G. Tappert et al. (Philadelphia: Fortress, 1959), s.v. "Laity," "Pastors," "Ordination," also "Church Servants," "Preachers," and "Bishops." In the older edition by H. E. Jacobs, *The Book of Concord,* s. v. "Ministers," "Ministry of Word and Sacraments," "Laymen," etc.

20. Cf. Leonhard Goppelt, "The Ministry in the Lutheran Confessions and in the New Testament," *Lutheran World* (= *LW*) 11 (1964): 410-11; Edmund Schlink, *Theology of the Lutheran Confessions,* trans. Paul F. Koehneke and Herbert J. A. Bouman (Philadelphia: Fortress, 1961), p. 104; Elert, op. cit., pp. 339-40; Peter Brunner, "Das Heil und das Amt," in *Pro Ecclesia: Gesammelte Aufsätze zur dogmatischen Theologie* (Berlin: Lutherisches Verlagshaus, 1962), pp. 293-309; English trans. Paul D. Opsahl, "Salvation and the Office of the Ministry," *LQ* 15 (1963): 99-117.

21. Schlink, op. cit., p. 202.

22. Loc. cit.

23. Ruben Josefson, "The Ministry as an Office in the Church," in *This Is the Church,* ed. Anders Nygren, trans. C. C. Rasmussen (Philadelphia: Muhlenberg, 1952), p. 272.

24. Schlink, op. cit., p. 243.

25. For this emphasis, cf. Schlink, op. cit., pp. 229ff., especially p. 241.

26. References in *The Book of Concord* (Tappert and Jacobs editions), Index, s. v. "Pastors."

27. Carlson, op. cit., pp. 121-126. In the "so-called Appendix to the Smalcald Articles (the Treatise on the Power and Primacy of the Pope [67])" Melanchthon asserts that "in an emergency even a layman absolves and becomes the minister and pastor of another."

28. Manuscript Lectures, as summarized in R. F. Weidner, *The Doctrine of the Ministry: Outline Notes Based on Luthardt and Krauth* (Chicago: Wartburg Publishing House, 1907), pp. 88-93.

29. For this paragraph, cf. Elert, op. cit., pp. 340-344.

30. Schlink, op. cit., p. 245.

31. Elert, op. cit., pp. 342-43, references in n. 5 to Luther.

32. Ibid., pp. 346-348.

33. Schlink, op. cit., p. 245.

34. Carlson, op. cit., p. 125, notes the use of this specific example of what laity can do, in arguing for absolution as the essential function of ministry.

35. "It is as norms for the proclamation of the church that the Confessions are taken seriously. Laymen usually employ the shortest and simplest creedal form, the Apostles' Creed, when they make a public confession of their faith. . . . Relatively few laymen have any real acquaintance with the Augsburg Confession. . . . Only very exceptional laymen have ever read the other sixteenth century documents in the Book of Concord, and they are neither required or expected to do so. But ministers of the church are. Because of their responsibilities of leadership, ministers are expected to have a fuller knowledge than laymen of the historical landmarks of the church's developing understanding of God's revelation of himself. They are also expected to embrace as their own the understanding of God's revelation to which these statements bear witness. This is so because ministers are called not to speak for themselves alone but to speak for the church . . . to proclaim good news." Theodore G. Tappert, "The Significance of Confessional Subscription," in *Essays on the Lutheran Confessions Basic to Lutheran Cooperation* (New York: National Lutheran Council, and The Lutheran Church–Missouri Synod, 1961), p. 28.

36. In the Catechism, the order of the last two is "laborers . . .," then "masters," but that comes from a literal following of the order of Eph. 6:5-9. Actually the table in the Catechism had previously reversed the order found in Eph. 5:22—6:4

and at 1 Peter 2:18; 3:1-7 (wives/husbands, children/parents) into the sequence given above—probably a sequence suggested by the "pastors/laity" arrangement.

37. Schlink, op. cit., p. 307, cf. p. 313; Goppelt, op. cit., pp. 421-424.
38. Goppelt, op. cit., p. 422.
39. Schlink, op. cit., pp. 246-247.
40. Elert, op. cit., p. 344.
41. Elert, op. cit., p. 353.
42. WA 19, 75, 5ff.; = PE 6, 173; = LW-AE, 53, 64.
43. Elert, op. cit., p. 354.
44. Wilhelm Pauck, "The Ministry in the Time of the Continental Reformation," in *The Ministry in Historical Perspective,* ed. H. Richard Niebuhr and Daniel D. Williams (New York: Harper, 1956), p. 116.
45. Ibid., but cf. use of the Latin *minister* in the confessions.
46. Elert, op. cit., p. 354.
47. Bernhard Lohse, "Priestertum, III. In der christlichen Kirche, 3. Protestantismus," in *RGG³,* 5:580.
48. Cf. Heinrich Schmid, *The Doctrinal Theology of the Evangelical Lutheran Church Verified from the Original Sources,* trans. C. A. Hay and H. E. Jacobs (Philadelphia: Lutheran Publication Society, 1899; repr. Minneapolis: Augsburg, 1961), par. 57, pp. 599-604, with references to the theologians cited above: Hollaz, *Examen* (1707), 1277; Hutter, *Loci Communes Theologici* (1619), 568, 581; Hollaz, 1320, and Baier, *Compendium* (1685), 773.
49. Schmid, paras. 58 and 59, pp. 604-616.
50. Examples are given in Weidner, op. cit., pp. 101-104.
51. Elert, op. cit., pp. 354-55. Elert writes (p. 355), "To be sure, one can offer no valid objection to the actual custom of carrying out the act of ordination only through ordained clerics (Enders [et al., *Luthers Briefwechsel*], 11, 40, 18ff.); but the derivation of this custom as a right from the clergy's 'power of jurisdiction' really gives to this power a content which no longer has anything to do with the Office of the Keys."
52. Ibid., pp. 355-56.
53. Ibid., p. 363; cf. Pauck, op. cit., p. 138.
54. Lohse, loc. cit.
55. C. Mirbt, "Pietism," in *The New Schaff-Herzog Encyclopedia of Religious Knowledge,* ed. S. M. Jackson (New York: Funk and Wagnalls), 9 (1911), p. 55. Cf. Philip Jacob Spener, *Pia Desideria,* trans. T. G. Tappert, Seminar Editions (Philadelphia: Fortress, 1964), p. 94: "No damage will be done to the ministry by a proper use of this priesthood. In fact, one of the principal reasons why the ministry cannot accomplish all that it ought is that it is too weak without the help of the universal priesthood."
56. E. Sehling, "Collegialism," in *Schaff-Herzog,* 3 (1909), p. 160.
57. Ragnar Askmark, *Ämbetet i den Svenska Kyrkan* (Lund: Gleerup, 1949); summary in English by C. G. Carlfelt in *LQ* 3 (1951): 318-19; and Conrad Bergendoff, "Wanted: A Theory of the Laity in the Lutheran Church," *LQ* 3 (1951): 83-90.
58. Schlink, op. cit., p. 244, n. 13; E. Friedberg, "Boehmer, Justus Henning," in *Schaff-Herzog,* 2 (1908), p. 211.
59. I. Ludolphy, "Hoefling, Johann Wilhelm Friedrich," in *Enc. Luth. Ch.,* p. 1032.
60. Schlink, op. cit., pp. 244-45.
61. Ibid., p. 244, n. 13.
62. Lohse, loc. cit.

63. Schlink, op. cit., p. 244, n. 12.
64. F. W. Hoft, "Vilmar, August Friedrich Christian," in *Enc. Luth. Ch.*, p. 2442.
65. I. Ludolphy, "Stahl, Friedrich Julius," ibid., p. 2256; Schlink, op. cit., p. 235, n. 6.
66. Hans Conzelmann, *An Outline of the Theology of the New Testament* (New York: Harper and Row, 1969), pp. 41-42.
67. Schlink, op. cit., p. 246, n. 16.
68. So Lohse, loc. cit., mentioning H. Asmussen and G. Merz as Lutherans advocating a "priestly" concept of office. For "high church" and "kerygmatic" views, cf. Jürgen Roloff, "The Question of the Church's Ministry in Our Generation," *LW* 11 (1964): 389-408, especially 398-402.
69. Cf. H. H. Walz, "Laienbewegung, christliche," in *RGG³*, 4:203-206.
70. That Lutheranism in America is inevitably varied follows from its variegated background in Europe and the fact that there were often "varied emphases and trends" in the Reformation and "no absolute uniformity"; what Willard D. Allbeck speaks of as "A Binocular View of Lutheranism in America," in *LQ* 14 (1962): 206-216, especially p. 214, applies above all to the ministry. In listing complicating factors above, I include the fact that conditions often militated against an educated ministry, but that is not to agree with Sidney E. Mead's contention ("The Rise of the Evangelical Conception of the Ministry in America [1607-1850]" in *The Ministry in Historical Perspective* [New York: Harper, 1956], p. 237) that the clergy who had previously been intellectual leaders were estranged from intellectual currents after the American Revolution; his point is less true of Lutheran clergy because of their tradition of training, but estrangement from the general culture in America was heightened for them by language barriers.
71. *The Doctrine of the Church in American Lutheranism*, The Knubel-Miller Lectures, 11 (Philadelphia: Board of Publication of the United Lutheran Church in America, 1956), p. 19.
72. *LQ* 3 (1951): p. 82.
73. Mead, op. cit., p. 217, citing J. H. St. J. Crevecoeur, *Letters from an American Farmer*, p. 64.
74. *The Journals of Henry Melchior Muhlenberg*, trans. T. G. Tappert and J. W. Doberstein (Philadelphia: Muhlenberg, 1942), 1:67. The context is struggles against itinerant interlopers, a quacksalver hired to preach by a congregation without a pastor, and the Moravian Count Zinzendorf who was ordaining Lutheran ministers on the strength of appointment by a Reformed preacher (p. 77). Cf. also, from a sociologist's standpoint, J. J. Mol, *The Breaking of Traditions: Theological Convictions in Colonial America* (Berkeley: Glendessary Press, 1968).
75. Bergendoff, *The Doctrine of the Church in American Lutheranism*, p. 27.
76. Ibid., pp. 20-23, with references in the notes. Falckner's ordination is interpreted differently by Theodore G. Tappert, in *Episcopacy in the Lutheran Church?* edited by I. Asheim and V. R. Gold (Philadelphia: Fortress, 1970), p. 163.
77. *Fraternal Appeal to the American Churches: With a Plan for Catholic Union on Apostolic Principles*, by Samuel Simon Schmucker, edited by F. K. Wentz, Seminar Editions (Philadelphia: Fortress, 1965), especially pp. 164-168.
78. T. A. Kantonen, "Laestadius, Lars Levi," pp. 1242-43, and A. K. E. Holmio, "Apostolic Lutheran Churches (in America)," p. 97, in *Enc. Luth. Ch.;* Bergendoff, *Church in American Lutheranism*, pp. 25-26.
79. Bergendoff, ibid.; G. H. Lenski, "Grabau, Johannes Andreas August," in *Enc. Luth. Ch.*, pp. 946-47; F. Meuser, "American Lutheran Church," ibid., p. 45.

80. *Minutes . . . Joint Synod of Ohio . . . 1870,* pp. 25-26, reprinted in *Documents of Lutheran Unity in America,* ed. Richard C. Wolf (Philadelphia: Fortress, 1966), no. 85, pp. 184-85.

81. *Church in American Lutheranism,* p. 24. Cf. E. C. Nelson, "American Lutheran Church," in *Enc. Luth. Ch.,* pp. 49-50, and "Eielsen Synod" and G. E. Lenski, "Eielsen, Elling," ibid., p. 769.

82. So Bergendoff in *LQ* 3 (1951):86.

83. On Loehe, in addition to encyclopedia articles and German literature listed there, cf. G. Ottersberg, "Wilhelm Loehe," *LQ* 4 (1952): 170-190; Bergendoff, *Church in American Lutheranism,* pp. 29-30.

84. Bergendoff, ibid., pp. 28-33; Arnold C. Mueller, *The Ministry of the Lutheran Teacher: A Study to Determine the Position of the Lutheran Parish School Teacher within the Public Ministry of the Church.* Authorized by the Board of Parish Education of The Lutheran Church–Missouri Synod (St. Louis: Concordia, 1964), pp. 52 ff.; cf. also encyclopedia articles and church histories.

85. As summarized in Mueller, ibid., pp. 52-53. Full translation of the 10 theses by D. H. Steffens, "The Doctrine of the Church and the Ministry," in *Ebenezer,* edited by W. H. T. Dau (St. Louis: Concordia, 1922), pp. 152-53, reprinted in Bergendoff, *The Doctrine of the Church in American Lutheranism,* pp. 31-32: (1) "The holy office of preaching (*Predigtamt*) or the ministry (*Pfarramt*) is not identical with that of the priesthood of all believers." This office is "no human institution," but is "instituted by God himself" (2) and is "not optional" (3). It is "no separate holy estate" (4). It is "conferred by God [*übertragen*] through the congregation" (6). "The holy ministry, indeed, has the right to judge doctrine; however, the laity also has this right" and thus has "seat and voice with the ministers in church courts and councils" (10). Fuller discussion in W. Dallmann, W. H. T. Dau, Th. Engelder, ed., *Walther and the Church* (St. Louis: Concordia, 1938), pp. 71-74 for the 10 theses.

86. Wolf, *Documents,* no. 93, p. 210; = *Synodal-Bericht,* 1873.

87. Ibid., No. 99, pp. 229-30.

88. Weidner, op. cit., pp. 107-110.

89. Cf. Richard R. Caemmerer, "The Universal Priesthood and the Pastor," *Concordia Theological Monthly* (= *CTM*) 19 (1948): 573-74. Bergendoff, *Church in American Lutheranism,* p. 35, notes "the powerful influence of the ministers and especially of the theological faculty, in the life of the Missouri Synod."

90. For the following section, cf. especially Mueller, op. cit., though the book is arguing one particular view, on authorized lines, however.

91. Bergendoff, *Church in American Lutheranism,* pp. 33-34.

92. Weidner, op. cit., p. 120. Of theologians in the General Council taking the third position, Weidner lists H. E. Jacobs as closer to Missouri in emphasis on the local congregation, and himself and C. P. Krauth as reflecting a less congregational view.

93. Bergendoff, *Church in American Lutheranism,* p. 34. One Danish group elected a senior member of its ministerium for life as "Ordainer."

94. T. F. Gullixson, "The Ministry," in *What Lutherans Are Thinking: A Symposium on Lutheran Faith and Life,* ed. E. C. Fendt (Columbus: Wartburg Press, 1947), pp. 289-306; Richard R. Caemmerer, "The Ministry of the Word," in *Theology in the Life of the Church,* ed. R. W. Bertram (Philadelphia: Fortress, 1963), pp. 215-232. The phrases quoted are from pp. 289 and 225, respectively.

95. Bergendoff, *LQ* 3 (1951): 86.

96. United Lutheran Church in America, Eleventh Biennial Convention, 1938, *Minutes,* pp. 65-73; the Statement on "The Call to the Ministry," approved at the Baltimore convention as a "guide to the church" has also been printed separately. ULCA, Eighteenth Biennial Convention, 1952, *Minutes,* pp. 543-556 (phrases quoted below from pp. 544-45, 554). Lutheran Church in America, Third Biennial Convention, 1966, *Minutes,* pp. 434-447 and passim (pp. 440-443 cited below; the work of George Lindbeck on this commission is especially singled out in the *Minutes,* p. 447).

97. Lutheran Church in America, 1966 Report, *Minutes,* p. 435. For part III, section A, below, one unpublished study has been basic: Dagny Ohlekopf, "The Church's Concept of the Place and Role of the Ministry," part of a study on the church and the office of the ministry in The American Lutheran Church, the Lutheran Church in America, and The Lutheran Church–Missouri Synod, carried out by the research assistant in the Division of Theological Studies of the Lutheran Council in the U.S.A. The material was made available to me in manuscript form before it went to the Lutheran Council or was available generally, by the kindness of Dr. Paul D. Opsahl. I cite by the pages of the typed manuscript of this significant study: for The ALC, pp. 63-76; for the LCA, pp. 92-128; for the LCMS, pp. 164-196. (Cited as Ohlekopf, "Ministry," and the initials of the church body for the section.) While the LCA may appear to be most in flux and most to reflect current change (so Ohlekopf concludes, "Ministry," LCA, p. 92), other Lutheran bodies are likewise examining the ministry. The 1959 convention of The Lutheran Church–Missouri Synod called for a study with special attention to the public ministry as over against the universal priesthood. In 1962 there was a "Special Study Commission on the Theological Foundations of the Ministry," which later turned its task over to a research committee at the St. Louis Seminary School for Graduate Studies. A "Church and Ministry" project was listed in 1965 convention reports but not for 1967 (Ohlekopf, "Ministry," LCMS, p. 197, n. 1).

98. Ohlekopf, "Ministry," ALC, pp. 63, 70. The "Definitions of Terms" in the *Handbook of The American Lutheran Church* (1965 ed.), p. 7, were not part of the Constitution and Bylaws, but were approved by that body's Joint Council and General Convention.

99. Ohlekopf, "Ministry," LCMS, pp. 164-167, "Brief Statement," Articles 31-33; in Wolf, *Documents,* no. 158, pp. 388-89. "Common Confession," Part I, in *Doctrinal Declarations* (St. Louis: Concordia, 1957), p. 76. *Reports and Memorials, Forty-Fourth Regular Convention,* LCMS, 1959, p. 102.

100. Ohlekopf, "Ministry," LCMS, pp. 167-169. Ordination and installation were held not essentially to differ.

101. Ibid., p. 178. Thesis 31 in Walther's essay, "The Proper Form of an Evangelical Lutheran Congregation . . ." in *Walther and the Church* (cited above, n. 85), pp. 104-5.

102. Bylaw 4.07. The Bylaws are sometimes more liberal than the Constitution, which renounces "serving congregations of mixed confession" or "taking part in . . . sacramental rites of heterodox congregations" (VI.2).

103. Ohlekopf, "Ministry," LCMS, pp. 185ff., on "Distinctions within the Concept of the 'Laity'" (more accurately: a "class" between pastors and laity?).

104. Ibid., p. 187. Cf. Mueller, op. cit., pp. 143, 145-46 (Lutheran teachers were generally given draft exemption, as "ministers of religion," and certain tax deductions).

105. Ohlekopf, "Ministry," LCMS, pp. 191ff.
106. Ibid., pp. 193ff. Note the symposium in the *American Lutheran*, cited below, n. 136.
107. Ohlekopf, "Ministry," ALC, p. 63. The "Statement on Ordination and Clergy Roster," (which draws on Luther and the Confessions, plus Joachim Heubach, *Die Ordination zum Amt der Kirche* [Berlin: Lutherisches Verlagshaus, 1956], and the work of the ULCA commission of 1952) appears in the *Reports and Actions of the Second General Convention*, The ALC, 1964, pp. 137-142. On "blessing" in ordination, cf. Schlink, op. cit., pp. 245-46, note 15. The book by Heubach, which sees ordination primarily as a theological matter, and only secondarily one of order, seeks to correct the older views of Georg Rietschel, said by Ewing (*LQ* 16 [1964]: 213) to have influenced the 1938 ULCA statement on ministry. On Rietschl, cf. I. Ludolphy in *Enc. Luth. Ch.*, p. 2061.
108. Paragraph 701.
109. Ohlekopf, "Ministry," ALC, pp. 64-65.
110. Ibid., p. 67. See the essay, "The Doctrine of the Church in the Lutheran Confessions," from the ALC/LCMS talks.
111. Ibid., pp. 67-68. *Reports and Actions*, 1964, pp. 139-140. The Luther reference is to WA 12, 191, 22; cf. 193, 35 ff. = LW-AE, 40, p. 37, cf. pp. 40-41.
112. Ohlekopf, "Ministry," ALC, pp. 69f.; The ALC *Handbook*, 1965, pp. 133-34, from the "United Testimony." A paper by D. N. Granskou was referred to on restricting the vote of nonparish clergy; this already held true in some LCA synods on the district (not "synod") level.
113. Ibid., p. 71; *Handbook*, pp. 136-39.
114. LCA *Minutes*, 1964, pp. 582-83.
115. So Ohlekopf, "Ministry," LCA, pp. 93-94.
116. Ibid., p. 93; LCA *Minutes*, 1966, p. 40. ". . . it might almost sound as if the ordained ministry were merely supplementary to all the rest. I regret the failure to call it distinctly the Ministry of Word and Sacraments, thus describing the inner substance of what ordination is and the holy authority it confers" (p. 41). There was also a fear expressed that a host of commissionings would encourage growing "professionalism" in lay church service and undercut voluntary service and in turn, the universal priesthood (p. 42). "A church which does not acknowledge the universal priesthood of all believers may find itself compelled to send ordained men, worker priests, into lay vocations for 'the church to be there'; ours doesn't" (p. 43).
117. Transcript of the discussion, cited by Ohlekopf, "Ministry," LCA, p. 94.
118. Ibid., p. 112 and p. 100. She was not correct in saying, however, that the choice seems to be having the pastor as president ex officio or electing him to the office. Some congregations had a long tradition of lay presidents for the council.
119. LCA *Minutes*, 1964, p. 676.
120. Ohlekopf, "Ministry," LCA, pp. 109-10. At the 1966 convention, the chair ruled that the pertinent paragraph ("n") of the "Standards of Acceptance into and Continuance in the Ministry of the Lutheran Church in America," is "procedural" and does not establish a cause for discipline other than that in Article VII, Section 4 of the Constitution; *Minutes*, p. 827.
121. Ohlekopf, "Ministry," LCA, pp. 116-17; 1964 *Minutes*, pp. 518-19.
122. Ohlekopf, "Ministry," LCA, p. 117, cf. 118-19. On lay readers (not "lay preachers") cf. 1964 *Minutes*, p. 313. Contrast the opinion of Otto W. Heick, s. v. "Lay Activity," *Enc. Luth. Ch.*, p. 1277: "In American Lutheranism, too, the

autonomy of the local church is fully accepted and the laity is in complete charge of all the affairs of the church" (!).

123. Ewing, *LQ* 16 (1964): 215. Text in *The Occasional Services* (1962), pp. 90-99, and *Service Book and Hymnal* (text edition, 1967), pp. 563-572. He does not go into the order employed in The Lutheran Church–Missouri Synod.

124. Ewing, ibid., p. 217 (italicized in his article).

125. Ibid., p. 221.

126. Cf. Gilbert P. Voigt, "The Protestant Minister in American Fiction," in *LQ* 11 (1959): 3-13. The general finding: these ministers "minimize liturgy, organizing ability, pulpit oratory, and, on the whole, even theological learning; they magnify sincerity, unselfish concern for the poor and outcast, fearless denunciation of evil from the pulpit, and wise, sympathetic counsel to the erring and perplexed" (p. 13). Among novels about Lutheran clergy are O. E. Rølvaag, *Giants in the Earth*, on an itinerant Norwegian minister in the Dakotas, revered by his people; James K. Paulding, *Koningsmarke*, a humble, unselfish, benevolent pastor among the Swedes in colonial Delaware, in contrast to his dour predecessor; and Christopher Morley, *Swiss Family Manhattan*, on a Swiss minister who goes to work for the League of Nations and ends up tending a gas station on Long Island. Add John Updike's short story reflecting a catechetical class in Eastern Pennsylvania, in *The Same Door*, "Pigeon Feathers" in *Pigeon Feathers and Other Stories*, and Pastor Fritz Kruppenbach in *Rabbit, Run*, and Conrad Richter, *A Simple Honorable Man*, about a pastor in Central Pennsylvania. W. E. Mueller, "Protestant Ministers in Modern American Novels, 1927–1958: The Searcher for a Role" (diss., University of Nebraska, 1961), was not available to me. I suspect that motion picture portrayals of clergymen would add little to help us. In the classification of ministers employed by R. S. Michaelsen, "The Protestant Ministry: 1850 to the Present," in *Ministry in Historical Perspective*, pp. 250-288, I find few categories in which to place Lutherans ("urban and rural" is rather obvious); the closest classification is "immigrant," but this category, according to Michaelsen, is but "similar to the place of the minister in the Negro community," i.e., as community leader, p. 269.

127. Cf., on Methodists, M. H. Leiffer, *The Layman Looks at the Minister* (New York: Abingdon-Cokesbury, 1947); Berndt Gustafsson, "People's View of the Minister and the Lack of Ministers in Sweden," in *Archives de Sociologie des Religions*, 22 (1966): 135-144, as cited in *Ministry Studies*, 1, 3 (October, 1967), p. 28. Edgar W. Mills, of the Ministry Studies Board, of the National Council of Churches, wrote me, September 9, 1969, that he knew of no studies dealing directly with Lutheran views of the difference between clergy and laity.

128. Cf. R. E. Sommerfeld, "Role Conceptions of Lutheran Ministers in the St. Louis Area" (diss., Washington University, 1957), summary in *Dissertation Abstracts of Research*, ed. R. J. Menges and J. E. Dittes (New York: Nelson, 1965), p. 94. Further, the dissertation by H. J. Bertness, University of Minnesota, 1955, on "Interests of [ALC] Lutheran ministers as measured by the Strong Vocational Interest Blank" (*Dissert. Abstr.*, 15 [1955]: 2094-2095; *Psychological Studies*, p. 24).

129. "The Lutheran Ministry: Origins, Careers, Self-Appraisal," in *The Cresset* 26 (1963), 9-17, also in *Information Service* 42 (1963), 1-8, summarizing a dissertation at the University of Chicago, 1963, "Ministers of the Lutheran Church–Missouri Synod: Origins, Training, Career-lines, Perceptions of Work and Reference." Phrases below come from pp. 13 and 15 of the *Cresset* article.

130. Cf. W. W. Schroeder, "Lay Expectations of the Ministerial Role: an Exploration of Protestant-Catholic Differentials," in *Journal of the Scientific Study of Religion* 2 (1963), 217-227 (summary in *Psychological Studies*, pp. 93-94). There are some statistics for 12 Lutheran congregations on how parishioners think ministers spend their time in C. Y. Glock and R. Stark, *Religion and Society in Tension* (Chicago: Rand McNally, 1965), pp. 141-150, but no comparative data from clergymen or from the past.

131. Walton Harlowe Greever, *The Minister and the Ministry*, Knubel-Miller Lectures, 1 (Philadelphia: Board of Publication of the United Lutheran Church in America, 1945).

132. Clarence C. Stoughton, *Set Apart for the Gospel*, Knubel-Miller Lectures, 2 (Philadelphia: Muhlenberg, 1946), pp. 1, 40.

133. R. P. Roth, "Ministry," p. 1581, and the article, "Keys, Office of" (reprinted from *Lutheran Cyclopedia*), p. 1207, in *Enc. Luth. Ch.*

134. Josefson, in *This Is the Church*, pp. 268-280, especially pp. 270, 276 for the five points he stresses; p. 273 on sacrifice; p. 277 on the ministry as a "divine order" (cf. also pp. 278, 279). It is when Josefson gets to his final points, on the ministry as "the fulcrum" and "a God-given order," that his citations from Luther cease.

135. Per Erik Persson, *Roman and Evangelical; Gospel and Ministry: An Ecumenical Issue*, trans. E. H. Wahlstrom (Philadelphia: Fortress, 1964), especially p. 89, and pp. 61-79 and 80-89 on the Roman and Evangelical views of ministry.

136. *American Lutheran* 46, 1 (1963): 12-15; 46, 2 (1963): 12-14, 25; 46, 3 (1963): 14-15, 24; 46, 4 (1963): 14-16, 23-24 (note the phraseology of the topic!: "Symposium on Authority—The Authority of the Ministry in Relation to the Laity"); *LW* 11 (1964): 389-462; *LQ* 18 (1966): 98-184; *Dialog* 8 (1969): 166-208.

137. R. R. Caemmerer, "The Universal Priesthood and the Pastor," *CTM* 19 (1948): 561-582.

138. H. G. Brueggemann, "The Public Ministry in the Apostolic Age," *CTM* 22 (1951): 81-109, favors the *Übertragungstheorie;* E. J. Moeller, "Concerning the Ministry of the Church," ibid., pp. 385-416, the alternate view sketched above. On the study of the ministry by commissions in The Lutheran Church–Missouri Synod, cf. above, n. 97.

139. Walter J. Bartling, "A Ministry to Ministers: An Examination of the New Testament *Diakonia*," *CTM* 33 (1962): 325-336.

140. Cited above, note 136. The examples noted are from Wayne C. Rydburg (M.D.), Vernon R. Schreiber (parish pastor), Harold Midtbo (layman), Oscar T. Doerr (attorney), and Fred A. Schurmann (layman), respectively.

141. William Horn, "The Image of the Ministry," *LQ* 13 (1961): 193-210; quotation from p. 207.

142. Robert E. Huldschiner, "The Lay Perversion of the Church," *LQ* 14 (1962): 217-229; quotation from p. 222. Cf. the comments of President Fry of the LCA, quoted above in §80.

143. As example of this concern for the laity, I have quoted from a Lutheran, Frederick K. Wentz, *The Layman's Role Today* (Garden City: Doubleday, 1963), cf. pp. 28-29, 163-166. Cf. also Wentz's article, "What Public Role for the Clergy?" *LQ* 18 (1966): 148-154. In the Knubel-Miller lecture series of the LCA (see above, notes 130-131) the emphasis in the first two on the "set-apart" ministry was followed by emphasis on the lay ministry: cf. nos. 13 and 18 in the series, *The Christian's Calling*, by Donald R. Heiges (1958), and *The Militant Ministry: People and Pastors of the Early Church and Today*, by Hans-Ruedi Weber (1963).

144. LCA *Minutes*, 1966, pp. 556-57; Donald R. Pichaske, *A Study Book on the Manifesto* (Philadelphia: Board of Publication of the LCA, 1967), especially pp. 166-174.

145. John Hall Elliott, *The Elect and the Holy: An Exegetical Examination of 1 Peter 2:4-10 and the Phrase* basileion hierateuma. Supplements to Novum Testamentum 12 (Leiden: Brill, 1966). See especially pp. xiii-xiv and 1-15 for connections with the general problem, pp. 219-226 for Elliott's conclusions, and pp. 225-26, n. 3, on the relation to Reformation and other subsequent interpretations of universal priesthood. For a favorable Catholic reaction to the general position that 1 Peter 2:4-10 does not support "universal priesthood," cf. R. Schnackenburg's review in *Biblische Zeitschrift* 12 (1968): 152-153; for somewhat more critical but generally favorable comments, cf. F. W. Danker in *CTM* 38 (1967): 329-332, and C. F. D. Moule, *Journal of Theological Studies* 18 (1967): 471-474. Elliott himself makes application of his findings in "Death of a Slogan: from Royal Priests to Celebrating Community," in *Una Sancta* 25 (1968): 18-31, emphasizing that the passage has nothing to do with universal priesthood or with "baptism as ordination" or with the individual; rather the community is stressed, election and holiness, and public proclamation of God's saving deeds (2:9) as witness to the world. But is this not close, after all, to the emphasis which some have seen in this "slogan" on the priestly witness and service of the whole community, in the sense of Romans 12, "our reasonable service"? "Celebrating community," especially if it is made to refer to celebrating eucharist, is something of an extrapolated phrase, in light of what 1 Peter itself says or fails to say (Elliott's dissertation, pp. 186-188, finds no connection between 2:5, 9 and a celebration of the eucharist; *hierateuma* refers rather to the response of believers: a holy life of obedience and well-doing before God and for human beings). Some of Elliott's remarks seem directed at an individualized concept of priesthood oriented to the local congregation, devoid of much feeling for the larger church or people of God; but this concept which he attacks is scarcely what all have meant by "general priesthood."

146. Horace D. Hummel, in *LQ* 18 (1966), especially pp. 104-106, 113, 116-17, 119.

147. Peter L. Kjeseth, p. 179, and Gerhard Krodel, pp. 198-99, n. 78, in *Dialog* 8 (1969).

148. See especially Krodel's survey in *Dialog* 8 (1969): 191-202, perhaps the best survey article currently available in English.

149. Martin J. Heinecken, "The Ministry, a Functional Office," *Lutheran Church Quarterly* 20 (1947): 432-441; "What Does Ordination Confer?" *LQ* 18 (1966), especially pp. 126 and 131.

150. Edgar Brown, *LQ* 18 (1966): 275-76.

151. H. Paul Santmire, "An Introduction to the Doctrine of the Ministry," *LQ* 16 (1964): 195-210 (his own summary on pp. 209-10). Phrases quoted above are from pp. 195, 198, 206-7.

152. Peter L. Kjeseth, "Baptism as Ordination," *Dialog* 8 (1969): 177-182. Kjeseth alludes to, and agrees with, the position expressed by J. Duss-von Werdt, on "What Can the Layman Do without the Priest?" in *Apostolic Succession,* ed. Hans Küng, Concilium 34 (New York: Paulist, 1968), p. 112: "in virtue of the universal priesthood, in principle, 'laymen' can do everything without priests."

153. Lutheran Council News Bureau, 69-41, p. 6, on the Lutheran World Federation conference at Cartigny, Switzerland, on "The Structures of the Congregation in

Mission" (3/28/69); and 69-91, p. 4, on the Evangelical Church in Württemberg (8/18/69). (Both proposals stem from regions where pietist emphasis on the universal priesthood has been strong.)

154. *Dialog* 8 (1969), in the "Symposium," p. 172, alluding to the Treatise on the Power and Primacy of the Pope, 62 and 67. On "presbyteral succession," cf. above, sections 22, 25, 40, 43, 45, 51, 55.7, 56, 58, 63.18, 67, 73, and 84.

155. Brunner, *LQ* 15 (1963): 99-117 (cited above, n. 20).

156. Ibid., p. 111.

157. Cf. *Dialog* 8 (1969), in the "Symposium," p. 168, where the view is attributed to Schlink; Roloff, in *LW* 11 (1964): 405-407. Roloff compares this position with that sketched in the section on ministry in *The Fourth World Conference on Faith and Order: The Report from Montreal 1963*, ed. P. C. Rodger and L. Vischer, Faith and Order Paper No. 42 (London: SCM, 1964), pp. 61-69, and contrasts the manner in which Montreal derives the "special ministry" from the ministry of all. Further, on reactions from a biblical standpoint on Küng's views in *The Church* (1967), that a church faithful to the New Testament need not be conditioned on ordination and that the reality of the eucharist in nonepiscopal churches is a distinct probability, cf. M. M. Bourke, "Reflections on Church Order in the New Testament," in *CBQ* 30 (1968): 493-511.

158. *Ministry in the Lutheran Church in America* (Philadelphia: LCA/Division for Professional Leadership, 1984), foreword by Lloyd E. Shenemann; includes "A Study of Ministry, 1980," pp. 9-24, on which see *LCAM*, Tenth Biennial Convention (Seattle, 1980), pp. 140-55; action, pp. 139, 155-58, 192-97; "Expectations of the Lutheran Church in America of Its Ordained Ministers," pp. 25-33; "God's People in Ministry," pp. 35-52; *LCAM*, Twelfth Biennial Convention (Toronto, 1984): 240-58.

2. The Ordination of Women: Exegesis, Experience, and Ecumenical Concern

1. Cf. E. Lohse, *Die Ordination im Spätjudentum und im Neuen Testament* (Göttingen: Vandenhoeck und Ruprecht, 1951); critique by A. A. T. Ehrhardt, "Jewish and Christian Ordination," *Journal of Ecclesiastical History* 5, 2, reprinted in *The Framework of the New Testament Stories* (Univ. of Manchester Press, 1963), pp. 132-50. J. Newman, *Semikhah [Ordination]* (Univ. of Manchester Press, 1950). E. Lohse, "Ordination, II. Im NT," *RGG*, 4:1672-73; *"rabbi, rabbouni," TDNT*, 6:961-65. Eduard Schweizer, *Church Order in the New Testament*, SBT 32 (London: SCM, 1961), §25, pp. 206-10. Heber F. Peacock, "Ordination in the New Testament," *Review and Expositor* 55 (1958): 262-74. J. Coppens, "Handauflegung," *Biblisch-historisches Handwörterbuch*, ed. B. Reicke and L. Rost (Göttingen: Vandenhoeck und Ruprecht, 1964), vol. 3, esp. cols. 633-35.

2. On the sense of the term today, cf. H. H. Bagger, "Pastor, Ordination of," in *Enc. Luth. Ch.*, 1857-59. For evidence that the ministry of today does not exist in the New Testament, cf. Gustav Wingren, *Kyrkans ämbete*, Ordet och kyrkan serie (Lund: Gleerups, 1958); cf. his "Church Order and Unity," *Church Quarterly Review* 161 (1960): 44-54.

3. So Lohse, *Die Ordination*, p. 101; Coppens.

4. So Ehrhardt.

5. Schweizer, §7k, p. 101: "for Paul . . . an ordination . . . is impossible."

6. Cf. Schweizer. That 1 Tim. 6:11-16 is a formulary of ordination paraenesis has been argued by E. Käsemann, in *Neutestamentliche Studien für Rudolf Bultmann* (Berlin, 1954), pp. 261-68, reprinted in *Exegetische Versuche und Besinnungen* (Göttingen: Vandenhoeck und Ruprecht), vol. 1 (1960), pp. 101-108.

7. Old Testament usage is discussed by Russell C. Prohl, *Woman in the Church: A Restudy of Woman's Place in Building the Kingdom* (Grand Rapids: Eerdmans, 1957), pp. 36-47. Prohl, a Lutheran clergyman from the Missouri Synod, wrote at Brite College of the Bible, Texas Christian University.

8. *Concerning the Ordination of Women* (Geneva: World Council of Churches, Department of Faith and Order and Department on Cooperation of Men and Women in Church, Family and Society, 1964), p. 31.

9. 1 Sam. 2:22 (but this may be a jibe at how lax things had gotten under the sons of Eli, women were serving "at the entrance to the tent of meeting"!): Exod. 38:8. Cf. *TDNT,* 5:962, n. 97.

10. *Concerning the Ordination of Women,* pp. 31-32.

11. For example, Emil Brunner, *Man in Revolt* (Philadelphia: Westminster, 1947), p. 354, disparages woman's tendency to indulge in "nature mysticism."

12. Horace D. Hummel, "The Holy Ministry from Biblical Perspective," *LQ* 18 (1966): 104-119; he notes how little secondary literature exists on the Old Testament and ministry, stresses how much a hermeneutical question is involved, and does not mention the issue of ordaining women. Cf. Raphael Loewe, *The Position of Women in Judaism* (London: SPCK, 1966), written as a supplement for *Women and Holy Orders.* His most striking suggestion: marriage should be a precondition for women ordained! A more positive sketch of the participation of women in the liturgical life of diaspora Judaism is given by J. Massingberd Ford, "The First Epistle to the Corinthians or the First Epistle to the Hebrews?" *CBQ* 28 (1961), pp. 413-14.

13. Peter Brunner, "The Ministry and the Ministry of Women," *LW* 6 (1959): 248.

14. Literature is extensive on the place of women in antiquity and in early Christianity. A pertinent survey on "the status of women in the New Testament world" is provided by Raymond T. Stamm, in "The Status of Women Workers in the Church," *LQ* 10 (1958): 139-45. Further: Johannes Leipoldt, *Die Frau in der Antiken Welt und im Urchristentum* (Leipzig: Koehler und Amelang, 1954). Connie Parvey, "Ordain Her, Ordain Her Not. . . ," *Dialog* 8, 3 (Summer 1969): 203-208: Paul said yes theologically, but tended to say no sociologically.

15. The "paternal" argument is discussed, and rejected as not significant, in *Concerning the Ordination of Women,* pp. 8, 22-24, and 64; Margaret E. Thrall, *The Ordination of Women to the Priesthood: A Study of the Biblical Evidence,* Studies in Ministry and Worship (London: SCM, 1958), pp. 80ff.; G. W. H. Lampe, "Church Tradition and the Ordination of Women," *The Expository Times* 76 (1964-1965): 123-25, to which there is a response in the same journal by J. Pretlove, p. 294; and Leonard Hodgson, "Theological Objections to the Ordination of Women," *The Expository Times* 77 (1965-1966): 210-13.

16. The Mariological argument has been advanced by E. Mascall, *Theology* 658 (1955), p. 103, quoted by Thrall, *Ordination of Women,* p. 80; Mrs. F. C. Blomfield, *Wonderful Order* (1955), summarized by Thrall, pp. 82-87; cf. Lampe, "Church Tradition," p. 124. It is usually in (Anglo-)Catholic circles that this approach is found. For a Protestant assessment of recent discussion about Mary, cf. Stephen Benko, *Protestants, Catholics, and Mary* (Valley Forge: Judson Press, 1968), where it is even discussed whether the historical mother of Jesus became a believer in Christ.

17. Even the difficult passage 1 Tim. 2:15 (on which, see below) "woman will be saved through bearing children . ." does not invoke Mary as model for the church.

18. The "apostolicity" argument occurs in many of the same quarters as that involving the divine paternity; for discussion, cf. *Concerning the Ordination of Women,* pp. 9, 33-35, 58, 69; Thrall, pp. 87-90; Lampe, pp. 124-25 (reply by Pretlove, p. 294); and Hodgson, pp. 210-11.

19. Cited by Hodgson, p. 210.

20. The relation of "the Twelve" (in Mark, or Matthew, or 1 Cor. 15:5) to "the apostles" (as developed in Luke-Acts, cf. 1 Cor. 15:7, 9) and the whole question of "apostleship" in early Christianity are too complex, and the literature too extensive, to allow discussion here. However, in Paul, where "the apostles" are a larger group than "the Twelve," it is possible that Junia or Julia (cf. NEB note), mentioned (in some manuscripts) at Rom. 16:7 as "eminent among the apostles," may be a "female *apostolos.*"

21. Krister Stendahl, *The Bible and the Role of Women: A Case Study in Hermeneutics,* trans. Emilie T. Sander, Facet Books, Biblical Series 15 (Philadelphia: Fortress, 1966), pp. 38-39, who notes also that nowhere in the New Testament is there any reference either to "the exclusively male character of the first celebration of the Last Supper."

22. For the argument, cf., for example, Harald Riesenfeld, "The Ministry in the New Testament," in *The Root of the Vine: Essays in Biblical Theology,* ed. Anton Fridrichsen and other members of Uppsala University (Westminster: Dacre Press, 1953), especially pp. 123-27 (". . . self-evident to the early Christian mind that the officer presiding over the assembled congregation, and therefore at the Eucharist, should be a male"), or P. Y. Emery, "Féminité de l'Église et féminité dans l'Église," *Études Théologiques et Religieuses* 40 (1965): 90-96 (woman's primary role is that of being a reminder of all the hidden realities when men, owing to their rationalistic inclinations, easily slight or forget them; summary in *New Testament Abstracts* 10 [1965-1966], number 649). It is also treated by Hodgson, pp. 212-13.

   This argument appeared to some extent in the debate in the Church of Sweden in the 1950s over the ordination of women. The 1951 statement by seven university teachers of New Testament, for example, held that "the minister represents Christ in the liturgy, and Christ cannot be represented by a woman," to which Nygren replied, "Christ is present in the service of the church . . . and does not need any re-presentation" (Sten Rodhe, "The Controversy over the Ordination of Women in Sweden," *LW* 4 [1957-58]: 394, 399).

23. On the "inferiority of women" argument, cf. *Concerning the Ordination of Women,* pp. 58 and 61, where present-day theologians of the Orthodox Church allude to "the period when women are 'impure' " (Lev. 12; 15:19ff.) and cite canons "prohibiting women-priests, based on this point of view," and even forbidding women to participate in the sacraments or enter church during this period (cf. the custom of "churching" a mother, 40 days after childbirth, also); hence the view that "biological rhythms fluctuate more in women than in men" (p. 61), and that since "spiritual life" and "sacramental vocation" are conditioned by "bodily functions," women are not meant, by their very nature physically, to be able to become priests, but are to fit "a more maternal rhythm" (F. C. Blomfield, as cited in Thrall, p. 102; the argument discussed and rejected, pp. 102-4).

24. One can readily see a clear tendentiousness in a characterization of women such as that offered by the church father Epiphanius: they are "a feeble race, untrustworthy, and of mediocre intelligence" (as quoted by Lampe, p. 124), but a not

too different argument, though less crassly put, can appear in current discussions; for example, J. J. Von Allmen, *Pauline Teaching on Marriage* (London: Faith Press, 1963), p. 13, n. 5: "a person's sex theologically conditions his or her place in the church," and that is the reason, rather than any prejudices of the time, why "there are ministries which the New Testament does not consider as being open to a woman." Peter Brunner, p. 272, points to "the theological doctrine of the sexual difference between man and woman" so that there is "conflict between being 'pastor' and being 'woman.' "

25. The "subordination" argument is especially stressed by Fritz Zerbst, *The Office of Woman in the Church: A Study in Practical Theology*, trans. A. G. Merkens (St. Louis: Concordia, 1955), pp. 69-81. The most impressive counterstatement, turning Genesis 1 (and Gal. 3:28) against Genesis 2-3, is M. E. Thrall's *The Ordination of Women to the Priesthood* (summary in *Concerning the Ordination of Women*, pp. 25-27, 30, with objections considered on p. 27; and in Stendahl, pp. viii, 28-32; cf. p. 39, n. 37, where Stendahl voices disagreement on some points). Thrall's argument is rejected by Peter Brunner, p. 264. "Subordination" in its varying meanings in the Pauline epistles is studied by Else Kähler, *Die Frau in den paulinischen Briefen* (Zurich: Gotthelf Verlag, 1960), briefly summarized by Stendahl, pp. 28-29, n. 29.

26. Gen. 2:18,20. *'ēzer* in Old Testament usually means "superordinate," not "subordinate."

27. Zerbst, p. 105, cited in *Concerning the Ordination of Women*, p. 26, and by Thrall, p. 94. For Lutheran discussions, it is significant that it is on the basis of the Confessions that Zerbst reaches his conclusion that there is nothing in the nature of the office of preaching and administration of the sacraments to exclude women from that office.

28. D. E. H. Whiteley, *The Theology of St. Paul* (Philadelphia: Fortress, 1964), pp. 222-23. "I myself have no doubt that the subordination of women is socially conditioned. . . . St. Paul would have employed different analogies if he had lived in a different civilization." Whiteley admits, however, that while the subordination of women in Col. 3:18-19 may be called functional, 1 Corinthians seems to make it a matter of status.

29. That Genesis 1 is assigned to the Priestly writer and Genesis 2 to the J source may help explain the differences in the two accounts, but is not necessary to the argument here.

30. Stendahl, pp. 28ff., emphasizes how, though the point was grounded in creation (Genesis 2) for early Christianity that woman was to be subordinate to her husband in the home and subordinate to male teachers in church, "in Christ" that "order of creation" has been transcended, so that there is now full religious equality, even in the *Haustafeln* or "tables of household duties" (cf. 1 Peter 3:7, "joint heirs of the grace of life"), and even when Paul reflects the traditional pattern, as in 1 Corinthians 11, he transforms it—"man is not independent of woman . . . in the Lord, for as woman was made from man, so man is now born of woman," 11:11-12.

31. "Two very different approaches can be found in two books by Lutherans. . . . Both base their study upon the Bible, using the same quotations from Genesis and Paul, but each comes out with different conclusions. Dr. Zerbst makes the more traditional conclusion that in the order of Creation there is a basic inequality between man and woman, that woman is under subjection. . . . [Russell C. Prohl, *Woman in the Church* (cited above, n.7), pp. 35, 47] concludes that 'there is no

law of creation which makes women in general subordinate to men in general
. . . . It is not true, as many believe, that the Bible subordinates woman as a sex
to man as a sex . . ." (Report on *Women in the Ministry* [mimeographed; Geneva:
World Council of Churches, Department on the Cooperation of Men and Women
in Church and Society, May, 1958], p. 2).

32. So Prohl, summarized in *Concerning the Ordination of Women*, p. 28; hence Prohl's
conclusion cited in the previous note. He holds there is a hierarchical order of
creation that holds in the family but not in the church. André Dumas, in *Concerning
the Ordination of Women*, p. 29, reverses this, however, to claim that for Paul
reciprocity holds in the family but hierarchy in the church! A recent Roman Catholic
study, however, concludes for Prohl's position: "the New Testament texts generally
adduced to support the impossibility of ordaining women are almost certainly
concerned with the relationship of wives to husbands." John O'Rourke, "Women
and the Reception of Orders," *Revue de l'Université d'Ottawa* 38 (1968): 295
(summary in *New Testament Abstracts* 13 [1968-69], no. 368).

The word *idios* ("one's own" [husband, wife]) occurs frequently in these passages (1 Cor. 14:35; Eph. 5:22, and so forth). Paul's aim was to maintain conventions in the family, in the face of contemporary misunderstandings about Christianity, not to give rules for church government or the sexes in society in general.

33. The *"imago"* argument is presented in *Concerning the Ordination of Women*, pp.
6 and 24 ff. On *"imago dei"* see, in addition to standard Bible dictionary articles,
C. F. D. Moule, *Man and Nature in the New Testament,* Facet Books, Biblical
Series 17 (Philadelphia: Fortress, 1967), pp. viii-xvii and the literature cited on
p. 24. See also Prohl, pp. 36-37.

34. The "all members are ministers" argument can be examined in *Concerning the
Ordination of Women*, pp. 6 and 15-17. The *locus classicus* at 1 Peter 2:4-10 for
"the priesthood of all believers" has been reexamined by John H. Elliott in *The
Elect and the Holy,* Supplements to Novum Testamentum 12 (Leiden: Brill, 1966),
with the conclusion that Exod. 19:6 ("you shall be to me a kingdom of priests")
is not employed here, or elsewhere, in support of, or in polemic against, the
Levitical priesthood, or in connection with Christ's priesthood (never mentioned
in 1 Peter), but to describe, in cultic terms, the mission of the church in the world
on the basis of election. The church is thus not in 1 Peter presented as a neo-
Levitical community—where women would be barred from the ministry; in the
Haustafeln of 1 Peter, women, though described as "the weaker sex," are now
"joint heirs of the grace of life" (3:7). Cf. Schweizer, *Church Order,* pp. 110-
12. For discussion in Germany over the relation of the pastoral office to the general
priesthood, cf. Gerhard Heintze, "Allgemeines Priestertum und besonderes Amt,"
Evangelische Theologie 23 (1963): 617-46, where the attempt of Joachim Heubach,
in *Die Ordination zum Amt der Kirche,* Arbeiten zur Geschichte und Theologie
des Luthertums 2 (Berlin, 1956), to outline a *theologia ordinationis,* is discussed
(pp. 636-38 with regard to New Testament material; p. 639, on the effort to exclude
women from "public" proclamation, while allowing them to teach catechetical
classes, and so forth, without realizing how the concept of "public" has changed,
for example, since Luther's day).

35. In addition to commentaries, cf. *Concerning the Ordination of Women*, pp. 49-
51; Stamm, p. 154; and especially Stendahl, pp. 32-35, who treats the passage
as "the 'breakthrough'" (p. 5, n. 4, cites literature where his position is disputed).
Secondary literature, especially in German, from 1900 to the 1940s, is conveniently
summarized by Zerbst, pp. 14-30; writers of that period in favor of ordaining

women often stressed Gal. 3:28 (Bäumer, Zscharnack, H. Jordan, M. Dibelius); to Zerbst's bibliography, add J. M. Robbins, "St. Paul and the Ministry of Women," *The Expository Times* 46 (1934-35): 185-88. Also, *Women and Holy Orders: Being the Report of a Commission Appointed by the Archbishops of Canterbury and York* (London: Church Information Office, 1966), p. 12; B. Gärtner, "Das Amt der Mann und die Frau," in *In Signo Crucis* (Uppsala, 1963); G. Krodel, "Forms and Functions of Ministries in the New Testament," *Dialog* 8, 3 (Summer 1969): 191-202.

36. A. Oepke, *"gynē," TDNT,* 1:777.

37. First Corinthians 12:13 may omit "male and female" because the "breakthrough" had already been achieved at Corinth; in fact, women prophesying in church were a problem there, which Paul takes up at 1 Cor. 11:2-16 and 14:34 (see below). Rom. 10:9 (in the context of chaps. 9-11, Christ and Israel) mentions only "Jew and Greek." Col. 3:11 brings in "barbarian, Scythian" instead, breaking the pattern of contrasting pairs (cf. E. Lohse, *Die Briefe an die Kolosser und an Philemon,* KEK IX/2 [Göttingen, 1968], pp. 207-8; trans. W. R. Poehlman and R. J. Karris, *Colossians and Philemon,* Hermeneia [Philadelphia: Fortress, 1971], pp. 143-44).

38. Ragnar Bring, *Commentary on Galatians,* trans. Eric Wahlstrom (Philadelphia: Muhlenberg, 1961), pp. 184-86, points to how the passage has been interpreted in two different directions: so as to lead to the abolition of social differences mentioned in the verse, or to retain differences in social life while applying the verse with reference to God, righteousness, and salvation. For the latter position, cf. the reply of Bishop Malmeström in the Swedish debate, reported by Rodhe, *LW* 4 (1957-58): 401, or the commentary by H. Schlier, *Der Brief an die Galater,* KEK (Göttingen, 1951), p. 130, n. 5: one must be guarded in drawing direct consequences for the ordering of ecclesiastical or political life; ecclesiastical office does not depend on baptism but on "being sent" (commentary written in 1949 before Schlier entered the Catholic church). Peter Brunner, p. 255, following Zerbst, rejects the "eschatological breakthrough" argument as leading to *Schwärmerei,* though he does hold that "one of the fundamental insights of the Lutheran Reformation" was that "the order of the church cannot stand in contradiction to her Gospel."

39. Besides the commentaries of C. K. Barrett, HNTC (1968); J. Héring (1949; Eng. tr., London: Epworth, 1962); H. Lietzmann, HNT 9 (1931), with supplementary notes by W. G. Kümmel, 1949; J. Weiss, KEK (1910); and F. W. Grosheide, New International Commentary (1953); among others, see John C. Hurd Jr., *The Origin of 1 Corinthians* (New York: Seabury, 1965), pp. 90-91, 182-86; and in the literature already cited, *Concerning the Ordination of Women,* pp. 45-47; Thrall, pp. 66-76; Kähler, pp. 43-70; Zerbst, pp. 31-45; Prohl, pp. 24-30.

A very particular type of treatment is given by Abel Isaksson, *Marriage and Ministry in the New Temple: A Study with Special Reference to Mt. 19. 3-12 and 1. Cor. 11. 3-16,* Acta Seminarii Neotestamentici Upsaliensis 24 (Lund, 1965), especially pp. 153-86. (On the general background and interests of some Swedish exegetes of the "Uppsala School," some of whose concerns were noted above in discussion of the debate in the Church of Sweden, cf. A. Rask, "Le ministere néotestamentaire et l'exégèse suédoise," *Istina* 7 [1960]: 205-32, summary in *New Testament Abstracts* 6 [1961-62], number 286—cultic, hierarchical concept of the ministry, a ministry instituted by Jesus himself.) On much of Isaksson's theorizing, reviewers have been unconvinced—for example, that Jesus and Paul shared a view that disciples were to abide by rules originally laid down for priests at the temple; that Jesus' teachings on marriage and divorce were inspired by Ezek. 44:22, rather than Genesis 1–2; and thus that the "exception clause" at Matt. 5:32 and 19:9 ("except for unchastity") referred originally to a woman who had lost her virginity prior to marriage and that such a ("divorced") woman could not marry a priest (that is, a disciple of Jesus; cf. pp. 146ff.). Reviews: J. Fitzmyer, *Theological Studies* 27 (1966): 451-54; G. Delling, *TLZ* 92 (1967): cols. 276-77; and J. M. Ford, *Journal of Theological Studies* 18 (1967): 197-200 (= *New Testament Abstracts* 11, numbers 702r, 804r; and 12, 162r). Madelein Boucher, "Some Unexplained Parallels to 1 Cor. 11:11-12 and Gal. 3:28: The New Testament on the Role of Women," *CBQ* 31 (1969): 50-58. S. Aalen, "A Rabbinic Formula in I Cor. 14:34," *Studia Evangelica* II, ed. F. L. Cross, Texte und Untersuchungen 87 (Berlin, 1964), pp. 513-25.

More sound, however, is Isaksson's view that 11:2-16 treats married prophetesses who speak under the Spirit at cultic gatherings and constitute a (possibly ordained!) part of the ministry at Corinth. Isaksson interprets the details to show that these women, in a congregation rich in the gifts of the Spirit, spoke prophecies mediated by angels, wearing some sort of emblem or band on the head as authority, long hair put up on the head as a sign of authority instead of a prophet's cloak (the veil is a sign of a prophetess, Ezek. 13:17-23), all with the authorization of the church there and the consent of the husband of each prophetess. Paul insists only that these prophetesses "appear in accordance with the directives Paul has given here," which are those in effect throughout the churches. M. B. Hansen basically agrees, in a review article in *Dansk Teologisk Tidsskrift* 29 (1966): 91-107 (= *New Testament Abstracts* 11, 804r), but interprets these Corinthian prophetesses to be acting wrongly, as if the life of the community were already in the kingdom-to-come; Paul rebukes this eschatological miscalculation by stressing "the traditions" and that the old order is not yet abrogated.

40. For what it is worth, the Augsburg Confession, Art. 28, cites 11:5 (that women cover their heads in the assembly, though the fact they pray or prophesy is not mentioned) and alludes to 1 Cor. 14:30 as examples of "good order" (Tappert edition, p. 90), but 1 Cor. 14:34-35 is never mentioned in the 16th-century confessional writings (so Peter Brunner, p. 248).

41. First Corinthians 11:3 is a keystone in the "subordination" argument discussed above. Cf. Riesenfeld, p. 125, on "the hierarchy of representation": in the sequence "God—Christ—man—woman," each of the last three is charged with representing the superior to the inferior; thus a male ministry must represent God and Christ to women. So also von Allmen, pp. 39ff., on "the 'man-as-captain-of-the-woman' idea" (p. 41); or Héring's remark in his commentary, "woman has no *raison d'être* in herself" (p. 106, as cited in von Allmen, p. 41, n. 20).

A particularly strong form of statement appears in the article on "head" (*kephalē*) in *TDNT,* 3:679-80, when Schlier takes the statement ontologically ("the origin and *raison d'être* of woman are to be found in man . . . .she points to man, and only with and through him to God. . . . Not merely as a Christian, nor historically, but ontologically and by nature woman lives of man and for him. . . . *Kephalē* implies one who stands over another in the sense of being the ground of his being. . . . It would be for Paul an abandonment of the foundations of creation if charismatically gifted women . . . were to pray or prophesy with their heads uncovered like men").

A similar view is upheld by Peter Brunner: "we have to do here with something which is central to the faith . . . the concept of subordination" (p. 263). First Corinthians 11:8 shows that man is both the head and the ruler of woman (never the reverse), and there can be no eschatological transformation of this structure, which is "in effect in the Christian church until the Last Judgment" (p. 268), even though in the world nowadays a Christian woman might be permitted to serve as a judge in a secular court over men. Brunner applies the *kephalē*-structure even to unmarried women who have no husband as "head." A pastor represents Christ, a woman cannot represent Christ (p. 271).

To Brunner (and Schlier, recalling a time when he served on a committee discussing the office of *Vikarin* in the Confessing Church), cf. the reply by Anna Paulsen, *LW* 7 (1960): 231-32, and the arguments of Thrall, pp. 66-76. The latter holds that a woman may (contrary to the hierarchy-of-representation principle) mediate the Christ-relationship to the husband in some cases (for example, 1 Cor. 7:14, "the unbelieving husband is consecrated through his wife"). This is denied by von Allmen (pp. 42-43, n. 23): "Nowhere in the New Testament is there to be found the least religious sublimation of the uterine complex"; woman is not "a mediatress between God and man"—or at least if she is, it is as a Christian, not as a woman (which—one may reply to von Allmen—is the point involved seemingly in 1 Corinthians 11, the prophetesses function as Christians who have the Spirit, not because they are women but, in that day, in spite of it!).

Concerning the Ordination of Women, p. 46, terms 11:3 not a ladder but an abiding social fact that is put into a new light.

Isaksson (p. 165, n. 2) sees here no reference to an "order of creation" nor to men and women in general, but simply a reference to husband and wife: the husband is his wife's lord. Hence the Corinthian prophetesses spoke in public only with their husband's consent. O'Rourke is typical of many exegetes who see 11:3ff. as referring to married women only (pp. 292-93: ". . . wives just because they are Christians are not to act in socially unacceptable ways").

42. The term is Peter Brunner's (p. 262).
43. Among interpretations: women wore veils as a sign of the husband's authority; or as protection against (evil) angels; or in view of the presence of angels at the church's worship; or to prevent reflecting the husband's glory at a time when only God's glory should be reflected; or because angels have spoken to her (cf. Isaksson, pp. 177ff.).
44. Stamm, p. 148.
45. Cf. Kähler, pp. 66-67: (1) the passage recognizes the place of the woman who prays or prophesies; (2) propriety is involved; the woman cannot just do as the man of the day does, but must wear a veil; (3) mutual dependence of man and woman is stressed; there are differences that come from God, providing boundaries, but the one also supplements the other. Vv. 11-12 is the high point of the section.
46. In addition to commentaries mentioned for 1 Corinthians 11, and *Concerning the Ordination of Women*, pp. 47-48; Thrall, pp. 76-79; Kähler, pp. 71-83; Zerbst, pp. 45-51, see especially the monograph on this passage by Gottfried Fitzer, *Das Weib Schweige in der Gemeinde: Über den unpaulinischen Charakter der mulier-taceat-Verse in 1. Korinther 14,* Theologische Existenz Heute 110 (Munich: Chr. Kaiser, 1963), which concludes for the interpolation of the verse under the influences of "early Catholicism" at the end of the first century A.D. (when office-bearers were being regarded as priests, the Communion service as a sacrifice, and women were becoming passive observers at the liturgy, and women generally were being regarded as inferior and responsible for sin), on the basis of textual, historical-critical, and theological reasons. The verses contradict 11:5—cf. K. Heim,

Die Gemeinde des Auferstandenen (Munich, 1949), pp. 204-5. Krodel, p. 199: probably an interpolation.

47. In the recent literature, the first view has been argued by Schmidthals, and the second view by P. Bachmann's commentary (4th ed. 1936) and Grosheide.

48. So Fitzer, with reasons detailed; the view goes back at least as far as J. S. Semler, and has been held, for example, by J. Weiss; Leipoldt, pp. 190-91, Oepke, in *TDNT* 1:787 ("perhaps"); and Barrett, p. 333 (but "not certain"). Thrall, 76ff., thinks the simpler solution is to regard the verses as authentic but out of context. Zerbst, pp. 50-51 does not feel this solution merits "earnest consideration." E. Schweizer, *Church Order*, p. 203, n. 783: "presumably a marginal gloss," comparing the addition in 7:5 of "fasting" (so KJV, not in RSV). V. P. Furnish, *Theology and Ethics in Paul* (New York: Abingdon, 1968), pp. 70-71, n. 4. In this case, the "ecumenical words," "as in all the churches of the saints," are not part of the interpolation but go with v. 33*a*, as in the NEB footnote. S. Aalen, "A Rabbinic Formula in I Cor. 14, 34," *Studia Evangelica II*, ed. F. L. Cross, Texte und Untersuchungen 87 (Berlin, 1964), pp. 513-25.

49. So Lietzmann; cf. Barrett. Some argue that "to speak" here is to be distinguished from "pray" and "prophesy" in Chap. 11. Zerbst, pp. 50ff., allows this as a possibility. Cf. also D. E. H. Whiteley, *The Theology of St. Paul*, pp. 223-25.

50. So, for example, *Concerning the Ordination of Women*, pp. 47ff., where to the sort of statement P. Brunner makes (that "Paul bids the women to keep completely still in the assemblies of the congregation"), pp. 260-61, it is objected that in our churches today women are scarcely kept completely still. So also O'Rourke, pp. 291-92, for example.

51. Kümmel, p. 190, quotes Dibelius's comment: "The juxtaposition of the two chapters demonstrates at the least that this command to silence is not an order for every situation and for all times, for it is limited even in the same letter by adjacent material in ch. 11." The phrase in v. 37, "a command from the Lord," is not to be referred to vv. 33*b*-36, as if a saying of Jesus were involved; it may refer to v. 38, a sentence of "holy law" from the early Christian community, or to the whole chapter—or (so Barrett) "command" may be a later insertion (cf. the manuscript evidence) and Paul's point that he speaks with the "mind of Christ."

52. On Ephesians 5 and 1 Peter 3, see commentaries, especially that by E. G. Selwyn on 1 Peter; also *Concerning the Ordination of Women*, pp. 43-44, and Kähler, pp. 88-140.

53. Nygren cited this argument in his speech against the government bill on ordaining women in Sweden; Rodhe, *LW* 4 (1957-58): 400.

54. So, for example, O'Rourke.

55. On 1 Tim. 2:11-14, cf. *Concerning the Ordination of Women*, pp. 51-55; Thrall, pp. 76-79; Kähler, pp. 146-61; Zerbst, pp. 51-56; Peter Brunner, pp. 259-60; and, among the commentaries, J. N. D. Kelly, *A Commentary on the Pastoral Epistles*, HNTC (1963); Hans Conzelmann, revision of Martin Dibelius, HNT 13; 4th ed., rev. (1966). N. J. Hommes, "Let Women Be Silent in Church. . .," *Calvin Theological Journal* 4 (1969): 5-22 (= *New Testament Abstracts* 13, Number 994).

56. So Kelly, pp. 65-66.

57. Kelly, p. 67.

58. The view is found in Judaism: "from a woman sin had its beginning, and because of her we all die" (Sir. 25:24). While the idea appears in Paul's undisputed letters at 2 Cor. 11:3 ("the serpent deceived Eve by his cunning"), Paul is explicit that

the entry of sin is through Adam (5:12-19), and Adam is not exonerated at the expense of Eve. Zerbst notes (and rejects) the unwarranted deductions sometimes made about women on the basis of this verse at 2:14, for example, that "the great guilt and sinfulness of woman and her moral and religious inferiority is also for Paul an article of faith" (pp. 54-55).

59. We pass over the debate as to whether v. 15 means childbearing only or also childrearing as the role laid down for woman. Kelly rightly rejects interpretations that see a reference here to Mary and the birth of a Savior in v. 15, or a general truth that "women will get safely through childbearing if. . ." (Moffatt). That only Christian mothers are referred to in the "if" clause, cf. Conzelmann, pp. 39-40.

60. So Stamm, rightly, p. 156.

61. Features of *"Frühkatholizismus"*: growth of (hierarchical) orders and structures in the church, which is becoming institutionalized; a "bourgeois morality"; eschatology becomes conventionalized; justification may be paid lip service as a slogan, but it is no longer understood or made central as in Romans; growth of "church law" and legalism. Note the phrase "by good deeds" (v. 10), on which see Conzelmann, p. 38 (good deeds are regarded in the Pastorals as a sign of true Christianity, whereas the genuine letters of Paul know only the singular and in a different sense).

62. Cf. Stamm, pp. 156-57 "Women do teach in our church schools. . . .Yet the writer of 1 Tim. 2:12 would call this a breaking of the Scripture."

63. So O'Rourke, for example, p. 294. Hommes sees vv. 11-12 as concerned with the decorum of a married woman at the church service; the passage does not preclude woman from office but rather "playing the boss" over a husband.

64. While some see here part of the repudiation by the Pastorals of the anticreational asceticism of the gnostic opponents, Kähler sees v. 15 reflecting "a powerful 'natural theology'" (p. 158), and most commentators take pains to show that the passage is not expounding "salvation via childbearing." It has been claimed, reading the passage in light of 1 Corinthians 11, that the entire chapter reflects the hierarchical subordination of 11:3, viz., God (2:3), Christ (2:5), man (2:8), woman (2:9)!

65. For details, cf. the excursus in Conzelmann, p. 40; for Thecla, cf. *Acts of Paul*, Chapters 37; 39; 41; 43. Zerbst, pp. 52-53, allows that even in 1 Timothy 2 women may have been allowed to teach in the quiet of the family circle, or, following Schlatter, that they might speak in the congregation when they again became calm after an experience of the Spirit (in this case, 1 Timothy modifies 1 Corinthians 14), and that women should be under the same condition as men: to pray "without anger" (v. 8); Zerbst criticizes Schlatter's exegesis and stresses subordination.

66. *Concerning the Ordination of Women*, p. 53. An additional question raised there is whether the treatment of the Old Testament given in vv. 13-14 can be regarded as a right use of Scripture today, especially for building doctrines.

67. Summaries are provided in *Concerning the Ordination of Women*, pp. 17-21; Zerbst, pp. 82-94 (with succeeding periods treated pp. 94-103); and Oepke, *"gynē,"* in *TDNT* 1: 787-89; further references in these treatments, as well as in Zerbst, pp. 14ff., on monographs on the topic early in the present century. C. H. Turner, "Ministries of Women in the Primitive Church; Widow, Deaconess, and Virgin," in *Catholic and Apostolic*, ed. H. N. Bate (London: Mowbray, 1931), pp. 316-51. J. Daniélou, *The Ministry of Women in the Early Church* (London: Faith Press, 1961). See also commentaries on specific verses cited, and Bible

dictionaries and treatments of "ministry," many of which are cited in Schweizer, *Church Order.* Some of the pertinent, recent literature in periodicals is cited below. See also *Women and Holy Orders,* pp. 14-16, and Prohl, pp. 73-76.

68. Thus the 1951 statement of New Testament teachers in Sweden, in response to the exegetical treatment by Erik Sjöberg in the report of the official government committee, cited in Stendhal, p. 7; cf. Rodhe's summary, *LW* 4 (1957-1958): 393-94.

69. Thus, for example, von Allmen, p. 43, n. 23: "each time these ministries to which women are ordained include the regular administration of the sacraments, one is falling into heresy." Or was the "restriction on the participation of women in church services" inherited from Judaism, one of the factors, Stamm asks, p. 149, "that led to the development of the heresies"? On the "heresy" argument, cf. Thrall, p. 113, and *Concerning the Ordination of Women,* pp. 35-36.

70. The possibility was noted above. Pro: C. H. Dodd, *Romans,* Moffatt Commentary (1932), p. 239, "Chrysostom . . . saw no difficulty in a woman-apostle; nor need we"; Prohl, p. 72. Con: O. Michel, *Römer,* KEK (⁴1966), pp. 379-80, the feminine form "Julia" or "Junia" is "not to be thought of." Rengstorf, "*apostolos,*" *TDNT,* 1:421: against *shaliah* background [the Hebrew term for "one sent" as agent] and legal view of women in Judaism, a woman "apostle" is not to be expected—a legal self-contradiction. Cf. also p. 431.

71. On deaconesses, cf. "*diakonos,*" *TDNT,* 2:93; A. Kalsbach, "Die altkirchliche Einrichtung der Diakonissen," *Römische Quartelschrift,* Beiheft 22 (1926). At 1 Tim. 3:8ff., Oepke decides for "official deaconesses" (*TDNT,* 1: 788), rather than a deacon's wife; so also O'Rourke, p. 294 ("official functions in the Church, . . . not necessarily . . . a sacramental Order"); Schweizer, *Church Order,* p. 86, n. 334; Conzelmann leaves the matter open. Krodel, deaconesses rather than deacons' wives (*Dialog,* p. 201, n. 105).

72. N. Chitescu, writing as a Roumanian Orthodox theologian, in *Concerning the Ordination of Women,* denies that such titles justify an order of women priests; they denote "the wives (and mothers) of priests and bishops, especially when they divorced so their husbands could enter the monastery" (p. 57, cf. 58, 63). Others take such terms differently. For citations, cf. the entries in *A Patristic Greek Lexicon,* ed. G. W. H. Lampe (Oxford: Clarendon, 1961–1968), for example, p. 358; *s. v. diakonos* C.; or G. Uhlhorn, *Christian Charity in the Ancient Church* (New York: Scribner's, 1883), pp. 170ff., and A. Ehrhardt, *The Framework of the New Testament Stories* (Cambridge: Harvard Univ. Press, 1964), pp. 308-9 (*venerabilis femina episcopa*).

73. So G. G. Blum, "Das Amt der Frau im Neuen Testament," *Novum Testamentum* 7 (1964): 142-61 (summary in *New Testament Abstracts* 9, Number 1060), who holds the early church made a deliberate decision, which should hold good today as well, not to ordain women. Stendahl, p. 40, counters that "the New Testament knows of no special argumentation about the ministry when it comes to the role of women in the church"—it speaks of her subordination in creation, but does not make special statements here about the sacraments.

74. So Dale Moody, "Charismatic and Official Ministries: A Study of the New Testament Concept," *Interpretation* 19 (1965): 169-81. (Summary in *New Testament Abstracts* 10, number 283.)

75. O'Rourke, p. 296: "prescinding from a possible definitive statement of the magisterium there does not seem present anything which would militate against woman's being advanced to lower Orders, specifically to the diaconate. . . ." Decrees

like that of Gelasius I (A.D. 494; Denzinger no. 1839) are discussed, with the notation that no appeal is made in these decrees to New Testament texts. Another recent Roman Catholic analysis is found in P. Grelot, *Le ministère de la Nouvelle Alliance* (Paris: Cerf, 1967), where ordination of women is specifically discussed. For Lutherans, similarly, the absence of confessional statements based on Scripture is noted by Peter Brunner, p. 248 (cf. 253), "the confessional standards of the Evangelical Lutheran Church . . . do not express themselves on the problem of the ordination of women to the pastoral ministry," and neither 1 Cor. 14:33*b*-36 nor 1 Tim. 2:11 are cited. Canons to which the Eastern Orthodox appeal are given in *Concerning the Ordination of Women*, pp. 57-60, 63; Anglican, p. 69. Though Thrall thought it necessary to argue (p. 113) that "if the ordination of women can be justified on the biblical bases . . . the evidence of tradition during the first three centuries should not be regarded as a decisive argument against it," it now appears that the tradition embodied in canons, decrees, and confessional writings is not so limiting, at least for some Roman Catholics and Lutherans, as her comment supposed.

76. Hence Stendahl's subtitle, "A Case Study in Hermeneutics." Opinions on the basis of the historical and exegetical evidence vary from declarations that the Bible forbids ordaining women to Schweizer's judgment that "no ministry in the New Testament is forbidden to any member of the Church" (*Church Order*, p. 203). Hence the judgment, "Most churches do not believe they can get any direct guidance from the Bible on the matter, the pertinent passages being interpreted very differently" (S. Rodhe, *LW* 5, [1958-59]: 398). So also the view expressed by J. R. Nelson, "Styles of Service in the New Testament and Now," *Theology Today* 22 (1965): 84-102, that the New Testament does not answer our questions here; "restorationalism" of supposed New Testament practices would be impossible (even if we knew those practices); the best we can gain from the New Testament is an insight into the diversity of ministries then which contributed to the upbuilding of the church.

The article on "Woman's Place in the Church" by three women, in *Enc. Luth. Ch.*, 3:2497a, states that "the problem seems to be one of Bible interpretation" and asks, "must the passages cited above be applied literally to our times or do we have to take into account the difference in woman's sociological position today and two thousand years ago and then seek to discover the actual meaning of the message for today?" That implies, though, that the problem is caused only by "modern change," when in reality there is a problem already in the diversity of the biblical data and the question of what shall be central in interpreting Scripture. It is also a misleading truism to point out that in time of emergencies, theological objections fade! While many turns in the development of ordination and customs about the ministry have doubtless been caused by practical necessity (for example, the decline of a female diaconate in the fourth century because of the growth of the practice of infant baptism meant it was no longer necessary to have deaconesses to baptize female adults), we are suggesting there is a hermeneutical aspect that ought to be involved in our decision—not just a series of pragmatic factors. On the hermeneutical question here, cf. Stendahl, pp. ix-xii and 8ff.

77. This is true even if the Pastorals be accounted deutero-Pauline; 1 Cor. 11 and 14:34 must still be brought into harmony. Lampe, p. 124, comments, "To cite Gal. 3:28 against 1 Corinthians and the Pastorals is not to play off one proof-text against another. As Luther found with the texts on justification, there are Scriptural passages which unmistakenly express the fundamental implications of the gospel itself, and this is one of them."

78. Compare the attempt at summation and drawing the consequences in *Concerning the Ordination of Women,* pp. 37-39, 55-56: no biblical basis exists for rejecting the ordination of women; building up the body of Christ as a regulative criterion, with a view to the church's mission; that "the relationship of man and woman in the N.T. is everywhere grafted into the manifold relationships of the body of Christ" is also binding on us; today's rising demand for partnership between men and women; in light of all this, "does the admission of women to full service in the Church help in its edification and in the fulfillment of its mission to the world?"

79. J. Leipoldt, *Die Frau in der antiken Welt und im Urchristentum,* pp. 234-35: the general New Testament picture is clear—women were not minimized or under-valued. But current customs and conditions had to be obeyed. Yet times have changed. Today who would insist that women be veiled at church services? "Every age has the duty to draw out of the basic principles of the Gospel the consequences that correspond to the times. In the case of the question of women, the decisive thing is the principle that before God man and woman are alike. Paul formulated that in a classic way (Gal. 3:28). But it was impossible in the ancient world to realize this; the whole contemporary social order stood in the way; one had to be satisfied with partial fulfillment. In the present it is especially pressing to take up the task again of whether a further fulfilling is commanded."

80. Many writers have recognized this eschatological aspect and the role of the Spirit in opening new possibilities. Thus Stendahl, pp. 36-37: we know we are not yet in the kingdom, but we need to see Paul's bold vision. E. Schweizer, *Church Order,* p. 204: it is God's Spirit who marks out in freedom the pattern that church order afterwards recognizes; it is therefore functional, regulative, serving, but not constitutive, and that is what is decisive. The Spirit, which ever could be counted on in new situations (cf. Acts 15:28; 1 Cor. 7:40), may be calling for new patterns today. Hence the church is to stay "open to God's active intervention," allowing for new ministries and new persons given grace for existing ministries. Against such a view, von Allmen warns, p. 15, "Do not make the Holy Spirit an excuse for turning everything upside-down."

81. Cf. W. Thüsing, "Dienstfunktion und Vollmacht kirchlicher Ämter nach dem Neuen Testament," *Bibel und Leben* 14 (1973): 77-88.

82. *Eucharist and Ministry,* Lutherans and Catholics in Dialogue IV, ed. Paul C. Empie and T. Austin Murphy (Washington, D.C.: Bishops' Committee for Ecumenical and Interreligious Affairs, and New York: U.S.A. National Committee of the Lutheran World Federation, 1970), p. 9.

83. The survey by André Lemaire, "The Ministries in the New Testament: Recent Research," *Biblical Theology Bulletin* 3 (1973): 133-66, emphasizes the consensus among exegetes *(a)* to begin with the "ministerial" rather than the "sacerdotal"; *(b)* that ministries are gifts bestowed on the church, *(c)* in great diversity, *(d)* emphasizing service; and that it is in light of these factors, examples of ministerial office are to be seen beginning to develop in the early church.

84. For essays and a literature survey 1965–1974, cf. *Women: New Dimensions,* ed. Walter J. Burghardt, s.j. (New York: Paulist, 1977). A survey of the situation in a number of churches is provided in Rachel Conrad Wahlberg's article, "The American Feminist Movement and the Churches," in *The Identity of the Church and Its Service to the Whole Human Being, Final Volume I, Summary—Analysis— Interpretation, Reports on 35 Self-Study Projects in 46 Churches* (Geneva: Lutheran World Federation, Department of Studies, 1977), pp. 412-53. Needless to say, there has been influence from "the feminist movements," and the literature

noted there is considerable. Wahlberg treats "The Gentle Revolution—The Roman Catholics," pp. 424-29; "Conflict—The Episcopal Crisis," 429-32; "The Methodical Lutherans," 432-37; "Methodist Women: A Vocal Majority," 437-38; "The Southern Baptists: Traditional and Individual," 439-40; "Presbyterians—and Reaction," 440-42; "United Church of Christ—Out Front," 443-45; "Christian Church (Disciples of Christ)—Affirmative Directions," 444-45; "Judaism—Small but Significant Changes," 445-47. Reflecting the Orthodox viewpoint, G. Barrois, "Women and the Priestly Office according to the Scriptures," *St. Vladimir's Theological Quarterly* 19 (1975): 174-92, finds that the biblical data do not support a thesis of the radical inferiority of women but authorize a prejudgment against their involvement in the hierarchic priesthood. See also Thomas Hopko, "On the Male Character of Christian Priesthood," ibid., pp. 147-73.

85. Among the surveys of the literature are "The Ordination of Women to the Priesthood: An Annotated Bibliography," by Ruth Tiffany Barnhouse, Michael Fahey, s.j., Bridget Oram, and Baily T. Walker, o.p., *Anglican Theological Review,* Supplementary Series 6 (June 1976): 81-106; R. T. Beckwith, "Recent New Testament Study," in *Why Not? Priesthood and the Ministry of Women, A Theological Study,* ed. Michael Bruce and G. E. Duffeld, rev. and augmented R. T. Beckwith (Appleford, Abingdon, England: Marcham Books, 1976), pp. 148-52; Letha Scanzoni and Nancy Hardesty, *All We're Meant to Be: A Biblical Approach to Women's Liberation* (Waco, Texas: Word Books, 1974). A good, brief summary is found in K. Thraede, "Trouble with Freedom: Summary of the Study on 'The Contribution of Women to the Life of the Early Christian Congregation,' " in *The Identity of the Church* (cited above, n. 84), pp. 366-72. See also, for the debate in Sweden, Krister Stendahl, *The Bible and the Role of Women: A Case Study in Hermeneutics,* trans. Emilie T. Sander, Facet Books, Biblical Series 15 (Philadelphia: Fortress, 1966).

86. On the theological arguments sketched above in Part A, IV. A., of this chapter, the following subsequent treatments are noteworthy:

A. 1—Richard A. Norris Jr., "The Ordination of Women and the 'Maleness' of the Christ," *Anglican Theological Review,* Supplementary Series 6 (June, 1976): 69-80, arguing that to say women as females cannot "represent" Christ is both theologically unsound and a departure from tradition.

A. 2—With reference to the argument that a clergyperson "represents" the (male) Christ and God, cf., for a Lutheran view, Per Erik Persson, *Repraesentatio Christi: Der Amtsbegriff in der neueren römisch-katholischen Theologie* (Göttingen: Vandenhoeck und Ruprecht, 1966).

A. 3—On the "patriarchy" argument, see Ruth Tiffany Barnhouse, "Patriarchy and the Ordination of Women," in *Toward a New Theology of Ordination: Essays on the Ordination of Women,* ed. Marianne H. Micks and Charles P. Price (Somerville, Mass.: Greeno, Hadden and Co., 1976), pp. 71-89.

A. 4—Against "subordination" and appeal to "orders of creation," so strongly urged in Lutheran Church–Missouri Synod discussion, cf. Edward H. Schroeder, "The Orders of Creation: Some Reflections on the History and Place of the Term in Systematic Theology," *CTM* 43 (1972): 165-78. Among significant subsequent studies, cf. Agnes Cunningham, *The Role of Women in Ecclesial Ministry: Biblical and Patristic Foundations* (Washington, D.C.: United States Catholic Conference, 1976). P.-L. Carle, "La femme et les ministères pastoraux selon l'Écriture," *Nova et Vetera* 47 (1972): 161-87, 263-90: 48 (1973): 17-36, 262-85 (summary in *New Testament Abstracts* 17 [1973]: 676, 1092; 18 [1974]: 1023), stresses the dignity of women in the New Testament but their consistent, later exclusion from ordination.

B. 1—On "image of God," cf. Susan E. Crane, "The Imago Dei: An Historical Approach," *Nexus* 19, 2 (Spring, 1976): 3-14.

87. *Origins: NC Documentary Service,* Feb. 3, 1977, pp. 518-24, with "A Commentary on the Declaration," pp. 524ff. (Separately published by the United States Catholic Conference, Washington, D.C., 1977.)

88. Cf. *Peter in the New Testament: A Collaborative Assessment by Protestant and Roman Catholic Scholars,* ed. R. E. Brown, K. P. Donfried, and J. Reumann (Minneapolis: Augsburg, and New York: Paulist, 1973), pp. 163-68; or *Papal Primacy and the Universal Church,* Lutherans and Catholics in Dialogue V (Minneapolis: Augsburg, 1974), p. 16. The terminology stems from Helmut Koester and James M. Robinson, *Trajectories through Early Christianity* (Philadelphia: Fortress, 1971), pp. 46, 56, 65, 66, 113, 238, 260, 266, 269ff., and 279. T. E. Crane, "The Petrine Trajectory in the New Testament," *Australasian Catholic Record* 53 (1976): 153-63, shows to what, in a less critical approach, the concept can lead.

89. "Exegetes, Honesty, and the Faith: Biblical Scholarship in Church School Theology," *Currents in Theology and Mission* (St. Louis) 5 (1978): 23-25.

90. Cf. Jean Colson, "Ecclesial Ministries and the Sacred," in *Office and Ministry,* Concilium 80 (New York: Herder and Herder, 1972), pp. 64-74, especially pp. 68-9, on absence of *hiereus* terminology in the New Testament); J. Blank, as summarized, with references, by M. Houdijk, ibid., pp. 137-40, and, likewise, W. Pesch, pp. 143-45; A. E. Harvey, "New Wine in Old Skins: II. Priest," *Expository Times* 84 (1972–73): 200-203; A. Vanhoye, "Sacerdoce commun et sacerdoce ministériel. Distinction et rapports," *Nouvelle Revue Théologique* 97 (1975): 193-207; Louis Weil, "Priesthood in the New Testament," in *To Be a Priest: Perspectives on Vocation and Ordination,* ed. R. E. Terwilliger and Urban T. Holmes III (New York: Seabury, 1975), pp. 64-65. Further literature in *CTM* 44 (1973): 6, and in Elisabeth Schüssler Fiorenza, *Priester für Gott,* Neutestamentliche Abhandlungen 7 (Münster, 1972), especially pp. 4-60.

91. E.g., H. Schlier, "Neutestamentliche Grundelemente des Priesteramtes," *Catholica* 27 (1973): 209-33 (where, however, the eschatological priesthood of Jesus Christ, and not Old Testament priesthood, is made the base); L. Shehan, "The Priest in the New Testament: Another Point of View," *Homiletic and Pastoral Review* 76 (1975): 10-23, stressing Rom. 15:15-16. Contrast Claude Wiéner, "Hierourgein" (Rom. 15, 16), *Studiorum Paulinorum Congressus* 1961, Analecta Biblica 17-18 (Rome: Pontifical Biblical Institute, 1963), vol. 2, pp. 399-404; J. A. Grindel, "The Old Testament and Christian Priesthood," *Communio/International Catholic Review* (Spokane) 3 (1976): 16-38.

92. R. Laurentin, in *Office and Ministry* (Concilium 80, cited above, n. 90), p. 14.

93. Cf. Rivkah Harris, "Woman in the Ancient Near East," *IDBS:* 960-63, especially 962 and the literature cited there.

94. Ibid., p. 962.

95. Phyllis Trible, "Woman in the OT," *IDBS,* p. 964, cf. pp. 962-66.

96. W. L. Holladay, "Jeremiah and Women's Liberation," *Andover Newton Quarterly* 12 (1972): 213-23.

97. Joyce Baldwin, "The Biblical Basis for Women's Ministry," in *Evangelicals and the Ordination of Women*, ed. C. Craston, Grove Booklet on Ministry and Worship 17 (Bramcote, England: Grove Books, 1973), p. 17. Cf. also her book, *Women Likewise* (London: Falcon, 1973). Baldwin, Dean of Women at Trinity College, Bristol, was a member of the Church of England Evangelical Council study group on women's ministry.

98. Ismar J. Pentz, "Women in Ancient Hebrew Cult," *Journal of Biblical Literature* 17 (1898): 111-48; Clarence J. Vos, *Women in Old Testament Worship* (Delft: Verenigde Drukkerijen Judels & Brinkman, 1968). Cf. also Numbers 30; 2 Kings 4:22-23. On the subject generally, cf. John H. Otwell, *And Sarah Laughed: The Status of Women in the Old Testament* (Philadelphia: Westminster, 1977), pp. 152-78, who concludes, "The woman's status in the cult was equal to that of the man," except for priesthood (p. 178).

99. *Women in Christian Tradition* (Notre Dame: University of Notre Dame Press, 1973). For reorientation generally, the following are helpful: Samuel Terrien, "Toward a Biblical Theology of Womanhood," *Religion in Life* 42 (1973): 322-33; K. D. Sakenfeld, "The Bible and Women: Bane or Blessing?" *Theology Today* 32 (1975): 222-33; Harvey H. Guthrie Jr., "The Bible, the Nature of the Church, and the Ordination of Women," in *To Be a Priest* (cited above, n. 90), pp. 155-62.

100. Phyllis Trible, *IDBS:* 965-66; "Depatriarchalizing in Biblical Interpretation," *JAAR* 41 (1973): 30-48; and "Eve and Adam: Genesis 2–3 Reread," *Andover Newton Quarterly* 13 (1973): 251-58.

101. Jersualem Talmud, Sotah, iii. 4, 19a. 7. Cf. J. Jeremias, *Jerusalem in the Time of Jesus*, trans. F. H. and C. H. Cave (Philadelphia: Fortress, 1969), p. 373, and the entire section on "The Social Position of Women," pp. 359-76.

102. Phyllis Trible, "God, Nature of, in the OT," *IDBS:* 368-69, and the literature cited there.

103. Cf. also Sir. 9:1-13; 25:13-26; 36:21-27; 42:12-14. "It is a woman who brings disgrace and shame" (42:14).

104. Mishna Sotah 3:4. Cf. Jeremias, *Jerusalem* (cited above, n. 101), pp. 372-75.

105. Baldwin, "Biblical Basis" (cited above, n. 97), p. 18.

106. Tavard (cited above, n. 99), p. 20. On the Essenes and the archeological evidence at Qumran, cf. H. Ringgren, *The Faith of Qumran: Theology of the Dead Sea Scrolls*, trans. Emilie T. Sander (Philadelphia: Fortress, 1963), p. 140. On the Theraputae, cf. Philo, *de vita contemplativa* 8 and 9 (68 and 83-89; Loeb ed., 9, pp. 155 and 165-69). On Josephus, cf. Robin Scroggs, "Paul and Eschatological Woman," *JAAR* 40 (1972): 290-91.

107. As argued by J. Massingberd Ford, "The First Epistle to the Corinthians or the First Epistle to the Hebrews?" *CBQ* 28 (1961): 413-14.

108. Edward R. Hardy, "The Priestess in the Greco-Roman World," in *Why Not?* (cited above, n. 85), pp. 56-62. Even Hardy, who holds "the early Church did not invite women to preside at the Eucharist"—contrast Raymond E Brown, *Priest and Bishop: Biblical Reflections* (New York: Paulist, 1970), pp. 40-43, where how little we know about who presided, e.g., in Corinth, is emphasized— rightly notes the variety, paucity, and generally lower level roles of women in Greco-Roman religion. To the point he makes about the remoteness of sacred prostitution from the world of that day, compared to the over-assumption of it by some writers (a point which, however, Hardy fails to apply to New Testament

Corinth), cf. Hans Conzelmann, *I Corinthians,* Hermeneia (Philadelphia: Fortress, 1975), p. 12, and his demolition of the fable about the "prostitutes in the Corinthian temple of Aphrodite," in a monograph cited in n. 97.

109. On the "holy body of priests" *(hierateuma),* cf. J. H. Elliott, *The Elect and the Holy: An Exegetical Examination of 1 Peter 2:4-10 and the Phrase* Basileion Hierateuma, Supplements to Novum Testamentum 12 (Leiden: Brill, 1966), with a critique by E. Best in *Novum Testamentum* 11 (1969): 270-93.

110. *The Position of Women in Judaism* (London: SPCK, 1966), written to supplement the 1966 Church of England study, *Women and Holy Orders,* p. 53, comparing Greek Orthodox practice for parish clergy. Further, S. Baron, *A Social and Religious History of the Jews* (New York: Columbia University Press, 1952), 1:111-14; 2:215-41; Leonard Swidler, *Women in Judaism* (Metuchen, N.J.: Scarecrow Press, 1976).

111. About the Twelve being all men there is no question. More dubious is whether they were termed "apostles" during Jesus' lifetime, and the extent to which the 12 apostles are a Lucan creation. I am not convinced by suggestions that the 70 (72), who appear only in Luke, included women.

112. "Declaration," 2 (as cited above, n. 87), p. 520. The "Commentary" adds, "With regard to women his attitude was a complete innovation: all the commentators recognize that he went against many prejudices, and the facts that are noted [regarding women, it is to be assumed] add up to an impressive total." It is a bit strong to say "a complete innovation," for we have seen some hints of a different view of women in ancient Israel and indeed the original will of God at creation, as presented in Genesis 1–2. The argument of the "Commentary" is that Jesus "did not shrink from other 'imprudences'" regarding Sabbath rules, but he did not bring women into the Twelve.

113. Leonard Swidler, "Jesus Was a Feminist," *South East Asia Journal of Theology* 13 (1971): 102-110.

114. Typical among recent commentators on Luke 8:1-3 are the following: E. Earle Ellis, *The Gospel of Luke,* rev. ed., New Century Bible (London: Marshall, Morgan and Scott, 1974), p. 124, holds their names suggest these women "were important in the Palestinian Church" and "may be a prototype of the 'deaconesses' "; F. W. Danker, *Jesus and the New Age: A Commentary on the Third Gospel* (St. Louis: Clayton, 1972), p. 101: "Non-conformist that he was, Jesus refused to permit tradition to make second-class citizens of women, whom he considered his sisters. His enemies would say, as in Luke 23:5, that it was poor judgment to flaunt custom in this way; Jesus would reply that those who hear and observe God's words belong to his family (8:21)."

115. If the latter story is read on a *Sitz-im-Leben-der-Kirche* level, it affirms the need to hear the word (a Lucan emphasis) and "the continuing right of women to full discipleship" (so Robin Scroggs, "Women in the NT," *IDBS:* 967). If on a *Sitz-im-Leben-Jesu* level, the former point still holds, and the remarkable openness of Jesus to treat women as sisters is again emphasized.

116. So "Declaration," 2 (as cited above, n. 87), p. 520, with further emphasis in the "Commentary," notes 30, 31, and 40. As noted in *CTM* 44 (1973): 8, n. 16, the mariological argument is found especially among Anglo-Catholics, like E. L. Mascall; to the literature cited there, add his *Women Priests?* (London: Church Literature Association, 1972), pp. 14-15 and passim (quoting C. S. Lewis). On the importance of "the Mary-myth" for our subject, especially among Catholics, cf. Elisabeth Schüssler Fiorenza, "Feminist Theology as a Critical Theology of Liberation," *Theological Studies* 36 (1975): 620-24.

117. *Mary in the New Testament: A Collaborative Assessment by Protestant and Roman Catholic Scholars*, ed. R. E. Brown, K. P. Donfried, J. Fitzmyer, and J. Reumann (Philadelphia: Fortress, New York: Paulist, 1978). Cf. Raymond E. Brown, "The Presentation of Jesus (Luke 2:22-40)," *Worship* 51 (1977): 2-10; and his fuller study, *The Birth of the Messiah: A Commentary on the Infancy Narratives in Matthew and Luke* (Garden City, N.Y.: Doubleday, 1977), especially pp. 462-66.

118. Luke concludes his picture of Mary with a reference to her "together with the women" and Jesus' brothers, involved in the worship life of the Jerusalem community (Acts 1:14). Cf. E. Leland, "Die Martha-Maria Perikope Lukas 10, 38-42," *Studia Theologica* 13 (1959): 70-85.

119. Cf. Scroggs, "Women in the NT," *IDBS:* 967. This is a point endorsed by all life-of-Jesus research. E.g., Günther Bornkamm, *Jesus of Nazareth*, trans. I. and F. McLuskey with J. M. Robinson (New York: Harper, 1960), pp. 79-81; Joachim Jeremias, *New Testament Theology, Part One: The Proclamation of Jesus*, trans. John Bowden (London: SCM, 1971), pp. 108-21, especially p. 121.

120. This is to claim that eucharistic origins lie, not simply in the Upper Room or post-Easter meals with the risen Christ (Acts 1:4, reading "eating"; Luke 24; John 20–21), but also in meals with Jesus during the earthly ministry, including the feeding miracles and table-fellowship with outcasts, publicans, and women.

121. William E. Hull, "Woman in Her Place: Biblical Perspectives," *Review and Expositor* 72 (1975): 5-17. It is oversimplified, at least to the degree that at points in the New Testament the "age to come" seemed to some to have already come, while for others the realities of the "old age" still obtained.

122. Wayne A. Meeks, "The Image of the Androgyne: Some Uses of a Symbol in Earliest Christianity," *History of Religions* 13 (1973-74): 167-68, citing Diogenes Laertius 1.33 (Thales): Lactantius *Divinae institutiones* 3.19 (Plato): cf. Tosefta, *Berakot* 7.18 (ed. Lieberman, p. 38; ed. Rengstorf, p. 52); Palestinian Talmud, *Berakot* 9.2; Babylonian Talmud, *Menahot* 43b.

123. Meeks, op. cit., p. 179.

124. R. H. Fuller, *The Foundations of New Testament Christology* (New York: Scribner's, 1965). Fuller's essay, "Pro and Con: The Ordination of Women in the New Testament," in *Toward a New Theology of Ordination* (cited above, n. 86), pp. 1-11, stresses how, with regard to its ministry, the early church felt free to adapt to the needs of the age.

125. So Raymond E. Brown, "Roles of Women in the Fourth Gospel," *Theological Studies* 36 (1975): 690. n. 7; reprinted in *Women: New Dimensions* (cited above, n. 84). On the history of the passage and how the view has arisen that the Seven are not "deacons" (never so called by Luke) but presbyters, elders, or counterparts to the apostles, cf. Ernst Haenchen, *The Acts of the Apostles: A Commentary* (Philadelphia: Westminster, 1971), pp. 264-69.

126. "Women Apostles: The Testament of Scripture," in *Women and Catholic Priesthood: An Expanded Vision, Proceedings of the Detroit Ordination Conference,* ed. Anne Marie Gardiner (New York: Paulist, 1976), p. 96. Mary Magdalene, who seems to have been particularly important, much later was termed "the apostle to the apostles" because of John 20:17-18; cf. Brown, "Roles . . ." (cited above, n. 125), pp. 692-93.

127. Meeks, "Image" (cited above, n. 122), p. 175, on the phrase *mater synagogae*. On the lectionary, cf. Tosefta, *Megilla* 4.11; Babylonian Talmud, *Megilla* 23a. George Foot Moore, *Judaism in the First Centuries of the Christian Era, The*

Age of Tannaim (Cambridge: Harvard Univ. Press, 1927), 2:131, adds, however, such reading by women was disapproved (in *Palestinian* Judaism?) "on grounds of propriety and no instance is reported."

128. Cf. David E. Aune, *The Cultic Setting of Realized Eschatology in Early Christianity*, Supplements to Novum Testamentum 28 (Leiden: Brill, 1972); "The Presence of God in the Community: The Eucharist in its Early Christian Cultic Setting," *Scottish Journal of Theology* 29 (1976): 451-59.

129. Scroggs, "Paul . . ." (cited above, n. 106), p. 291, referring to H. Schlier, *Der Brief an die Galater,* KEK (Göttingen: Vandenhoeck und Ruprecht, 1965), pp. 174-75. Schlier emphasizes the sacramental context, but does not specifically analyze a liturgical fragment here, and (175, n. 4) holds ecclesiastical office rests on "sending," not directly on baptism.

130. The phrases are those of Scroggs, *IDBS:* 966 (his article, cited in n. 106, pp. 291-92, speaks of "the societal-leveling quality of baptism" in early Hellenistic Christianity) and of Meeks, "Image" (cited above, n. 122), pp. 180-81. On the topic as a whole, cf. Elaine H. Pagels, "Paul and Women: A Response to Recent Discussion," *JAAR* 42 (1974): 538-49.

131. Scroggs, "Paul . . ." (cited above, n. 106), p. 292, n. 29; Meeks, "Image" (cited above, n. 122), p. 181, note 77, citing Windisch and Stendahl (cited above, n. 85), p. 32.

132. Cf. also Eph. 6:8; Ign. *Smyr.* 1.2; Gospel of Philip 49. On the major passages, see M. Bouttier, "Complexio Oppositorum: sur les Formules de I Cor. xii. 13; Gal. iii 26-8; Col. iii 10, 11," *NTS* 23 (1976-77): 1-19.

133. So Hans Kosmala, "Gedanken zur Kontroverse Farbstein-Hoch," *Judaica* 4 (1948): 227-29. If the rabbis involved, R. Judah and R. Meir (texts cited in n. 127 above), are reflective of a tradition early enough, the baptismal liturgy could have been influenced by the Jewish blessing, and must stem from Jewish Christianity, in Palestine or the diaspora.

134. Meeks, "Image" (cited above, n. 122), pp. 183-89.

135. Ibid., pp. 185, 188, citing Col. 2:11, 3:9-10; Eph. 4:24.

136. Ibid., pp. 189-97; note Meeks's reservations about finding a ritual *hieros gamos* in Eph. 5:22-33, p. 206.

137. Ibid., pp. 197-205; Scroggs, "Paul . . ." (cited above, n. 106), pp. 292-93, who stresses that for the church of this period baptism nullified "value judgments based on the distinctions in human society," but *not* the distinctions themselves between male and female.

138. Scroggs, ibid., p. 284; *IDBS:* 966; Meeks, "Image . . ." (cited above, n. 122), pp. 197-206; *CTM* 44 (1973): 26-28; M. Bertetich, "Las mujeres en la vida y los escritos de San Pablo," *Revista Biblica* 38 (1976): 15-48.

139. Cited by Scroggs, p. 290, from *Contra Apionem* 2.201 (2.24). Genesis 3:16 is assumed. But the Niese and Loeb editions bracket the words as a possible (Christian) gloss, intruding into a discussion on marriage laws. In any case, the reference is to husband and wife, not to men/women generally. The tension for Paul between his "Hellenistic Judaism and his basic Christian theological stance" on this issue of the place of women is emphasized by Scroggs, p. 291.

140. So Schmithals and others, as summarized, e.g., in W. Marxsen, *Introduction to the New Testament,* trans. G. Buswell (Philadelphia: Fortress, 1970), pp. 52-56.

141. Cf. the analysis of Galatians in connection with liberation theology by James Bergquist, in *The Church Emerging: A U.S. Lutheran Case Study*, ed. J. Reumann (Philadelphia: Fortress, 1977), pp. 225-28.

142. Meeks, "Image" (cited above, n. 122), pp. 197-98. J. M. Ford, "Biblical Material Relevant to the Ordination of Women," *Journal of Ecumenical Studies* 10 (1973): 669-94, urges that *prostatis* denotes "authority" (over many, and Paul too?).

143. Meeks, p. 198; *CTM* 44 (1973): 27. L. Caddeo, "Le 'diaconesse,' " *Richerche Bibliche e Religiose* 7 (1972): 211-25, opts for a female diaconate in the first century and "women (ministers)" at 1 Tim. 3:11.

144. Romans 16:6, 12 *(kopiaō)*; cf. Phil. 4:2-3 *(synathleō)*.

145. *CTM* 44 (1973): 27, n. 70; E. S. Fiorenza, "Women Apostles" (cited above, n. 126), p. 96.

146. So commentators (Bachmann, Robertson, and Plummer) and translators (Moffatt), though Barrett and Conzelmann, *1 Corinthians* (cited above, n. 108), p. 107, take it as a passive, despite its form. The point is simply that an apostle need not have baptized at Corinth (1:14, 16), and who did, we do not know, especially in the case of women. Or did the "baptizer" say the words of the formula while the person self-administered his/her immersion? W. F. Orr and J. A. Wather, *1 Corinthians,* Anchor Bible (New York: Doubleday, 1976), pp. 198-99, recognize the middle force.

147. Cf. Brown, "Roles . . ." (cited above, n. 125), p. 689, n. 2, "We know very little about who presided at the Eucharist in NT times." Further, Myles Bourke, "Reflections on Church Order in the New Testament," *CBQ* 30 (1968): 499-507.

148. "Declaration," 3 (cited above, n. 87), p. 521. The Commentary cites in support I. de la Potterie, *Titres missionnaires du chrétien dans le Nouveau Testament* (Paris: Desclée de Brouwer, 1966), pp. 29-46, esp. 44-45.

149. 1 Thess. 3:2 reads variously in MSS:

    (1) "fellow-worker of God in the gospel of the Christ"—D, 33, Old Latin MSS, Ambrosiaster, Pelagius, Ps-Jerome (a fairly weak attestation, but adopted in the United Bible Societies Greek New Testament); NEB;

    (2) "fellow-worker in the gospel of Christ"—B, 1962, apparently Ephraem;

    (3) "servant *(diakonos)* of God in the gospel of Christ"—Aleph, A, P, Psi, 5 minuscule MSS, some Old Latin MSS, Vulgate, several ancient versions, and some church fathers; RSV;

    (4) "servant and fellow-worker of God in the gospel of the Christ"—G, 2 Old Latin MSS; a conflation;

    (5) "servant of God and our fellow-workers in the gospel of the Christ"—D, K, many minuscules, lectionaries, some fathers; KJV; obviously a conflation.

    If (1) is read, the others are attempts to ease the offensiveness of calling a new convert like Timothy "*God's* fellow-worker," either by omitting "God's" (2) or substituting "servant" (3, 5) with "God's." The problem for the scribes, however, was not with calling a woman *God's* fellow-worker but with assigning the phrase to anyone save Paul (and Cephas and Apollos, 1 Cor. 3:4-9, 22; cf. 1:12). Metzger urges "great caution" on the passage, in *The Text of the New Testament* (Oxford University Press, 1964), pp. 240-42, but in *A Textual Commentary on the Greek New Testament* (New York: United Bible Societies, 1971) follows the "B" level rating in the UBS Greek NT, i.e., "some degree of doubt," on an A-to-D scale of increasing uncertainty.

150. A suggestion by Georg Bertram, *"synergos, synergeō," TDNT,* 7:874-875. Those who dedicate themselves to ministering to the community "share in God's own work, with its toil and labour," as workers for God, helpers of the community, but not its lords. E. Earle Ellis, in an informative article, "Paul and His Co-Workers," *NTS* 17 (1970-7I): 437-52, does not reflect de la Potterie's distinction (see n. 148), nor does he discuss women especially among these fellow workers; cf. pp. 440-41 and the chart on 438. For a picture in a particular community, cf. W. Derek Thomas, "The Place of Women in the Church at Philippi," *Expository Times* 83 (1971-72): 117-19.

151. On the sense of "source" or "origin," rather than "lordship," cf. S. Bedale, "The Meaning of *kephalē* in the Pauline Epistles," *Journal of Theological Studies* 5 (1954): 211-15, followed in Barrett's commentary; Scroggs, "Paul . . ." (cited above, n. 106), pp. 298-99, n. 41; and others.

152. Scroggs, ibid., p. 301: "Since in the created order man had assumed . . . a dominating role based on his priority in creation, but since in the eschatological age there is no such priority, woman must show by the head covering that she has left that old order and now lives in the new." "The *exousia* upon her head 'on account of the angels' " (11:10) is the badge of realized eschatology.

153. The above analysis follows Scroggs, ibid., pp. 298-302, and rejects the analysis by William J. Martin, "I Corinthians 11:2-16: An Interpretation," in *Apostolic History and the Gospel* (Festschrift for F. F. Bruce), ed. W. W. Gasque and R. P. Martin (Grand Rapids: Eerdmans, 1970), pp. 231-41, who accepts a role of silence and subordination for women, since they "act the part of the church" in worship, while man "personates" God and Christ. Martin takes the references to be to "hair," not a "veil," as does J. B. Hurley in "Man and Woman in I Corinthians" (Cambridge University dissertation, 1973). On the broader issue, cf. G. B. Caird, "Paul and Women's Liberty," *Bulletin of the John Rylands Library* 54 (1971-72): 268-81; and A. Feuillet, "La dignité et le rôle de la femme d'après quelques Textes pauliniens," *NTS* 21 (1974-75): 157-91. The attempt by W. O. Walker Jr., "1 Corinthians 11: 2-16 and Paul's Views Regarding Women," *JBL* 94 (1975): 94-110, to cover Scroggs's position by arguing 11:2-16 is a later interpolation, composed of three separate pericopes (3, 8-9, 11-12; 4-7, 10, 13; 14-15), has been answered by Jerome Murphy-O'Connor, "The Non-Pauline Character of 1 Corinthians 11: 2-16?" *JBL* 95 (1976): 615-21.

154. *CTM* 44 (1973): 18-22. Scroggs, "Paul . . ." (cited above, n. 106), p. 284, repeats reasons for regarding 14:33*b*-36 as a later gloss. Similarly, Gerhard Krodel, "Forms and Functions of Ministries in the New Testament," *Dialog* 8 (Summer 1969): 199, n. 87. T. R. W. Longstaff, "The Ordination of Women: A Biblical Perspective," *Anglican Theological Review* 57 (1975): 316-27, accepts 14:33*b*-36 as Paul's accommodation to that time and place.

155. *CTM* 44 (1973): 20-22, where efforts to neutralize the effects of 1 Tim. 2:11-14 are noted: it is dismissed as deutero-Pauline, or is said to prove too much, or deals with wives, not women generally. Haye van der Meer, *Women Priests in the Catholic Church? A Theological-Historical Investigation,* trans. Arlene and Leonard Swidler (Philadelphia: Temple University Press, 1973), pp. 23-25, terms it the text "most useful for dogmatic theologians," but notes the church has not enforced v. 12 (no gold or jewelry) the way it has vv. 9-11, and calls attention to the "conditioned, time-limited situation" of such texts.

156. "Declaration," 4 (as cited above, n. 87), p. 521; to prophesy is allowed. G. W. Knight, "The New Testament Teaching on the Role Relationship of Male and

Female with Special Reference to the Teaching/Ruling Functions in the Church," *Journal of the Evangelical Theological Society* 18 (1975): 81-91, would limit the role of women to diaconal tasks and to teaching women and children.

157. See the analysis in Scroggs, "Paul . . ." (cited above, n. 106), pp. 294-97, and *IDBS:* 966-67.

158. Scroggs, "Paul . . .," p. 297.

159. Ibid., p. 296. Paul still maintains an "eschatological reservation" against the gnosticizing view that the eschaton has fully come, but this reservation makes sense only in the light of the more important fact that "the new has come" (2 Cor. 5:17). Cf. my remarks in *Creation and New Creation: The Past, Present, and Future of God's Creative Activity* (Minneapolis: Augsburg, 1973), pp. 89-99.

160. Ibid., "Paul . . .," p. 284; *IDBS:* 968. The article by William Lillie, "The Pauline House-tables," *Expository Times* 86 (1974-75): 179-83, rightly notes how in Colossae the attempt was to restore a balance between enthusiasm and order, but even in this hierarchical arranging of the household, there is a tendency toward reciprocal rights and some equality.

161. *IDBS:* 968.

162. Cf. Edward Schweizer, *Church Order in the New Testament,* SBT 32 (London: SCM, 1961), pp. 117-124, cf. 125-30, especially 124; Raymond E. Brown, *The Gospel according to John I–XII,* Anchor Bible 29 (Garden City: Doubleday, 1966), pp. cv-cxi; Brown, "Roles . . ." (cited above, n. 125), p. 690. Note the significant statement by Meeks, "Image" (cited above, n. 122), p. 207, so applicable to John's Gospel, "In a sense, every kind of 'realized eschatology' is a metaphysical rebellion."

163. Brown, "Roles . . .," ibid., pp. 690-91.

164. Ibid., pp. 691-92.

165. Ibid., pp. 692-93. Gnostic and apocryphal circles often make Mary Magdalene "the most prominent witness to the teaching of the risen Lord," and Rabanus Maurus (9th cent.) terms her *apostola apostolorum* (apostle [fem.] of the apostles) and *evangelista* (evangelist, fem.) of the resurrection. On her importance as a "liberated woman," cf. Fiorenza, "Feminist Theology" (cited above, n. 116), pp. 624-26.

166. Brown, "Roles . . .," pp. 693-94.

167. Ibid., p. 694. Brown also uses the scene in 20:1-18, alongside 10:3-5, to show that Mary Magdalene is "in the same category of relationship to Jesus," namely, among "his own," as the Twelve are (13:1).

168. Ibid., pp. 695-98; cf. n. 116 above.

169. Ibid., p. 699.

170. See pp. 105-110 of this essay.

171. Schweizer, *Church Order* (cited above, note 162), includes no section on Mark. T. J. Weeden, *Mark—Traditions in Conflict* (Philadelphia: Fortress, 1971), pp. 101-17, holds that Mark uses traditions to shape an "anti-appearance-tradition narrative" against his theological opponents; the fact that the women never tell Peter and the (Jerusalem, relatives-of-Jesus) disciple-group (16:8*b*) robs the latter of their apostolic credentials. J. D. Crossan, *The Passion in Mark,* ed. W. H. Kelber (Philadelphia: Fortress, 1976), pp. 135-52, goes the logical next step: Mark created 16:1-8 in order to contrast the faith of the Marcan community (16:6-7) with the failure of Jerusalem Christianity and of the women who are Jesus' relatives (16:7-8). G. W. Trompf, "The First Resurrection Appearance and the

Ending of Mark's Gospel," *NTS* 18 (1971-72): 308-30, is representative of a more widely held view which is positive about the women: Mark reflects a tradition where the first appearance (with the authority that brought) was to women. E. L. Bode, *The First Easter Morning: The Gospel Accounts of the Women's Visit to the Tomb of Jesus,* Analecta Biblica 45 (Rome: Biblical Institute Press, 1970), pp. 25-47, feels the silence of the women is an apologetic device to keep the apostles free of any dependence on hysterical women for their authority.

172. So Fiorenza, "Women Apostles" (cited above, n. 126), p. 94. On Matthew's church, cf. Schweizer, *Church Order* (cited above, n. 162), pp. 51-62. For the emphases on Cephas, cf. the assessment in *Peter in the New Testament* (cited above, n. 88), pp. 75-107.

173. Cf. Schweizer, *Church Order,* pp. 63-76.

174. *CTM* 44 (1973): 22-26, where the passages which follow are discussed. On the nature of the "leaders" in Hebrews 13, cf. Otto Michel, *Der Brief an die Hebräer,* KEK (Göttingen: Vandenhoeck und Ruprecht, 1966), pp. 529-30. On the "orders of creation" so invoked in this discussion, cf. E. H. Schroeder, cited above, n. 86, under A. 4.

175. Cf. Louis Weil, "Priesthood in the New Testament," in *To Be a Priest* (cited above, n. 90), p. 68, reflecting R. E. Brown, *Priest and Bishop* (cited above, n. 108), pp. 21-43.

176. The examples above are meant to be suggestive. Each one, of course, could be discussed in detail. The point is simply that the early Christian documents are remarkably little concerned about "validating" ministries, especially given the variety we now know to have characterized Christianity in its first two generations or so. Cf. Schweizer, *Church Order* (cited above, n. 162), for further problems of "order."

177. Particularly relevant is "Responsible Use of the Scriptures," by Schuyler Brown and Richard W. Corney, in *Pro and Con on the Ordination of Women: Report and Papers from the Anglican-Roman Catholic Consultation* (New York: Seabury Professional Services, 815 Second Avenue, n.d.), pp. 39-56.

178. So Brown, "Roles. . ." (cited above, n. 125), pp. 688-89.

179. *The Ordination of Women: A Report Distributed by Authorization of the Church Body Presidents as a Contribution to Further Study, Based on Materials Produced through the Division of Theological Studies of the Lutheran Council in the U.S.A.,* condensed by Raymond Tiemeyer (Minneapolis: Augsburg, 1970), pp. 8, 52.

180. Donald F. Winslow, "Priesthood and Sexuality in the Post-Nicene Fathers," *The St. Luke's Journal of Theology* 18 (1975): 352-65; further, "Sex and Anti-Sex in the Early Church Fathers," in *Male and Female: Christian Approaches to Sexuality,* ed. Ruth Tiffany Barnhouse and Urban T. Holmes III (New York: Seabury, 1976), pp. 28-38.

181. *Women Priests* (cited above, n. 155); Joan Morris, *The Lady Was a Bishop: The Hidden History of Women with Clerical Ordination and the Jurisdiction of Bishops* (New York: Macmillan, 1973).

182. Connie Parvey, "Ordain Her, Ordain Her Not . . .," *Dialog* 8, 3 (summer 1969): 203-208.

183. Cf., e.g., Dale Moody, "Charismatic and Official Ministries: A Study of the New Testament Concept," *Interpretation* 19 (1965): 169-81. Involved, of course, is the substance of the 19th-century debate between Rudolf Sohm and Adolf Harnack over whether in early Christianity "office" and "ministry" were originally charismatic, or "church law" and "structures" were there from the outset.

Generally, (German) Lutheran discussion endorsed the latter or Harnack position; cf. my references in Chap. 1, above, p. 40.

184. Kilian McDonnell, "Ways of Validating Ministry," *Journal of Ecumenical Studies* 7 (1970): 209-65.

185. The sequence in the Augsburg Confession is particularly striking on this point. After articles on God, original sin, and the Son of God, there is exposition of Justification, followed by Article 5 on "The Office of the Ministry," beginning "In order that we may obtain this faith, the ministry of teaching the Gospel and administering the sacraments was instituted." *The Book of Concord,* ed. T. G. Tappert et al. (Philadelphia: Muhlenberg Press, 1959), pp. 30-31. In connection with the 450th anniversary of the Augsburg Confession in 1980, the proposal has been made that the *Confessio Augustana* be declared an ecumenical statement of the Church of Rome also.

186. As Lutherans have done in the U.S. dialogue with Roman Catholics, affirming the judgment that "the ordained Ministers of the Roman Catholic church are engaged in a valid Ministry of the gospel announcing the gospel of Christ and administering the sacraments of faith as their chief responsibilities." *Eucharist and Ministry* (cited above, n. 82), p. 22.

187. Cf. *CTM* 44 (1973): 29-30. The "eschatological question" continues to seem to me the most significant and the most neglected. See the attempt at a more careful statement in the book *Creation and New Creation* (cited above, n. 159), pp. 89-99.

188. So van der Meer, *Women Priests* (cited above, n. 155), p. 6. Cf. "Commentary" (cited above, n. 87), p. 524. As (Lutheran) *Forum Letter* 6,4 (April 18, 1977), p. 5, protests, "Commentary" errs in its understanding of Swedish Lutheranism when it holds there was "no strictly theological problem" here because the Church of Sweden "had rejected the sacrament of Order," and only with Anglican ordination in Hong Kong in (1944), 1971 and 1973 had there been ordinations of women "within communities that considered that they preserved the apostolic succession of Order."

189. Van der Meer, *Women Priests,* p. 7.

190. Stendahl (cited above, n. 85) especially gives a picture of the excellence of the level of debate.

191. Cf. Michael D. Hamilton and Nancy S. Montgomery, editors, *The Ordination of Women: Pro and Con* (New York: Morehouse-Barlow Co., 1975) for a calm, balanced appraisal of the Episcopalian debate which by 1977 had become a battle where the Presiding Bishop of the Church had to appeal to his fellow-bishops for a vote of confidence after he declared he personally disagreed with the church decision to ordain, and where separate synods of an "Anglican Church of North America" were being formed.

192. Cf. James E. Adams, *Preus of Missouri: A Report on the Great Lutheran Civil War* (New York: Harper and Row, 1977).

193. Details in Stendahl (cited above, n. 85), pp. viii-ix.

194. I have relied here on press releases, especially from the Lutheran World Federation. Canada provides an interesting example. The Canada Section of the LCA and the Evangelical Lutheran Church of Canada (of ALC origins) ordain women. The Lutheran Church–Canada (affiliated with the Missouri Synod) does not. In their merger negotiations (1977) they proposed that the clergy roster of the merged church would include all ordained persons of the merging churches and that the new church would ordain both men and women; but no congregation should be

expected to accept an ordained woman as pastor if that is against the particular congregation's understanding of Scripture. Such a stance recognizes the pluralism in practice found in Sweden (by dioceses) and endorsed in the U.S. Lutheran Council study. [This merger proposal failed, and the Lutheran Church–Canada did not become part of the Evangelical Lutheran Church in Canada subsequently formed.] Contrast the handling of the problems in church mergers like South India.

195. For a socio-theological portrait of the LCA, cf. Philip Hefner, "The Identity and Mission of the Church: Theological Reflections on the Concrete Existence of the Lutheran Church in America," in *The Church Emerging* (cited above, n. 141), pp. 139-81.

196. The figure is given by Marjorie Garhart, *Women in the Ordained Ministry, A Report to the Division for Professional Leadership, Lutheran Church in America* (Philadelphia: LCA/DPL, 1976), p. 2. The survey by Burnice Fjellman, "Women in the Church," in *Centennial Essays: Augustana Lutheran Church 1860–1960,* ed. E. Engberg et al. (Rock Island: Augustana Press, 1960), pp. 200-226, looked to the possibility of women as theologians, but does not mention ordination.

197. The commission reports are summarized in part in *Eucharist and Ministry* (cited above, n. 82), pp. 262-63. Garhart (cited above, n. 196), p. 3, especially singles out Professors Martin J. Heinecken and Edmund Steimle, of the Philadelphia Seminary.

198. Contrary to the statement in the Translators' Foreword, p. xiii, of van der Meer, *Women Priests* (cited above, n. 155), one of these papers has appeared in print: that on Scripture, in *CTM* for January, 1973 (repr. above as Chap. 2A). Others included one on the Confessions and Luther, by Stephen G. Mazak Sr. (never published, only two pages); Fred Meuser, "The Lutheran Tradition and the Ordination of Women"; Ronald L. Johnstone, "Sociological Factors"; Harold I. Haas, "Psychological Factors"; Robert W. Bertram, "What Theological Reasons Are Being Given Pro and Con on the Ordination of Women," and a summary of ecumenical praxis, by Paul D. Opsahl. On Luther's own views—of interest, but not in the status of confessions for Lutherans—cf. Gerta Scharffenorth, "Friends in Christ: The Relation between Men and Women according to Luther," in *The Identity of the Church . . . Final Volume I* (cited above, n. 84), pp. 373-411.

199. See above, n. 86. Further, *CTM* 44 (1973): 25-26, on the *"kephalē-principle,"* which was envoked by Scharlemann. The letter of April 9, 1970, from Professor Scharlemann to Missouri Synod President J. A. O. Preus, which is commonly credited with starting the investigation at Concordia Seminary, St. Louis, which led to the disruption of that school and church, specifically refers to dispute over "the orders of creation"; cf. *Exodus from Concordia: A Report on the 1974 Walkout* (St. Louis: Concordia Seminary Board of Control, 1977), p. 152.

200. The mild tone of the resolution was intended as a gesture toward those unable, for scriptural reasons, to accept ordination of women. The impromptu summaries by Drs. Meuser and Reumann produced a surge of feeling which led to the resolution to have all three churches send a common summary of the report to all pastors. Curiously, the tape recording of the proceedings has disappeared from the LCUSA archives.

201. See above, n. 179.

202. Letter to Synod clergy, as quoted in *Lutheran Witness Reporter,* 6, 13 (July 5, 1970), p. 1.

203. *Minutes, Fifth Biennial Convention of the Lutheran Church in America,* 1970 (Philadelphia: Board of Publication of the LCA), pp. 433, 539; cf. 441-450, "The Role of Women in the Life of the Church." The report notes the threat to fellowship with other Christians which such a step as ordaining women could bring, but also is aware of "the grassroots revolt that is an actuality" among Roman Catholics in favor of the step, p. 450.

204. The Rev. Elizabeth A. Platz, then of the Maryland Synod.

205. The 1965 LCMS convention had declared "women suffrage in the church as contrary to Scripture only when it violates" the principles found in 1 Cor. 14:34-35 and 1 Tim. 2:11-15 (that women may not "exercise authority over men"), adding that Gal. 3:28 "does not cancel the order God has established at the time of creation but sanctifies and hallows it"; see *Proceedings of the 46th Regular Convention of the Lutheran Church–Missouri Synod, 1965,* p. 103, Resolution 2-36. The 1967 convention showed "some disagreement" over meaning and application of this resolution; *Convention Proceedings . . . 1967,* p. 89, Resolution 2-05. For the 1969 action, see *Proceedings . . . 1969,* p. 88, and the *Convention Workbook,* pp. 514-22, on Resolution 2-17. Further, Schroeder, as cited above in n. 86. It is likely, however, that "official Missouri" will try to reverse the decision on women's suffrage. See, in the publication of the LCMS Seminary at Fort Wayne (formerly Springfield, Ill.), Douglas Judisch, "Theses on Woman Suffrage in the Church," *Concordia Theological Quarterly* 41 (1977): 36-45; he concludes that passage after passage in the Bible denies women the right to vote and thus to "rule" over men.

   It should be remembered that the Lutheran Church–Missouri Synod has a larger number of parochial school teachers than any other church in the United States outside the Roman Catholic. There has long been debate over whether these teachers are part of the (ordained) Ministry. If they are, the LCMS would immediately have more ordained women than any other U.S. church! Cf. A. C. Mueller, *The Ministry of the Lutheran Teacher: A Study to Determine the Position of the Lutheran Parish School Teacher within the Public Ministry of the Church* (St. Louis: Concordia, 1964), especially pp. 162-71; and *Eucharist and Ministry* (cited above, n. 82), pp. 259-60, 266-67.

206. Address to the Religious Newswriters Association in Chicago, May 17, 1977.

207. Figures from the LCA/DPL. Of the 54, two more were serving coordinator roles for groups of congregations, one was vice pastor in a congregation under synodical administration, and one on leave from call.

208. Garhart (cited above, n. 196), pp. 5-15. Domination of male imagery and language in liturgy was a particular concern of an international Lutheran consultation on "Women and Worship" at Madison, Wisconsin, in April, 1977. Such language, it was said, ought to be "more inclusive of the experience and images of women," and "while respecting the biblical witness in the naming of God," participants asked a reduction of the "overwhelmingly male references and imagery about God, particularly the use of male pronouns." "Hierarchial assumptions . . . convey a message that contradicts the Good News." The consultation report has been published as *Women and Worship: Rooted in the New Creation,* ed. Constance F. Parvey (New York: Lutheran World Ministries, 1977).

209. Garhart, ibid., pp. 15-17, 26-33.

210. Ibid., p. 40.

211. E. Wilbur Bock, "The Female Clergy: A Case of Professional Marginality," *American Journal of Sociology* 5 (1967): 531-39, shows that, while between 1900

and 1960 clergywomen increased by 38% in numbers, they give less evidence of professionalization and more of being marginal after these decades.

212. So Ralph W. Klein, "The Ordination of Women in the Lutheran Church," a radio interview on KFUO, St. Louis, printed in *Currents in Theology and Mission* 4 (1977): 151.

213. "Declaration," Introduction (as cited above, n. 87), p. 519.

214. Bishop Hall, as quoted by Colin Craston, in *Evangelicals* (cited above, n. 97), p. 5. For a negative judgment on this "guinea-pig treatment" of women, cf. Beckwith and Duffield, in *Why Not?* (cited above, n. 85), p. 155.

215. Note Krister Stendahl's contention, correct in my view, that women's suffrage is the issue; once women are allowed to vote in the church, it is difficult, on biblical grounds, to exclude them from ordination. *The Bible and the Role of Women* (cited above, n. 85), p. 39, especially n. 38.

216. Cf. *Papal Primacy and the Universal Church,* Lutherans and Catholics in Dialogue V (Minneapolis: Augsburg, 1974), p. 20.

217. So W. A. Bretherton, in *Women's Ministry: A Valid Ministry,* ed. Ruth Wintle (London: CPAS 1975), as cited by Beckwith, in *Why Not?* (cited above, n. 85), p. 150.

218. So Craston, in *Evangelicals* (cited above, n. 97), pp. 10-11.

219. So Fiorenza, in *Women and Catholic Priesthood* (cited above, n. 126), pp. 99-100. Cf. her book, *Der vergessene Partner, Grundlagen, Tatsachen und Möglichkeiten der beruflichen Mitarbeit der Frau in der Heilssorge der Kirche* (Düsseldorf, 1964), pp. 87-94.

220. So Craston, *Evangelicals* (cited above, n. 97), p. 7. Cf. Peter Kearney, "New Testament Incentives for a Different Ecclesial Office," in *Office and Ministry,* Concilium 80 (cited above, n. 90), pp. 50-63.

221. Joseph A. Burgess, *Can Women Serve in the Ordained Ministry?* (Minneapolis: Augsburg, 1973), p. 7; C. Tatton, "Some Studies of New Testament *diakonia,*" *Scottish Journal of Theology* 25 (1972): 423-34.

222. Frederick H. Borsch, "The Authority of the Ministry," in *Toward a New Theology of Ordination* (cited above, n. 86), pp. 12-22, especially p. 18.

223. Garhart (cited above, n. 196), p. 1.

224. "Declaration," Introduction, 4, 5, 6 (as cited above, n. 87), pp. 518, 522, 523.

225. Ibid., Introduction, p. 519, citing the Pastoral Constitution on the Church in the Modern World, *Gaudium et Spes,* 29; in Walter M. Abbott, ed., *The Documents of Vatican II* (New York: Guild, America and Association Presses, 1966), p. 228.

226. Among Cullmann's many works, see *Christ and Time: The Primitive Christian Conception of Time and History* (Philadelphia: Westminster, rev. ed. 1964), and *Salvation as History* (New York: Harper and Row, 1967). Further, Jean Frisque, *Oscar Cullmann: Une théologie de l'histoire du salut* (Tournai, Belgium: Casterman, 1960).

227. Cf. the old *Thesaurus Ecclesiasticus e patribus graecis,* by J. C. Suicer (Amsterdam, 1728), or G. W. H. Lampe, editor, *A Patristic Greek Lexicon* (Oxford: Clarendon Press, 1961–1968), under the pertinent Greek terms. I have dealt with the theme in several articles: "*Oikonomia* = 'Covenant'; Terms for Heilsgeschichte in Early Christian Usage," *Novum Testamentum* 3 (1959): 282-99; "Oikonomia-Terms in Paul in Comparison with Lucan Heilsgeschichte," *NTS* 13 (1966–67): 147-67; "Heilsgeschichte in Luke: Some Remarks on Its Background and Comparison with Paul," in *Studia Evangelica IV,* Texte und Untersuchungen

102 (Berlin: Akademie-Verlag, 1968), pp. 86-115. That I hold, contrary to Cullmann, that *oikonomia* comes to mean "Heilsgeschichte" only *after* the New Testament and not already in the canonical writings does not affect the argument which follows.

228. In addition to the lexica cited, cf. G. L. Prestige, *God in Patristic Thought* (1936; London: SPCK, paperback 1964), pp. 57-66.

229. E.g., A. Alegro, "La mujer en camino de realizarse," *Revista Biblica* 38 (1976): 3-13; J. Konings, "A Mulher no Novo Testamento," *Revista de Cultura Biblica* 12 (1975): 5-16; Eng. summaries in *New Testament Abstracts* 21 (1977): 220, 232.

230. S. Runciman, *The Eastern Schism* (Oxford, 1955), as noted by D. J. Geanakoplos, *Byzantine East and Latin West* (New York: 1966), p. 74, n. 58.

231. Cited above, n. 127; s.v. *oikonomia*, D. 2-6, pp. 942-43.

232. J. Darrouzès, "Les documents byzantines du XIIᵉ siècle sur la primauté romaine," *Revue des Études Byzantines* 23 (1965): 42-88. Further, John H. Erickson, "*Oikonomia* in Byzantine Canon Law," in *Law, Church, and Society: Essays in Honor of Stephan Kuttner,* ed. Robert Somerville and Kenneth Pennington (Philadelphia: Univ. of Pennsylvania Press, 1977).

233. Cf. Metropolitan Axomes Methodios (Fouyas), "*Peri tēn 'ekklēsiastikēn oikonomian,'* " in *Ekklēsiastikos Pharos* (Addis Ababa) 58 (1976): 5-24 (with Eng. summary and bibliography). My 1957 dissertation, "The Use of *Oikonomia* and Related Terms in Greek Sources to about A.D. 100 as a Background for Patristic Applications," will be published in *Ekklēsiastikos Pharos,* beginning in 1978, as a contribution to this discussion.

234. McDonnell, ". . . Validating Ministry" (cited above, n. 184), pp. 261-63.

235. Lampe, *Patristic Lexicon* (cited above, n. 227), s.v. *oikonomia*, D. 4. Athanasius *Epp.* 62 and 63; cf. Basil, *Ep.* 204, discussed in J. F. Bethune-Baker, *Introduction to the Early History of Christian Doctrine* (London: Methuen, 1903), p. 214, n. 1.

236. *Ep.* 313 (443 E).

237. In addition to the lexica and Prestige (cited above, n. 228), cf. J. Reumann, "*Oikonomia* as 'Ethical Accommodation' in the Fathers, and its Pagan Background," *Studia Patristica III,* Texte und Untersuchungen 78 (Berlin: Akademie-Verlag, 1961), pp. 370-79. The 12th-century *Lexicon* of Johannes Zoneras (ed. J. A. H. Tittmann, Leipzig, 1808), 2, 1435, defines *oikonomikon pragma* along these lines and cites as an example the circumcision of Timothy by Paul.

238. Chrysostom, *Expos. in Gal.* 2.4. (10.688A), with further references in Lampe, *Patristic Lexicon* (cited above, n. 227), s.v. *oikonomia*, D. 6.

239. *Hom.* 61. 1 Cor. 9:19-23 was often cited as justification for such an approach.

240. *Hom.* 127 on Matthew.

241. *Orthod. fidei* 123.

242. *Ep.* 228.

243. *Hom.* 31, on Matt. 15:21.

244. On the argument, greatly compressed above, see Guthrie, in *To Be a Priest* (cited above, n. 90), pp. 158-62. In place of the obvious "subordination" patterns which appear in the New Testament, the church has long since transcended that of "Jew and Gentile," and more recently of "slave and free." We have learned centuries ago not to take the subordination of Christ expressed in such passages as 1 Cor. 11:3 or 15:28 ontologically, and more recently we have, as Christians,

acknowledged, in various ways, the rights of people and individual conscience against the state and even against church government. Now, can we transcend the even longer patterns (which similarly have appeared in the Bible and all our traditions) regarding the subordination of women?

3. The Title *Bishop*

1. *Eucharist and Ministry,* Lutherans and Catholics in Dialogue IV (New York: U.S.A. National Committee of the Lutheran World Federation, and Washington, D.C.: Bishops' Committee for Ecumenical and Interreligious Affairs, 1970), pp. 14-15, 173-75.

2. Cf. Arthur Carl Piepkorn, ibid., pp. 108-9, "the unitary character of the sacred ministry"; for the Lutheran confessions the one "holy order" is "the presbyterate-episcopate of the New Testament." Similarly in Günther Gassmann, "The Ordained Ministry and Church Order," in *The Lutheran Church Past and Present,* ed. Vilmos Vajta (Minneapolis: Augsburg, 1977), p. 172; the essay, pp. 163-84, is an excellent survey of the Reformation position and subsequent historical developments in the entire world of Lutheranism, for pastoral office and episcopal office.

3. E.g., M. H. Shepherd Jr., "Bishop," *IDB* (New York and Nashville: Abingdon, 1962), 1:441-43.

4. Leonhard Goppelt, "Church Government and the Office of Bishop in the First Three Centuries," in *Episcopacy in the Lutheran Church? Studies in the Development and Definition of the Office of Church Leadership,* ed. Ivar Asheim and Victor R. Gold (Philadelphia: Fortress, 1970), pp. 1-29.

5. Cf., e.g., Eduard Schweizer, *Church Order in the New Testament,* SBT 32 (London: SCM, 1961).

6. *Lutheran–Episcopal Dialogue: A Progress Report* (Cincinnati: Foreward Movement Publishers, 1973), pp. 20-22, 24, 32.

7. Cf. Joseph A. Fitzmyer, s.j., "Jewish Christianity in Acts in Light of the Qumran Scrolls," in *Studies in Luke-Acts, Studies presented in honor of Paul Schubert,* ed. L. E. Keck and J. L. Martyn (Nashville and New York: Abingdon, 1966), pp. 247-48, reprinted in Fitzmyer's *Essays on the Semitic Background of the New Testament,* Sources for Biblical Study 5 (Missoula, Mont.: Society of Biblical Literature and Scholars' Press, 1974), pp. 293-94.

8. See the discussion in Jean-Francois Collange, *L'épître de Saint Paul aux Philippiens,* Commentaire du Nouveau Testament Xa (Neuchatel: Delachaux & Niestlé, 1973), pp. 39-42; trans. A. W. Heathcote, *The Epistle of Saint Paul to the Philippians* (London: Epworth, 1979), pp. 37-41.

9. For an analysis in the context of Lutheran–Roman Catholic discussion about the ministry, cf. Jerome D. Quinn, "Ministry in the New Testament," in *Eucharist and Ministry* (cited above, note 1), pp. 96-98; further, pp. 24-25, 99-100.

10. Cf. Rudolf Schnackenburg, "Apostolicity: The Present Position of Studies," *One in Christ* 6 (1970): 243-73.

11. Cf. Raymond E. Brown, s.s., *Priest and Bishop: Biblical Reflections* (New York: Paulist, 1970), pp. 47-86, "Are the Bishops the Successors of the Apostles?"

12. So Raymond E. Brown, s.s., *The Community of the Beloved Disciple* (New York: Paulist, 1979), especially pp. 6, 86-87, 99-103, 146, 158-62, 164, 166.

13. Cf., e.g., in the Lutheran–Catholic dialogue, *Eucharist and Ministry* (cited above, n. 1), pp. 138-177, 216-26; and *Papal Primacy and the Universal Church,* Lutherans and Catholics in Dialogue V, ed. Paul C. Empie and T. Austin Murphy (Minneapolis: Augsburg, 1974), pp. 48-58.

14. Theodore G. Tappert, "Lutheran Ecclesiastical Government in the United States of America," in *Episcopacy in the Lutheran Church* (cited above, n. 4), pp. 155-74, where documentation and bibliography for the section above are given.
15. George Lindbeck, in a paper at a colloquy on the Augsburg Confession, 1979. In English, cf. Avery Dulles and George A. Lindbeck, "Bishops and the Ministry of the Gospel," in *Confessing One Faith: A Joint Commentary on the Augsburg Confession by Lutheran and Catholic Theologians*, ed. G. W. Forell and J. F. McCue (Minneapolis: Augsburg, 1982), pp. 147-72, especially 149 and 155. On this view consult further Wilhelm Maurer, *Historical Commentary on the Augsburg Confession*, trans. H. George Anderson (Philadelphia: Fortress, 1987).
16. Cf. the *Progress Report* (cited above, note 6), Carl S. Meyer, pp. 99-116, especially also on reactions toward episcopacy by American Lutherans. The position remains clear: "the historic episcopate is not *iure divino*"; "the notion that the historical form of the Church is guaranteed by unbroken continuity in the episcopal office is heresy in the Lutheran Church" (Bishop Hans Lilje); "the only point at which all Lutheran Churches agree on the question of Church polity is that one could not argue for the historic episcopate by divine right" (Jerald C. Brauer). Nonetheless, Lutherans and Episcopalians hoped together in the dialogue for "an *episcopē* which will be an *episcopē* of the apostolic Gospel" (p. 22).
17. For the "Malta Report," see *LW* 19 (1972): 259-73, especially 268-70.
18. Subtitled *The Report of the Conversations 1970–72 Authorized by the Lambeth Conference and the Lutheran World Federation* (London: SPCK, 1973), sections 79-82, pp. 18-19; in the U.S. *Progress Report* (cited above, n. 6), pp. 159-60.
19. *Lutherans in Ecumenical Dialogue: An Interpretive Guide* (New York: Lutheran Council in the U.S.A., 1977), pp. 30 and 29.
20. *One Baptism, One Eucharist, and a Mutually Recognized Ministry: Three Agreed Statements*, Faith and Order Paper No. 73 (Geneva: World Council of Churches, 1975), pp. 36-39, 53-56, especially sections 26, 30-37, 93-100, 104. The Faith and Order Paper No. 111, *Baptism, Eucharist and Ministry* (1982) builds on this document; see Chap. 5, below.
21. *In Quest of a Church of Christ Uniting*, Consultation on Church Union, Princeton, New Jersey, 1976.
22. Jerald C. Brauer, in his "afterword" to the LWF volume *Episcopacy in the Lutheran Church* (cited above, n. 4), pp. 197-211, suggests adoption of the title—and even of the historic episcopate (but modified, "on different grounds," p. 211), for the "well-being of the church—'that they might be one.'"

4. "Authority" in Ministry: The "Teaching Office" according to the New Testament

1. Helmut Koester and James M. Robinson, *Trajectories in Early Christianity* (Philadelphia: Fortress, 1971); German, *Entwicklungslinien durch die Welt des frühen Christentums* (Tübingen: J. C. B. Mohr, 1971).
2. For objections to the term *trajectory* see J. Reumann, "Exegetes, Honesty and the Faith," *Currents in Theology and Mission* 5 (1978): 23-25. Compare R. E. Brown, K. P. Donfried, J. A. Fitzmyer, and J. Reumann, *Mary in the New Testament* (Philadelphia: Fortress, and New York: Paulist, 1978), p. 25, n. 36.
3. See Klaus Wegenast, "Lehre," in *Theologisches Begriffslexikon zum Neuen Testament*, ed. L. Coenen et al. (Wupperthal: Brockhaus, 1970), 2:852-867; cited hereafter from the subsequent English trans., "Teach," *The New International*

Dictionary of New Testament Theology, ed. Colin Brown (Grand Rapids: Zondervan, 1978, 3:759-781.

The verb *katēcheō,* rare in secular Greek and missing in the LXX, may have been introduced by Paul as a term for "the person who teaches the word" (Gal. 6:6), and could thus be "the earliest evidence we have for a 'full-time' teaching office in the early church" (p. 771); cf. also 1 Cor. 14:19; Rom. 2:18; Luke 1:4; Acts 18:25 especially.

The usual New Testament word for "handing on" a tradition is *paradidōmi.* It is employed not only for Jewish *halakah* (Mark 7:13; Acts 6:14) but also for narratives about Jesus which Christians transmitted (Luke 1:2) and confessions of faith (1 Cor. 11:23; 15:3; cf. 11:2 and Jude 3) and fixed commands (2 Peter 2:21).

Paideuō/paideia (New International Dictionary of New Testament Theology article by Dieter Fürst) means "teach, instruct, educate," often with a note of discipline or suffering (1 Cor. 11:32; Eph. 6:4, of parents; 2 Tim. 3:16, of Scripture; Titus 2:11-13; Heb. 12:5-9). Inclusion of this term suggests teaching as a work of God includes the development of persons as children of God through agencies other than professional teachers.

4. See especially *The Semantics of Biblical Language* (New York: Oxford University Press, 1961), though there is a considerable subsequent literature.

5. But is it as clear and simple as Rengstorf (in *TDNT* 2:138) implies? 2 Thess. (2:15) and the Pastoral Letters, written as much in a Hellenistic context as Paul's unquestioned letters, do have a Jewish sense for *didaskein* as "teaching established traditions." Wegenast, "Teach," p. 764, suggests a more persuasive reason than the Hellenistic context: for Paul, "to teach" implied transmitting "the traditions of the fathers" (Gal. 1:12,14; Rom. 2:21); therefore he himself avoided it as a term.

6. Wegenast, "Teach," p. 763, after proceeding more redaction-critically, concludes that often in the Synoptics "the rabbinic sense of *didaskō* (i.e., that of the Heb. *limmad*) has been replaced by the meaning 'to proclaim salvation.' "

7. For example, Wegenast points out in connection with *didaskalia* that the LXX avoided the term because "its primary meaning in profane Greek is intellectual training with a view to knowledge, whereas Israel saw teaching as meaning the law of God, to which the only appropriate response was obedience" (p. 769). On the other hand, the Pastoral Letters show no inhibitions about using *didaskalia* (p. 771).

8. First Corinthians 2:13 is a kind of parallel to John 6:45 (about being "taught by the Father," *didaktoi Theou*) when it says: "We impart this [God's revelation] in words not taught by human wisdom but taught by the Spirit [*didaktois Pneumatos*], interpreting spiritual truths to those who possess the Spirit."

9. *The Apostolic Preaching and Its Developments* (London: Hodder and Stoughton, 1936); *Gospel and Law: the Relation of Faith and Ethics in Early Christianity* (New York: Columbia University Press, 1951).

10. Cf. Victor Paul Furnish, *Theology and Ethics in Paul* (Nashville: Abingdon, 1968), pp. 224-27.

11. *Apostolic Preaching,* p. 7. But cf. *Gospel and Law,* p. 10: *didachē* is "a course of instruction in morals."

12. *Apostolic Preaching,* especially p. 17 for a summary of the *kērygma* recovered from the Pauline epistles, and pp. 21-24 for the Jerusalem *kērygma;* on pp. 25-26 the differences are discussed.

13. Cf. Hans Conzelmann, *An Outline of the Theology of the New Testament,* trans. John Bowden (New York: Harper and Row, 1969), pp. 62ff., 87ff.

14. So Conzelmann in "On the Analysis of the Confessional Formula in I Corinthians 15:3-5," *Interpretation* 20 (1966): 15-25, and his commentary on the passage in KEK, *Der erste Brief an die Korinther* (Göttingen: Vandenhoeck und Ruprecht, 1969), trans. J. W. Leitch, *1 Corinthians*, Hermeneia (Philadelphia: Fortress, 1975). What is at issue between Paul and the Corinthian opponents are the implications of a credo which they both accept.

15. "Didache, Kerygma, and Euangelion," *New Testament Essays: Studies in Memory of Thomas Walter Manson 1893-1958*, ed. A. J. B. Higgins (Manchester: Manchester University Press, 1959), pp. 306-314. The quotations are from pp. 307, 312.

16. Cf. *Theology of the New Testament*, trans. Kendrick Grobel (New York: Scribner's, 1951), 1:86: out of the kerygma grew both (1) formulas which crystallized into creeds and (2) the literary form we call the gospel-book, made up of "the kerygma of the death and resurrection of Jesus," visualized by narratives, cult aetiologies, miracle stories, and apophthegms. Bultmann holds that the "sayings of the Lord" were handed down separately from the "christological kerygma" and were combined in "the gospel [book]," first sparingly by Mark, then more by Matthew and Luke. On this view, "Jesus in the role of 'teacher'" (on which, for the "historical Jesus," cf. R. Bultmann, *Jesus and the Word*, trans. Louise Pettibone Smith and Erminie Huntress [New York: Scribner's, 1934]) now in the gospel-writing stage "had become more important again" (p. 86).

   Behind the topic lies the problem posed (but not yet solved) in Robert A. Bartels, *Kerygma or Gospel Tradition—Which Came First?* (Minneapolis: Augsburg, 1961). This monograph raises the perennial question whether there was an authoritative body of teaching material attributed to Jesus in the early church which was "non-christological," if not "non-kerygmatic"; cf. the debate over a Q source and, more negatively, Howard M. Teeple, "The Oral Tradition That Never Existed," *JBL* 89 (1970): 56-68, who denies there was "a widespread oral tradition that originated with Jesus' teaching." Such a viewpoint raises the question of "norm" and "canon within the canon" in a way that Lutherans and Catholics alike have not usually had in mind.

17. *The Essential Nature of New Testament Preaching* (Grand Rapids: Eerdmans, 1960). Cf. also Robert C. Worley, *Preaching and Teaching in the Earliest Church* (Philadelphia: Westminster, 1967).

18. Peter F. Ellis, *Matthew: His Mind and His Message* (Collegeville, Minn.: Liturgical Press, 1974), p. 21.

19. *TDNT* 2:164. Wegenast, "Teach," pp. 762-763, cf. 769, concludes each Synoptic evangelist uses *didaskein* in the senses of "teach" *and* "preach."

20. J. Reumann, "The Kerygma and the Preacher," *Dialog* 3 (1964): 27-35, especially 32-33, where further literature is cited; *Jesus in the Church's Gospels* (Philadelphia: Fortress, 1968), pp. 30-36.

21. "*Didache* as a Constitutive Element of the Gospel-Form," *CBQ* 17 (1955): 345.

22. Cf. e.g. W. D. Davies, *Paul and Rabbinic Judaism* (London: SPCK, 1948), pp. 136ff.; C. H. Dodd, "Ennomos Christou," in *Studia Paulina, Festschrift de Zwaan* (Haarlem, Holland: 1953), pp. 96-110, reprinted in *More New Testament Studies* (Grand Rapids: Eerdmans, 1968), pp. 134-48; David L. Dungan, *The Sayings of Jesus in the Churches of Paul: The Use of the Synoptic Tradition in the Regulation of Early Church Life* (Philadelphia: Fortress, 1971).

23. So already Alfred Seeberg, *Der Katechismus der Urchristenheit* (Leipzig: Deichert, 1903, reprinted Munich: Kaiser, 1966); Philip Carrington, *The Primitive Christian Catechism* (New York: Cambridge University Press, 1940); E. G. Selwyn, *The First Epistle of Peter* (London: Macmillan, 1946), Essay II, pp. 363-466.

24. Examples and discussion in J. Reumann, "Is Writing Confessions Possible Only Where Scripture Speaks?" *The Confession-Making Process,* Studies Series (New York: Lutheran Council in the U.S.A., Division of Theological Studies, 1975), pp. 25-29. The aim would be neither to restrict church teaching solely to reiteration of scriptural passages nor to allow statements on any basis whatever, but within the scriptural-confessional framework to allow for new insights under the Spirit, but always normed by the New Testament gospel.

25. Maurice F. Wiles, *The Divine Apostle: The Interpretation of St. Paul's Epistles in the Early Church* (New York: Cambridge University Press, 1967), especially Chapter II.

26. Wegenast, "Teach," p. 774; cf. 770 (German, p. 860, "Paul always preserves a freedom with the tradition," omitted in the more conservatively oriented English rendering); and K. Wegenast's *Das Verständnis der Tradition bei Paulus und in den Deuteropaulinen,* Wissenschaftliche Monographien zum Alten und Neuen Testament 8 (Neukirchen: Neukirchener Verlag, 1962).

27. "The Office of Teaching," p. 193, citing Rengstorf on possible origins in Jewish Christianity. Otherwise H. Greeven, "Propheten, Lehrer, Vorsteher bei Paulus," *ZNW* 44 (1952-1953): 1-43 (evidence from Hellenistic Judaism). See also n. 5 above.

28. Conzelmann, *1 Corinthians,* p. 215, where references are cited; C. K. Barrett, *The First Epistle to the Corinthians,* HNTC (New York: Harper and Row, 1968), p. 295; Wegenast, "Teach," p. 768.

29. Lutherans and Catholics in Dialogue IV (Washington: Bishops' Committee for Ecumenical and Interreligious Affairs, and New York: USA National Committee of the Lutheran World Federation, 1970), p. 10, n. 6 (cited by Fitzmyer in "The Office of Teaching," n. 19). See also the "Common Statement" in *Teaching Authority and Infallibility in the Church,* p. 17, section 10, and n. 20.

30. E. Käsemann, "Sentences of Holy Law in the New Testament" (1954), trans. W. J. Montague in *New Testament Questions of Today* (Philadelphia: Fortress, 1969), pp. 66-81. For criticism of the theory and even the form-critical analysis, see Klaus Berger, "Zu den sogennanten Sätzen Heiligen Rechts," *NTS* 17 (1970-1971): 10-40, and David Hill, "On the Evidence for the Creative Role of Christian Prophets," *NTS* 20 (1973-1974): 262-274.

31. E. J. Tinsley, *The Imitation of God in Christ* (Philadelphia: Westminster, 1960), pp. 134-165. Some criticism of the Old Testament derivation of the imitation theme is voiced by W. P. De Boer, *The Imitation of Paul* (Grand Rapids: Eerdmans, 1962).

32. R. Bultmann, "Glossen im Römerbrief," *TLZ* 72 (1947): 202, reprinted in his *Exegetica* (Tübingen: Mohr [Siebeck], 1967), p. 283, first spotted the possibility of a later gloss here. The view is followed in the commentaries of Leenhardt (1957) and Michel (1966) and by Wegenast, "Teach," p. 773, and *Verständnis der Tradition,* p. 179 (a mystery-religions concept that *persons* are "handed over" to a form of doctrine). J. C. O'Neill, *Paul's Letter to the Romans,* Pelican New Testament Commentaries (Baltimore: Penguin, 1975), takes all of 6:16-20 as a gloss. On the other hand, the commentaries by Käsemann (1973) and C. E. B. Cranfield (1975, pp. 323-325, but cf. p. 5) accept the phrase as Paul's, from baptismal paraenesis, to stress obedience.

33. Wegenast, "Teach," p. 771. Is it significant that in the Pauline corpus *didaskalia* in the plural has a pejorative sense ("doctrines of demons," 1 Tim. 4:1; cf. Col. 2:22, "human doctrines"), while the singular denotes (Paul's) gospel teaching?

34. *Jesus and His Contemporaries* (London: SCM, 1973), especially Chaps. 3, 4, and 6.

35. See Howard Clark Kee, *Jesus in History: An Approach to the Study of the Gospels* (New York: Harcourt, Brace and World, 1970), Chap. 3, "Jesus as God's Eschatological Messenger: The Q Document," pp. 62-103; H. E. Tödt, *The Son of Man in the Synoptic Tradition,* trans. D. M. Barton (Philadelphia: Westminster, 1965), especially pp. 246-269 and 293-296 on how the teaching of Jesus continued after Easter in Q circles with new authority; Siegfried Schulz, *Q: Die Spruchquelle der Evangelisten* (Zurich: Theologischer Verlag, 1972), who divides Q into earlier and later layers, with the implication that words spoken by Christian prophets in the period of post-Easter enthusiasm came to be assigned to the earthly Jesus prior to his exaltation. In any case, teaching authority in Q would be charismatic and based on (future) eschatology. Compare the authoritative statements of Christian prophets noted above in this essay (II.A.4 and n. 30).

36. Cf. Wegenast, "Teach," p. 762.

37. So Willi Marxsen, *Mark the Evangelist,* trans. R. A. Harrisville (Nashville and New York: Abingdon, 1969). Cf. Mark 8:35 and 10:25 with parallels, to see how Mark parallels "Jesus" and "the gospel."

38. *Paul on Preaching* (London: Sheed and Ward, 1964), p. 68; O. Glombitza, "Die Titel *didaskalos* und *epistatēs* für Jesus bei Lukas," *ZNW* 49 (1958): 275-278. Unlike Matthew, who often removes "teacher" from his sources, Luke simply takes the title over and adds *didaskalos* four times (7:40; 11:45; 12:13; 19:39); three times he substitutes *epistata* (8:24,45; 9:49): see Wegenast, "Teach," p. 767.

39. G. Bornkamm, "End-Expectation and Church in Matthew," in G. Bornkamm, G. Barth, and H. J. Held, *Tradition and Interpretation in Matthew,* trans. Percy Scott (Philadelphia: Westminster, 1963), p. 41.

40. Cf. Krister Stendahl, *The School of St. Matthew,* 2d ed. (Philadelphia: Fortress, 1968). Wegenast, "Teach," pp. 767-68 (German, p. 858), stresses Matthew's "Auseinandersetzung mit dem Rabbinat" as reason for his avoiding the title. On the christological aspects, cf. F. Hahn, *The Titles of Jesus in Christology,* trans. H. Knight and G. Ogg (New York and Cleveland: World, 1969), pp. 75-78; with Haenchen, he takes 23:8 as formed by the community.

41. G. Barth, *Tradition and Interpretation in Matthew,* pp. 159-164, "The Antinomians in Matthew."

42. Wegenast, "Teach," p. 763 (cross-references omitted); cf. 767-768.

43. This is to take *kai idontes auton prosekynēsan, hoi de edistasan,* not in the usual rendering, "And when they saw him they worshiped him; but *some* doubted" (RSV, emphasis added), leaving it open as to whether the "some" are a group beyond the Twelve (laity?) who have slipped up to the mountain top unnoticed, or two or six or whatever out of the eleven themselves; but rather as "they worshiped and they doubted," i.e., both reactions came from the same group. So Benjamin J. Hubbard, *The Matthean Redaction of a Primitive Apostolic Commissioning: An Exegesis of Matthew 28:16-20,* Society of Biblical Literature Dissertation Series 19 (Missoula, Mont.: SBL and Scholars' Press, 1974), pp. 75-77.

44. Cf. Eduard Schweizer, *Church Order in the New Testament,* Studies in Biblical Theology 32, trans. Frank Clarke (London: SCM, 1961), pp. 51-62.

45. Wegenast, "Teach," p. 770 (more literally translated above from the German, p. 859).
46. On the "gospel function" (truth), which is the norm for even the "Petrine function" (unity of the universal church), cf. *Papal Primacy and the Universal Church*, Lutherans and Catholics in Dialogue V (Minneapolis: Augsburg, 1974), pp. 11, 20-21, especially §§26 and 28. One finds an exposition of the Galatians 2 theme of "the truth of the gospel" in *Peter in the New Testament*, ed. R. E. Brown, K. P. Donfried, J. Reumann (Minneapolis: Augsburg, and New York: Paulist, 1973), pp. 24-32, especially p. 30 (on exegesis); see the essay in *Teaching Authority and Infallibility in the Church* by Karlfried Froehlich, "Fallibility Instead of Infallibility? A Brief History of the Interpretation of Galatians 2:11-14," pp. 259-69, on subsequent interpretations. Further, Peter Stuhlmacher, *Das paulinische Evangelium. I. Vorgeschichte*, Forschungen zur Religion und Literatur des Alten und Neuen Testaments 95 (Göttingen: Vandenhoeck und Ruprecht, 1968), pp. 38, 62-108, especially 70-71: "Paul understands his gospel as revelation itself, that is, he understands it as tradition-affirming but as not bound to what were pre-Pauline normative traditions."
47. The Common Statement, pp. 11-38 in the volume cited at the beginning of this essay, is followed by Roman Catholic and Lutheran reflections, pp. 39-68.
48. *The Ministry in the Church* (Geneva: Lutheran World Federation, 1982; German ed. 1981).
49. *The Lutheran Understanding of Ministry: Statement on the Basis of an LWF Study Project* (Geneva: Lutheran World Federation, Department of Studies, 1983).
50. *Papal Primacy and the Universal Church*, Lutherans and Catholics in Dialogue V (Minneapolis: Augsburg, 1974).

5. Current Crisis Questions about Ministries

1. Faith and Order Paper No. 111 (Geneva: World Council of Churches, 1982).
2. *A History of the Ecumenical Movement 1517–1948*, ed. Ruth Rouse and Stephen Charles Neill, 2d ed. (Philadelphia: Westminster), vol. 1 (1967), p. 414.
3. *One Baptism, One Eucharist and a Mutually Recognized Ministry: Three Agreed Statements*, Faith and Order Paper No. 73 (Geneva: World Council of Churches, 1975). Cited hereafter by paragraph §, usually in Part III, The Ministry.
4. *The Supper of the Lord: The New Testament, Ecumenical Dialogues, and Faith and Order on Eucharist* (Philadelphia: Fortress, 1985), Fig. 1, pp. 82-83, for the chart. The depiction of a stream with tributaries has been used in a chart by Jeffrey Gros, f.s.c., of the Commission on Faith and Order of the National Council of Churches, New York.
5. *The Fourth World Conference on Faith and Order: The Report from Montreal, 1963*, ed. P. C. Roger and L. Vischer (London: SCM, 1964), p. 52: "we exist as Christians by the Tradition of the Gospel (the *paradosis* [handing on] of the *kerygma* [apostolic proclamation]) testified in Scripture, transmitted in and by the Church through the power of the Holy Spirit" (partially quoted in *BEM*, p. ix). This Tradition (capital "T," equated with the Gospel) stands over all subsequent ":traditions" (lower case).
6. Cf. *Supper of the Lord*, p. 141, for references and details.
7. As listed by Nils Ehrenström and Günther Gassmann, *Confessions in Dialogue: A Survey of Bilateral Conversations among World Confessional Families, 1959–1974*, Faith and Order Paper No. 74 (Geneva: World Council of Churches, 3d ed., 1975).

8. See the Supplementary Study by Yves Congar, o.p., "One Mediator," in *The Ministry in the Church,* from the Roman Catholic–Lutheran Joint Commission (Geneva: LWF, 1982), pp. 108-14.

9. Bibliographical data on each in n. 12 below, where the process and contents of these responses are further discussed.

10. E. Schlink, "Apostolic Succession," in his *The Coming Christ and the Coming Church* (Philadelphia: Fortress, 1968), pp. 186-233; earlier in *Encounter* 25 (1964): 50-83 and *Kerygma und Dogma* 7 (1961): 79-114, as well as Schlink's *Der kommende Christus und die kirchlichen Traditionen* (Göttingen: Vandenhoeck und Ruprecht, 1961): 169-95.

11. E.g., *The Ministry in the Church,* §§59-66.

12. *A Response to* Baptism, Eucharist and Ministry (New York: LCA Department for Ecumenical Relations, n.d.). *The Response of The American Lutheran Church to* Baptism, Eucharist and Ministry (Minneapolis: Office of the Presiding Bishop, n.d.). The LCA document is reprinted in *Churches Respond to BEM: Official responses to the "Baptism, Eucharist and Ministry" text, Vol. 1,* ed. Max Thurian, Faith and Order Paper No. 129 (Geneva: World Council of Churches, 1986): 28-38.

13. *The Report of the Task Force on Theology* was published by the Commission for a New Lutheran Church, through the Office of its Coordinator, in Minneapolis, and received wide circulation. *The Progress Reports* came from the same office and were also published in the magazine or newspaper of each church.

14. *The New Church Debate: Issues Facing American Lutheranism,* ed. with introduction by Carl E. Braaten (Philadelphia: Fortress, 1983). Sections 3 and 4 deal with Ordained Ministry and Bishop. Walter R. Bouman proposed in his lecture that Lutheranism's understanding of the gospel might not be adequate for a full definition of the church and its ministries, and that the "many ministries of the New Testament" arise not from one ministry but from the community's gifts (pp. 67-68).

15. As quoted in *Lutheran Perspective* 14,3 (November 24, 1986), p. 1. For reader reaction to Tietjen's letter see 14,5 (January 19, 1987), p. 5, and 14,6 (February 9, 1987), p. 5.

16. J. M. R. Tillard, o.p., "What Priesthood Has the Ministry?" French in *Nouvelle Revue Théologique* 105 (1973): 481-514; *One in Christ* 9 (1973): 237-69.